National Security Cultures

This edited collection examines changes in national security cultures in the wake of international events that have threatened regional or global order, and analyses the effects of these divergent responses on international security.

Tracing the links between national security cultures and preferred forms of security governance, the work provides a systematic account of perceived security threats and the preferred methods of response with individual chapters on Canada, China, France, Germany, Italy, Japan, Mexico, Russia, the UK and the USA. Each chapter is written to a common template exploring the role of national security cultures in shaping national responses to the four domains of security governance: prevention, assurance, protection and compellence. The volume provides an analytically coherent framework evaluating whether cooperation in security governance is likely to increase among major states, and if so, the extent to which this will follow either regional or global arrangements.

By combining a theoretical framework with strong comparative case studies this volume contributes to the ongoing reconceptualization of security and definition of threat and provides a basis for reaching tentative conclusions about the prospects for global and regional security governance in the early twenty-first century. This makes it ideal reading for all students and policy-makers with an interest in global security and comparative foreign and security policy.

Emil J. Kirchner is Professor of European Studies and Jean Monnet Chair at the University of Essex, UK.

James Sperling is Professor of Political Science at the University of Akron, Ohio.

National Security Cultures offers a tightly argued, deeply researched, and empirically encompassing analysis. It establishes the enduring imprints Westphalian and post-Westphalian state structures have on governance in East and West. And it tracks the variable effects of national security cultures on policies spanning the full governance spectrum. An impressive achievement that will become required reading in the field of security studies.

Peter J. Katzenstein,
Walter S. Carpenter, Jr. Professor of International Studies,
Cornell University
USA

The result of empirical research conducted by an impressive international team of scholars, this is a rigorous and systematic examination of national security cultures across a wide swath of the world. The authors follow a common framework in an exemplary collaborative project which reveals important insights into the fundamental question of the relationship between culture and security policy and the extent to which security concepts in the West can be transferred to other regions.

Stephen F. Szabo
Executive Director of the Transatlantic Academy,
USA

Emil Kirchner and James Sperling have produced a welcome addition to the literature on national security cultures by applying the concept to the pressing problem of global and regional security governance.

Country experts, area specialists, and international relations theorists with an interest in these topics will all want to consult this volume.

John S. Duffield
Professor of Political Science Georgia State University,
USA

Interest in security governance has risen and fallen in the past ten years; now again on the rise, the concept is in great need of theoretical exposition and empirical grounding; and that is what this book achieves. In a welcome and highly ambitious study, the focus on security governance – so often constrained to Europe – is examined globally. In all these contexts, it is an exceptionally important book.

Stuart Croft
Professor of International Security,
Warwick University, UK

National Security Cultures

Patterns of global governance

**Edited by Emil J Kirchner and
James Sperling**

LONDON AND NEW YORK

First published 2010 by Routledge
2 Park Square, Milton Park, Abingdon, Oxon, OX14 4RN

Simultaneously published in the USA and Canada
by Routledge
270 Madison Avenue, New York, NY 10016

Routledge is an imprint of the Taylor & Francis Group, an informa business

Typeset in Times New Roman by
Pindar NZ, Auckland, New Zealand
Printed and bound in Great Britain by
CPI Antony Rowe, Chippenham, Wiltshire

British Library Cataloguing in Publication Data
A catalogue record for this book is available from the British Library

Library of Congress Cataloging in Publication Data
National security cultures: patterns of global governance / edited by Emil J
Kirchner and James Sperling.
    p. cm.
  Includes index.
  1. Security, International. 2. National security. 3. National security—
International cooperation. I. Kirchner, Emil Joseph. II. Sperling, James.
  JZ5588.N36 2010
  355'.033—dc22   2009049052

ISBN 13: 978-0-415-77742-1 (hbk)
ISBN 13: 978-0-415-77743-8 (pbk)
ISBN 13: 978-0-203-85061-9 (ebk)

To Tristan, Stefan and Victoria

Contents

List of illustrations   ix
List of contributors   xiii
Preface   xvi
Acknowledgements   xix
List of abbreviations   xx

1 **National security cultures, technologies of public goods supply
   and security governance**   1
   JAMES SPERLING

PART I
Europe   19

2 **France: a departure from exceptionalism?**   21
   BASTIEN IRONDELLE AND SOPHIE BESANCENOT

3 **Germany: the continuity of change**   43
   SEBASTIAN HARNISCH AND RAIMUND WOLF

4 **Italy: hard tests and soft responses**   66
   PAOLO FORADORI AND PAOLO ROSA

5 **United Kingdom: how much continuity? How much change?**   85
   MARTIN A. SMITH

6 **European Union: moving towards a European security culture?**   103
   EMIL J. KIRCHNER

PART II
North America 125

7 **Canada: facing up to regional security challenges** 127
OSVALDO CROCI

8 **Mexico: current and future security challenges** 152
ROBERTO DOMINGUEZ

9 **United States: a full spectrum contributor to governance?** 172
JAMES SPERLING

PART III
Eurasia 211

10 **China: power, complementarity and reflexivity** 213
ANTHONY COATES

11 **Japan: from deterrence to prevention** 245
HARUHIRO FUKUI

12 **Russia: a global power?** 265
DEREK AVERRE

13 **Conclusion: structure, agency and the barriers to global security governance** 287
HAN DORUSSEN, EMIL J. KIRCHNER AND JAMES SPERLING

Index 303

Illustrations

Figures

1.1	A typology of threats	6
1.2	Challenges of governance	8
1.3	Policies of governance	9
2.1	Total aid and bilateral aid 1990–2007	28
2.2	Percentage of aid related to GNI	28
2.3	Inquiries into illegal situation of foreigners and actual deportations	30
2.4	French expenditure for defence and homeland security	31
2.5	Homeland security spending	32
3.1	German ODA	52
6.1	EU countries' contribution to ODA/DAC	111
7.1	Personnel operational tempo to overall strength 1980–2004, increasing demand vs falling capacity	136
8.1	Remittances to Mexico	158
11.1	Japanese ODA disbursements 1997–2006	252
11.2	Membership of crime organizations	256
11.3	Number of criminals arrested for serious crimes 2005	256
11.4	MOE budget 1980–2005	257

Tables

1.1	Key characteristics of (post-)Westphalian states	4
1.2	National security cultures	12
2.1	French participation in UN peacekeeping operations	36
2.2	French defence expenditure	38
3.1	Current UN assurance missions with German personnel contributions	48
3.2	German contribution to EU-led assurance missions 2003–7	50
3.3	Migration flows, Germany 1991–2006	53
3.4	Number of procedures against organized crime	55
3.5	German contribution to EU-led compellence missions 2003–7	57

3.6	German defence expenditure	58
4.1	The Carabinieri's participation in international police missions 2008	70
4.2	Italy in ESDP civilian operations	71
4.3	Italy in OSCE missions	71
4.4	Italian ODA: net disbursement in US dollars	73
4.5	Residence permits issued 1996–2007	74
4.6	Crimes reported to the judiciary by the police 1997–2007	75
4.7	Italian defence expenditure	78
4.8	Italian participation in current UN operations	80
4.9	Italian participation in ESDP military operations	81
4.10	Italian participation in NATO missions as of 1 July 2008	81
5.1	Annual UK 'security' spending by government department 2003–8	86
5.2	UK personnel contributions to OSCE field missions 2000–9	88
5.3	UK personnel contributions to EU peacekeeping and stabilization operations 2003–7	88
5.4	Total UK ODA net spending 1997–2006	90
5.5	UK aid disbursement priorities 2004–7	91
5.6	Migration inflows to the UK 2000–6	92
5.7	Inflows of asylum seekers to the UK by nationality 2000–5	92
5.8	Spending on UK intelligence agencies 2004–8	94
5.9	Central government grant to selected regional police forces in England 2000–11	94
5.10	UK defence spending 1990–2007	97
5.11	Aspects of the UK approach to security governance	99
6.1	Overview of ESDP civilian missions	107
6.2	Percentage of EU member states' contributions to OSCE field operations	108
6.3	Budgets for EU policies of assurance and prevention	109
6.4	Stability Pact allocations: total assistance by donors 2001–5	109
6.5	Asylum applications	113
6.6	Inflows of foreign population by nationality	113
6.7	Number of individuals tried for terrorism charges (in selected EU countries) 2005 and 2006	114
6.8	Europol and Eurojust budgets activities 2000–7	115
6.9	Overview of ESDP military missions	116
6.10	EU countries' defence expenditures and force strength 2005–7	118
7.1	Canadian security culture	128
7.2	Canadian government's threat perceptions after September 11	131
7.3	Canadian ODA spending	132
7.4	Incremental cost of Canadian peace-support missions 1989–2009	137
7.5	Canadian Security Intelligence Services: full-time equivalent employees and financial resources	141
7.6	Canadian defence expenditures 1985–2008	143
8.1	Crime statistics for Mexico 1998–2007	161
8.2	Spending per capita on public security	163

8.3	Drug trafficking and drug-related crime in Mexico 1997–2007	163
9.1	US national security culture	175
9.2	Assurance programmes, International Affairs budget 2001–10	179
9.3	Contributions and arrears to UN 2001–8	180
9.4	Bilateral and multilateral development assistance to Afghanistan and Iraq, 2002–8	182
9.5	Political and economic stabilization programmes 2001–10	185
9.6	US Official Development Assistance	187
9.7	Non-proliferation: cooperative threat reduction and defence nuclear non-proliferation programmes	189
9.8	Terrorism	193
9.9	Resources devoted to securitized crimes	196
9.10	NATO troop commitments to KFOR, ISAF and OEF 2008	200
10.1	Government expenditure, public security and policing (USDm)	215
10.2	Criminal cases reported to public security organs	216
10.3a	Contributions to ongoing UNPKO, People's Republic of China	220
10.3b	Contributions to completed UNPKO, People's Republic of China	221
10.4	Chinese engagement in the ASEAN Regional Forum, the Shanghai Cooperation Organisation and Six Party Talks	226
10.5	Examples of ARF 'Track One' inter-sessionals hosted by China since 1997	227
10.6	Institutionalization of the Shanghai Cooperation Organization	229
10.7	Chinese defence spending 1978–2009	231
10.8	People's Republic of China, force levels	232
10.9	Significant PRC military acquisitions since 2005	234
10.10	Official scientific and technological activities and spending, 2001–7	236
10.11	The duality of China's national security culture	238
11.1	Japanese troop contributions to UN assurance missions	251
11.2	Japanese contributions to UN peacekeeping operations budget, 2000–6	251
11.3	Inflow of asylum seekers into Japan	253
11.4	Japanese policing agencies	254
12.1	Draft Russian defence expenditure 2009–11	269
12.2	Russian contributions to multilateral assurance missions 2008	270
12.3	Power agencies in the federal budget	274
12.4	Share of total funding by security category 1999–2010	276
12.5	Structure of federal budget expenditure 2005–10	277
12.6	Russian budget expenditure on health care and sport	277
12.7	Recorded crimes	278
12.8	Criminality in 2008	279
12.9	Russian nuclear forces in January 2009	281
12.10	Estimated Russian military expenditure 1999–2008	282
13.1	Constituent elements of security governance system	288
13.2	A typology of security governance systems	289

13.3 Burden-sharing of deployment and contributions to UN initiatives relative to population, wealth and size of the economy (Kendall rank-order tests) 298

List of contributors

Emil J. Kirchner is Professor of European Studies and Jean Monnet Chair at the University of Essex. He is also Associate Editor of the *Journal of European Integration*. His current main interests include European security policy, regional and global governance, and cross-border cooperation. He is coauthor of *EU Security Governance* (Manchester University Press, 2007) and *Global Security Governance: Competing Perceptions of Security in the 21st Century* (Routledge, 2007). He has published articles in the *Asia Europe Journal*, *Contemporary Security Strategy*, *European Foreign Affairs Review*, *German Politics*, the *Journal of Common Market Studies*, *International Organization* and *West European Politics*.

James Sperling is Professor of Political Science at the University of Akron. He is coauthor of *EU Security Governance* (Manchester University Press, 2007) and *NATO: Decline or Renewal?* (Palgrave, forthcoming). He has also authored and coauthored articles on European and German security that have appeared in the *British Journal of Political Science*, *Contemporary Security Strategy*, *European Foreign Affairs Review*, *German Politics*, *International Affairs* and *International Organization*.

Derek Averre is Senior Lecturer at, and currently Director of, the Centre for Russian and East European Studies, University of Birmingham, UK. His main research interests are Russian foreign and security policy, Russia-Europe relations, arms control and non-proliferation issues in the USSR successor states. He is coeditor of *New Security Challenges in Postcommunist Europe* (Manchester University Press, 2002). He has also published articles in *Demokratizatsiya*, *European Security*, *International Affairs* and *Problems of Post-Communism*.

Sophie Besancenot graduated in 2007 from a Dual Master's Degree in International Relations from the Free University of Berlin and Sciences Po, Paris. After having worked as a research assistant for the Parisian office of Friedrich Ebert Foundation, she is now a PhD candidate at the European University Institute in Florence. Her interests include European security cultures, human security and post-conflict reconstruction.

Anthony Coates was awarded his PhD from Essex University in 2009, where he has taught introductory politics and managed learning innovations projects for several years. His thesis investigated regionalization and security governance, comparing European, Southeast Asian and African settings. In addition to advancing this work for publication, he is currently exploring textual-analysis methods for assessing foreign policy behaviours.

Osvaldo Croci is Professor of International Politics at Memorial University in St. John's, Newfoundland. His research interests focus on foreign and security policies in the Atlantic area, particularly those of Canada and Italy. Together with Amy Verdun, he has recently edited *The Transatlantic Divide: Foreign and Security Policies in the Atlantic Alliance from Kosovo to Iraq* (Manchester University Press, 2006); and *The European Union in the Wake of Eastern Enlargement: Institutional and Policy-making Challenges* (Manchester University Press, 2006).

Roberto Dominguez is Assistant Professor in the Department of Government at Suffolk University, Boston. He is a research associate at the Miami European Union Center and was editor of the journal *Relaciones Internacionales* (UNAM, Mexico). His recent publications include *European Union Foreign Policy: A Study in Structural Transition* (Edwin Mellen Press, 2008) and coeditor of *The Lisbon Fado: The EU under Reform* (Miami European Union Center, 2009).

Han Dorussen is Professor at the University of Essex and Associate Editor of the *Journal of Peace Research*. His research focus is on international relations, international and comparative political economy and applied game theory. He is coeditor of *Economic Voting* (Routledge, 2002). He has published articles in *Public Choice*, *International Organization*, the *Journal of Peace Research*, the *Journal of Conflict Resolution*, *European Union Politics* and *Electoral Studies*.

Paolo Foradori is Lecturer of Political Sociology at the University of Trento, Italy, and Marie Curie Fellow at the Center for Nonproliferation Studies of the University of Monterey, California. His research interests are in the field of conflict analysis, European foreign and security policy, and non-proliferation of weapons of mass destruction. He has coedited *Managing a Multilevel Foreign Policy: The EU in International Affairs* (Lexington Books, 2007).

Haruhiro Fukui is Professor Emeritus at the University of California, Santa Barbara, and former director of the Hiroshima Peace Institute. His recent publications include: 'Japan: recasting the post-war security consensus', in E. J. Kirchner and J. Sperling (eds) *Global Security Governance: Competing Perceptions of Security in the 21st Century* (Routledge, 2007); 'Japan: Why Parties Fail, Yet Survive', in K. Lawson and P. Merkl (eds) *When Parties Prosper: The Uses of Electoral Success* (Lynn Rienner, 2007); and (coauthored) 'Japan', in M. Kesselman *et al.* (eds) *Introduction to Comparative Politics*, 5th edn (Cengage Learning, 2010).

Sebastian Harnisch is Professor of Political Science at the Ruprecht Karls University of Heidelberg. His research interests are in German and American foreign policy, European affairs, theories of international relations, non-proliferation of weapons of mass destruction and Korean affairs. He is author of *International Politics and Constitution and Foreign Policy Learning* (Nomos, 2006) and *US Policy vis-à-vis the Korean Peninsula* (Leske and Budrich, 2000). He has also published articles in the *Asian Survey*, *Pacific Review*, *German Politics*, *Zeitschrift für Internationale Beziehungen* and *Zeitschrift für Politikwissenschaft*.

Bastien Irondelle is a Tenured Research Fellow at the Center for International Studies and Research, CERI-Sciences Po, and Lecturer in political science since 2005. He is the Deakin Fellow at the European Studies Centre, St Antony's College, University of Oxford for 2009–2010. His research interests include military transformation and armed forces reforms in Europe (mainly France, UK and Germany) and changes in the governance of the defence field. He is interested in European Security and Defence Policy with a focus on public opinion, ESDP networks, Europeanization and agenda-setting. He has co-edited the volume *European Security Since the Fall of the Berlin Wall* (University of Toronto Press, forthcoming) and has also published articles in *Journal of European Integration*, *Journal of European Public Policy*, and *Security Studies*.

Paolo Rosa is Associate Professor of Political Sociology, Department of Sociology and Social Research, University of Trento, Italy. His research interests include the sociology of the state, international relations theory, foreign policy analysis, and Italian and Chinese foreign policy. He is author of *Sociologia politica delle scelte internazionali. Un'analisi comparata delle politiche estere nazionali* (Laterza, 2006), coauthor of *Immagini del mondo. Introduzione alle relazioni internazionali* (Vita e Pensiero, 2008) and coeditor of *Managing a Multilevel Foreign Policy: The EU in International Affairs* (Lexington Books, 2007).

Martin A. Smith is Senior Lecturer in Defence and International Affairs at the Royal Military Academy Sandhurst. His main research interests are in the fields of international and European security. He is the coauthor of *The Kosovo Crisis and the Evolution of Post-Cold War European Security* (Manchester University Press, 2003), *Russia and NATO since 1991: From Cold War through Cold Peace to Partnership?* (Routledge, 2006). His articles have appeared in, *inter alia*, *Contemporary Security Policy*, *European Security*, *International Peacekeeping*, the *Journal of Strategic Studies* and *West European Politics*.

Raimund Wolf is a PhD student at the Ruprecht Karls University of Heidelberg. He graduated with a MA in Political Science from the University of Trier. His research interests include American, British and German foreign policy, security and military studies, and theories of international relations. He is currently writing his dissertation on the politics of US military policy during transition periods.

Preface

National Security Cultures: Patterns of Global Governance is part of an existing research project emanating from the Network on Global and Regional Governance (GARNET). The main aims of the overall research project are fourfold: to provide some conceptual clarification on the meaning of European security governance; to investigate whether elite perceptions on security threats and the appropriate means to respond to those threats converge or diverge among ten major powers spanning three geopolitical spaces: Europe, North America, and the Asia-Pacific; to determine the extent to which security and defence burdens are shared equally among EU member states; and to examine whether the national security cultures of ten countries, as well as that of the EU, have an impact on the way countries conduct their security and defence affairs, i.e. whether they prefer unilateral, bilateral or multilateral forms of engagement and the type of instruments they prefer to use (military versus non-military). The last of these research aspects is the focus of this book, which builds on and extends a number of published works from the GARNET research project, including 'The Challenge of European Security Governance' (2006), *Global Security Governance* (2007), *Global Threat Perceptions* (2007), *EU Security Governance* (2007), 'Sharing the Burden of Collective Security in the European Union' (2009) and 'Security Governance in a Westphalian World' (2009).

This edited volume examines the reasons for and implications of changes in national security cultures, and explores the extent and scope for international security governance in light of those changes. Major states have responded differently to international events such as the end of the Cold War, the terrorist attacks of 11 September 2001 (9/11), and the wars in Iraq, Afghanistan and elsewhere that have threatened regional or global order. Divergent responses among the world's major powers to these events reflect not only disparate resource constraints, but also national security cultures that favour a civilian response to a military one even in those cases where risk and threat assessments are not dissimilar. The linkage between national security cultures and the preferred form of security governance remains relatively unexplored and underdeveloped conceptually and empirically. The primary focus of each chapter is on the barriers and opportunities posed by national security cultures to regional and global security governance with respect to the national understanding of the external environment, the preferred instruments of statecraft (coercive versus persuasive), the pattern of interaction (unilateral, bilateral or multilateral) and institutional choice.

Each contribution explores the role of national security cultures in shaping national responses to security governance challenges with reference to four domains of governance: prevention, assurance, protection and compellence. A key common assumption is that national security cultures predict and determine the importance countries place on certain policy domains (e.g. prevention over compellence) or choice of policy instrument (e.g. the military rather than the civilian). These differences and outcomes provide the empirical basis for assessing the post-Westphalian hypothesis and national security culture hypotheses. The post-Westphalian hypothesis predicts that the fundamental change in the nature of the state found in specific regions of the world not only demarcates the range of security cultures found in specific states but also provides a structural explanation of why some states prefer unilateral rather than multilateral responses, uphold preventive rather than pre-emptive measures, or rely upon 'soft' rather than 'hard' power reflexively. While the composition of the national security cultures of these ten countries, as well as the points of convergence and divergence between them, are of intrinsic interest, those security cultures also establish the limits of regional and global security cooperation.

The nature of national security cultures is one of the variables that affect the prospects for international security governance. A third hypothesis relates to the impact that the technology of public goods supply has on the prospects for the collective provision of security governance. This hypothesis allows us to account for the impact that the intrinsic nature of the collective good has on the prospects for effective security governance; it contributes to our understanding of variations in their level of 'publicness' in the (a)symmetry of threats (i.e. the costs associated with any failure to provide security) and in costs (i.e. the marginal costs of providing security). The heterogeneity of the security challenges facing the ten countries encodes different technologies of publicness, which Todd Sandler (Sandler 1992: 36) defined as the 'manner in which each country provision or subscription levels are aggregated to yield a group provision or consumption level' of the public good. These technologies determine whether a collective international response is possible, either by all the ten countries (summation technology); is affected by lack of cooperation by some countries (weakest link technology); or depends on the contributions of the United States or the five permanent members of the UN Security Council (best-shot production technology).

In the Introduction to the volume, the content and implications of these hypotheses are fully developed and its Conclusion provides a partial statistical test of the technologies of public goods supply as a barrier to security governance and as an alternative hypothesis to the national security culture hypothesis for understanding and explaining national variations in security governance policies. There we return to these hypotheses and address the overriding objectives of this volume, namely establishing the likely parameters of security governance cooperation among ten of the world's major powers and differentiating national foreign policy behaviour with respect to the governance categories of prevention, assurance, protection and compellence. The national security culture and technology of public goods supply hypotheses are also assessed. We provide a partial statistical test of the technologies of public goods supply hypotheses. Our goal is to determine whether the intrinsic nature of collective goods hinders or facilitates cooperation and to demonstrate that national security cultures do function as an independent or intervening variable in determining national security policies and the level of security governance cooperation.

Characteristic of these research outputs has been an extensive empirical investigation, comparative analysis, and reliance upon a large team of international scholars, which has promoted international contacts and interchanges and hence furthered the cause of the GARNET network. *National Security Cultures* is the final volume produced under the aegis of the GARNET network.

Emil J. Kirchner and James Sperling,
October 2009

References

Kirchner, E.J. 'The Challenge of European Security Governance', *Journal of Common Market Studies*, 44(5): 947–68.

Kirchner, E.J. and Sperling, J. (2007) *Global Security Governance: Competing Perceptions of Security in the 21st Century*, Abingdon, UK: Routledge.

Kirchner, E.J. and Sperling, J. (eds) (2007) 'Global Threat Perception: Elite Survey results from Canada, China, the European Union, France, Germany, Italy, Japan, Russia, the United Kingdom and the United States', *GARNET Working Paper* 18/07, May. Available online at: http://www.garnet-eu.org (accessed 15 January 2009).

Kirchner, E.J. and Sperling, J. (2007) *EU Security Governance*, Manchester, Manchester University Press.

Dorussen, H., Kirchner, E.J. and Sperling, J. (2009) 'Sharing the Burden of Collective Security in the European Union. Research Note', *International Organization*, 63(4): 789–810.

Sandler, T. (1992) *Collective Action: Theory and Application*, New York: Harvester Wheatsheaf.

Sperling, J. (2009) 'Security Governance in a Westphalian World', in Wagnsson, C., Sperling, J. and Hallenberg, J. (eds) European Security Governance: The European Union in a Westphalian World, Abingdon, UK: Routledge.

Acknowledgements

The book has benefited from a number of financial sources, organizational arrangements and personal contributions. Financial assistance was secured primarily through the European Commission 6th Framework Programme, which resulted in the Network on Global and Regional Governance (GARNET). Two workshops were organized to prepare and monitor the research for this edited collection. The first took place at Suffolk University in Boston (US) in April 2008. We are grateful for the financial and organizational support from Suffolk University. The second workshop was held at the United Nations University Centre for Regional Integration Studies (UNU-CRIS) in Bruges (Belgium) in October 2008, with that institution's gracious financial support and much appreciated facilities. We are particularly indebted to Luk van Langenhove, the Director of UNU-CRIS, for his support. A number of people have provided useful comments, either in participating in workshops, or through communicating helpful suggestions, including the four anonymous reviewers of the book proposal. We are especially thankful in this respect to John Berg, Sven Biscop, Simone Chun, Judith Dushku, Sebastian Royo, Reimund Seidelmann, Stephen Szabo, Rodrigo Tavares, James Walsh, Mark Webber and Marcin Zaborowski. Particular thanks are also due to Susan Sydenham for her fantastic editorial assistance, to Katja Mirwaldt for compiling the abbreviations, to Max Paiano for compiling the index and to Oistein Harsem and Andrea Hurley for their helpful collection of data for the chapters on the EU and United States, respectively.

Emil J. Kirchner and James Sperling,
October 2009

Abbreviations

ACP	African, Caribbean and Pacific
ADB	Asian Development Bank
AEW	Airborne Early Warning
AFD	French Development Agency
AFP	Agence France Presse
AIFI	Integrated Automated Fingerprint Identification system
AMIS	African Union's enhanced Mission to the Darfur region of Sudan
AMM	Aceh Monitoring Mission
ANP	Afghanistan National Police
AOR/AOE	Logistics and Fleet Replenishment Ships
APC	Armoured Personnel Carrier
APEC	Asia Pacific Economic Consortium
ARATS	Association for Relations across the Taiwan Strait
ARF	ASEAN Regional Forum
ARTF	Afghan Reconstruction Trust Fund
ASBM	Anti-Ship Ballistic Missiles
ASCM	Anti-Ship Cruise Missiles
ASEAN	Association of Southeast Asian Nations
ASW	Anti-Submarine Warfare
ATA	Anti-Terrorism Act
AU	African Union
BBC	British Broadcasting Corporation
BBK	Federal Office of Civil Protection and Disaster Assistance (Germany)
BINUB	United Nations Integrated Office in Burundi
BKA	Federal Criminal Police Office (Germany)
BMD	Ballistic Missile Defence
BMDP	Ballistic Missile Defence Programme
BMI	Federal Ministry of the Interior (Germany)
BMU	Federal Ministry for the Environment, Nature Conservation and Nuclear Safety (Germany)
BMVG	Federal Ministry of Defence (Germany)

CAD	Canadian dollars
CANSOFCOM	Canadian Special Operations Forces Command
CANOSCOM	Canadian Operational Support Command
CAR	Central African Republic
CARDS	Community Assistance for Reconstruction, Development and Stabilisation
CBC	Canadian Broadcasting Corporation
CBRN	chemical, biological, radiological or nuclear weapons
CCM	Centre for the Prevention and Control of Disease (Italy)
CDC	Centers for Disease Control and Prevention (US)
CDU	Christian Democratic Union (Germany)
CEFCOM	Canadian Expeditionary Force Command
CEPOL	European Police College
CFAF	United Forces for Federal Support (Mexico)
CFE	Conventional Forces in Europe
CFSP	Common Foreign and Security Policy
CGP	Clean Government Party (Japan)
CIA	Central Intelligence Agency (US)
CICID	Committee for International Cooperation and Development (France)
CIDA	Canadian International Development Agency
CIMIC	Civilian-Military Cooperation (Italy)
CIR	Intelligence Interagency Committee (France)
CIS	Commonwealth of Independent States
CIU	Central Intelligence Unit (Kosovo)
CNCI	Comprehensive National Cybersecurity Initiative (US)
CNTF	Counter-Narcotics Trust Fund (US)
COFOG	Classification of Functions of Governments (France)
COMEXI	Mexican Council of International Affairs
CONTEST	Counter-Terrorism Strategy (UK)
CPC	Communist Party of China
CPCTC	China Peacekeeping/Civilian Police Training Centre
CPOT	Consolidated Priority Organization Target List (US)
CPR	Cyberspace Policy Review (US)
CSBM	Confidence and Security Building Measure
CSCE	Conference on Security and Co-operation in Europe (see OSCE)
CSI	US Container Security Initiatives
CSIS	Canadian Security Intelligence Service
CSTO	Collective Security Treaty Organisation
CSU	Christian Social Union (Germany)
CTAG	Counter Terrorism Action Group
CTBT	Comprehensive Test-Ban Treaty
CTF	Combined Task Force
CWC	Chemical Weapons Convention

DAC	Development Assistance Committee (Japan)
DAC	Development Assistance Cooperation
DAFC	Department of Aid to Foreign Countries (China)
DCI	Development Cooperation Instrument
DDG	Guided Missile Destroyers
DEA	Drug Enforcement Administration (US)
DFAIT	Department of Foreign Affairs and International Trade
DfID	Department for International Development (UK)
DGCID	Directorate-General for International Cooperation and Development (France)
DMTAP	Directorate of Military Training Assistance Programme
DOD	Department of Defense (US)
DRC	Democratic Republic of Congo
DST	Directorate of Territorial Surveillance (France)
EAS	East Asia Summit
EAU	Engineer Aviation Unit
EC	European Community
ECHO	European Community Humanitarian Office
EDC	European Defence Community
EDF	European Development Fund
EEA	European Environment Agency
EIDHR	European Initiative for Democracy and Human Rights
ENP	European Neighbourhood Policy
ENPI	European Neighbourhood Policy Instrument
EPRUS	Office for Preparation and Response to Health Emergencies (France)
ESDP	European Security and Defence Policy
ESF	Economic Stabilization Fund (US)
ESS	European Security Strategy
EU Artemis	European Union Military Operation in the Democratic Republic of Congo
EU NAVAR	Military naval operation against piracy
EU Proxima	European Union Police Mission in the Former Yugoslav Republic of Macedonia
EU-3	UK, France and Germany
EUBAM	EU Border Assistance Mission
EUFOR	European Union Force
EUFOR Althea	European Forces in Bosnia and Herzegovina
EUFOR Concordia	European Union Military Operation in the Former Yugoslav Republic of Macedonia
EUI	European University Institute
EUJUST LEX	European Union Integrated Rule of Law Mission for Iraq
EUJUST Themis	EU Rule of Law Mission to Georgia
EULEX Kosovo	European Union Rule of Law Mission in Kosovo
EUMM	EU Monitoring Mission in Georgia

EUPAT	EU Police Advisory Team in the Former Yugoslav Republic of Macedonia
EUPM	European Union Police Mission in Bosnia and Herzegovina
EUPOL AFG	EU Police Mission Afghanistan
EUPOL COPPS	EU Police Mission in the Palestinian Territories
EUPOL	European Union Police Mission
EUPT	European Union Planning Team
EUROFOR	European Operational Rapid Force
EUROGENDFOR	European Gendarmerie Force
EUROJUST	European Union Judicial Cooperation Unit
EUROMARFOR	European Maritime Force
EUROPOL	European Police Office
EURST	European Union Reinforced Support Team
EUSEC DR Congo	EU Advisory and Assistance Mission for Security Reform in the Democratic Republic of Congo
EUSR	European Union Special Representative
Exim	Export-Import Bank of China
FAI	Federal Agency of Investigations
FBI	Federal Bureau of Investigation (US)
FCO	Foreign and Commonwealth Office (UK)
FDI	Foreign Direct Investment
FFG	Guided Missile Frigates
FinCEN	Financial Crime Enforcement Network (US)
FOCAC	Forum on China-Africa Cooperation
FPP	Federal Preventive Police
FRONTEX	European Agency for the Management of Operational Cooperation at the External Borders of the Member States of the European Union
FSB	Federal Security Service (Russia)
FSKON	Federal Service for the Control over the Circulation of Drugs (Russia)
FSO	Federal Protection Service (Russia)
FSTEK	Federal Service for Technical and Export Control (Russia)
FYR	Former Yugoslav Republic
FYROM	Former Yugoslav Republic of Macedonia
G8	Group of Eight
GKKE	Common Church and Development Conference (Germany)
GNI	Gross National Income
GUSP	Main Directorate for Special Programmes (Russia)
HLSC	High Level Specialized Committee (Mexico)
HQ	Headquarters
IAEA	International Atomic Energy Agency
IBET	Integrated Border Enforcement Teams

IBJ	Immigration Bureau of Japan
IBRD	International Bank for Reconstruction and Development
ICBM	Intercontinental Ballistic Missile
ICC	International Criminal Court
ICTY	International Criminal Tribunal for the former Yugoslavia
IDRC	International Development Research Centre
IFOR	NATO Implementation Force in Bosnia and Herzegovina
IFS	Instrument for Stability
IISS	International Institute for Strategic Studies
IMATT	International Military Assistance Training Team (Sierra Leone)
IMIE	International Mission for Iraqi Elections
IMMHE	International Mission for Monitoring Haitian Elections
INF	Intermediate-Range Nuclear Forces
INP	Iraqi National Police
INTERPOL	International Criminal Police Organization
IOSC	Information Office of the State Council (China)
IPA	Instrument for Pre-Accession Assistance
IRBM	Intermediate Range Ballistic Missiles
IRFFI	International Reconstruction Fund Facility for Iraq
IRRF	Iraq Relief and Reconstruction Fund
ISAF	International Security Assistance Force in Afghanistan
ISPI	Institute for International Political Studies
ISTAT	Italian National Statistics Institute
JCG	Japan Coast Guard
KFOR	NATO Force in Kosovo
LACM	Land-attack Cruise Missiles
LDP	Liberal Democratic Party (Japan)
LOFTA	Law and Order Trust Fund (US)
LTM	Long-term Mission
MAE	Ministry of Foreign Affairs (France)
MChS	Ministry of Civil Defence, Emergencies and Liquidation of Natural Disasters (Russia)
MFO	Multinational Force and Observers
MHLW	Ministry of Health, Labour and Welfare (Japan)
MI5	Military Intelligence, Section 5 (UK)
MILOB	military observer
MINUK	United Nations Interim Administration Mission in Kosovo
MINURCAT	United Nations Mission in the Central African Republic and Chad
MINURSO	United Nations Mission for the Referendum in Western Sahara
MINUSTAH	United Nations Stabilization Mission in Haiti
MIRVed	Multiple Independently Targetable Reentry Vehicle

MLF	Multinational Land Force
MNTF–W	Multinational Task Force West
MoD	Ministry of Defence
MOE	Ministry of the Environment (Japan)
MOFA	Ministry of Foreign Affairs (Japan)
MONUC	United Nations Mission DRC
MP	Military Police
MSDF	Maritime Self-Defence Force (Japan)
MSU	Multinational Specialised Unit
MVD	Ministry of Internal Affairs (Russia)
NAFTA	North American Free Trade Agreement
NAO	National Audit Office (UK)
NATO	North Atlantic Treaty Organization
NBC	Nuclear, Biological and Chemical
NGO	Non-governmental Organization
NIS	National Intelligence Strategy (US)
NMI	National Migration Institute
NORAD	North American Air/Aerospace Defence Command
NORTHCOM	US Northern Command
NPA	National Police Agency (Japan)
NPSS	National Public Security System
NPT	Non-Proliferation Treaty
NRC	NATO-Russia Council
NSD	National Security Division (US)
NSS	National Security Strategy (US)
NTM-I	NATO Training Mission – Iraq
OAH	Operation Allied Harmony (FYROM)
OAS	Organization of American States
ODA	Official Development Assistance
ODG	Office for Democratic Governance
OECD	Organisation for Economic Cooperation and Development
OEF	Operation Enduring Freedom (Afghanistan)
OIF	Operation Iraqi Freedom
ONUMOZ	United Nations Operation in Mozambique
ONUSAL	United Nations Observers Mission in El Salvador
OSCE	Organization for Security and Co-operation in Europe
PAMECA	Police Assistance Mission of the European Community to Albania
PAP	People's Armed Police (China)
PAPF	People's Armed Police Force (China)
PB	peacebuilding
PK	peacekeeping
PKO	peacekeeping operations
PLA	People's Liberation Army (China)
PLAAF	People's Liberation Air Force (China)

PLAN	People's Liberation Navy (China)
PPH	Prefectural Police Headquarters (Japan)
PPP	Puebla-Panama Plan
PRI	Institutionalized Revolutionary Party
PRT	Provincial Reconstruction Team
PRT/FSB	Provincial Reconstruction Team/Forward Support Base
PSI	US Port Security Initiatives
PSO	Peace-support Operation
R&D	Rights and Democracy (Canada)
R&D	Research and Development
RATS	Regional Anti-Terrorism Structure
RC	Reconstruction
RCC	Regional Command
RCTS	Regional Counter Terrorism Structure
RC-W	Regional Command West
RMA	Revolution in Military Affairs (China)
RMB	Renminbi (Chinese currency)
RRM	Rapid Reaction Mechanism
SAD	Stewards of the American Dream
SALIS	Strategic Airlift Interim Solution
SAP	Stability and Association Policy
SAT	Special Assault Teams (Japan)
SCO	Shanghai Cooperation Organisation
SDF	Self-Defence Forces (Japan)
SEE	South Eastern Europe
SEED	Support for East European Democracy
SFOR	Stabilisation Force in Bosnia and Herzegovina
SGDN	General Secretariat for National Defence (France)
SIPRI	Stockholm International Peace Research Institute
SLBM	Submarine-Launched Ballistic Missile
SOCA	Serious Organised Crime Agency (UK)
SORT	Strategic Offensive Reduction Treaty
SPD	Social Democratic Party (Germany)
SRBM	Short-Range Ballistic Missiles
SSBN	Ballistic missile submarines
SSK	Diesel attack submarines
SSN	Nuclear attack submarines
SSR	Security Sector Reform (France)
START I-Treaty	Strategic Arms Reduction Treaty
SVR	Foreign Intelligence Service (Russia)
TAC	Treaty of Amity and Cooperation
TFF	Task Force Fox (FYROM)
TFH	Task Force Harvest (FYROM)
TFI	Office of Terrorism and Financial Intelligence (US)
TRT	Terrorism Response Team (Japan)

UN	United Nations
UNAMA	United Nations Assistance Mission in Afghanistan
UNAMI	United Nations Assistance Mission for Iraq
UNAMIC	United Nations Advance Mission in Cambodia
UNAMID	African Union/United Nations Hybrid Operation in Darfur
UNDGITF	United Nations Development Group Iraq Trust Fund
UNDOF	United Nations Disengagement Observer Force
UNDP	United Nations Development Program
UNDPKO	United Nations Department for Peacekeeping Operations
UNFICYP	United Nations Peacekeeping Force in Cyprus
UNHCR	United Nations High Commissioner for Refugees
UNIFIL	United Nations Interim Force in Lebanon
UNIKOM	United Nations Iraq-Kuwait Observation Mission
UNIOSIL	United Nations Integrated Office in Sierra Leon
UNMEE	United Nations Mission in Ethiopia and Eritrea
UNMIH	United Nations Mission to Haiti
UNMIK	United Nations Interim Administration Mission in Kosovo
UNMIL	United Nations Mission in Liberia
UNMIN	United Nations Mission in Nepal
UNMIS	United Nations Missions in Sudan
UNMISET	United Nations Mission of Support in East Timor
UNMIT	United Nations Integrated Mission in Timor-Leste
UNMOGIP	United Nations Military Observer Group in India and Pakistan
UNOCI	United Nations Operation in Côte d'Ivoire
UNODC	United Nations Office on Drugs and Crime
UNOMIG	United Nations Observer Mission in Georgia
UNOMIL	United Nations Observer Mission in Liberia
UNOMSIL	United Nations Observer Mission in Sierra Leone
UNPBF	United Nations Peacebuilding Fund
UNPKO	United Nations Peacekeeping Operations
UNPROFOR	United Nations Protection Force
UNRIC	United Nations Regional Information Centre
UNSC	United Nations Security Council
UNTAC	United Nations Transitional Authority in Cambodia
UNTAET	United Nations Transitional Administration in East Timor
UNTAG	United Nations Transition Assistance Group
UNTSO	United Nations Truce Supervision Organization
USD	US dollars
VLCC/ULCC	Very-large or Ultra-large Crude [oil] Carriers
VV MVD	Internal troops of the MVD (Russia)
WBITF	World Bank Iraq Trust Fund
WEU	Western European Union

WHO	World Health Organization
WMD	Weapons of Mass Destruction
WWII	World War II
XFOR	Extraction Force (Kosovo)

1 National security cultures, technologies of public goods supply and security governance

James Sperling

National Security Cultures has two primary goals. The first is to understand the impact of national security cultures on four categories of national security governance policies: assurance (post-conflict interventions), prevention (pre-conflict interventions), protection (internal security) and compellence (military intervention). The second is to assess the barriers and opportunities for collective action among the major powers in the provision of global and regional security governance. The study is predicated upon two assumptions: first, states can no longer be treated as homogeneous actors; and second, regional and global security governance is an (impure) collective good. The first assumption brings forward the problem of reconciling state structure and the agency of national elites in the definition and execution of security policies, particularly within a comparative framework. The second recognizes that security governance represents a bundle of policies which may individually or jointly exacerbate or mitigate the problem of collective action.

This Introduction seeks to answer four major questions: does the coexistence of states ranging from the Westphalian to post-Westphalian necessarily complicate global or regional security cooperation? What implications does that coexistence have for the process of securitization regionally or globally? Are the security governance tasks of post-Westphalian states fundamentally different from those of Westphalian states or do they merely engender different forms of security cooperation? Do national security cultures shape national security policy choices and is the technology of public goods supply relevant to understanding the challenges of effective security governance in the contemporary international system?

Security governance and the emergence of the post-Westphalian state

The importance of domestic constitutional orders as the determinant of international order has long been factored into the study of international relations as a causal variable across the theoretical spectrum (e.g. Thucydides 1954; Machiavelli 1998; Kant 1939; Hilferding 2006; Carr 1964; Rosecrance 1963). Philip Bobbitt (2002), for example, has linked the historical evolution of the European state system to changes in domestic constitutional form. The democratic peace hypothesis similarly maintains that a specific form of constitutional order, a liberal democracy, guarantees global or regional peace and stability (Owen 1994; Oneal and Russet 1997; Ward and Gleditsch 1998; Lipson 2003; Barnett 2008).[1] More recently, a group of scholars has made an effort to develop and elaborate a 'capitalist' peace hypothesis as an alternative to the democratic peace hypothesis. Stochastic analyses generally support the hypothesis, but the data supporting it are largely drawn from the European and Anglophone worlds.

The empirical support for these hypotheses rests on the circumscribed empirical base of the European system (broadly conceived), thereby precluding from consideration the more fundamental change that is taking place – the rise of the post-Westphalian state in a largely Westphalian world (Caporaso 1996 and 2000; Falk 2002). The post-Westphalian hypothesis better explains the emergence of a European (and perhaps transatlantic) security community, than does reliance upon an evolutionary form of constitutional or economic order in constant historical flux. Conversely, the persistence of the Westphalian state elsewhere better explains the continuing force of anarchy and the persistence of the balance of power, concerts and impermanent alliances as regulators of interstate conflict.

Westphalian sovereignty forms a significant barrier to cooperation generally, and security governance specifically (Jervis 2002; Keohane 1984, 2001). John Herz (1957) identified territoriality as the key characteristic of the Westphalian state and characterized it as the 'hard shell' protecting states and societies from the external environment. Territoriality is increasingly irrelevant, particularly in Europe. States no longer enjoy the 'wall of defensibility' that leaves them relatively immune to external penetration. The changed salience and meaning of territoriality has not only expanded the number and categories of security threat, but changed the assessment of instrumental rationality of the 'soft' and 'hard' elements of power, as well as the normative assessment of both.

Westphalian states remain chiefly preoccupied with protecting autonomy and independence, retaining the historic gate-keeping role between internal and external transactions, and avoiding external interference in domestic constitutional arrangements. The Westphalian state may be distinguished from the post-Westphalian state by reference to three separate but interrelated changes engendering the emergence of the latter. The first points to the qualitative erosion of the state's ability and desire to act as a gate-keeper between internal and external flows of people, goods and ideas. In the post-Westphalian state, there has been a qualitative change in the nature and volume of flows across national boundaries, as well as a change in the nature and height of the technical and normative barriers to controlling those flows contrary to the preferences of individual or corporate agents. The second acknowledges that in post-Westphalian states there has been a voluntary acceptance of mutual governance between states and the attending loss of autonomy in order to maximize the welfare benefits of those cross-border flows and to meet common challenges or threats to national welfare. Similarly, for the Westphalian state, encroachments on national territoriality and autonomy are involuntary, the barrier to intervention is technically and normatively surmountable, and unwanted external encroachments reflect disparities in relative power. The third dimension of difference derives from the asymmetrical status of international law for Westphalian and post-Westphalian states. For the post-Westphalian state, international law qualifies sovereignty in novel and meaningful ways: first, international law defines the (il)legitimacy of a government's sovereign prerogatives against their own citizenry (and a corresponding 'duty to intervene' when international law governing human rights is grossly violated); and second, states acknowledge the existence and legitimacy of extra-national adjudication of disputes and voluntarily comply with decisions of international or supranational courts and other institutionalized dispute resolution mechanisms. These developments fundamentally separate Westphalian from post-Westphalian states; the latter accept the circumscribed legal autonomy of the state vis-à-vis the citizen as natural and legitimate. The evolution of the European state system, particularly the trajectory of the European Union (EU), provides the empirical evidence supporting the post-Westphalian hypothesis and its relevance for understanding the limits and possibilities of security governance cooperation in the twenty-first century.

The post-Westphalian hypothesis challenges the assumptions that states can be treated as homogenous actors; that there is a single, homogeneous international society of states; and that states confront the same structural constraint, namely the distribution and concentration of power. The Westphalian and post-Westphalian states face an alternative set of objective security vulnerabilities, and are compelled to practise an alternative form of statecraft, instrumentally and substantively. Post-Westphalian states, while not indifferent to territorial integrity, have largely abandoned their gate-keeper role owing to the network of interdependencies formed by economic openness, the political imperative of welfare maximization, and democratic political principles. Autonomy and independence have been devalued as sovereign imperatives in order to meet the welfare demands made on the state and the expectations of individual agents. Post-Westphalian states are more vulnerable to the influence of non-state actors – malevolent, benevolent, or benign – in international politics. Non-state actors fill or exploit the gaps left by the (in)voluntary loss or evaporation of sovereignty attending the transformation of the state, while others are purposeful repositories for sovereignty ceded, lent, pooled or forfeited. The changing nature of the security agenda, particularly its functional expansion and the changing agency of threat, necessitates a shift from coercive to persuasive security strategies (Kirchner and Sperling 2007).

European states have progressively stripped away the prerogatives of sovereignty and eliminated the autonomy once afforded powerful states by exclusive territorial jurisdiction. A specific constellation of events led to the emergence of the post-Westphalian state within Europe: the growing irrelevance of geography and borders, technological innovations, particularly the revolution in information technologies and the digital linking of national economies and societies, a convergence around transnational meta-norms of inalienable civil liberties, democratic governance and an irreversible economic openness. The ease with which domestic disturbances are transmitted across national boundaries *and* the difficulty of deflecting those disturbances underline the strength and vulnerability of the post-Westphalian state: the ever expanding spectrum and depth of interstate and inter-societal interactions provide greater levels of collective welfare than would otherwise be possible. Yet the very transmission belts facilitating those welfare gains also serve as diffusion mechanisms (Hanrieder 1978; Most and Starr 1980; Ruggie 1986; Siverson and Starr 1990), which in turn hinder the state's ability to inoculate itself against exogenous shocks or malevolent actors. Those actors, in turn, are largely immune to sovereign jurisdiction as well as strategies of dissuasion, defence or deterrence. Consequently, broad and collective milieu goals have been substituted for particularistic national security goals, conventionally conceived. Perforated sovereignty has rendered post-Westphalian states incapable of meeting their national security requirements alone; security has become a structurally conditioned (impure) collective good. These developments, in conjunction with the emergence of failed states and the growing autonomy of non-state actors, have produced a changed threat environment that initiated and pushed forward the securitization of policy arenas heretofore exclusively defined in terms of domestic welfare or law and order.

Thus, Westphalian and post-Westphalian states differ along four dimensions: the degree of penetration by state and non-state actors and the consequences of that penetration for national authorities; the nature and extent of the securitization process; the level of sovereign control, *de facto* and *de jure*; and the referent for calculating security interests (see Table 1.1). The existence of two general categories of states with fundamentally dissimilar structural characteristics suggests the need for the analysis of regional security systems as the appropriate unit of analysis, although it poses a significant barrier to a unified system-level of theory

Table 1.1 Key characteristics of (post-)Westphalian states

	Westphalian state	Post-Westphalian state
Penetration	The degree of penetration by non-state and state actors is limited and revocable	The degree of penetration by non-state and state actors is extensive and irrevocable
Critical threats	State security largely defined by threats to territorial integrity, autonomy from external influence, and power maximization	State security largely defined by the vulnerabilities of the state attending the voluntary and structural erosion of sovereignty; states are primarily oriented towards milieu goals
Sovereign control	State functions as effective gate-keeper between internal and external flows; disinclination to surrender sovereignty to individual agents domestically or to international institutions	There is a *de facto* erasure of sovereign boundaries and governments are unable to act as effective gate-keepers between internal and external flows; there exists a sanctioned loss of sovereign control to individual economic agents and a willingness to transfer sovereignty to international institutions
Interest referent	Interests are narrow and self-regarding	Interests are constituted by a broad, other-regarding set of criteria

(Powell 1991: 1305). With the post-Westphalian state, the emergence of highly institutionalized forms of security governance becomes comprehensible, particularly the European security community formed by the European Union (EU), as does the persistent Westphalian embrace of power-based forms of security governance elsewhere.

Threats in the contemporary international system

The vulnerabilities of the post-Westphalian state and the securitization process that those vulnerabilities have engendered require an alternative conceptualization of threat and the concomitant proliferation of security policies. That states today now embrace an expanded national security agenda is no longer contested, but the precise boundary between a security threat and a challenge to domestic governance is not yet fixed. Barry Buzan, Ole Wæver and Jaap de Wilde (1998: 21), despite their embrace of a broadened security agenda, limit security to those threats that are 'about survival [and pose] an existential threat to a designated referent object'. This suggested demarcation is too restrictive given the novel vulnerabilities facing the post-Westphalian state and the inevitable prominence of non-state actors as the primary agent of threat. A comprehensive approach to security governance must also include threats posed to systemic or milieu goals of states, the legitimacy or authority of state structures, or national social cohesiveness and integrity. These three categories of threat are of particular concern for post-Westphalian states, because these threats cannot be reduced to a state-centric security calculus where the state is both subject and object of the analysis. Instead, the new security agenda demands a more nuanced and complicated treatment of the security problem: the state is only one agent and target of security threats. Non-state actors play an important role as agents of insecurity; and security is sought for society, the state and the milieu goals embraced by international society or a well-defined group of states. There has been a relative diminution of the state, both as a target and source of threat.

Thus, a typology of threats, which bears directly on the problem of security governance and the validity of the post-Westphalian hypothesis, defines threats along two dimensions: the target of the threat (state or society or milieu) and the agent of threat (state or non-state) (see Figure 1.1). This threat typology underscores the relative complexity and intractability of the systemic requirements of security for two reasons: first, states play a relatively minor role as protagonists in the present security system, and agency is attributed overwhelmingly to non-state actors beyond the reach of states and the 'hard' instruments of state-craft; and second, threats against the state are indirect rather than direct, and now purposely target society or envelop the regional milieu. Malign transnational non-state actors, the agents of threat that target societal rather than state structures, are of greatest concern to post-Westphalian states, while a state-centric calculus continues to frame the security concerns of the Westphalian state (Sperling 2009). Many of the new security challenges threaten social structures or cohesion. Still others target institutionalized governance structures or the milieu goals of states in a specific

		Target of threat		
		State	*Society*	*Milieu*
Agent of threat	State	Traditional war: • conventional war • nuclear war	Institutions: • weak civil institutions • cyber warfare	Impure public good: • macroeconomic instability • energy infrastructure
	Non-state	Asymmetric war: • terrorism	Individuals: • migratory pressures • transnational organized crime • health	Pure public good: • environmental degradation • non-governance

Figure 1.1 A typology of threats

region, particularly where national political systems are democratically governed and national economies adhere to a form of liberal or social democratic capitalism. Where these conditions present themselves, the state itself is largely bypassed as a target of threat. As problematically, states are the least likely source of threat thereby denying national authorities a well-defined threat referent.

The confluence of post-Westphalian vulnerabilities and non-governance in weak or failed Westphalian states requires a reconceptualization of the governance functions performed within any regional security system. The difficulty of managing these security threats derives from two conditions: the inability of governments to control territory owing to the state's involuntary loss of *de facto* sovereignty and voluntary abnegation of *de jure* sovereignty; and the problem of non-governance in areas of the world devoid of *de facto* sovereign jurisdiction. Security governance provides a conceptual framework capturing both aspects of this dynamic.

Security governance, governance functions and systems of governance

Why security governance? The fundamental problem of international politics – and security provision in particular – is the supply of order and the regulation of conflict without the resort to war. Westphalian anarchy provides states the benefits of autonomy and independence, but precludes the emergence of global or even regional governance to manage the attending liabilities of chronic insecurity and conflict that sometimes leads to war. The regulation of international politics, particularly the management of disorder, can be best thought of as a problem of governance as well as non-governance.[2] The alternative forms of interstate regulation that have emerged and receded historically (balance of power, collective defence or concert) can neither account for nor ameliorate the range of threats states face today, largely owing to their inherent limitations, the most important of which is a preoccupation with the military aspect of security and the unspoken assumption that all states still share the Westphalian preoccupation with autonomy, influence and the aggregation of power.

A conceptual reliance upon alliances or concerts for understanding the require-ments and modes of national security is obsolete, at least in the European and possibly in the wider transatlantic geopolitical space. Alliances and concerts, as either formal or informal institutions, have been rightly regarded as mechanisms for regulating disequilibria in the international system.[3] The theory of alliances has been traditionally focused on determining or explaining patterns of interstate alignments; such a focus is not particularly relevant to our understanding the security dilemmas facing the post-Westphalian state or providing a rationale for choosing one form of governance rather than another to meet the novel security challenges of the twenty-first century. Similarly, concerts have had the limited preoccupation of minimizing the potential for conflict between the Great Powers and limiting mutual interference in one another's domestic affairs. Not only have the source of threat and the security objectives of the state changed in fundamental ways, but the nomenclature of alliances and concerts is increasingly irrelevant to the problem of security governance. Both systems of international conflict regula-tion remain overly state-centric, tend to depend upon the existence and relevance of power disequilibria among a well-defined set of states, and cannot account for the subcontracting of sovereign responsibilities to international or supranational institutions. Consequently, the formulation and execution of security policy can-not be disciplined or translated into the traditional rubric of sovereign jurisdiction or assessments of the capabilities and intentions of identifiable adversaries with a state identity. Only security governance provides a conceptual framework clarify-ing and capturing within group security challenges as well as those posed by a variegated set of 'others'.

Security governance has been expansively defined as 'an international system of rule, dependent on the acceptance of a majority of states that are affected, which through regulatory mechanisms (both formal and informal), governs activities across a range of security and security-related issue areas' (Webber 2002: 44). This definition is elastic enough to accommodate analytical frameworks treating institu-tions as mechanisms employed by states to further their own goals (Koremenos *et al.* 2001: 761–99); states as the primary actors in international relations where some states are 'more equal than others' (Waltz 1978; Gilpin 1981); power relation-ships determined not only by underlying material factors, but norms and identities (Checkel 1998; Hopf 1998; Barnett and Duvall 2005); and states as constrained by institutions with respect to proscribed and prescribed behaviour (Martin and Simmons 1998; March and Olsen 1998). This broad conceptual definition of secu-rity governance permits an investigation of the role institutions play in the security domain, particularly the division of labour between states and international or supranational institutions, the proscribed and prescribed instruments and purposes of state action, and the consolidation of a collective definition of interest and threat.

The conceptualizations of security governance generally fall into one of four broad categories: as a general theory of state interaction (Webber 2002, 2007; Webber *et al.* 2004); as a theory networks (Krahmann 2003); as a system of international and transnational regimes (Young 1999; Kirchner 2007); and as a heuristic device for recasting the problem of security management in order to accommodate the coexistence of alternative forms of conflict regulation, the rising number of non-state actors considered relevant to national definitions of security, and the expansion of the security agenda (Holsti 1991; see also Sperling 2003, 2007, 2008). Security governance possesses the virtue of conceptual accommodation: it allows for hierarchical and heterarchical patterns of interaction as well as the disparate substantive bundling and normative content of security institutions. Security governance possesses the additional virtue of neither precluding nor necessitating the privileging of the state or non-state actors in the security domain; it leaves open the question of whether states are able to provide security across multiple levels and dimensions unilaterally or whether states are compelled to work within multilateral or supranational institutional frameworks. Most important, the concurrent emergence of the post-Westphalian state and broadening of the contemporary security agenda constitute the key rationales for adopting the concept of governance rather than the more established security frameworks and concepts. Moreover, the emergent role of the EU as a security actor – and a corresponding erosion of state prerogatives in this policy domain – requires a more plastic framework allowing the simultaneous consideration of EU (and the structural characteristics of its member states) with other states in the system, particularly the late-Westphalian states of Northeast Asia and North America as well as the Westphalian states of Eurasia and the southern and eastern Mediterranean.[4]

Governance functions

One approach to the problem of disentangling and understanding the current threat environment focuses on how those threats are manifested. In this case, security challenges may be defined by the arena of conflict (state, society or milieu) and the instruments of conflict resolution (coercive or persuasive). When combined, these variables produce a typology presenting six distinct categories of security

		Instruments of statecraft	
		Coercive	*Persuasive*
Arena of conflict	State	Avoidance of interstate conflict by coercive means (sanctions and deterrence)	Avoiding civil conflict or collapse of internal authority in weak or failed states
	Society	Protection of society from transnational criminal organizations	Institutionalization of democratic norms
	Regional or global milieu	Resolution of interstate and intrastate conflict by coercive means (direct intervention)	Strengthening regional or global governance institutions

Figure 1.2 Challenges of governance

challenge: resolving interstate conflicts; resolving intrastate conflicts; preventing the criminalization of national economies; avoiding the collapse of weak or failing states; institutionalizing democratic norms and institutions regionally; and constructing effective systems of regional governance (see Figure 1.2). These policy challenges overlap in many instances and are inseparable in practice. In some cases they require the simultaneous application of the coercive and persuasive instruments of statecraft; in many cases the distinction between intrastate and interstate conflicts is unhelpful; and in still others, the policy challenges and tasks are sequential.

A second approach to security governance identifies the tasks of security governance as the institutional and normative frameworks supporting multilateral peacekeeping, peace-making and peace-enforcement operations (Kirchner 2007). There is a great deal of value to be gained from adopting this approach, but it is limiting owing to its exclusion of those internal security governance functions that present the most intractable threats in the contemporary state system, namely those posed to civil society. This latter category of threat, which increasingly requires external cooperation, is most directly affected by the presence or absence of an effective form of security governance.

Although both typologies provide a window on the governance tasks attending the expanded security agenda, a functional categorization of security policy not only captures both the external and internal tasks of governance, but explicitly captures the distinction between pre-conflict and post-conflict interventions. Such an approach combines the functional and instrumental requirements for meeting these security challenges. Security governance performs two functions – institution-building and conflict resolution – and employs two sets of instruments – the persuasive (economic, political and diplomatic) and the coercive (medium to high-intensity military interventions and internal policing). Taken together, four categories of security governance emerge: assurance, prevention, protection and compellence (see Figure 1.3).[5]

Policies of assurance identify efforts aimed at post-conflict reconstruction and

		Instruments	
		Persuasive	*Coercive*
Functions	Institution-building	Prevention	Protection
	Conflict resolution	Assurance	Compellence

Figure 1.3 Policies of governance

attending confidence-building measures. Three general policies of assurance are addressed in the contributing chapters to this collection: policing and border missions; post-conflict monitoring missions; and economic reconstruction aid. In each instance, three questions are posed: what budgetary and personnel contributions are made to the operation? Does the country under consideration betray a geographic bias in its governance policies? Does the country prefer to act bilaterally or multilaterally? Policies of prevention capture efforts to prevent conflict by building or sustaining domestic, regional or international institutions that contribute to the mitigation of anarchy and the creation of order. Common policies of prevention include arms control and non-proliferation measures as well as technical assistance for internal political and economic reform, ranging from establishing civil-military relations consistent with the Euro-American norm to enhancing the prospects for democratic governance to aiding the development of market economies.

Policies of protection describe internal and multilateral efforts to fulfil the traditional function of protecting society from external threats. There are five general categories of protection policies: health security, border control, terrorism, organized crime and environmental degradation. The country-specific analyses will reveal whether those issues have been securitized and if so, the relative importance of each category of threat, measured primarily by budgetary expenditures and policy initiatives seeking to manage threats (e.g. improved health surveillance or funds devoted to medical research) or to eradicate it (e.g. increases in personnel or budgetary resources to combat crime or terrorism). Policies of compellence capture the tasks of conflict resolution via military intervention, particularly peace-making and peace enforcement. As the traditional focus of security analyses, the country-specific studies will assess national contributions to unilateral, bilateral and multilateral interventions to restore or create regional order or to remove a direct military threat to national security. Policies of compellence raise an important question: do some states rely disproportionately upon the military instrument relative to the other three categories of security governance?

These four tasks of security governance are often pursued concurrently; it is also clear that economic and military instruments may be relied upon to achieve not dissimilar goals. Arguably there *is* an elective affinity between policy instruments and a specific form of governance challenge, and post-Westphalian states exhibit a substantive normative reliance upon the civilian instruments of statecraft and disinclination to rely upon military force.

Effective security governance: national security cultures and technologies of public goods supply

Kalevi J. Holsti (1991), Emmanuel Adler and Michael Barnett (1998), Robert O. Keohane (2001) and Robert Jervis (2002), among others, have considered the domestic and systemic requirements for effective security governance. With the exception of Holsti, who addressed the necessary and sufficient conditions for system stability (defined as the absence of war), these scholars have been preoccupied with the preconditions for the emergence and persistence of a democratic security community. The international system neither constitutes a democratic security community nor does it come close to meeting the conditions necessary for one to emerge. Regional security subsystems range from rudimentary systems of governance (e.g. the Pacific balance of power) to more complex forms of governance (e.g. the EU security community). Within each regional subsystem, which is in turn anchored by the major powers investigated in this collection, there are variations in national security policies and preferred forms of governance. These nations' security governance policies – in form or content – and the limits of interstate cooperation can be best explained by variations or similarities in national security cultures.

National security cultures provide the lens through which national authorities refract the structural position of the state in the international system; it explains the subjective understanding of objective threats to national security, the instruments relied upon to meet those threats, and the preference for unilateral or multilateral action. When national security cultures clash or merely impede the ability to translate threats into a common frame of reference, highly institutionalized forms of security governance are unlikely to emerge and cooperation is likely to be tactical and infrequent rather than strategic and routinized. But even where national security cultures significantly overlap (i.e. threats are treated as common and are understood with respect to cause and effect, and multilateral cooperation is preferred to bilateral or unilateral action), states may nonetheless be incapable of meeting those threats individually or collectively. The second barrier to multilateral cooperation, then, is found in the differentiated nature of the security goods under consideration; variations in the technology of public goods supply function as an intervening variable that can mitigate or exacerbate the problem of collective action despite the presence of compatible or security cultures.

Security culture

National security cultures pose a potential barrier to effective security governance. There are those who treat national strategic cultures as relatively fixed and incorrigibly national (Lindley-French 2002; Rynning 2003; Longhurst and Zaborowski 2005), while others (Meyer 2006; Eilstrup-Sangiovanni and Verdier 2005; Matlary 2006) detect instead a convergence of cultures. While these two orientations are oppositional, it is of little practical consequence if divergent cultures cannot explain the dynamic of disparate subjective understandings of material interests or if the negative consequences of ideational opposition are illusory.

National security cultures may be defined according to four criteria: the worldview of the external environment; national identity; instrumental preferences; and interaction preferences.[6] The worldview of the external environment refers to the elite consensus on the underling dynamic of the international system, the importance and viability of state sovereignty, and the definition of security threats. National identity captures the extent to which national elites have retained an 'egoist' definition of the national interest or the extent to which the elites have embedded the national interest in a broader, collective 'we' defined against some 'other'. Instrumental preferences demarcate those states which retain the traditional reliance upon the 'hard' instruments of statecraft and the coercive use of economic power, as opposed to those states relying on the 'soft' instruments of power, particularly international law, economic aid, and the creation of binding normative frameworks that constitute national threat perceptions and interests and define the parameters of (il)legitimate policy options. Interaction preferences, which refer to the level of cooperation favoured by a state when seeking to ameliorate a security threat, fall along a continuum marked at one end by unilateral action and at the other by a reflexive multilateralism within highly formalized institutional structures.

Post-Westphalian and Westphalian states have significantly different, if not oppositional, security cultures (see Table 1.2). Disparate security cultures pose

Table 1.2 National security cultures

	Elements	Westphalian	Post-Westphalian
Worldview of external environment	Refers to the elite consensus on the underling dynamic of the international system, the importance and viability of state sovereignty, and the definition of security threats	Competitive international system populated by sovereign, autonomous states preoccupied with territorial integrity; interstate interaction is largely zero-sum	Cooperative international system populated by states largely indifferent to sovereign prerogatives, territorially secure and welfare maximizing; interstate interaction is generally joint-sum
Identity	Captures the way in which national elites define the nation vis-à-vis the external world	Elites retain an 'egoist' definition of the national interest and define the nation in opposition to an 'other' posing an existential threat	Elites denationalize the national interest; the national is embedded in a broader collective 'we' rather than in opposition to an 'other'
Instrumental preferences	Identifies preferred instruments of statecraft which can be assessed in relation to the typology of power	Realist power resources, particularly a reliance upon the coercive instruments of statecraft	Direct and indirect institutional power, preference for reliance upon persuasive instruments of statecraft
Interaction preferences	Refers to the preference for unilateral, bilateral, and multilateral cooperation in addressing security threats	Ranges from preference for unilateralism to conditional and temporary bilateralism or multilateralism	Ranges from preference for multilateral cooperation within institutions to abnegation of sovereign prerogatives to empower institutional rather than national action

a largely self-evident barrier to interstate cooperation across the four security governance policies: states will disagree not only on what constitutes a threat, but the appropriate means for ameliorating it. Common security cultures only produce cooperation when they tend towards the post-Westphalian variant whereas the Westphalian variant may or may not impede cooperation. In the former, states are likely to view multilateralism as the strategy of choice reflexively, to securitize a not dissimilar range of threats and to adopt policy options that minimize social and economic dislocations internally or in the target state or region. Westphalian security cultures, on the other hand, are similar insofar as they target the maximization of power, rely upon military power to achieve their goals, and acknowledge a circumscribed range of threats. Despite that commonality, however, the security cultures themselves do not provide the basis for routinized cooperation since they internalize and act in a manner consistent with the imperatives of anarchy as understood by realists and neorealists alike. Just as divergences in the security cultures within the transatlantic subsystem inhibit sustained, institutionalized cooperation on a range of security governance policies, the American, Chinese and Russian security cultures, for example, virtually preclude sustained or institutionalized security governance with one another, particularly with respect to the policies of assurance, prevention and protection.

Each country chapter will assess the three hypotheses linking this conceptualization of security culture to the content and form of national security policies:

- H_1: *National security cultures account for the securitization of threats and the preferred instruments relied upon to meet them.*
- H_2: *'Post-Westphalian' security cultures mitigate the problem of collective action, while 'Westphalian' security cultures intensify the problem of collective action in the provision of security.*
- H_3: *National security cultures produce preferences for specific forms of security governance systems that, in turn, facilitate or inhibit international cooperation.*

Technology of public goods supply

The heterogeneous security governance challenges encode different technologies of public goods production, which may be defined as 'the manner in which [actors'] provision or subscription levels are aggregated to yield a group provision or consumption level' of the public good (Sandler 1992: 36). There are three basic technologies of publicness: summation, weakest link and 'best shot'.

Summation represents the simplest case: the provision of the collective good is simply dependent upon the substitutability of the actors providing the good insofar as the definition of the privileged group is not dependent upon the identity of any individual member of the collective; the amount of the good supplied is simply determined by the sum of the individual contributions of the group. Weakest link technology exists where the smallest level of the good provided by an individual actor determines the absolute level of the public good available to all.[7] 'Best shot' technology obtains where the amount of the public good provided to the collective depends upon the largest effort of an individual state (Sandler 1992: 36–37). These alternative technologies of public goods production can help explain barriers to effective security governance across the entire range of security governance policies and the unwillingness of states to relinquish sovereign prerogatives, even when an optimal policy response requires it. Moreover, those different technologies explain why governance structures are asymmetrically developed even where state structures and security cultures should reinforce rather than inhibit effective security governance.

Weakest link technology complicates the policies of protection: the defection of one state from an agreed-upon common or coordinated policy – on rules of evidence, penal law, information-sharing or common epidemiological surveillance and protocols – will hamper the ability of others to combat the common threats posed by organized crime, terrorism or pandemics, natural and otherwise. 'Best shot' technology defines the policies of compellence: the unwillingness of any state or group of states from participating in a military intervention, for example, is unimportant so long as a major state with power projection capabilities does so. Finally, summation technology is relevant for understanding the relative ease of implementing policies of assurance and prevention, particularly within the EU, the UN or the OSCE: individual member state contributions to those institutions' policies are compulsory and assessed according to an agreed-upon scale of national contributions that predetermines each member's contribution to any undertaking. Within these institutional fora, defection can be made a costly option. In most cases, mechanisms exist to ensure an optimal supply of the good once the institution or member states jointly define its content. These three technologies of public goods production generate a central hypotheses:

- H_1: *Burden-sharing in global security governance will vary across governance policies and regions depending upon the specific technology of public goods supply.*

This hypothesis is assessed in the concluding chapter with respect to national contributions to UN programmes and operations across the spectrum of security governance policies.

Conclusion

If the world's major powers may be placed along a continuum demarcated by Westphalian and post-Westphalian states, then each state will face different, yet overlapping, vulnerabilities and insecurities which, in turn, may produce alternative and possibly competing national security agenda. Similarly, the ability of national elites to meet those vulnerabilities and insecurities will be shaped and limited by the imperatives, prescriptions and proscriptions of the national security culture. The precise variations in state structure and national security culture between two or more states will create a context that is (un)favourable to bilateral or multilateral security cooperation. The problem of collective action in the provision of regional and global security governance is similarly complicated by an important, often overlooked, intervening variable, namely the various technologies of public goods supply. Even where there is a positive, reinforcing correspondence between the structural characteristics and national security cultures of the cooperating states, the production technologies for specific categories of public goods can either ease or complicate the dilemma of collective action in the security sphere. The contributions to *National Security Cultures* provide the basis for a systematic comparison of the major world powers' security governance policies along these three dimensions.

Notes

1 Edward Mansfield and Jack Snyder (2007) also demonstrate that states in the early stages of democratization are as likely to be war prone as not, while Kal Holsti (1995) rejects the emphasis on democratic constitutional orders and suggests instead that the absence of domestic legitimacy, regardless of constitutional form, is the better indicator of bellicosity.
2 See Wagnsson and Hallenberg (2009) on pre-Westphalian states as a form of non-governance.
3 For the period 1648–1945, see Langer (1950); Taylor (1954); Holsti (1991); and Schweller (1998). For the post-war period, see Wolfers (1959); Osgood (1962); Liska (1962); and Walt (1987).
4 Late-Westphalian states are transitional states that share many of the structural characteristics of the post-Westphalian state, but retain the instrumental and normative orientations of the Westphalian state. The United States is a case on point (see Chapter 9).
5 This typology is applied in a qualitative study of the EU by Kirchner and Sperling (2007) and in a quantitative analysis by Dorussen *et al.* (2009).
6 This definition builds on the conceptualizations of security culture found in Berger (2003); Banchoff (1999); Duffield (1998); and Katzenstein (1996).
7 A factor aggravating the collective action problem of providing public goods with a weakest link production technology is an inability (or unwillingness) to expel or sanction a chronic free-rider.

References

Adler, E. and Barnett, M. (1998) 'A Framework for the Study of Security Communities', in Adler, E. and Barnett, M. (eds) *Security Communities*, Cambridge: Cambridge University Press.

Banchoff, T. (1999) *The German Problem Transformed: Institutions, Politics and Foreign Policy, 1945–1995*, Ann Arbor, MI: University of Michigan Press.

Barnett, M. and Duvall, R. (eds) (2005) *Power in Global Governance*, Cambridge: Cambridge University Press.

Berger, T. (2003) *Culture of Anti-Militarism: National Security in Germany and Japan*, Baltimore, MD: Johns Hopkins University Press.

Bobbitt, P. (2002) *The Shield of Achilles: War, Peace, and the Course of History*, New York: Anchor Books.

Buzan, B., Wæver, O. and de Wilde, J. (1998) *Security: A New Framework for Analysis*, Boulder, CO: Lynne Rienner.

Caporaso, J. (1996) 'The European Union and Forms of State: Westphalian, Regulatory or Post-Modern?', *Journal of Common Market Studies*, 34(1): 29–52.

—— (2000) 'Changes in the Westphalian Order: Territory, Public Authority, and Sovereignty', *International Studies Review* (Special Issue: Continuity and Change in the Westphalian Order), 2(2): 1–28.

Carr, E.H. (1964) *The Twenty Years' Crisis, 1919–1939: An Introduction to the Study of International Relations*, New York: Harper Torchbooks.

Checkel, J.T. (1998) 'The Constructivist Turn in International Relations Theory', *World Politics*, 50(2): 324–48.

Duffield, J.S. (1998) *World Power Forsaken: Political Culture, International Institutions, and German Security Policy after Unification*, Stanford, CA: Stanford University Press.

Eilstrup-Sangiovanni, M. and Verdier, D. (2005) 'European Integration as a Solution to War', *European Journal of International Relations*, 11(1): 99–135.

Falk, R. (2002) 'Revisiting Westphalia, Discovering Post-Westphalia', *Journal of Ethics*, 6: 311–52.

Gilpin, R. (1981) *War and Change in World Politics*, Princeton, NJ: Princeton University Press.

Hanrieder, W.F. (1978) 'Dissolving International Politics: Reflections on the Nation-State', *American Political Science Review*, 72(4): 1276–87.

Herz, J.H. (1957) 'The Rise and Demise of the Territorial State', *World Politics*, 9(4): 473–93.

Hilferding, R. (2006) *Finance Capital: A Study of the Latest Phase of Capitalist Development*, Abingdon, UK: Routledge.

Holsti, K.J. (1991) *Peace and War: Armed Conflicts and International Order, 1648–1989*, Cambridge: Cambridge University Press.

—— (1995) 'War, Peace and the State of the State', *International Political Science Review*, 16(4): 310–39.

Hopf, T. (1998) 'The Promise of Constructivism in International Relations Theory', *International Security*, 23(1): 171–200.

Jervis, R. (2002) 'Theories of War in an Era of Leading Power Peace', *American Political Science Review*, 96(1): 1–14.

Kant, I. (1939) *Perpetual Peace*, Butler, N.M. (ed.), New York: Columbia University Press.

Katzenstein, P.J. (ed.) (1996) *The Culture of National Security*, New York: Columbia University Press.

Keohane, R.O. (1984) *After Hegemony: Cooperation and Discord in the World Political Economy*, Princeton, NJ: Princeton University Press.

—— (2001) 'Governance in a Partially Globalized World', *American Political Science Review*, 95(1): 1–13.

Kirchner, E.J. (2007) 'Security Governance in the European Union', *Journal of Common Market Studies*, 44(5): 947–68.

Kirchner, E.J. and Sperling, J. (2007) *EU Security Governance*, Manchester: Manchester University Press.

Koremenos, B., Lipson, C. and Snidal, D. (2001) 'The Rational Design of International Institutions', *International Organization*, 55(4): 761–99.

Krahmann, E. (2003) 'Conceptualising Security Governance', *Cooperation and Conflict*, 38(1): 5–26.

Langer, W.L. (1950) *European Alliances and Alignments*, 2nd edn, New York: Random House.

Lindley-French, J. (2002) 'In the Shadow of Locarno: Why European Defence is Failing', *International Affairs*, 78(4): 789–811.

Lipson, C. (2003) *Reliable Partners: How Democracies Have Made a Separate Peace*, Princeton, NJ: Princeton University Press.

Liska, G. (1962) *Nations in Alliance: The Limits of Interdependence*, Baltimore, MD: Johns Hopkins University Press.

Longhurst, K. and Zaborowski, M. (2005) *Old Europe, New Europe and the Transatlantic Security Agenda*, Abingdon, UK: Routledge.

Machiavelli, N. (1998) *The Discourses*, Crick, B. (ed.) and Walker, L.J. and Richardson, B. (trans.), London: Penguin Classics.

Mansfield, E. and Snyder, J. (2007) *Electing to Fight: Why Emerging Democracies Go To War*, Cambridge, MA: MIT Press.

March, J.G. and Olsen, J.P. (1998) 'The Institutional Dynamics of International Political Orders', *International Organization*, 52(4): 943–69.

Martin, L.L. and Simmons, B.A. (1998) 'Theories and Empirical Studies of International Institutions', *International Organization*, 52(4): 729–57.

Matlary, J.H. (2006) 'When Soft Power Turns Hard: Is an EU Strategic Culture Possible?', *Security Dialogue*, 27(1): 105–21.

Meyer, C.O. (2006) *The Quest for a European Strategic Culture: Changing Norms on Security and Defence in the European Union*, Basingstoke, UK: Palgrave Macmillan.

Most, B.A. and Starr, H. (1980) 'Diffusion, Reinforcement, Geopolitics, and the Spread of War', *American Political Science Review*, 74(4): 932–46.

Oneal, J.R. and Russett, B.M. (1997) 'The Classic Liberals Were Right: Democracy, Interdependence, and Conflict, 1950–85', *International Studies Quarterly*, 41(2): 267–93.

Osgood, R.E. (1962) *NATO: The Entangling Alliance*, Chicago: University of Chicago Press.

Owen, J.M. (1994) 'How Liberalism Produces the Democratic Peace', *International Security*, 19(1): 87–125.

Powell, R. (1991) 'Absolute and Relative Gains in International Relations Theory', *American Political Science Review*, 85(4): 1202–20.

Rosecrance, R. (1963) *Action and Reaction in World Politics: International Systems in Perspective*, New York: Little, Brown.

Ruggie, J.G. (1986) 'Continuity and Transformation in the World Polity: Toward a Neo-Realist Synthesis', in Keohane, R.O. (ed.) *Neorealism and its Critics*, New York: Columbia University Press.

Rynning, S. (2003) 'The European Union: Towards a Strategic Culture?', *Security Dialogue*, 34(4): 479–96.

Schweller, R. (1998) *Deadly Imbalances: Tripolarity and Hitler's Strategy of World Conquest*, New York: Columbia University Press.

Siverson, R.M. and Starr, H. (1990) 'Opportunity, Willingness, and the Diffusion of War', *American Political Science Review*, 84(1): 47–67.

Sperling, J. (2003) 'Eurasian Security Governance: New Threats, Institutional Adaptations', in Sperling, J., Kay, S. and Papacosma, S.V. (eds) *Limiting Institutions? The Challenge of Eurasian Security Governance*, Manchester: Manchester University Press.

—— (2007) 'Regional or Global Security Cooperation? The Vertices of Conflict and Interstices of Cooperation', in Kirchner, E.J. and Sperling, J. (eds) *Global Security Governance: Competing Perceptions of Security in the 21st Century*, Abingdon, UK: Routledge.

—— (2008) 'State Attributes and System Properties: Security Multilateralism in Central

Asia, Southeast Asia, the Atlantic and Europe', in Bourantonis, D., Ifantis, K. and Tsakonas, P. (eds) *Multilateralism and Security Institutions in an Era of Globalization*, Abingdon, UK: Routledge.

—— (2009) 'Security Governance in a Westphalian World', in Wagnsson, C., Sperling, J. and Hallenberg, J. (eds) *European Security Governance: The European Union in a Westphalian World*, Abingdon, UK: Routledge.

Taylor, A.J.P. (1954) *The Struggle for Mastery of Europe, 1848–1918*, Oxford: Clarendon Press.

Thucydides (1954) *The History of the Peloponnesian War* (rev. edn), Finley, M.I. (ed.) and Warner, R. (trans.), London: Penguin Classics.

Wagnsson, C. and Hallenberg, J. (2009) 'Conclusion: Farewell to Westphalia? The Prospects for EU Security Governance', in Wagnsson, C., Sperling, J. and Hallenberg, J. (eds) *European Security Governance: The European Union in a Westphalian World*, Abingdon, UK: Routledge.

Walt, S. (1987) *The Origins of Alliances*, Ithaca, NY: Cornell University Press.

Waltz, K. (1978) *Theory of International Politics*, New York: Random House.

Ward, M.D. and Gleditsch, K.S. (1998) 'Democratizing for Peace', *American Political Science Review*, 92(1): 51–61.

Webber, M. (2007) *Inclusion, Exclusion and the Governance of European Security*, Manchester: Manchester University Press.

—— (2002) 'Security Governance and the "Excluded" States of Central and Eastern Europe', in Cottey, A. and Averre, D. (eds) *New Security Challenges in Central and Eastern Europe: Securing Europe's East*, Manchester: Manchester University Press.

Webber, M., Croft, S., Howorth, J., Terriff, T. and Krahmann, E. (2004) 'The Governance of European Security', *Review of International Studies*, 30(1): 3–26.

Wolfers, A. (ed.) (1959) *Alliance Policy in the Cold War*, Baltimore, MD: Johns Hopkins University Press.

Young, O.R. (1999) *Governance in World Affairs*, Ithaca, NY: Cornell University Press.

Part I
Europe

2 France

A departure from exceptionalism?

Bastien Irondelle and
Sophie Besancenot

Since the 2007 election of President Nicolas Sarkozy, several reform processes regarding French security policy are underway.[1] The 2008 White Paper on Defence and National Security (*Livre blanc* 2008) develops a national security strategy that gives more priority to national security issues than to military ones; indeed, intelligence is given pride of place at the expense of nuclear deterrence, the former cornerstone of French security policy. Sarkozy announced several changes: first, he committed himself to bringing France and NATO closer together with the objective of French full participation in the alliance; second, he envisioned drawing the era of the *domaine resérvé* to a close, wherein the sphere of foreign and defence policy is under the exclusive control of the Chief of State; third, he agreed to endow the Parliament with new powers for the use of force – even though this had lain at the heart of the executive prerogative – through the July 2008 Constitutional amendments. These elements of 'rupture', as proclaimed in Sarkozy's motto, seem to illustrate a normalization process of French security culture and governance in terms of two dynamics: a transition to a post-Westphalian approach, and also a trend towards a departure from 'French exceptionalism' (Erlanger and Bennhold 2008). Nevertheless, France's pattern of international projection has not abated. Instead, France's 'return to Europe' and the objectives of French international missions to promote and defend human rights were re-asserted in the first announcements of the newly elected President on 6 May 2007.

What underlies this mixture of continuing exceptionalism and increasing normalization? To what extent has French security culture been changing? What are the consequences of this change towards the securitization of threats and towards the instruments France chooses to favour? Does the broad threat assessment in the 2008 White Paper reveal that 'new issues' have been securitized, thus giving birth to a comprehensive vision of security developed in France, and thereby outdating the classical Westphalian one? Do current French threat perceptions reveal that the post-Westphalian French state admits the unconditional need for cooperation on both international and European levels?

The aim of this chapter is twofold. First, it will provide a detailed account of the changes in France's security culture since the end of the Cold War and the terrorist attacks of 11 September 2001 (9/11) and its main sequels (invasion of Iraq, war in Afghanistan). Second, it will analyse the consequences of these changes both with regard to the instruments relied upon and chosen by France to meet the threats in question, and also the preference for international security governance systems. In order to evaluate the changes in French security culture, this chapter is not based on discourse analysis methodology (Kempin 2008; Rieker 2006). Official discourses are neither sufficient nor relevant in many instances. France has always presented itself as a promoter of human rights but this has often not been translated into substantive action. By contrast, the following analysis focuses on concrete policy choices (guidelines, priorities, resource allocation) by way of comprehensive data collection concerning the main security domains studied and identified in the introductory chapter: assurance, prevention, protection and compellence. The developments of French security culture are first evaluated through a theoretical prism, and an assessment of French behaviour and priorities in the four aforementioned policy dimensions ensues. It is argued that even if 'new domains' (mainly within prevention and assurance) have been securitized, this integration tends towards what can be called a 'pragmatic Europeanization' rather than a substantial civilian normalization and absolute preference for multilateral fora.

Explaining changes in French security culture

Legacies

French foreign policy has long been characterized by its constant and 'exceptional' features, aimed at guaranteeing its status as a great power, which, according to some observers, was 'stolen' by France after World War II. The main Gaullist legacy was to reinvigorate French exceptionalism and the French rank in international affairs (Gordon 1993). French exceptionalism in global security governance rests on three pillars: the idea of *La Grandeur* (Gordon 1993; Vaïsse 1998); the legacy of the 1789 Revolution and its Declaration of the Rights of Man and of the Citizen, endowing France with a mission to promote and defend universal values of human rights; and independence, entailing distant relationships with its allies, notably the US from 1958 onwards. France considered its relationship with the US and NATO according to the motto of '[f]riend, ally, but not aligned' (Védrine 1996). The Gaullist consensus typified this stance, and it has since been crystallized to the point of becoming a cross-party and enduring security culture. Even in 1995, Alain Juppé declared: 'Through imagination, determination, and a desire to hold its rank in the world, France can affirm itself as it wishes to be – a great power' (Treacher 2003: 65). This doctrine is related to a very classical perception of threats, and to the desire that France remain established as a classical 'military power', valuing coercion and overseas intervention as foreign policy instruments. French security culture is based on the sacrosanct principle of autonomous decision-making and independent defence capabilities. Nuclear deterrence is thus at once the instrument, the symbol and the masterpiece of the French exceptionalism that allowed France to remain a great power during the Cold War and enabled her to pursue independent foreign policy. French security culture gives priority to military and diplomatic responses over civilian and preventive responses. Yet, after the Cold War, there was a need for a reappraisal of the country's national security strategy. Already in 1994, France became aware of the existence of transnational threats, but there had been no global re-assessment since the mid-1990s. According to recent reports from the French Ministry of Defence, the French population is now more vulnerable to threats than it was in the 1990s. The 2008 White Paper's main guidelines are that '[s]ecurity interests are assessed globally without restricting the analysis to defence issues', and that there is a 'growing interconnection between threats and risks and a continuity between internal and external security'. It is also asserted that '[k]nowledge and intelligence are our first line of defence' (*Livre blanc* 2008).

The 2008 White Paper tries to prioritize these 'new threats' according to two criteria: probability of occurrence and scope of the crisis that it could provoke. The probability of terrorist attacks is assessed as high; their scope as varied in degree (low to severe). Cyber-attacks are also deemed to be very probable, but their seriousness would be more limited (low to high). Ballistic attacks from great or emerging powers are not very probable (low to average) but their scope can be severe. Pandemics are considered of average probability and their scope would be middle to severe. Natural or industrial disasters are assessed as average to high probability; scope middle to severe. An increase in organized crime is also seen as very probable, but its scope cannot be assessed. The 2006 survey on threat perceptions of French civil servants, security experts and members of parliament are convergent with the conclusion of the 2008 White Paper. New 'non-military' threats such as natural disasters, pandemics, cyber-attacks, terrorism and environmental issues are prioritized at the expense of traditional military threats such as conventional war, regional conflicts (Tardy 2007a; Irondelle and Foucault 2008).

Changes in French security culture: much ado about nothing?

There are several competing theories explaining the French security trajectory after the Cold War. This chapter focuses on the most general theories: realism and constructivism. From a realist standpoint, French security culture and governance are driven by the approach 'if we want things to stay as they are, things will have to change' (Di Lampedusa 1972: 29). According to a constructivist account, French security culture and governance have been deeply changed by European Union (EU) membership and the development of international norms.

For realists, France could be considered the ideal type of a Westphalian state. Indeed, France is often portrayed as the realist state par excellence. Barry Posen classifies France as a second-rank consequential power (Posen 2006). Others understand France as a true realist state, with a high level of state power, thanks to the strong centralization and autonomy of the state apparatus in the hands of a president with much room to manoeuvre, compared with other European democracies, in deciding what is the national interest in the power politics of international relations (Rynning 2001). According to realists, the supreme goals of French foreign policy remain unchanged, because they are derived from the enduring national interest as defined by the Gaullist legacy (Gordon 1993). With the end of the Cold War, traditional strategies became outdated, and there has been a need for pragmatic adaptation. The downsizing of the nuclear investment and the increase of the investment in intelligence, the professionalization of the Army, and the end of the national procurement of armaments dogma can all be seen as instrumental adaptations to the new era of world geopolitics (Keiger 2005: 142–3; Gautier 1998). In the 1990s, cooperation and conventional force projection became gradually more important at the expense of deterrence based on nuclear weapons: in 1996 France embarked upon a real 'strategic revolution' when signing the Comprehensive Test Ban Treaty and promoting a 'European pillar' to NATO (Irondelle 2003a; Rynning 2001).

Furthermore, realists point out that this adaptation corresponds to an acknowledgement by France that its disproportionate status in the post-Cold War world has been in decline since 1989. The fact that France was the greatest contributor to the United Nations can be seen as a strategy of power maximization: France needed to consolidate its permanent seat on the UN Security Council. Moreover, France continues to project its disappointed ambitions onto the European level, seeing Europe as a power-multiplier: a strong Europe with weak institutions serves the French national interest. In order to continue to master the process and preserve its independence, France mainly promotes the idea of enhanced cooperation and itself as a pioneer group in Europe, and opts for 'light reintegration' into NATO. But for realists, all the French changes after the Cold War are no more than tactical shifts according to the 'same objectives, different tactics' paradigm that is used to explain French policy towards European integration (Drake 2006), the relationship between European defence policy and NATO (Treacher 2003), or French preferences towards the world order (Hoffmann and Kempin 2007).

However, are all of these changes only due to instrumental adaptation to international and domestic constraints? Is the revival of multilateralism only the choice of the weak? Nowadays, even if it operates within a set of constraints, France has two conflicting goals: independence and multilateralism (Meunier 2008: 243). The 2003 invasion of Iraq crystallized defining elements of French foreign policy, which are UN legitimacy, the preference for a multipolar world, and independence from the us (Meunier 2008: 248). The constructivist understanding of French security culture highlights the substantial normalization process that deeply affected France to these ends. Constructivist authors pay more attention to ideational and cultural factors, and particularly to the influence of the EU, the role of which is ignored by realists (Wong 2006). Europeanization is 'a set of processes through which the political, social and economic dynamics of European integration become part of the logic of domestic discourses, identities, public structures and public policies' (Irondelle 2003b: 211). According to Pernille Rieker, the EU has developed a holistic approach to security, which not only constrains, but also shapes the way France approaches its security. Having no security legacy of its own, the EU developed a peculiar and innovative security approach, blurring the distinction between internal and external security, as well as that between civilian and military instruments. Rieker does not deny that there is also an instrumental adaptation to a new geopolitical environment, but mainly shows, with the help of discourse analysis, that French identity, in 'Europeanizing' itself, has also 'civilianized' itself (Rieker 2006; Kempin 2008).

Hypotheses on French security culture and global security governance

Two hypotheses put forward in the introductory chapter are particularly relevant to understand the relationship between French security culture and international security governance.

- H_1: *National security culture accounts for the securitization of threats and the preferred instruments relied upon to meet them.*

A vast literature deals with securitization issues both theoretically and empirically. In order to operationalize the concept of securitization in the French case, a three-step approach is proposed here. The first step of securitization occurs when the issue is framed as a security one. The most obvious criterion is whether the issue is framed as a threat in the national security strategy or, in the French case, in the 2008 White Paper. The second step concerns the relevant service that tackles the peculiar issue: is there a transfer of prerogatives from a civilian to a security department? Such a transfer would clearly indicate that securitization is underway. This transfer can be permanent or can occur only for specific periods in case of crisis (for instance, in case of a national emergency due to a huge pandemic, security services take charge, yet they are not in charge in conventional circumstances). The third step is militarization, which means the participation of the military in the management of the issue either in normal times or in times of crisis. Traditional French security culture tends toward securitization, which, in the case of France, often implies militarization.

- H_3: *National security culture produces preferences for specific forms of security governance systems that, in turn, facilitate or inhibit international cooperation.*

French security culture puts emphasis on autonomy and sovereignty, which is most evident in two forms: strict intergovernmentalism for the Common Foreign and Security Policy (CFSP) in the EU, and qualified membership in NATO. France is a key player in security multilateralism, being present in all the main multilateral security institutions. But French security culture clearly prefers forms of multilateralism and international cooperation that rely upon a statutory hierarchy of states, as in the case of the UN Security Council or the Non-Proliferation Treaty – or, alternatively, that rely on informal political 'directorates' like the EU-3 (Germany, the UK and France) in negotiations with Iran (Giegerich 2006; Harnisch 2007). Unilateral response remains a politically viable option that France does not hesitate to use. France has revived its national interventionism tradition since the 2002 intervention in Ivory Coast. French military action in Chad and the Central

African Republic in 2006 has confirmed the return of unilateral interventionism, in contradiction to the French policy of involvement of European partners for the crisis management of African conflicts.

Further sections of this chapter will test these hypotheses and theoretical arguments concerning the extent to which change and continuity prevail in French national security culture and its consequences for global security governance. This will be done by scrutinizing four policy dimensions consisting of the policies of assurance, prevention, protection and compellence.

Policies of assurance

An integration of 'assurance' as a core policy function in French security culture would demonstrate a growing trend towards normalization: the preferred frameworks are multilateral. Yet, the remnants of French exceptionalism can be identified in an instrumental use of multilateralism, for example through a strong regional focus, 'symbolic' participation in some of the operations, or what has been called a 'bilateral approach' to multilateralism in post-conflict reconstruction. This field is however blurred with other policy fields because an apparently stabilized situation can easily return to its previous, conflictual state. In particular, Afghanistan has demonstrated the difficulty to speak of purely post-conflict stabilization missions. Thus, military doctrine has to take into account the possible versatility of conflicts and the final step towards reconstruction might be indefinitely delayed.

Policing and peacekeeping missions

Since the Balkans conflict, French involvement in policing and peacekeeping missions is a growing trend. Policing missions are always undertaken in various multilateral frameworks, be it in the context of the UN (UNMIK in Kosovo), NATO (KFOR in Kosovo) or the EU (for whom the majority of missions are civilian). Of these three frameworks, the preferred ones for police missions are the EU and the UN. France was a pillar and an engineer of the EU Gendarmerie Force, whose main goal is to provide military police forces for European missions. The EU launched 15 civilian and police missions in all of which France was present, except in Eujust Lex in Iraq. France provides around 10 per cent of the total EU personnel for civilian missions.

In the policing and peacekeeping policy area, there are no unilateral or bilateral missions. The deployment of Gendarmes under national command for unilateral operations is not related to policing missions but mainly to the role of the Gendarmerie as the military police of French Armed Forces. In some cases, French participation is often symbolic and motivated by the need to strengthen French status in the UN. France's participation in OSCE missions follows the same political logic: France participates in the maximum number of operations but with limited numbers of experts. In 2006, France had 42 experts engaged in 14 out of a total of 19 OSCE missions. In 2008, 28 experts were engaged in 12 of the 19 OSCE missions. Besides making significant contributions to UN peacekeeping missions in military terms (see the 'Compellence' section below), France has also provided 136 civilian police officers to the 12 UN peacekeeping operations in which it has participated since 1974.

To conclude, even if a better integration of civilian-military missions is sought, a military *'ad hoc'* approach still dominates the field of 'assurance policies'.

Policies of prevention

In French military strategy, prevention is one of the five main strategic functions of the Armed Forces. Whereas the general definition of prevention policy would include diplomatic, financial and aid policy tools to prevent conflict, French prevention policy includes defence diplomacy, military cooperation, and the training of foreign Armed Forces. Although some analysts see a kind of Europeanization in French security policy with the adoption of a more comprehensive security strategy, as alluded to above, the recent 2008 White Paper and particularly the French White Paper on Foreign and European Policy (Juppé and Schweitzer 2008) confirm the absence of prevention in French security policy, or a very narrow conception of it as a classical security concern. Moreover, the 2008 White Paper displays a very militarized and national-security-oriented conception of prevention: 'the aim of prevention is to avoid the emergence or the aggravation of threats to our national security' (*Livre blanc* 2008). The main prevention tools are: military bases, the fight against criminal trafficking outside Europe, an increase in African peacekeeping capabilities, arms control, and the fight against the proliferation of weapons of mass destruction.

It is clear that the prevention items have been securitized and even militarized, notably in the case of migration, at the expense of a more civilian and comprehensive approach, as promoted by Scandinavian countries, for instance. But it should be noted that there are strong disagreements between bureaucracies on the fate of prevention policies, notably between political and strategic services of the Ministry of Foreign Affairs (MAE), with the Ministry of Defence more concerned with conflict prevention and short-term policies, and the Aid and Cooperation Department of the MAE (DGCID) or the French Development Agency (AFD) more concerned with 'structural prevention' and long-term perspectives.

Aid

About one-third of aid goes to multilateral institutions and two-thirds goes to bilateral financing: this distribution has remained approximately stable since 1990 (Figure 2.1). The geographical distribution has not undergone many changes: the share allotted to Asia has increased at the expense of Oceania. Yet, all in all, the huge share devoted to Africa remains a constant feature of French bilateral aid. In 2003, France was the third donor globally in absolute terms, but only ranked ninth, with 121 dollars per inhabitant (Cohen 2006: 199–200). From 1994 until 2000, aid dramatically decreased, and subsequently increased. Nevertheless, as a percentage of GNI, it remains very low in comparison with the 1990 level (Figure 2.2).

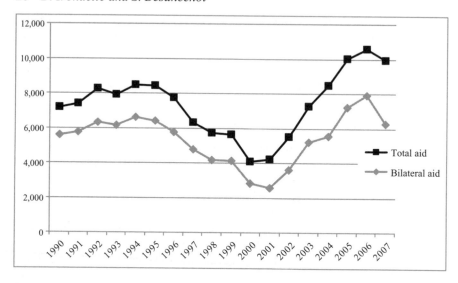

Figure 2.1 Total aid and bilateral aid 1990–2007

Source: OECD.stat 2008

*   Total aid = bilateral aid + multilateral aid

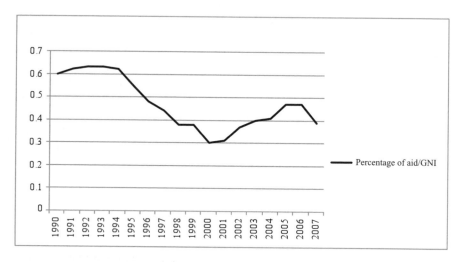

Figure 2.2 Percentage of aid related to GNI

Source: OECD.stat 2008

Aid management underwent a full overhaul in 2004 and now three Ministries have a pivotal role in this Inter-ministerial Committee for International Cooperation and Development (CICID): the Ministry of Foreign Affairs (via its DGCID), the Ministry of Finance, and the newly created Ministry of Identity, Immigration and Development Solidarity. The AFD has become the pivotal operator in development aid, and it has gradually enlarged its area of intervention: it is both a specialist financial institution and a development bank. But AFD ranks third in terms of overall aid volume behind the Ministry of Finance, which controls 40 per cent of French assistance, notably macroeconomic and financial aid, debt relief and contributions to international financial institutions. The Ministry of Foreign Affairs with its DGCID is responsible for around 30 per cent of all French aid.

French aid policy relies on two main pillars: economic development and cultural influence, and is not clearly linked to prevention (Von Kapp-Herr and Moreau 2008: 7). 'Cultural influence' can include democratization and the promotion of the rule of law, but it has ambiguous links with the promotion of *Francophonie*, mainly geared towards the former African colonies. In his La Baule Discourse, President François Mitterrand made aid conditional on democratic change. However, in the 1990s, there was a tendency to consider governments militarily allied to France as intrinsically democratic and to ignore civil society groups in certain countries. Since then, foreign policy and aid have been traditionally intertwined. France has reiterated its intention to 'Europeanize' its Africa policy, but it has refrained from major changes. Democratization policies are included in the 'governance' field: a partnership approach is privileged and investment goes mainly to civil sectors (police, justice). Although France traditionally has many links to armies of the South (especially in francophone Africa), France has been reluctant to adopt Security Sector Reform (SSR) as a doctrine. Whereas there are no official texts that mention SSR (Wulf 2005), France supports ESDP-sponsored SSR missions. Moreover, France receives a black mark from international aid and development NGOs for its egotistical defence of EU export subsidies within the framework of the Common Agricultural Policy in agricultural trade negotiation.

Immigration

After strong growth between 1995 and 2003, inflows of immigrants slowed down since 2004. In 2007, Africa remained the principal region of origin, with one-third of new immigrants coming from Algeria and Morocco. As indicated in Figure 2.3, interpellation and deportation numbers have generally been on the increase since 2001. France increasingly considers immigration to be destabilizing for its domestic population; societal capacity of absorption of immigrant populations without friction is limited, as the exceptional scores of the extreme right candidate Jean-Marie Le Pen in 2002 have shown. There is a growing perception that immigration flows will explode in years to follow: environmental immigrants and the demographic explosion in Mediterranean countries and Sub-Saharan Africa are becoming salient issues in political debates. Across the political spectrum, a new concept has emerged: 'co-development', which is the other side of the coin of the harsh limits on immigration in France. Since 2004, the *police aux frontières* has been tasked with reinforcing the tracking of illegal immigration, and the investigatory *Brigades Mobiles de Recherche* saw their role extended (Ministère de l'Intérieur 2004). This re-organization of police services has been dubbed by journalists as the 'creation of an immigration police force' (*Le Monde* 2005). Ultimately, the creation of a

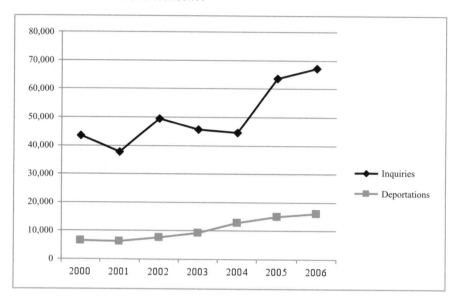

Figure 2.3 Inquiries into illegal situation of foreigners and actual deportations

Source: Secrétariat général du comité interministériel de contrôle de l'immigration 2007

new Ministry of Identity, Immigration and Development Solidarity illustrates how immigration issues have been securitized. Laws passed in recent years all tend towards a greater 'selection' of immigrants (*immigration choisie*). Allegedly, this securitization is also linked to 'co-development' and to the prevention of conflicts in the South. But this policy is mainly intended to attract skilled labour and ignores the 'brain drain' issue. To facilitate integration, a language and culture test has become mandatory. There has been a strong push for a multilateral approach to migration, and the French Presidency of the EU launched a 'European Pact on Migrations and Asylum', signed by the 27 members in July 2008. The launching of the Union of the Mediterranean in July 2008 can also be broadly explained by the desire to handle the migration issue in closer partnership with the countries of the Southern Mediterranean.

To conclude, the prevention sector of security governance has been gradually securitized, from the definition of a 'priority zone' for aid to the gradual involvement of police and even the military in the struggle against illegal immigration, notably in the Mediterranean Sea; recent policy initiatives varyingly point to securitization, albeit at very different levels.

Policies of protection

Protection is the 'great winner' of the 2008 White Paper, which is not only devoted to defence but also to 'national security', the latter being the most important. The 2008 White Paper introduces the doctrine of 'resilience' defined as the capability of public authorities and French society to respond to a major crisis and rapidly restore normal functioning (*Livre Blanc* 2008: 59–60). This approach is directly borrowed from British security policy. The crisis might be provoked by a major terrorist attack, a cyber-attack, a natural disaster or a health pandemic. The French budget for homeland security (police and Gendarmerie) amounts to 13.3 billion Euros (2000 constant) and only 3.8 per cent is devoted to capital expenditure. In the UK it represents 8.11 per cent for a total budget of 17.36 billion Euros (Foucault and Irondelle 2008). Figure 2.4 shows the evolution of France's expenditure for defence and homeland security (public order and safety) in Classification of Functions of Governments (COFOG) data in terms of share of total public expenditure. Yet, interestingly enough, despite this increase, France remains relatively circumspect in Europe in terms of security expenditure (Figure 2.5).

Environment

In France, the protection of the sea against threats related to pollution is the duty of the Gendarmerie and the Army. In the case of natural and industrial disasters, the Army is also entitled to intervene to complement civil actions. But securitization remains limited: this policy has more to do with 'prevention'. From 2002 to 2005, the percentage of the Defence Budget allotted to environmental measures remained low (roughly 1 per cent) (Paulin and Nexon 2007). There is no mention in the 2008 White Paper of what has been called 'Ecoterrorism' (pollution is seen as a 'natural catastrophe' and not as a man-made threat).

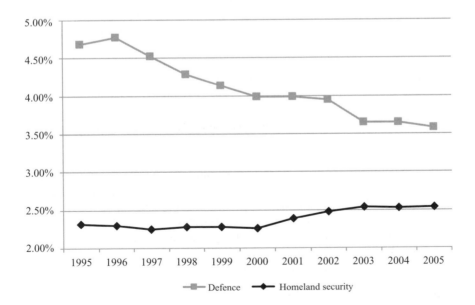

Figure 2.4 French expenditure for defence and homeland security

Source: Eurostat (Foucault and Irondelle 2008)

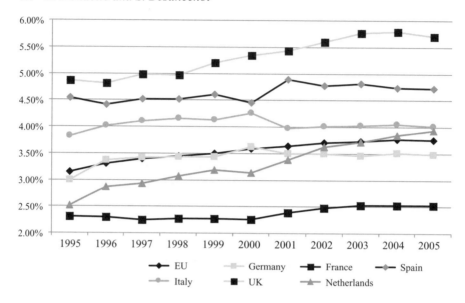

Figure 2.5 Homeland security spending

Source: Eurostat COFOG data (Foucault and Irondelle 2008)

Two Ministries are in charge of risk prevention: the Ministry of Ecology, Development and Sustainable Planning and the Ministry of Research. There is a notable transfer of funds into research on the impact of different types of pollution. While, under the Kyoto Protocol, most European countries committed themselves to reducing their emissions by 8 per cent between 1990 and 2012, France only committed itself to reduce its emissions to their 1990 level (0 per cent) on the grounds that, based on the structure of its energy supply, its margins were narrower than those of other European countries. Most reductions will have to come from tertiary activities and transportation. According to the Ministry of Foreign Affairs, 'France's predicted CO_2 emissions make her one of the few European countries to be on schedule for meeting its Kyoto commitments' (Ministry of Foreign Affairs 2009). Lastly, the Ministry of the Economy is involved in the contribution to global funds (Global Environment Fund, Montreal protocol). France has also integrated environment into its public development aid concept: the Ministry of Foreign Affairs funds environmental initiatives through bilateral and multilateral aid in the Priority Zone. France has been a great promoter of the creation of an 'Organization of the United Nations for the Environment'. This organization would be established with a mandate of capacity-building for the countries of the South.

Health security and pandemics

Only 4 per cent of French development aid is devoted to health security. Of this, about 65 per cent goes to multilateral initiatives and funds and 35 per cent to bilateral funding (Ministry of Foreign Affairs 2004). France is the leading contributor to the Global Fund against AIDS. Various ministries are involved in Health Security policies: the Ministry of Foreign Affairs, the Ministry of Health and Social protection, the Ministry of Economy and Finance, the French Development Agency and the Ministry of Education and Research.

Natural pandemics (Asian influenza/Chikungunya in La Réunion, the French department in the Indian Ocean) are also matters of concern. Large-scale pandemics (with high levels of lethality) and a bioterrorist attack were among the 12 scenarios studied by the Commission in charge of writing the 2008 White Paper. In the Autumn of 2004, a confidential defence plan was prepared, which was made public in May 2005; this has been followed up with a parliamentary mission to inquire into risks and crisis reaction mechanisms. Stockpiles of vaccines and masks were also constituted. The parliamentary report calls for 'first a European, and then an international place' (preferably the WHO) to answer growing 'biosecurity' threats. It calls for a 'right to health intervention' (*droit d'ingérence sanitaire*) with two main components: 'the right to information' and 'the right to medical protection' for those Southern countries under direct threat (Door 2006: 16).

Bioterrorism

Bioterrorism was recognized by the 2008 White Paper as a real 'threat' to French citizens, even if the difficult mastery of the technology for launching a large-scale attack makes such an event on French soil rather improbable. The prevention means examined are manifold (non-proliferation, control of dual-use materials exports, securitization of sensitive areas, water surveillance, construction of a network of epidemiological surveillance), yet none seems to be sufficient for adoption.

The 'Biotox plan' was passed in 2001 and aims at improving interministerial coordination (mainly between the Interior Ministry and the Ministry of Health) in case of a biological attack. France has a national institute devoted to the prevention of diseases and to research (Centre Pasteur). A recent law (2007) created an Office for Preparation and Emergencies (EPRUS). In 2008, it received 23.4 million Euros for acquiring stockpiles. With the 'Smallpox Plan', stockpiles of vaccines have already been constituted, covering 65 million days of antibiotics, 72 million vaccinations against smallpox and 60 million anti-radiation tablets of iodine. On the 'securitization' side, there is growing awareness of the need to instil greater cooperation between civil and military sectors, or between the Ministry of the Interior and the Ministry of Defence, as already proposed in the Biotox plan. Moreover, the 2008 White Paper foresees the creation of a new interministerial committee to coordinate the struggle against nuclear, radiological, bacteriological and chemical threats under the Secrétariat Général de la Défense Nationale (SGDN). About 300 to 400 million Euros will be invested in the modernization of alert mechanisms and risk prevention in view of nuclear, chemical, radiological and bacterial attacks.

The relevance of several multilateral possibilities is currently being examined. In the parliamentary report, a strong disagreement is stated with excessive American investment in the struggle against bioterrorism ('disproportionate with regard to the health system'). Spending on stockpiles is considered as very costly and 'unproductive'. A European approach is thus strongly favoured. Rather than a communalization of anti-bioterrorism politics across the EU, there were efforts to improve the coordination between reaction plans and to share information.

Terrorism

In 2006, the White Paper on Terrorism was the first attempt to elaborate a comprehensive strategy in fighting terrorism. 'Global terrorism', associated with 'fundamentalist Islam', is ranked as a strategic threat (*Livre blanc* 2006). Terrorism is the main threat assessed by the 2008 White Paper. France has several counter-terrorist agencies with overlapping mandates and competitive relationships in the areas of domestic intelligence and the fight against terrorism.

It is impossible to assess the number of individuals tasked with the fight against terrorism because these data are kept secret. Yet, according to some sources, there would be 4,000 personnel at the Directorate of Territorial Surveillance (DST) and 13,000 persons employed in the various intelligence services (civilian and military). In the context of the war against terrorism, France has mainly sought to work within the existing institutional framework and there is no such institution as a 'Department of Homeland Security'. The SGDN, attached to the Prime Minister, is in charge of the coordination of means and missions, with a specialized Intelligence Interagency Committee (CIR). The Ministry of Defence, the Ministry of the Interior, the Ministry of Justice and the Ministry of Foreign Affairs are all involved in the struggle against terrorism via different agencies.

All in all, terrorism remains mainly a policing and judicial problem. The extensive role of the judiciary is essential in the struggle against terrorism. The French terrorism doctrine evolved from a 'sanctuary doctrine' to an 'accommodation doctrine' (1987–94) and then to a prevention doctrine in the mid-1990s after the various Islamist terrorist attacks in France in the 1990s. Since then, French anti-terrorism policy has been aimed at dismantling networks before they act and has been a pioneer in international cooperation in the struggle against terrorism. The system based on the *juge d'instruction* (examining magistrate) has proven very efficient in the prevention of terrorist acts. Judges and the DST have gradually gained mutual confidence. Since 1998, investigating magistrates decided to work directly with the intelligence service, in particular the DST, on Islamist terrorism. Contrary to the United States federal system, the country's centralization has also proven to be a great advantage in tackling terrorism (Shapiro and Suzan 2003). Moreover, there is an increasing role of the military in the foreign dimension of the fight against terrorism (e.g. Afghanistan), as well as with regard to special covert operations.

Organized crime

In France, the first appearance of the term 'organized crime' dates back to a 1993 parliamentary report on the mafia, but until the recent Perben II Law (2004) there was no mention of this term in official documents. There are therefore no statistics integrating this category. France converges with other European countries and favours an 'organizational definition' of organized crime rather than a definition based on the natures of crimes themselves.

Even if its link to organized crime remains fuzzy, it can be acknowledged that France has increasingly securitized illegal immigration by connecting it to organized crime. Estimations of illegal immigration vary in France. There are up to 500,000 illegal immigrants in the country; the strongest disagreements surround the flow, not the 'stock', of illegal immigrants. As mentioned above, illegal immigration is strongly challenged. France's struggle against organized crime comprises several chapters: the fights against drug trafficking, against corruption and money laundering, and against counterfeiting and piracy. Organized crime and terrorism are strongly linked in the 2008 White Paper.

In all of these efforts, there has been an impetus to strengthen multilateral approaches, and especially to improve coordination with other European countries. France also actively participates in European Justice and Home Affairs and in INTERPOL coordination initiatives. Within INTERPOL, France has pushed for the sharing of data on the sexual exploitation of children. The 2008 White Paper even recommends the creation of a 'European narcotics survey and coordination centre in the Mediterranean' which would 'build upon the experiments of the operation centres from the West Indies and Portugal'. Additionally, to fight against terrorism and organized crime, France wishes to develop European capabilities and favours the creation of a 'European Operational Centre for Civil Protection'.

Policies of compellence

After assurance, prevention and protection, the cores of state prerogatives must be considered: the use of force. The two hypotheses presented in the first section of this chapter are polarized on this particular sector: one identifies a pattern of strong 'civilianization' and domestication of the use of force; the other sees a constant preference for it, because being able to intervene unilaterally is part of French 'exceptionalism'. In order to confront these theories with the latest evolutions in policy, there is a need to look at both military missions and resource allocation since the end of the Cold War.

Projections of force (operations)

The French Armed Forces are currently intervening militarily in 29 missions within different institutional frameworks, almost always with a UN mandate (France's diplomatic corps strongly insist on the UN mandate imperative). The exception is unilateral action in Africa according to defence cooperation agreements, for instance in Chad, where 70 per cent of French operations are multinational. In January 2009, around 13,000 French soldiers were deployed in military operations, involving around 2,000 soldiers each: Lebanon (1,600), EUFOR Chad (2,100 and 57 per cent of the total EU military personnel), KFOR (2,000), Afghanistan (3,300)

Table 2.1 French participation in UN peacekeeping operations

	1992	1993	1995	1996	2000	2004	2007
French contribution	4,794	9,119 1st rank	7,386	395	481	561 23rd rank	1,980 10th rank
UN total	38,144	76,461	68,894	25,598	37,967	58,756	83,271
Percentage	12.5	11.9	10.7	1.5	1.2	1.0	2.3

Source: Tardy 2007b

and the Ivory Coast (2,000). By 2009, France was the fourth largest contributor to NATO forces. As of 30 June 2008, France had participated in 12 out of 17 UN peacekeeping operations and had deployed 1,974 military personnel (136 civilian police officers, 26 military observers and 1,812 soldiers,) the vast majority being engaged in the United Nations Interim Force in Lebanon (UNIFIL – 1,626 military personnel). France's contributions towards peacekeeping operations amounted to 7.51 per cent of the total cost (553 million Euros between July 2008 and June 2009). Nevertheless, this 'comeback' in the UN in terms of massive participation in UN peacekeeping efforts is largely due to the UNIFIL II in Lebanon. After the active French participation, both doctrinally with the right to intervene and operationally with the massive deployment of French blue helmets, there was a lack of French participation in UN peacekeeping. Table 2.1 clearly shows the U-turn taken by France in the mid-1990s due to the failure of UNPROFOR in Bosnia and the transfer to a NATO peace enforcement operation in 1995–96, which began to change again after 2006.

The French government decides on the framework in which it will deploy its soldiers and military assets, be it within the EU, the UN or NATO, according to political, diplomatic, strategic and military parameters. France even placed its special forces under direct American command in the beginning of the United States-led 'Operation Enduring Freedom' in Afghanistan in 2001. The French political trend is to develop EU missions under UN mandate. Concerning foreign military operations, 'in order to promote ESDP, priority is given to common efforts with European Union partners' (Patry and Gros 2007). The EU has led five military operations since 2003: two in the Balkans (Concordia and Althea) and three in Africa (DRC, Artemis, Chad). France provides 35 per cent of the European military forces deployed. French troops represent 58 per cent of the forces for African operations, but only 8.5 per cent for European operations.

France is one of the countries that most often uses force for military operations abroad. According to Anthony Forster's typology, France and the United Kingdom are the unique 'expeditionary warfare' models of Armed Forces in Europe (Forster 2006). France is without doubt one of the European countries that put the most emphasis on military force in its international policy. But the 2008 White Paper ranks military intervention only in fifth position in the 'hierarchy of defence roles and missions', after intelligence (called knowledge and anticipation), prevention, deterrence and protection. Whereas deterrence had a pivotal role in the 1972 White

Paper, the keyword of the 1994 White Paper and the 1996 military reform was 'intervention'. In 2008, 'knowledge-based security' had become the heart of the new doctrine.

France's ambition is to preserve the full spectrum of its capabilities, even for high-intensity warfare and large-scale operations. But in June 2008 the loss of ten soldiers during a Taleban ambush in Afghanistan has shown that the current French intervention policy is limited by a lack of effective military means: France is definitively punching above its weight. According to the 2008 White Paper, France will be able to launch 'special operations' (to free hostages or pursue terrorists) on an unilateral basis, and 'middle-scale' operations such as the evacuation of French people in hostile environments, or selective and targeted operations as a response to a direct action against French interests. But 'significant' operations for peacekeeping or peace enforcement are only conceived of in bilateral or multilateral terms, and 'major' operations in alliance or coalition.

The re-organization of the Armed Forces, voted for in 2008 and to be concluded in 2013, will lead to a reduction of 54,000 defence personnel, 46,500 soldiers and 6,500 civilian personnel. The Air Force will lose 25 per cent of its personnel and 25 per cent of its combat aircraft, the Army 17 per cent of its personnel and the Navy 11 per cent of its personnel.

Defence budget

Since the end of the Cold War defence budgets have indeed been severely reduced and the share of military expenditure in GDP has drastically decreased from an average 3.3 per cent for the 1990–94 period to 2.4 per cent in 2007, according to NATO sources (NATO 2009); and from 3.6 per cent in 1988 to 3 per cent in 1995 and 2.3 per cent in 2007, according to SIPRI data (SIPRI 2009). See Table 2.2 on p. 37.

But these data give quite an optimistic picture of French defence expenditure since they take into account pensions and the Gendarmerie (a military police force whose military missions are small part of its activities). Therefore, national data may be used to obtain a more accurate analysis. The French MoD uses NATO data to elaborate a comparison between France and its main partners in terms of military expenditure, but NATO data are reprocessed by French experts to exclude pensions and to exclude 95 per cent of the Gendarmerie budget allocation, the remaining 5 per cent of which corresponds to the effective military missions undertaken by the Gendarmerie (Ministry of Defence 2008). With this measurement, the share of military expenditure in GDP was 1.64 per cent in 2007, with a defence budget totalling 30.5 billion Euros. Furthermore, in France there is often a massive difference between the voted budget and the executed budget. Despite ritual official speeches on the imperative to maintain the French defence potential, the defence budget remains subject to economic restrictions. Military expenditure, particularly equipment expenditure, has often been used as a 'variable of budgetary adjustment' since the end of the Cold War. Thus the discrepancy between planned defence spending in the five-year Military Programming Bill (Loi de

Table 2.2 French defence expenditure

	1990–94	1995–99	2000–4	2005	2006	2007
Share of GDP	3.3%	2.9%	2.5%	2.5%	2.4%	2.4%
Total[a]				38,699	38,650	38,673
Personnel		58.2%	59.6%	58%	56.5%	55.9%
Equipment		21.3%	19.7%	21.3%	23.2%	22.4%
Infrastructure		3.9%	4.6%	4.7%	3.8%	4.1%
Other		16.4%	16%	15.9%	16.5%	17.6%
Per capita[b]				568	563	560

Source: NATO 2009

Notes:
[a]   Millions of Euros, 2000 prices
[b]   USD, 2000 prices and exchange rates

programmation militaire), and the expenditure really executed each year (Loi de finances rectificatives) is a recurrent phenomenon of the French military budget. It is the concrete and budgetary expression of the gap between French ambitions and available means. Furthermore, French military planning has to manage the legacy of the major equipment originating from the Cold War period (Rafale fighter-jet programme, nuclear aircraft carrier, Leclerc heavy tank, Tigre attack helicopters). This problem is not specific to France; it also affects the United Kingdom, for instance. It is nevertheless exacerbated in the context of French security culture, obsessed by France's rank and determined by the institutional dominance of the President in military policy-making.

The objective of French policy-makers in planning future expenditure and military capabilities is to maximize France's political-military rank within international military coalitions, rather than to maximize operational military power on the ground. The combination of these cultural and institutional factors led to defence-equipment choices that give priority in resource allocations to prestigious equipment and 'highly political' programmes. This led to two structural deficiencies of the French Armed Forces: on the one hand, a limited number of operating military units turning the French Armed Forces into a 'prototype', given the phased reduction in quantities of ordered equipment and the delays in eventual delivery, and, on the other hand, increasing quantities of ill-maintained equipment. The transition to all-volunteer Armed Forces implies an increase in defence expenditure for personnel in France, from 51 per cent in 1994 to 53 per cent in 2002, at the expense of capital expenditure – the share of which is declining in the French budget, from 49 per cent to 42.5 per cent in the same period (Ministry of Defence 2008). Since 2002, this trend has been reversed thanks to the priority given to equipment expenditure planned in the military programming bill of 2003–8. France has spent about 2 billion Euros since 2004 on military research and development, after a strong decline from the peak in 1996 of 4.19 billion Euros.

The distribution of expenditure across military services undergoes strong inertia effects in France and has been amazingly stable since 1988. From 1988 to 2008, the share of each branch (Gendarmerie, Air Force, Army, Navy) in the defence budget remains almost the same. It is even more striking when capital expenditure from data of the French MoD is considered: the Navy absorbed 24.4 per cent of French capital expenditure in 1988, 25 per cent in 1999 and 25 per cent in 2008; the Army's share was 22.2 per cent in 1988, 21 per cent in 1999 and in 2008; the Air Force's was 24.7 per cent in 1988, 24 per cent in 1999 and in 2008. The main change has been decreasing investment in the nuclear field. Indeed, the nuclear share of the defence equipment budget has dropped from 40 per cent to 21 per cent since 1990, and the nuclear share of the defence budget fell from 16.9 per cent to 8.75 per cent between 1990 and 1999 (Tertrais 2007). According to the 2008 White Paper, the defence budget will remain stable in real terms from 2009 to 2012 and then will increase by 1 per cent a year. The savings resulting from the downsizing of the Armed Forces will theoretically be invested in the procurement of military equipment.

Conclusion

'Exceptionalism' remains the core of French security culture and governance but is increasingly tempered by a normalization process that puts the emphasis on multilateral rather than unilateral options, and on civilian rather than military instruments. New issues have been integrated and normative and cultural changes cannot be neglected, as a constructivist logic would show. But the key dynamic remains the pursuit of national interest, constrained by both domestic factors (mainly financial constraint and capabilities) and international-structural ones. Thus, the transition towards the post-Westphalian model is most advanced in the areas dependent upon capabilities and with strong financial constraints. There is a need to define more precisely what 'normalization' means in the context of the French model. If normalization means pragmatic Europeanization and a 'greater influence of protection' over the military, then French policy can be considered as following a growing trend of normalization since the end of the Cold War. This trend has simply been accelerated since the accession to power of the former Interior Minister, Nicolas Sarkozy. His closest advisers do not originate from traditional 'corps', which sustain the traditional French meaning of power (military and diplomatic corps), but from 'non-traditional' sectors of State administration. Indeed, a key adviser to Sarkozy, Claude Guéant, is a 'policeman' with no ties to the military. Priority is thus given to intelligence, which is more adapted, adaptable and less costly than force.

However, normalization in the meaning of Ronja Kempin (whereby human rights and belief in multilateralism have replaced 'grandeur' as the major foreign policy doctrine) cannot be identified as a key pattern. *Realpolitik* has been revived in the relationship with Russia (with a very pragmatic Sarkozy-Medvedev plan during the Georgian crisis); in relationships with the African continent where continuity prevails despite declarations to the contrary; and with China or Libya, where economic interests over-determine French foreign policy. To conclude, in terms of the first hypothesis, it is true that France, in the four sectors covered, sometimes favours multilateral initiatives, but they remain instrumental and *ad hoc*, and a general 'belief' in them cannot be identified. The second hypothesis is only partially confirmed: when new threats are securitized, they tend not to be as militarized as might first be imagined. But nor are they considered as only to be tackled by strictly preventive and civilian means, as they would be in a clear-cut post-Westphalian security culture, such as one finds in Nordic countries. Rather, an increasing 'culture of protection' is developing in France, which nonetheless does not contradict the fundamentals of the Westphalian state.

Note

1   The authors wish to thank Damien Bright for his helpful comments on a previous draft.

References

Cohen, D. (ed.) (2006) *La France et l'aide publique au développement*, Paris: Conseil d'analyse économique.

Di Lampedusa, G. (1972) *The Leopard*, London: Collins and Harvill Press.

Door, J.-P. (2006) *Rapport fait au nom de la mission d'information sur la grippe aviaire: mesures préventives*, Paris: Assemblée Nationale.

Drake, H. (2006) 'France: An EU Founder Member Cut Down to Size?', *Journal of European Integration*, 28(1): 89–105.

Erlanger, S. and Bennhold, S. (2008) 'French Shifting Strategic Policy', *International Herald Tribune*, 16 June.

Forster, A. (2006) *Armed Forces and Society in Europe*, Basingstoke, UK: Palgrave.

Foucault, M. and Irondelle, B. (2008) *Etude comparative des budgets des forces de sécurité intérieure de l'Union européenne, rapport pour l'Observatoire Economique de la défense*, Ministère de la défense.

Gautier, L. (1998) *Mitterrand et son armée*, Paris: Grasset.

Giegerich, B. (2006) 'E3 Leadership in Security and Defence Policy', *CFSP Forum*, 4(6): 5–7.

Gordon, P. (1993) *A Certain Idea of France: French Security Policy and the Gaullist Legacy*, Princeton, NJ: Princeton University Press.

Harnisch, S. (2007) 'Minilateral Cooperation and Transatlantic Coalition Building: The EU-3 Iran Initiative', *European Security*, 16(1): 1–27.

Hoffmann, S. and Kempin, R. (2007) 'France and the Transatlantic Relationship: Love Me, Love Me Not ...', *Working Paper FG 2*, SWP Berlin, April.

Irondelle, B. (2003a) 'Gouverner la défense. Analyse du processus décisionnel de la réforme militaire', PhD thesis, Institut d'Etudes Politiques de Paris.

—— (2003b) 'Europeanization without the European Union', *Journal of European Public Policy*, 10(2): 208–26.

Irondelle, B. and Foucault, M. (2008) *Opinion publique et sécurité en Europe*, Paris: Centre d'Etudes en Sciences Sociales de la Défense.

Juppé, A. and Schweitzer, L. (2008) *La France et l'Europe dans le monde, Livre blanc sur la politique étrangère et européenne de la France*, Paris: MAE.

Keiger, J. (2005) 'Foreign and Defense Policy: Constraints and Continuity', in Cole, A., Le Galès, P. and Lévy, J. (eds) *Developments in French Politics 3*, New York: Palgrave Macmillan.

Kempin, R. (2008) *Frankreichs neue Sicherheitspolitik von der Militär zur Zivilmacht*, Baden-Baden: Nomos.

Le Monde (2005) 'Création d'une nouvelle police de l'immigration pour traquer les clandestins', 11 August.

Livre blanc (2006) *La France face au terrorisme: Livre blanc du Gouvernement sur la sécurité intérieure face au terrorisme*, Paris: La Documentation française.

—— (2008) *Défense et sécurité nationale: Le Livre blanc*, Paris: La Documentation française and Odile Jacob.

Meunier, S. (2008) 'France and the World, from Chirac to Sarkozy', in Cole, A., Le Galès, P. and Lévy, J. (eds) *Developments in French Politics 4*, New York: Palgrave MacMillan.

Ministère de l'Intérieur (2004) 'Développement de l'investigation par la police aux frontières contre les filières d'immigration, les réseaux d'aide au séjour irrégulier sur le territoire et le travail clandestin organisé', Circulaire NOR/INT/C/04/00116/C (17 September). Available online at: http://www.libertysecurity.org/IMG/pdf/INTC0400116C.pdf (accessed 22 February 2009).

Ministry of Defence (2008) *Annuaire Statistique de la Défense 2007/2008*.

Ministry of Foreign Affairs (2009) 'Environmental diplomacy'. Available online at: http://www.diplomatie.gouv.fr/en/france-priorities_1/environment-sustainable-development_1097/environmental-diplomacy_4155/climate_4596/index.html (accessed 30 August 2009).

—— (2004) 'Participation de l'APD française aux objectifs du millénaire pour le développement'. Available online at: http://www.diplomatie.gouv.fr/fr/IMG/pdf/Strat_sector_sante.pdf (accessed 22 February 2009).

NATO (2009) 'Financial and Economic Data Relating to NATO Defence', Press Release, PR/CP 2009, 19 February.

OECD (2008) 'International Migration Outlook'. Available online at: http://www.oecd.org/dataoecd/56/44/41255405.pdf (accessed 22 February 2009).

Paulin, C. and Nexon, E, (2007) 'Investissement en sécurité globale', Paris: Fondation pour la recherche stratégique, Coll. Synthèse.

Patry, J.-J. and Gros, P. (2007) 'Les opérations extérieures: de l'interposition à la stabilisation', in Fondation pour la recherche stratégique, *Annuaire stratégique et militaire 2006–2007*, Paris: Odile Jacob.

Posen, B. (2006) 'The European Security and Defence Policy: Response to Unipolarity', *Security Studies*, 15(2): 149–86.

Rieker, P. (2006) 'From Common Defence to Comprehensive Security: Towards the Europeanization of French Foreign and Security Policy?', *Security Dialogue*, 37(4): 509–28.

Rynning, S. (2001) *Changing Military Doctrine. President and Military Power in Fifth Republic France 1958–2000*, New York: Prager.

Secrétariat général du comité interministériel du contrôle de l'immigration (2007) *Les orientations de la politique d'immigration*, Paris: La Documentation française.

Shapiro, J. and Suzan, B. (2003) 'The French Experience of Counter-terrorism', *Survival*, 45(1): 67–97.

SIPRI (2009) *The SIPRI Military Expenditure Database (France)*. Available online at: http://milexdata.sipri.org/result.php4 (accessed 22 February 2009).

Tardy, T. (2007a) 'National Threat Perception: Survey Results from France', Garnet

Working Paper 18.5. Available online at: http://www.garnet-eu.org/fileadmin/documents/working_papers/1807/5%20France.pdf (accessed 22 February 2009).

—— (2007b) 'La France à l'ONU et les opex: ressource ou contrainte', in Irondelle, B. (ed.) *L'action militaire extérieure de la France: enjeux et perspectives*, Actes du colloque 14–15 juin 2007, Paris, CERI-Sciences Po/CNRS, 14 August.

Tertrais, B. (2007) 'Dissuasion nucléaire. Enjeux et défis pour 2007–12', *Annuaire Stratégique et Militaire 2006–7*, Paris: Odile Jacob.

Treacher, A. (2003) *French Interventionism: Europe's Last Global Player?* London: Ashgate.

Vaïsse, M. (1998) *La Grandeur: La politique étrangère du général de Gaulle*, Paris: Fayard.

Védrine, H. (1996) *Les mondes de François Mitterrand à l'Elysée: 1981–1995*, Paris: Fayard.

Von Kapp-Herr, A. and Moreau, J. (2008) 'Les aides publiques au développement en France et en Allemagne: perspectives comparées', *Visions franco-allemandes 13*. Available online at: http://www.ifri.org/files/Vision_franco_allemande13.pdf (accessed 22 February 2009).

Wong, R. (2006) *The Europeanization of French Foreign Policy: France and the EU in East Asia*, London: Palgrave Macmillan.

Wulf, H.(2005) *Réforme du secteur de la sécurité dans les pays en développement et les pays en transition*. Available online at: http://www.berghof-handbook.net/uploads/download/french_wulf_dialogue2.pdf (accessed 22 February 2009).

3   Germany

The continuity of change

Sebastian Harnisch and Raimund Wolf

Introduction

The history of Germany's reluctant security policy – the aversion to exercise military power and the preference for multilateral diplomatic action – has often been told. And yet, 20 years after unification a paradox becomes apparent. The Federal Republic's security trajectory still features several characteristics of a 'civilian power' security culture: it has been a key protagonist of the European Security and Defence Policy (ESDP), of several diplomatic conflict resolution initiatives (e.g. the Fischer Plan, the Bonn conference on Afghanistan, the E-3 initiative, the Berlin conference on the Israeli–Palestinian conflict) and one of the main opponents of the US-led intervention in Iraq. And Berlin even pursues security policies in some areas – e.g. the Iraq case or the question of Ballistic Missile Defence – where costs for its vital alliance with the US are sizeable. At the same time, since 1990 German governments from the left and right have displayed a new robustness in security affairs, both in word and deed. In particular, German armed forces have been deployed in ever more dangerous military campaigns despite 'Germany's security culture of reticence'. After the attacks of 11 September 2001 (9/11), Germany's executive has also centralized its anti-terrorism policies and institutions, thereby shedding basic principles of Germany's federalist and fragmented policy process which emerged after the dramatic failure of the separation of powers during the Nazi period.

The resulting ambivalence in German security policy is widely criticized, both at home and abroad. At home, pacifistic groups, the Left Party, 'Die Linke', and members of the Liberal Party assailed both CDU and SPD-led governments for militarizing Germany's foreign policy and nurturing a police state domestically. Abroad, continuous US administrations and some European allies have pushed very hard, often in public, for a much stronger German military role and a less restrictive data exchange policy to detain terrorist suspects. Government officials therefore often maintain that Germany already carries a burden but will do more to live up to its increased international responsibility.[1]

What underlies this mixture of continuing reticence and increasing robustness? Why is Germany's cooperation in some areas of security governance almost a given but highly controversial in others? Do changes in German security behaviour reflect common patterns of convergence of compatibility among the ten countries under review in this book or do they correspond to the different modes of public goods production?

There are several competing explanations for Germany's ambivalent security trajectory. The most common realistic assertion holds that Germany's new robustness can be traced back to unification and an increase in material power that translates into a broader spectrum of policy choices ranging from autonomous external action to more coercive action within existing institutions.

However, this realistic explanation based only on material factors is both incomplete and misleading. To begin with, depicting Germany as a re-emerging 'great power' does not tell us in which direction this 'great power' is heading and it may mislead us into generalizing a trend in military deployment which may not be representative of the whole spectrum of security governance. Therefore, the comparative security policy perspective taken here and the conceptualization of security governance as consisting of different production modes – i.e. assurance, prevention, protection and compellence – are introduced to overcome these deficiencies. Furthermore, this chapter will analyse the reasons for and implications of changes in Germany's security culture and assess the extent and scope for international security governance in light of those changes.

The chapter has a different take on Germany's security behaviour. The ambivalent security trajectory, we argue in the first section, is a function of two historic trends in German foreign and security policy, neither of which can be directly inferred from Germany's material capacities. We posit that German security governance is ambivalent because Germany is a parliamentarian democracy with both a strong civil-society and civilian domestic culture and a strong inclination towards European integration and cooperation with transatlantic partners. Therefore, to restate the claim of the realist argument, ambivalent support for more robust security policy action derives from an enduring domestic culture of reticence, while increased military deployment can be explained through allied countries' perceptions and requests that a 'more powerful Germany' must shoulder a bigger share of the common burden. Our argument trades on the hypothesis that Germany's post-Westphalian security accounts for the securitization of economic and social threats and the preference of non-military policy instruments, while some changes in its security culture have mitigated collective action problems in certain policy areas. We posit that recent changes – Europeanization, increased robustness and domestication – do facilitate pooling security capabilities on a European and, to a lesser degree, an international level while inhibiting delegation of competences due to domestic constitutional and societal constraints (for further details see the introductory chapter of this book).

In the second section, we develop our theoretical argument based on the distinct German security culture and institutional setting, and in the third section we show that German security governance exhibits some key characteristics that other nations lack. Brief histories of the domestic debates on compellence and protection will uncover direct evidence of the importance of cross-cutting domestic and external expectations in Germany's post-Cold War security policy.

In the final section, we conclude that recent changes in Germany's security culture and governance have increased the country's ability to contribute to international security governance, although this contribution is limited due to several enduring key characteristics. We assert that Germany's contribution could be even stronger if international security governance were more 'Europeanized' and thereby more readily acceptable to the German public.

German security culture and recent trends in security governance: the argument

A plausible realist interpretation of Germany's post-World War II security policy holds that the conquered and occupied state had no other choice than to bandwagon with the US against the conventional threat of the Soviet Union. In classical realist alliance theory, the benefits of enhanced deterrence through US and allied forces on German territory outweighed the costs of sacrificing autonomy and unilateral or bilateral policy options. While sovereignty costs may not have been a major consideration for the semi-sovereign German state in the 1950s, relative gains in power and status in the aftermath of German unification set the stage for a more muscular and unilateral security policy (O'Brian 1992). Two prominent variants of realist interpretations can be identified: a structural realist argument, which posits that a moderate improvement of Germany's power position will result in intensified autonomy-seeking policies; and a modified neorealistic argument, which stipulates that the moderate power increase will induce influence-maximizing behaviour (Baumann, Rittberger and Wagner 2001).

Indeed, unilateralism and utilitarian considerations towards military action seem to have pervaded several German security policy decisions in the 1990s:

- the unilateral recognition of Slovenia and Croatia (1991) (Layne 1993: 37);
- participation in the NATO-led Kosovo intervention without proper United Nations Security Council mandate (1998); and
- opposition towards the US-led Iraq intervention (2002).

These are the most cited incidents of a new German assertiveness (Schöllgen 2004; Hedstück and Hellmann 2003).

While the desire to maintain discretion and influence in security affairs certainly contributes to Germany's ambivalence toward full-scope multilateral action and international law, the realist explanation does not tell the whole story. It fails to account for the decision-making process and the resulting policy change of each decision. A more plausible explanation of these episodes includes tracing the domestic debate that led up to the decision and the subsequent German behaviour. In the case of the Kohl government's recognition of Croatia and Slovenia 14 days ahead of the other European Union countries, domestic pressure by conservative newspapers as well as Germany's low-key Balkan policy after the intense external criticism of its decision by its partners do present a more convincing account. In the case of the Kosovo intervention, domestic political factors played a considerable role: first, with regard to the question of more migration by war refugees from Kosovo to Germany; and second with regard to the moral obligation to prevent genocide even if that meant breaking with the principle of 'nie wieder Krieg' (Harnisch and Longhurst 2006: 52). In the case of the opposition to the Iraq War, Chancellor Gerhard Schröder, who was in the middle of a close re-election campaign, responded to widespread popular sentiments which opposed the US administration's war-prone foreign policy.

Hence, we hold that Germany's security governance can be understood best by taking both institutional and ideational factors into account. Germany was shaped as a liberal parliamentarian democracy with an intense commitment to domestic civil rights and a strong inclination to international law and integration due to the catastrophe of the Third Reich (Pradetto 2006). The founding fathers and mothers of the Grundgesetz, the German Constitution, took the view that the young German democracy had to be anchored, or locked-in, as liberal theoreticians call it (Moravcsik 2000), both domestically and externally so that a democratic political culture could gain ground in a society still haunted by its totalitarian past. Furthermore, post-war German elites actively pursued a foreign policy based on two fundamental principles: 'never again war' and 'never again alone' (Dalgaard-Nielsen 2006). During the East-West conflict this institutional and ideational framework held the German ship of state on a steady course of a very close alignment with Western liberal democracies. As a consequence, clear commitment to international integration as well as scepticism towards robust means of foreign policy became pillars of German security culture, stabilized and reinforced by a strong institutional setting. Every major foreign policy change thus led to an intense domestic debate when domestic and foreign expectations diverged. In most cases, the opposition appealed to the Federal Constitutional Court, challenging the constitutionality of the government's course (re-integration into Western Europe; re-armament; executive emergency powers; Ostpolitik; NATO-Doppelbeschluss) (Harnisch 2006).

From this perspective, Germany's ambivalent security trajectory in the 1990s is an effort to balance two elements of its embedded security culture which increasingly mismatch. On the one hand, Germany tries to live up to external expectations for policy change as part of its commitment to international cooperation. On the other hand, it strives to maintain its institutional integrity as well as its reluctance towards robust means that are deeply rooted in society and parts of the elite. Thus, international expectations for 'normalization' are constrained by domestic expectations and institutions to keep its distinct post-World War II security policy (Longhurst 2004; Harnisch *et al.* 2004; Maull 2006). The most prevalent trends in security governance in the 1990s and beyond do reflect this pattern. The first of these is that German openness vis-à-vis international law has been particularly strong in the EU. In the context of unification, further integration became a primary instrument of German policy-makers to calm anxieties by its neighbours and to coin the EU economic and currency union, as well as the Common Foreign and Security Policy (CFSP), according to German needs (Miskimmon 2007). Second, while integration tends to beget integration, the formation of a common currency and political union triggered a substantial domestic response by the legislative and judiciary to limit the executive's gains of autonomous action on the European level. Europeanization, i.e. 'a set of processes through which the political, social and economic dynamics of European Integration become part of the logic of domestic discourses, identities, public structures and public policies' (Irondelle 2003: 211) and domestication, 'the limitation of executive prerogatives in foreign policy through normative and procedural restrictions that tie back further integration to the preservation of domestic norms and separation of powers' (Harnisch 2006) are now two common characteristics of Germany's security policy. Third, Germany's new robustness in security governance can hardly be linked to a new great-power status as a realistic interpretation would have it. German military means lag behind its potential, are firmly embedded in multilateral frameworks and mostly assigned to humanitarian tasks. In addition, many security efforts are tightly constrained by constitutional oversight. When looking at parliamentarian debates and executive actions, immaterial factors, i.e. ethnic and legal considerations, more than power purposes, affect decisions on force projection and criminal prosecution.

Assurance

Our first policy area of concern is assurance. A simple realist account may assume that Germany contributes either almost no or plenty of resources to international missions. A realist influence maximization logic suggests that Germany would send no or very few personnel in UN missions, because sovereignty costs are higher than in the EU, where Germany's relative weight is higher in securing influence over the missions' goal and overall policy direction. Instead, most liberal interpretations of foreign policy stress that liberal democracies spread their domestic conflict-resolution pattern outward for two reasons: first, because they believe in their superior effectiveness due to domestic experience; second, because foreign policy can be legitimized more efficiently when it resonates with domestic norms (Hawkins *et al.* 2006; Gurowitz 2006). Thus, a simple liberal explanation would hold that Germany would pool or even delegate assets wherever domestic norms are served. If German security governance is ambivalent here, this may seem puzzling, because post-conflict reconstruction and attending confidence-building measures are believed to be preferred instruments of a 'civilian power' (Maull 1990/91; Harnisch and Maull 2001). And yet, in the German case the relationship between liberal and civilized democracy and assurance behaviour is more complex than both assumptions suggest. In our reading, Germany's ambivalent assurance pattern derives from the interplay of both ideational and institutional factors.

With regard to international policing missions, Germany plays an active role, at least rhetorically. Berlin has pledged 910 officers for the 5,000-officer police component of the ESDP in the context of its leading role in institutionalizing a civilian component of the policy (Bund-/Länder-Arbeitsgruppe Internationale Polizeimissionen 2007). Yet, there is an almost equal spread of German participation between EU and UN policing missions (see Tables 3.1 and 3.2).[2] Furthermore, Germany's geographic force projection pattern reveals a strong European bias,

Table 3.1 Current UN assurance missions with German personnel contributions

Mission (location)	Est.[a]	Major aspects of mandates[b]	German personnel[c]
UNDOF (Golan Heights)	1974	Supervise the implementation of the agreement and monitor ceasefire	N/A
UNIFIL (Lebanon)	1978	Confirming Israeli withdrawal, restoring peace and security; since 2006 maintaining ceasefire	905
MINURSO (Western Sahara)	1991	Monitoring ceasefire and organizing/ conducting a referendum	N/A
UNOMIG (Georgia)	1993	Supervise the implementation of the agreement and monitor ceasefire	15
MONUC (DR Congo)	1999	Support the implementation of peace agreement and monitoring ceasefire	N/A
UNMIK (Kosovo)	1999	Monitoring and institutional build-up and support	143
UNMEE (Ethiopia/Eritrea)	2000	Monitoring ceasefire	2
UNMIL (Liberia)	2003	Supporting the implementation of peace agreement and ceasefire	5
UNOCI (Côte d'Ivoire)	2004	Monitoring ceasefire and disarmament	N/A
UNMIS (Sudan)	2005	Supervise and support the implementation of peace agreement	46
UNMIT (Timor-Leste)	2006	Consolidating stability and support institutional build-up	N/A
MINURCAT (CAR/Chad)	2007	Consolidating stability, protecting return of refugees	N/A
UNAMID (Darfur)	2007	Support the implementation of peace agreement	2

Source: Zentrum für Internationale Friedenseinsätze 2008

Notes:
a   Based on UN 2008
b   Based on UNRIC 1999, UN Information Service 2008 and mission factsheets
c   German personnel by end of 2007, based on SIPRI 2008

lending credence to the ideational liberal argument. This regional bias changed only recently. In contrast to its strong multilateral military projection pattern, German police officers do not participate in the integrated European Police Units or the French-led European Gendarmerie Force, the reason being that German constitutional law separates police and military functions, thereby banning paramilitary forces.

German constitutional law also requires UN mandates (or mandates by other systems of collective security) and German forces have been actively participating in deployments by other regional institutions (percentage shares ranging from 5 to 15 per cent of all contributions) since the early 1990s.[3] However, in recent years German contributions to the ESDP missions have been growing stronger than others, i.e. thereby setting a Europeanization trend in Germany's assurance policy.

A realist interpretation of this data may conclude that Germany prefers regional institutions where it retains a disproportionate influence. Our findings suggest otherwise. First, while the creation of ESDP goes back to European frustration with US military preponderance during the Kosovo intervention, an autonomous, but limited, European military capacity is a collective goal of most EU member states, both weak and strong. Second, Germany has not been eager to play a leadership role in ESDP in general or its missions in particular, e.g. the Congo mission where the Grand Coalition was reluctant to participate at all due to domestic opposition, in the end participating with a minor contribution (Mölling 2007: 10). Third, and most important, Berlin's preference for ESDP derives from the 'civilian profile' of those missions which are almost all post-conflict and therefore subsequent to NATO and or US-led deployments. Hence, Germany's assurance policy has become Europeanized because of the 'civilian character' of those missions and of the European Security Strategy in general, which fits the German security culture more closely (Berenskoetter and Giegerich 2006).

Prevention

Germany's prevention policy trajectory since unification is (broadly defined) consistent with its traditional security culture in the three areas of rhetoric, institutions and funding. Under the Red-Green coalition (1998–2003), Germany developed a comprehensive concept for conflict prevention to be implemented through national, European and other fora. The 2004 Action Plan is the main national policy document. Institutionally, German governments, responding to emerging crises in Europe, Africa and Asia, have also set up several new agencies: the Center for International Peace Operations (est. 2002) and several specific interministerial working groups and NGO liaison committees (Fincke and Hatakoy 2004: 71). Furthermore, Germany has actively supported the establishment of the new EU agency to coordinate border security operations (FRONTEX) in Warsaw. It has also been one of the leading protagonists for setting up the International Criminal Court (ICC), which serves both a deterrent and pacifying function in cases of massive human rights abuses.

Germany's strong support for Official Development Assistance (ODA) appears to confirm the importance of the 'civilian' tradition: as shown in Figure 3.1, while the percentage share of economic and reconstruction aid has been somewhat lower (approx. 0.33 per cent) than for the post-colonial powers France and the UK over the 1990s (approx. 0.4 per cent), it still tops that of the US and Japan (approx. 0.25 per cent). More consistently with the multilateral tradition and the Europeanizing trend, Germany donates more and more aid through multilateral channels, especially the EU.[4] Similarly, German ODA focuses on social infrastructure and services.[5]

Table 3.2 German contribution to EU-led assurance missions 2003–7

Mission	German personnel contribution by year Number (% of mission total)					Average per year
	2003	2004	2005	2006	2007	
EU Proxima (Macedonia)		25 (15.5%)	21 (14.9%)			15.2%
EUJUST Themis (Georgia)		N/A	N/A			
EUPAT (Macedonia)			4 (13.8%)	4 (12.5%)		13.2%
AMM (Aceh)			9 (7.6%)	4 (14.8%)		11.2%
EU support to AMIS II (Darfur)			5 (17.9%)	6 (22.2%)	6 (12%)	17.4%
EUPM (Bosnia-Herzegovina)	85 (18.1%)		29 (15.4%)	19 (11.4%)	23 (12.9%)	15%
EUSEC (DR Congo)				1 (3.1%)	1 (2.6%)	2.9%
EUJUST LEX (Iraq)			1 (8.3%)	1 (4.5%)	1 (5%)	5.9%
PAMECA (Albania)			4 (25%)		3 (20%)	22.5%
EU BAM (Rafah)			6 (8.5%)	5 (7%)	4 (5.1%)	6.9%
EUSR (Georgia)				1 (11.1%)	1 (10%)	10.6%
EU Border Assistance (Moldova/Ukraine)*					7 (10%)	
EUPT (Kosovo)				3 (10.3%)	5 (13.9%)	12.1%
EUPOL (Kinshasa)			N/A	N/A	N/A	
EUPOL (Congo)					N/A	
EUPOL COPPS (Palestinian Territories)				N/A	N/A	
EUPOL (Afghanistan)					N/A	

Sources: SIPRI Database 2004–7, Council of the EU 2008; Missiroli 2003; information from mission websites and reports 2005, 2007, 2008, 2009; information received from the General

Secretariat of the Council of the EU, 2005, 2006, 2007; information received from the Chief of Press and Public Information Office, AMM, 2006, 2007; information received from EUFOR Althea Spokesperson, 2006; information received from Deputy Press and Public Information Officer, EU BAM Rafah, 2007

Note:
* Seconded personnel only. The table does not include EULEX Kosovo, which was launched in 2008

However, when looking at the top recipients of German aid it becomes clear that commercial interests also play a strong role in assurance policies.[6]

Moreover, in the past decade Germany's prevention policy has had a functional and geographical focus. Functionally, one of the most important initiatives has been a common EU action against small arms proliferation. Berlin has also funded demilitarization and demobilization programmes in Niger, Sierra Leone, Mozambique and South Africa, as well as in the Caucasus, Balkan and Central Asian regions. At the same time, several coalition crises over the past decade about arms exports to sensitive regions indicate that commercial interests also do figure prominently in crisis prevention policies (GKKE 2003: 40ff.)

Geographically, Southeastern Europe has been a key region for German prevention efforts, but Afghanistan has also drawn much attention since 2001. In 1999, the Red-Green coalition launched the so-called 'Stability Pact for Southeastern Europe', to coordinate international aid and promote cooperation among former enemies. Consequently, Berlin contributed 650 million Euro to the Pact (2000–3) and another 240 million Euro in bilateral aid to the participating countries. In Afghanistan, again the Red-Green government launched a major post-conflict prevention initiative with the so-called Petersberg Conference, which started the political process to form a government and draft a constitution through a *loya jirga* (national assembly). Following up on the diplomatic engagement, Berlin spent USD 511 million of its ODA in Afghanistan (2001–6) and planned to further increase its spending from 2008 on (Weiss 2008). By far the largest German aid contribution has gone into Serbia and Kosovo; e.g. German ODA for Serbia (1999–2006) alone amounted to USD 1,308 million (OECD 2008b).

More recently, Berlin has been engaged in the so-called EU3+3 Process, in which the UNSC-5 and Germany use diplomatic mediation and some sanctions to persuade Iran to cease sensitive nuclear activities and clear up its safeguards record. The initiative itself and Germany's involvement is consistent with the Europeanizing trend in prevention policies, because the EU-3 (UK, France and Germany) started the mediation in April 2003 – right after the transatlantic and European dispute on Iraq – to ensure that diplomacy can run its course before coercive measures are applied (Harnisch 2007).

But make no mistake; when looking at Germany's performance in specific cases, the findings are less impressive. In Afghanistan, German police officers led the international efforts to establish an Afghanistan National Police (ANP). In fact, the programme trained some 5,000 officers (middle and upper ranks) and drilled some 15,000 officers in short-term courses. And yet, the programme failed in providing

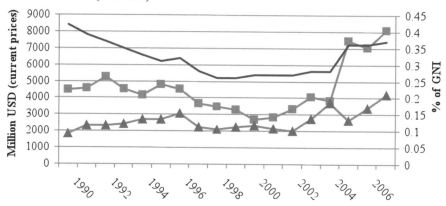

Figure 3.1 German ODA

Source: OECD 2008a

enough regular police officers so that Germany had to ask the EU to take over the mission in 2007 (Kempin 2008).

We find that the most important changes in Germany's prevention policy have occurred in regulating the flow of inward and outward migration (see Table 3.3). To begin with, Germany had one of the most liberal and permissive asylum laws because of its totalitarian past. At the same time, it has one of the most restrictive citizenship laws in the EU. Substantial changes occurred after unification, when a very large number of East Europeans of German descent – the so-called *Aussiedler* and *Übersiedler* – immigrated, a period during which a very significant number of war refugees from former Yugoslavia also arrived (Green 2006).

During this period, the conservative Kohl government pressed to further integrate migration policies in the EU in order to share the burden. However, when the effort failed and the government succeeded in limiting the permissive constitutional asylum provision, Germany grew more hesitant to delegate migration policy competences. In 2000, the Red-Green coalition tried – and at first failed – to change the very restrictive German citizenship law, but finally succeeded in getting a watered-down version adopted (Kruse *et al.* 2003). The latest immigration law reform, passed by the Grand Coalition in 2007, was adjusted to EU guidelines and set further restrictions by limiting subsequent immigration of dependants. In the public debate, language abilities as well as general knowledge of the German political system are increasingly considered as preconditions for migration, indicating increased societal pressure for an activist integration policy.

In sum, when looking at the balance of asylum requests, the number of individuals granted asylum and the number of deportees, Germany's policy has become more restrictive and more Europeanized.

Table 3.3 Migration flows, Germany 1991–2006

Year	Migration[a]			Asylum	
	Immigration	Emigration	Balance	Total applications	Rejected applications
1991	925,345	497,540	+ 427,805	256,112	128,820
1992	1,211,348	614,956	+ 596,392	438,191	163,637
1993	989,847	710,659	+ 279,188	322,599	347,991
1994	777,516	629,275	+ 148,241	127,210	238,386
1995	792,701	567,441	+ 225,260	127,937	117,939
1996	707,954	559,064	+ 148,890	116,367	126,652
1997	615,298	637,066	− 21,768	104,353	101,886
1998	605,500	638,955	− 33,455	98,644	91,700
1999	673,873	555,638	+ 118,235	95,113	80,231
2000	649,249	562,794	+ 86,455	78,564	61,840
2001	685,259	496,987	+ 188,272	88,278	55,402
2002	658,341	505,572	+ 152,769	71,124	78,845
2003	601,759	499,063	+ 102,696	50,563	63,002
2004	602,182	546,965	+ 55,217	35,607	38,599
2005	579,301	483,584	+ 95,717	28,914	27,452
2006	558,467	483,774	+ 74,693	21,029	17,781
Total	11,633,940	8,989,333	+ 2,644,607	2,060,605	1,740,163

Source: Bundesamt für Migration und Flüchtlinge 2007: 16, 89, 95

Notes:
[a] Migration data do not include cross-border movements by German citizens and illegal migration. Although there are no reliable estimates of illegal migration flows, some indicators point to a significant increase of illegal migration during the early 1990s (Lederer and Nickel 1997: 35–42)
[b] A direct comparison with total asylum applications is misleading, since not all applications are resolved in the year of application and time lags must be taken into consideration

To explain Germany's recent ambivalence towards international cooperation, insights can be drawn again from a liberal approach that takes both ideational and institutional factors into account. From this perspective, Germany's permissive asylum law came under tremendous pressure through the Yugoslav wars, aggravated by societal concerns about massive inflows of East European migrants of German descent. The government failed to adequately share the refugee burden within the EU by aligning migration policy competences with the EU level. Domestic actors, most prominently the second German chamber, the Bundesrat, then blocked the executive from shedding national competences. The Bundesrat, i.e. the conservative opposition to the Red-Green government, also played a crucial role in vetoing the modernization of Germany's citizenship law. In a nutshell, domestic opposition played a vital role in Germany's parliamentarian democracy in shaping preventive policies and the resulting international cooperation.

Protection

Germany's multilateral efforts to fulfil the traditional function of protecting society from external threats arguably best mirrors the ambivalent nature of its current security policy. While recognizing the need for international cooperation to tackle health threats, environmental problems and terrorism, as well as organized crime, Germany's contribution to security governance differs significantly over the issue areas, because domestic veto players curb the executive's thrust for enhanced competences.

Germany is a forerunner and strong advocate of environmental protection measures in the EU, as well as in other international organizations (Sprinz 2006; Jänicke 2006). The commitment to environmental protection is a continuous feature of German post-Cold War policy but it became even stronger under the Schröder and Merkel governments.[7] The efforts are in accordance with the firm securitization of the environment issue by successive governments since the 1980s and public opinion, which strongly supports environmental engagement. Internationally, Berlin took an active role in promoting and framing the UN agreements established in Rio de Janeiro in 1992, and it fervently supported the Convention on Biological Diversity as well as the global climate policy resulting in the Kyoto Protocol 1997. Berlin also self-confidently challenged the US resistance to a successor agreement in Bali 2008 (Fuller and Rosenthal 2007). Furthermore, the Merkel government made environmental issues one of their top priorities during the EU and G8 presidencies in 2007 (BMU 2008; Harnisch 2009).

While the rhetoric and negotiation stance are highly supportive of environmental protection measures, two flaws mark German environment policy. First, Berlin's compliance with international agreements is mixed. Germany shows a strong performance on global climate policy, where it lived up to its agreed cuts in greenhouse gas emissions which are the largest by any EU member state. Between 1990 and 2005, emissions were reduced by 18.7 per cent and the agreed reduction of 21 per cent seems to be attainable by 2010 (Umweltbundesamt 2007; EEA 2007). However, the adoptions of the Convention on Biological Diversity as well as some European agreements fell short of the ambitious rhetoric (Wurzel 2002). Reluctance by various industries and complex decision-making procedures made implementation difficult (Sprinz 2006). Second, since environmental policies are strongly Europeanized, German positions are subject to finding extensive consensuses within the EU, which reduced their consistency and ambition. In sum, however, Germany's contribution to international environmental protection is remarkable.

In comparison, the findings in the fight against organized crime and terrorism are more mixed. Organized crime ranks low in terms of its securitization and received little public attention in the past. When the risk of international organized crime

Table 3.4 Number of procedures against organized crime

■ First reporting　■ Follow-ups

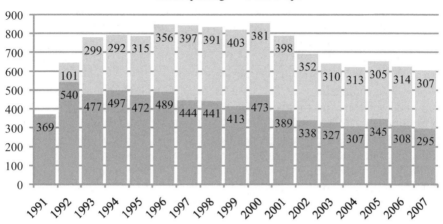

Source: BKA 2007: 7; BMI 2006: 455

Note: The first annual report on organized crime was prepared in 1991 and thus no follow-up cases are reported for this year

grew substantially with deeper European integration and successive reduction of border controls, Germany participated in the creation of EUROPOL as a European law enforcement agency and central information pool for cross-border criminality in 1992. The fight against organized crime has also been the subject of several bilateral agreements with states outside the EU recently, such as Turkey (2003) or Vietnam (2006). Furthermore, annual reports on organized crime by the Federal Criminal Police Office indicate that the measures taken are successful, since reported incidences of organized crime have declined since 2000 (see Table 3.4).

With the terrorist attacks in New York in 2001, Madrid in 2004 and London in 2005, and the coordinated fight against terrorism, organized crime took a back seat. The terrorist attacks in 2001 – three of the attackers were living and plotting in Germany – marked a watershed in German threat perception and caused significant domestic and international measures to meet the challenge (Rau 2004; Lange 2006). Almost immediately after the attack, German officials expressed solidarity with the US and willingness to take the necessary steps. The Parliament approved two substantial anti-terror packages which aimed at strengthening air and border security as well as reducing limitations on terrorist prosecution. Public opinion shifted significantly towards more robust measures, but a majority favours domestic measures, such as poverty reduction, over increased defence spending (Bulmahn 2008: 35). The second package also significantly improved the communication between federal and state levels, as well as between intelligence and enforcement agencies. In 2004 the 'Gemeinsame Terrorabwehrzentrum' was established, which coordinates various enforcement agencies, thereby breaking with Germany's long-held principle of a separation of police and intelligence services (Knelangen 2007). Additionally, the terrorist threat fostered personnel growth in the federal law enforcement agencies, Federal Crime Agency and Federal Police, which had been underway since the early 1990s (Möllers and van Ooyen 2008).[8]

The 9/11 attacks also boosted German participation in international cooperation on criminal and security issues. Accordingly, Berlin drives EU efforts to prosecute international terrorists and dry up their international financial flows. The US and Germany established close bilateral and multilateral cooperation to fight terrorism more effectively, e.g. through intelligence-sharing.

However, cooperation with the US faces major obstacles because of institutional limits and societal concerns about US violations of Germany's tough personal data protection laws (Miko and Froehlich 2004). Domestic resistance vis-à-vis executive autonomy-seeking in protection policies is considerable. Cases in point are the failed attempt of the federal government to enact a law allowing for the forceful downing of hijacked airplanes as well as the intense debate on phone and internet tapping. Hence, the domestication of the executive's security policies results in conflicts over Germany's full-fledged participation in international anti-terrorism cooperation. This trend continues under the Grand Coalition, although the Merkel government holds a two-third majority in the Bundestag (Harnisch 2009).

Germany's efforts on health protection remained by and large national over recent decades. Starting with 9/11 and fuelled by subsequent acts of terror using anthrax, as well as recent incidences of animal epidemics (e.g. BSE and SARS), Germany's government and society became more sensitive to health risks due to epidemics or biological attacks. Hence, the federal government decided to store vaccines and to prepare mechanisms for a timely and structured vaccination in case of a potential epidemic (BBK 2005, 25). And yet, preparations are limited to domestic adjustments and international agreements while overall policy planning is absent. A 2005 simulation of a biological terrorist attack with decision-makers from ten Western states clearly showed the deficiencies of cooperation in cases of epidemics: it soon became a case of 'dog eat dog' (Kleine-Brockhoff 2005).

In sum, German contributions to policies of protection are mixed. While the commitment to environmental issues puts Berlin in a leading role, policies on terrorism and biological attacks clearly display an ambivalent pattern between domestic constraints and allied expectations.

Compellence

It is often argued that increasing participation in military operations since unification proves that Germany has become a 'normal' country and some pundits even suggest that Chancellor Gerhard Schröder, who opposed the US intervention in Iraq, deliberately sought to demystify the military during his tenure (Baumann and Hellmann 2001; Geis 2005; Hellmann 2004; Wagener 2006). Indeed, as Baumann and Hellmann (2001: 78) argue: 'German policy makers did not just respond to a changing nature of the international system and to conflicting international and societal expectations ... They also managed to shape the public discourse in Germany and to establish new facts by slowly raising the scope of German military deployments, repeatedly moving beyond the established domestic consensus.'

And yet, there is little evidence that Germany's discourse formations (ideational structure) or parliamentary system (institutional structure) have supported or will support power politics in terms of autonomy-seeking or influence-maximizing behaviour (Harnisch 2005, 2009; Overhaus 2007; Meiers 2007). While the Bundeswehr has been deployed in some 15 countries, deployments have regularly addressed humanitarian crises and/or clear breaches of international law rather than strategic interests in resources or the counterbalancing of upcoming competitors, e.g. Russia. In our view, deployment has often been motivated by civilian power norms – as problematic as this may be – and constrained by institutional factors. Indeed, when analysing the patterns of deployment, we find that Bundeswehr missions have become ever more robust over time while the contingents remained multilaterally embedded. More recently, the Bundestag has strengthened its mandating power – through the *Parlamentsbeteiligungsgesetz* – and attached an increasing number of operational and financial caveats (Mair 2007; Wiefelspütz 2008; Harnisch 2009). One might argue that some deployments have been driven by more mundane 'national interests', such as limiting the flow of refugees from Kosovo or signalling cooperation to the US after the Iraq dispute by sending additional troops to Afghanistan. But in-depth studies of Germany's domestic deployment debates clearly indicate that mandates reaped large parliamentarian support because of their close fit with the civilian power tradition and drew substantial opposition when these where in doubt (Meiers 2007: 636). In sum, German force-projection patterns broadly followed an international trend towards more and more dangerous contingencies during the 1990s, but domestic legitimization and deployment patterns do not support the realists' argument. Details of German contributions to ESDP military missions are listed in Table 3.5.

Explanations stressing institutional constraints and ideational parameters enjoy more success, especially when explaining the idiosyncrasies of the German

Table 3.5 German contribution to EU-led compellence missions 2003–7

Mission	German personnel contribution by year Number (% of mission total)					Average per year
	2003	2004	2005	2006	2007	
EU Concordia (Macedonia)	26 (7.65%)					
EU Artemis (DR Congo)	N/A					
EUFOR Althea (Bosnia-Herzegovina)		1,227 (21.1%)	1,014 (17.9%)	861 (16.2%)	235 (10.9%)	16.5%
EUFOR (DR Congo)				745 (33%)		

Source: SIPRI Database 2004–7, Council of the EU 2008

Note: The table does not include the bridging mission EUFOR Chad/RCA from 2008 to 2009 which included four German personnel (Council of the EU 2008)

Table 3.6 German defence expenditure

	1990–94	1995–99	2000–4	2005	2006	2007
Share of GDP	2.1	1.6	1.4	1.4	1.3	1.3
Rate of change in defence spending	–7.2	–0.7	–0.8	–0.6	–1.0	–0.6
Distribution of defence expenditure:						
Personnel	57.4%	61.5%	60.0%	58.3%	57.1%	56.6%
Equipment	13.5%	11.8%	14.0%	14.2%	15.0%	15.3%
Infrastructure	4.9%	4.8%	4.3%	3.7%	3.6%	3.7%
Other	23.9%	21.9%	21.7%	23.9%	24.3%	24.3%
Defence spending per capita*	609	344	343	325	322	320

Source: NATO 2007b

Note:
* In USD (2000 prices and exchange rates)

compellence policies. Thus, the Grand Coalition has repeatedly withstood allies' calls for an increase in defence expenditures. Instead, as indicated in Table 3.6, the military budgets have been steadily declining since 1990, thus capping the Bundeswehr's capacity to transform into an intervention force with additional assets in long-distance deployment, armoured vehicles, etc. Although defence budgets of most Western European states dropped after the dissolution of the Soviet Union, German spending is remarkably lower than the budgets of France or Britain. While it may be argued that the gap in expenditure is caused solely by additional burdens for states with nuclear arsenals, it seems more plausible that this gap reveals a continuous German reluctance to robust military means based on its distinct security culture (Harnisch 2009). The impact of security culture is furthermore evident in the government's decade-old commitment to the Bundeswehr as a conscription army, rejecting an all-volunteer force because it may disconnect from the society at large (BMVG 2006: 14, 81, 83).

Or take force structure: Simply put, German armed forces are either too big to be adequately funded or their force structure is too narrow to be projected substantially as critical assets such as logistics are missing (IISS 2008: 97). Lastly, the Grand Coalition of CDU/CSU and Social Democrats has rejected such pointed criticism as 'the Germans must learn to kill' by keeping clear limits to German participation in frontline missions (*Spiegel* cover, 20 November 2006). Even as NATO Secretary General Jaap de Hoff Scheffer has called national caveats which threaten NATO's operational effectiveness 'poison', Germany has insisted on setting tight limits to its deployments, especially in Afghanistan. Hence, repeated demands for increased German support by NATO officials and allies has left the German position by and large unchanged (Cooper and Kulish 2008). The German contribution to the International Security Assistance Force (ISAF) is limited in number (currently up to 3,500, to be upgraded to up to 4,500) and confined to Kabul and the northern region, and only German special forces participate in Operation Enduring Freedom (OEF) combat missions against Taleban insurgents. But even these forces may not engage in combating the poppy industry in the north.

In sum, in comparison with other leading NATO/EU nations, Germany's armed forces are much less deployable, projectable and sustainable. In fact, it will not meet NATO usability standards that 40 per cent of each land force should be structured, prepared and equipped for deployed operations and 8 per cent for sustained operations at any one time in the foreseeable future (Meiers 2007: 627).

Conclusion

The most plausible explanation for Germany's continued ambivalent security governance between robustness and reticence rests on the liberal-institutionalist argument which stresses the distinct security culture strongly institutionalized at home and abroad. This is hardly surprising, since Germany's parliamentary democracy was consciously anchored in a unique constitutional framework and deliberately opened vis-à-vis international law (Katzenstein 2005: 305). The findings of this analysis of German participation in security governance can be summarized as follows:

- Germany's culture of reticence is changing slowly but considerably across different issues and therefore also across modes of public goods production. The causal pathway can be described as interaction between the domestic learning processes and institutional or bilateral socialization.
- Changes to German contribution patterns started to Europeanize after the Kosovo intervention and substantially increased after 9/11, and most notably after the US-led intervention in Iraq. We argue that Germany's security culture clearly fits better the emerging European security culture – not the least because Berlin can also shape the latter – than the perceived US security culture as interpreted during the George W. Bush administrations.
- Europeanization has become the preferred strategy to overcome domestication in Germany's security policy, but absolute limits – as defined by the Bundestag and the Federal Constitutional Court – are clearly identifiable.
- Reflecting upon our hypothesis linking security culture and international security governance, the German case presents a paradox: on the causal claim that security culture accounts for securitization and instrumental preferences, we find that cultural changes – Europeanization – have driven regional security governance, which often figures as a building block for global security governance. On the causal claim that post-Westphalian security cultures produce specific forms of security governance, however, the German case shows that changes in culture – and their societal underpinnings – may bring about different governance structures and even block some. Notably, more European security

governance has come together with more pooling and less delegation of German competences and capacities.

While these theoretical and empirical claims deserve more rigorous testing across issue areas and countries, our analysis suggests that the recent financial meltdown may well boost the Europeanization trend as the US's global financial stewardship is waning. In addition, current rescue schemes and secondary effects in the material economy will certainly hurt Germany's export-oriented economy and limit resources that may be spent on security governance beyond financial markets. Germany's pressure to water down the European agreement on carbon dioxide reduction efforts during the EU summit in Poznan (November 2008) may already indicate a decreasing willingness to contribute to costly international security governance in the face of a struggling economy.

Notes

1 With regard to Afghanistan, among other countries, Chancellor Merkel has argued that Germany is providing security for 40 per cent of the Afghan population and sustaining over 250 civilian reconstruction projects (Merkel 2006). In addition, the 2008 Afghanistan Concept of the Federal Government promotes a comprehensive approach, focusing on civil-military cooperation in the reconstruction effort (Bundesregierung 2008).

2 Since 1990, Germany has participated in nine UN missions (totalling 4,184 officers), nine EU and three WEU missions (totalling 949 officers) (Bund-/Länder-Arbeitsgruppe Internationale Polizeimissionen 2008).

3 Germany contributes significantly to the NATO-led KFOR (Kosovo) and ISAF (Afghanistan). By the end of 2007 the Federal Republic contributed 2,374 personnel to KFOR and 3,210 personnel to ISAF. Additionally, Germany supports OSCE missions in Macedonia, Georgia, Moldova, Tajikistan, Bosnia and Herzegovina, Albania, Kosovo, Serbia and Montenegro (OSCE 2008; NATO 2007a, 2008).

4 Germany has devoted an annual average of approx. 56 per cent of its multilateral ODA to the EC/EU since 1990. The share ranges from 42.59 per cent (1990) to 83.66 per cent (2005). Furthermore, Germany is the largest contributor to European aid funding in absolute terms (OECD 2008a, OECD 2006: 42).

5 For the purpose of social infrastructure and services Germany spent 33 per cent of its overall ODA in 1993–94, 39 per cent in 1998–99 and 40 per cent in 2003–4 (all based on two-year averages). Although the importance of economic infrastructure and services is slowly declining, it ranked second among the major purposes during most of the observed years, with a share of 22 per cent in 1993–94, 19 per cent in 1998–99 and 16 per cent in 2003–4 (OECD 2006: 91).

6 The major recipient of German ODA from 1990–2006 was China; Nigeria ranks third, India eighth and Indonesia tenth (OECD 2008b).

7 The active role of Germany owes much to steps taken during the 1980s. These measures resulted in comparative technological and structural advantages on environmental issues (Wurzel 2002).

8 The Federal Crime Agency gained more than 1,000 additional personnel and employed a total of 4,840 in 2008. The Federal Police included 39,000 personnel in 2008, 6,000 more than in 1992 (Möllers and van Ooyen 2008: 30).

References

Baumann, R. and Hellman, G. (2001) 'Germany and the Use of Military Force: "Total War", the "Culture of Restraint", and the Quest for Normality', *German Politics*, 10(1): 61–82.

Baumann, R., Rittberger, V. and Wagner, W. (2001) 'Neorealist Foreign Policy Theory', in Rittberger, V. (ed.) *German Foreign Policy since Unification: An Analysis of Foreign Policy Continuity and Change*, Manchester: Manchester University Press.

BBK [Bundesamt für Bevölkerungsschutz und Katastrophenhilfe] (2005) *Problemstudie: Risiken für Deutschland, Gefahrenpotentiale und Gefahrenprävention für Staat, Wirtschaft und Gesellschaft aus Sicht des Bevölkerungsschutzes*, Teil 1, Bad Neuenahr-Ahrweiler.

Berenskoetter, F. and Giegerich, B. (2006) 'From NATO to ESDP? Tracing Shifts in German Institutional Preferences after the End of the Cold War', paper prepared for the fourth Convention of the Central and East European International Studies Association (CEEISA), Tartu, Estonia, June 2006.

BKA [Bundeskriminalamt] (2007) *Organisierte Kriminalität. Bundeslagebild 2007, Pressefreie Kurzfassung*, Wiesbaden.

BMI [Bundesministerium des Innern] (2006) *Zweiter Periodischer Sicherheitsbericht*, Berlin.

BMU [Bundesministerium für Umwelt, Naturschutz und Reaktorsicherheit] (2008) *Umweltpolitische Bilanz der deutschen EU-und G8-Präsidentschaft 2007*, Berlin.

BMVG [Bundesministerium der Verteidigung] (2006) *Weißbuch 2006 zur Sicherheitspolitik Deutschlands und zur Zukunft der Bundeswehr*, Berlin. Available online at: http://www.bmvg.de/fileserving/PortalFiles/C1256EF40036B05B/W26UYEPT431INFODE/WB_2006_dt_mB.pdf?yw_repository = youatweb (accessed 20 March 2009).

Bulmahn, T. (2008) *Bevölkerungsbefragung 2008. Sicherheits-und verteidigungspolitisches Meinungsklima in Deutschland: Kurzbericht*, Strausberg: Sozialwissenschaftliches Institut der Bundeswehr.

Bundesamt für Migration und Flüchtlinge (2007) *Migrationsbericht des Bundesamts für Migration und Flüchtlinge im Auftrag der Bundesregierung. Migrationsbericht 2006*. Available online at: http://www.bamf.de/cln_011/nn_442522/SharedDocs/Anlagen/DE/Migration/Publikationen/Forschung/Migrationsberichte/migrationsbericht-2006, templateId = raw,property = publicationFile.pdf/migrationsbericht-2006.pdf (accessed 20 September 2008).

Bund-/Länder-Arbeitsgruppe Internationale Polizeimissionen (2007) *Ziviles Krisenmanagement der Europäischen Union. Informationsblatt*. Available online at: http://www.bundespolizei.de/cln_109/nn_268544/DE/Home/ – Startseite/IPM/Infoblaetter/ – Infoblatt – ZKM,templateId = raw,property = publicationFile.pdf/_Infoblatt_ZKM.pdf (accessed 21 September 2008).

—— (2008) *Auslandseinsätze der deutschen Polizei*. Informationsblatt Historie. Available online at: http://www.bundespolizei.de/cln_109/nn_268544/DE/Home/ – Startseite/IPM/Infoblaetter/ – Infoblatt – HistorieAuslandseinsaetze,templateId = raw,property = publicationFile.pdf/_Infoblatt_HistorieAuslandseinsaetze.pdf (accessed 21 September 2008).

Bundesregierung (2008) *Das Afghanistan Konzept*, Berlin. Available online at: http://www.auswaertiges-amt.de/diplo/de/Aussenpolitik/RegionaleSchwerpunkte/AfghanistanZentralasien/Downloads/080909-Afghanistan-Konzept2008.pdf (accessed 13 October 2008).

Cooper, H. and Kulish, N. (2008) 'As Afghanistan Flounders, US Asks Europe for More', *The New York Times*, 7 February 2008.

Council of the European Union (2008) *European Security and Defence Policy – Operations*.

Available online at: http://www.consilium.europa.eu/cms3_fo/showPage.asp?id = 268&lang = en (accessed 20 August 2008).

Dalgaard-Nielsen, A. (2006) *Germany, Pacifism and Peace Enforcement*, Manchester: Manchester University Press.

EEA (2007) *Greenhouse Gas Emission Trends and Projections in Europe 2007: Tracking Progress towards Kyoto Targets*, EEA-Report No. 5/2007, Copenhagen.

Fincke, G. and Hatakoy, A. (2004) 'Krisenprävention als neues Leitbild der deutschen Außenpolitik: Friedenspolitik mit zivilen und militärischen Mitteln?', in Harnisch, S., Katsioulis, C. and Overhaus, M. (eds) *Deutsche Sicherheitspolitik: Eine Bilanz der Regierung Schröder*, Baden-Baden: Nomos Verlag.

Fuller, T. and Rosenthal, E. (2007) 'At Divided Climate Talks, Consensus That US Is at Fault', *The New York Times*, 14 December.

Geis, A. (2005) *Die Zivilmacht Deutschland und die Enttabuisierung des Militärischen*, HSFK-Standpunkte 2/2005, Frankfurt am Main.

GKKE [Gemeinsame Konferenz Kirche und Entwicklung] (2003) *Rüstungsexportbericht 2003 der GKKE*, Bonn. Available online at: http://www3.gkke.org/publikationen/2003/ (accessed 6 April 2009).

Green, S. (2006) 'Zwischen Kontinuität und Wandel: Migrations-und Staatsangehörigkeitspolitik', in Schmidt, M. and Zohlnhöfer, R. (eds) *Regieren in der Bundesrepublik Deutschland: Innen-und Außenpolitik seit 1949*, Wiesbaden: VS Verlag.

Gurowitz, A. (2006) 'The Diffusion of International Norms: Why Identity Matters', *International Politics*, 43(3): 305–41.

Harnisch, S. (2005) 'Deutsche Außenpolitik auf dem Prüfstand. Die Kultur der Zurückhaltung und die Debatte über nationale Interessen', in Streitkräfteamt, Informations-und Medienzentrale der Bundeswehr (ed.) *Reader Sicherheitspolitik*, Ergänzungslieferung 3/05: 10–24.

——(2006) *Internationale Politik und Verfassung: Zur Domestizierung des sicherheits-und europapolitischen Prozesses der Bundesrepublik Deutschland*, Baden-Baden: Nomos Verlag.

——(2007) 'Minilateral Cooperation and Transatlantic Coalition Building: The EU3-Iran Initiative', *European Security*, 16(1): 1–27.

——(2009) 'Die Außen-und Sicherheitspolitik der Großen Koalition', in Zohlnhöfer, R. and Egle, C. (eds) *Bilanz der Großen Koalition*, Wiesbaden: VS Verlag.

Harnisch, S. and Longhurst, K. (2006) 'Understanding Germany: The Limits of "Normalization" and the Prevalence of Strategic Culture', in Taberner, S. and Cooke, P. (eds) *German Culture, Politics, and Literature into the 21st Century: Beyond Normalization*, New York: Camden House.

Harnisch, S., Katsioulis, C. and Overhaus, M. (eds) (2004) *Deutsche Sicherheitspolitik: Eine Bilanz der Regierung Schröder*, Baden-Baden: Nomos Verlag.

Harnisch, S. and Maull, H.W. (eds) (2001) *Germany as a Civilian Power: The Foreign Policy of the Berlin Republic*, Manchester: Manchester University Press.

Hawkins, D.G., Lake, D., Nielson, D. and Tierney, M. (2006) *Delegation and Agency in International Organizations*, Cambridge: Cambridge University Press.

Hedstück, M. and Hellmann, G. (2003) *'Wir machen einen deutschen Weg.' Irak-Abenteuer, das transatlantische Verhältnis und die Risiken der Methode Schröder für die deutsche Außenpolitik*. Available online at: http://www.soz.uni-frankfurt.de/hellmann/mat/irak.pdf (accessed 21 September 2008).

Hellmann, G. (2004) *Wider die machtpolitische Resozialisierung der deutschen Außenpolitik*, WeltTrends 12/42: 79–88.

IISS [International Institute for Strategic Studies] (2008) *European Military Capabilities: Building Armed Forces for Modern Operations*, London: IISS.

Irondelle, B. (2003) 'Europeanization without the European Union? French Military Reforms 1991–96', *Journal of European Public Policy*, 10(2): 208–26.

Jänicke, M. (2006) 'Umweltpolitik: Auf dem Weg zur Querschnittspolitik', in Schmidt, M. and Zohlnhöfer, R. (eds) *Regieren in der Bundesrepublik Deutschland: Innen-und Außenpolitik seit 1949*, Wiesbaden: VS Verlag.

Katzenstein, P.J. (2005) 'Conclusion: Semisovereignty in United Germany', in Green, S. and Paterson, W. (eds) *Governance in Contemporary Germany: The Semisovereign State Revisited*, Cambridge: Cambridge University Press.

Kempin, R. (2008) 'Polizeiaufbau in Afghanistan', in Schmidt, P. (ed.) *Das international Engagement in Afghanistan: Strategien, Perspektiven, Konsequenzen*, Berlin: SWP. Available online at: http://www.swp-berlin.org/common/get_document.php?asset_id = 5196 (accessed 17 September 2008).

Kleine-Brockhoff, T. (2005) 'Wenn die Pocken kommen', *Die Zeit*, 15 January 2007. Available online at: http://images.zeit.de/text/2005/05/N-Terrorspiel (accessed 12 October 2008).

Knelangen, W. (2007) 'Die deutsche Politik der Terrorismusbekämpfung', in Jäger, T., Höse, A. and Oppermann, K. (eds) *Deutsche Außenpolitik: Sicherheit, Wohlfahrt, Institutionen und Normen*, Wiesbaden: VS Verlag.

Kruse, I., Orren, H. and Angenendt, S. (2003) 'The Failure of Immigration Reform in Germany', *German Politics*, 12(3): 129–45.

Lange, H.-J. (2006) 'Innere Sicherheit und Wandel von Staatlichkeit', in Schmidt, M. and Zohlnhöfer, R. (eds) *Regieren in der Bundesrepublik Deutschland: Innen-und Außenpolitik seit 1949*, Wiesbaden: VS Verlag.

Layne, C. (1993) 'The Unipolar Illusion: Why New Great Powers Will Rise', *International Security*, 17(4): 5–51.

Lederer, H.W. and Nickel, A. (1997) *Illegale Ausländerbeschäftigung in der Bundesrepublik Deutschland*, Bonn: FES.

Longhurst, K. (2004) *Germany and the Use of Force: The Evolution of German Security Policy 1989–2003*, Manchester: Manchester University Press.

Mair, S. (ed.) (2007) *Auslandseinsätze der Bundeswehr: Leitfragen, Entscheidungsspielräume und Lehren*, Berlin: SWP. Available online at: http://www.swp-berlin.org/common/get_document.php?asset_id = 4355 (accessed 23 September 2008).

Maull, H.W. (1990/91) 'Germany and Japan: The New Civilian Powers', *Foreign Affairs*, 69(5): 91–106.

—— (2006) 'Die prekäre Kontinuität, Deutsche Außenpolitik zwischen Pfadabhängigkeit und Anpassungsdruck', in Schmidt, M and Zohlnhöfer, R. (eds) *Regieren in der Bundesrepublik Deutschland: Innen- und Außenpolitik seit 1949*, Wiesbaden: Verlag für Sozialwissenschaften.

Meiers, F.-J. (2007) 'The German Predicament: The Red Lines of the Security and Defence Policy of the Berlin Republic', *International Politics*, 44: 623–44.

Merkel, A. (2006) 'Sollen wir umdrehen und wegrennen?', *Frankfurter Allgemeine Zeitung*, 24 November.

Miko, F.T. and Froehlich, C. (2004) *Germany's Role in Fighting Terrorism: Implications for US Policy*, CRS Report for Congress, RL32710.

Miskimmon, A. (2007) *Germany and the Common Foreign and Security Policy of the European Union: Between Europeanisation and National Adaption*, London: Palgrave.

Missiroli, A. (2003) 'Euros for ESDP: Financing EU Operations', *Occasional Papers*, No. 45, Institute for Security Studies, Paris.

Möllers, M. and van Ooyen, R. (2008) 'Bundeskriminalamt, Bundespolizei und "neue" Sicherheit', *Aus Politik und Zeitgeschichte*, 48: 26–32.

Mölling, C. (2007) *EU-Battlegroups. Stand und Probleme der Umsetzung in Deutschland und für die EU*, Berlin: SWP.

Moravcsik, A. (2000) 'The Origins of Human Rights Regimes: Democratic Delegation in Postwar Europe', *International Organization*, 54(2): 217–52.

NATO (2007a) 'ISAF Fact Sheet'. Available online at: http://www.nato.int/isaf/docu/epub/pdf/isaf_leaflet.pdf (accessed 20 September 2008).

—— (2007b) 'NATO-Russia Compendium of Financial and Economic Data Relating to Defence'. Available online at: http://www.nato.int/docu/pr/2007/p07–141.pdf (accessed 15 December 2008).

—— (2008) 'Kosovo Force'. Available online at: http://www.nato.int/kfor/index.html (accessed 20 September 2008).

O'Brian, C.C. (1992) 'The Future of "the West"', *The National Interest*, 30: 3–10.

OECD (2006) *OECD Journal on Development*, 7(2), Paris.

—— (2008a) 'ODA by Donor', OECD.Stat.

—— (2008b) 'ODA by Recipient by Country', OECD.Stat.

OSCE (2008) 'Field Operations'. Available online at: http://www.osce.org/about/13510.html (accessed 25 October 2008).

Overhaus, M. (2007) 'Institutionalist Foreign Policy Analysis – The Case of German Security Policy in NATO After September 11, 2001', paper prepared for the 48th Annual ISA Convention, Chicago.

Pradetto, A. (2006) 'The Polity of German Foreign Policy: Changes since Unification', in H.W. Maull (ed.) *Germany's Uncertain Power: Foreign Policy of the Berlin Republic*, Basingstoke, UK: Palgrave MacMillan.

Rau, M. (2004) 'Country Report: Germany', in Walter, C., Vöneky, S., Röben, V. and Schorkopf, F. (eds) *Terrorism as a Challenge for National and International Law: Security versus Liberty?*, Berlin: Springer Verlag.

Schöllgen, G. (2004) 'Die Zukunft der deutschen Außenpolitik liegt in Europa', *Aus Politik und Zeitgeschichte*, B11, 9–16.

SIPRI (2008) 'Multilateral Peace Operations Database'. Available online at: http://conflict.sipri.org/SIPRI_Internet/index.php4 (accessed 20 September 2008).

Sprinz, D.F. (2006) 'Germany's International Environmental Policy', in Maull, H. (ed.) *Germany's Uncertain Power. Foreign Policy of the Berlin Republic*, Basingstoke, UK: Palgrave.

Umweltbundesamt (2007) 'Treibhausgas-Emissionen in Deutschland'. Available online at: http://www.env-it.de/umweltdaten/public/theme.do?nodeIdent = 3152 (accessed 12 October 2008).

UN (2008) 'List of Operations 1948–2008'. Available online at: http://www.un.org/Depts/dpko/list/list.pdf (accessed 20 September 2008).

UN Information Service (2008) 'Friedensicherung der Vereinten Nationen'. Available online at: http://www.unis.unvienna.org/pdf/peacekeeping_background_de.pdf (accessed 20 September 2008).

UNRIC (1999) 'Friedensicherung der Vereinten Nationen – 50 Jahre'. Available online at: http://www.unric.org/html/german/50jahre/dpi1999.htm (20 September 2008).

Wagener, M. (2006) 'Normalization in Security Policy? Deployments of Bundeswehr Forces abroad in the Era Schröder, 1998–2004', in Maull, H. (ed.) *Germany's Uncertain Power: Foreign Policy of the Berlin Republic*, New York: Palgrave.

Weiss, D. (2008) 'Deutschland am Hindukusch', *Aus Politik und Zeitgeschichte*, 43: 6–14.

Wiefelspütz, D. (2008) *Der Auslandseinsatz der Bundeswehr und das Parlamentsbeteiligungsgesetz*, Frankfurt am Main: Verlag für Polizeiwissenschaft.

Wurzel, R.R.W. (2002) *The Europeanisation of German Environmental Policy: From Environmental Leader to Member State under Pressure?*, FFU report 09/2002, Berlin.

Zentrum für Internationale Friedenseinsätze (2008) 'International and German Personnel in EU, UN, OSCE, NATO and Other Field Missions as of August 2008'. Available online at: http://www.zif-berlin.org/fileadmin/uploads/analyse/dokumente/veroeffentlichungen/ Mission_Update_August_08_final.pdf (accessed 21 September 2008).

4   Italy

Hard tests and soft responses

Paolo Foradori and Paolo Rosa

National security cultures are key determinants in shaping a country's strategic preferences. In this chapter we will consider how Italy's security policy and behaviour in the international arena are influenced by the specific ideational and cognitive characteristics rooted in its security culture. In particular, we will consider: 1) how national security culture accounts for the securitization of threats and the preferred instruments relied upon to meet them; and 2) how security culture produces preferences for specific forms of security governance systems that, in turn, facilitate or inhibit international cooperation.

The analysis is structured in three parts. The first provides an overview of Italian security culture from the end of World War II on, with a specific focus on the post-Cold War period. The second part is an in-depth empirical investigation of the Italian role in the global governance system, discussing the four dimensions of assurance, compellence, prevention and protection. In the light of the analyses made in the first two parts, the conclusion of the chapter assess the compatibility of the Italian security culture with the international security system, and its strengths and weaknesses as a contributor.

Italian security culture

Italy is a highly industrialized modern country and a member of the G8. There are no structural factors to impede the country's pursuit of an active diplomatic and strong security policy. Italy could aspire to be recognized as a medium-great power, like France, Germany and the UK. Nonetheless, Italy still performs at a much lower level in the global security governance system than the other medium-great powers. This is largely due to the country's security culture, which significantly influences its attitude to the use of force, inducing it to opt for low-profile strategies based on diplomatic and 'soft' power instruments, and essentially rejecting the threat or actual use of coercive means.

Italy's security culture is a result of the country's history, its formative experiences during the building of the nation-state, and national endowments and characteristics.[1] The most relevant factors shaping the country's security culture are: the lack of a significant military and imperial tradition, modest success on the battlefield, the negative experience of interwar fascism, defeat in WWII, subordination to the US in security matters during the Cold War period, and the exclusion (until the end of the 1990s) of defence matters from the political agenda.

In Italian security culture, war is deemed an aberration and not a 'normal' feature of the relations between states. Significantly influenced by Catholic and left-wing traditions, the Italian attitude to security is close to the idea of 'just war'. Both Catholic and leftist political thought identify a series of limits to the legitimate use of force: these limits essentially lead to the idea that the only possible 'just war' is that of self-defence, or that of an oppressed country against its oppressor. Italy repudiates the most extreme forms of nationalism and constitutionally rejects war as an instrument to regulate disputes. The current security culture and defence structures are heavily influenced by the desire of the members of the first Republican Parliament and Constitutional Assembly to put the fascist heritage behind them once and for all. To prevent any possible return to authoritarianism, the Italian Parliament was given the power to exercise considerable control over the executive. Aggressive nationalism was rejected in favour of a multilateral and peaceful foreign policy. Article 11 of the Constitution allows for the limitation of national sovereignty in order to create an international order capable of ensuring 'peace and justice among nations'.

This decision meant that Italy referred most of its defence responsibilities and, to some extent, the definition of threats, to the US and NATO during most of its post-WWII history. Italy was a security-consumer rather than a security-producer throughout the Cold War.

Within Italian security culture, the enemy is not considered an 'implacable adversary', to be confronted with overwhelming military force. In interstate relations cooperation prevails over conflict and hence international relations are not zero-sum. A foreign policy based on coercion is bound to fail and resorting to the use of force creates further problems, without addressing the causes of conflict. Diplomacy is therefore considered to be much more effective. Central to this approach is the concept of 'civilian power'. Italy's strategic tradition and its instrumental preferences for meeting its security threats remain connected to a comprehensive, integrated and multidimensional approach in which priority is given to 'soft power' strategies. Coercive methods are considered to be a last resort.

This approach is very evident in the Italian participation in the ISAF mission in Afghanistan, the most dangerous of missions in which the Italian army is currently involved. Here too, Italy has tried to prioritize, as much as possible, the civilian component of the mission, through its work on the promotion of the rule of law and security-sector reform. As the President of the Italian Republic, Giorgio Napolitano, said before NATO's Political Committee of the Parliamentary Assembly, Italian intervention in Afghanistan must operate according to principles and 'guidelines favourable to the civilian, and not just the military development, of the mission in Afghanistan, until the objectives have been reached which can allow for the establishment of peace and institutional stability in that country'.[2]

Given this image of international relations, the Italian security culture has developed a precise hierarchy of strategic preferences.[3] Diplomatic settlement/accommodation is the preferred option when facing security challenges. The second preference is for a defensive attitude and offensive strategies are a last resort, to be undertaken only in a multilateral context if possible.

Multilateralism is a key characteristic of the Italian security culture. The principal international institutions – the UN, EU, OSCE and NATO – are, always and without question, the reference point for Italian international action and the source of legitimacy for all Italian military interventions.

This security culture resulted in a peculiar model of civil-military relations. The Italian Armed Forces were held in low esteem after WWII, and conscripts were often ill-trained and ill-equipped. It was only at the end of the 1970s – with the so-called 'promotional laws' (Perani and Pianta 1992) – that Italy began undertaking a serious modernization of its military establishment. The low standing of the Armed Forces – especially in the eyes of the left-wing parties – meant that the country opted for a conscript army instead of a professional one, since the latter was felt to be more in tune with a right-wing ideology and so a potential threat to the newly established and still fragile democratic system. Since the pursuit of an offensive strategy is strictly connected to a professional army (Kier 1996), the very fact of having a conscript army has led Italy to adopt defensive strategic preferences.

The end of the Cold War signalled a thaw in Italy's domestic politics and the re-opening of the debate about foreign policy and defence, making it necessary to review the security architecture, which had been based on the defence of the territory and on a static and unidirectional conception of security threats, framed by the perspectives of the East–West conflict. A new phase in Italy's foreign and security policy began, characterized by a more assertive, pro-active and visible role on the global scene. This shift was the continuation of a trend that began in the mid-1980s, when the government tried to introduce a rapid reaction force of some 12,000 troops to perform force projection tasks. Even in this case, over and above the budgetary constraints which made this ambition rather unrealistic, the biggest obstacles were cultural. This is evidenced by the fact that an attempt was made to conceal the creation of this force amidst other budget entries which were less unpopular, both with the public and politicians (Caligaris and Santoro 1986).

The characteristics of the Italian security culture made it quite easy for the Italian Armed Forces to adapt *culturally* to the new security scenario post-1989. If the end of the Cold War deprived Italy of its enemy and caused a sort of legitimacy crisis in the Armed Forces, they found a new and to a large extent more suitable *raison d'être* through more active engagement in crisis management aimed at promoting peace and stability in post-conflict societies. The attainment of security is thus regarded as dependent not only on disarmament and other measures of security cooperation but, more importantly, on the long-term achievement of structural stability in the societies and polities concerned.

The conversion of the Armed Forces to this new mission has required a considerable restructuring effort by Italian security policy-makers, in order to modernize and reach the necessary standard for the achievement of new tasks which require a high capacity for mobility, readiness and interoperability. The move from conscription to a professional army is in line with this.

The Italian contribution to security governance

In this section we present an in-depth empirical investigation of Italy's contribution to the system of global governance, in its four dimensions of assurance, prevention, protection and compellence.

Assurance

The civilian emphasis within Italian security culture fits comfortably into the assurance category; an area of intervention based on the limited use of coercion in low-intensity, post-conflict, humanitarian and reconstruction contexts, often under a multinational cover. Assurance operations include peace-support operations with lightly armed personnel and exclude warfare/combat/hostility (though there may be sporadic high-intensity military engagements in the course of some robust peace-keeping missions, which will be considered in the Compellence section below). Italian engagement in assurance also reflects the holistic and multidimensional approach to security issues which defines the country's security culture.

Italy plays an important role, and has steadily gained a reputation, in international police missions (Table 4.1). Policing has become a fundamental component of peace operations and peace-building, and suits the civilian nature of the Italian security role perfectly. The Italian Carabinieri, a sort of Gendarmerie, are particularly renowned and in demand. They have both police skills and military discipline, training and equipment. Their special skills and training mean they are particularly deployed in situations that call for the 'presence not only of civilian police to maintain law and order but also of a stronger force that would be able to use military force when and if needed' (Aprile and Marco 2005: 23). The current NATO mission in Iraq, where Italian Carabinieri are training high-ranking Iraqi police, is particularly difficult. Thanks to the efforts of the Carabinieri, Italy is a founding member of, and the principal contributor to, the European Gendarmarie, whose headquarters in Vicenza was opened in 2006.

Italy contributes to the civilian dimension of the European Security and Defence Policy (ESDP) through the deployment of civilian personnel such as judges, legal experts and public officials (Table 4.2).

The Italian contribution to multinational operations under the aegis of the OSCE is also significant (Table 4.3).

The Italian security culture demonstrates both its continued influence and its intrinsic contradictions most clearly in situations where the line between assurance and compellence is fuzzy, as in Afghanistan. Italy has always seen its role in the Afghan conflict as that of a contributor to stability in the area; it does not consider itself at war with the Taleban or anyone else. The Italians are concentrating mainly on the justice sector and the promotion of the rule of law (increasing Afghan capacity to carry out a sustainable reform of the justice system, a technical assistance programme for the Afghan ministries, the rehabilitation and support of the Afghan justice and prison system), education and emergency aid for returnees, and infrastructure (bridges and roads).[4]

Table 4.1 The Carabinieri's participation in international police missions 2008

Name	Location	Personnel
EUFOR	Bosnia	87
HQ EUFOR	Bosnia	4
EUPM	Bosnia	13
Military Police Italian Army	Bosnia	4
UNFICYP	Cyprus	4
HQ UNFIL	Lebanon	11
Internat'l Military Police at HQ UNFIL	Lebanon	41
Military Police at UNFIL	Lebanon	4
EUFOR Tchad/DRC	Chad	4
EUPOL DRC	DRC	4
MSU/KFOR	Kosovo	261
HQ KFOR	Kosovo	11
Military Police MNTF–W	Kosovo	24
UNMIK CIU	Kosovo	3
EUPT	Kosovo	2
Military Police Staff RCC Kabul	Afghanistan	21
Military Police PRT/FSB	Afghanistan	19
Staff at RC-W	Afghanistan	2
Aviation unit EAU	Afghanistan	5
EUPOL	Afghanistan	12
Training INP	Iraq	41
Total personnel contribution		577

Source: Carabinieri (2009)

Prevention

Italy's main activities in the area of prevention have focused on developmental assistance and migration flow policies. Italy's international aid policies are, for the most part, born out of humanitarian impulses ('to guarantee respect for human dignity and ensure that all peoples benefit from economic growth'), concentrating on the fight against world poverty and assistance to developing countries, especially in the process of institution-building. More recently, new emergencies have 'given aid an even more fundamental role in Italian foreign policy',[5] both

Table 4.2 Italy in ESDP civilian operations

Name of mission	Location	Italian personnel
EULEX KOSOVO	Kosovo	172
EUMM GEORGIA	Georgia	15
EU BAM RAFAH	Palestine	4
EUSEC RD CONGO	Democratic Republic of Congo	5
EUJUST Themis	Georgia	10
AMM Aceh Monitoring Mission	Indonesia	1
Total personnel contribution		207

Source: European Union (5 June 2009)

Table 4.3 Italy in OSCE missions

Name of mission	Location	Italian personnel
Spillover Monitor Mission to Skopje	Macedonia	7
LTM Moldova	Moldova	1
LTM to Bosnia and Herzegovina	Bosnia and Herzegovina	12
LTM to Croatia	Croatia	4
LTM in Kosovo	Kosovo	20
LTM to Serbia	Serbia	5
LTM to Montenegro	Montenegro	1
Total personnel contribution		50

Source: ADISM DATASET, http://www.fscpo.unict.it/adism/dataItaly.pdf (accessed 22 April 2009)

Note: LTM = Long-term mission

as a means for maintaining international peace and for managing the flow of immigrants to Europe, and particularly Italy. Although a distinction is still drawn between development and security, a clear conviction is emerging that long-term sustainable security can never be won without economic development (Foradori and Rosa 2007).

Italy concentrates its development aid – which takes into account the guide-lines and commitments agreed in multilateral fora (the UN, EU, etc.) – in Africa; in countries where Italy has taken on international commitments (Afghanistan, Lebanon); and in areas with which the country has historical ties (Latin America, the Middle East and the Mediterranean). Particular attention is paid to the 'near abroad' – North Africa (Egypt, Tunisia, Algeria, Morocco), the Near and Middle

East (the Palestinian territories, Lebanon, Jordan, Syria, Iran, Iraq, Yemen), the Balkan Peninsula (Albania, Bosnia Herzegovina, Macedonia, Serbia and Montenegro). In line with Italian foreign policy, the declared objective of Italian aid is that of ensuring better standards of living for local populations, and of promoting stability in neighbouring countries.[6]

The areas prioritized are: the environment and the common goods, with a focus on rural development, organic and conventional agriculture; research into alternative and renewable energy sources; gender politics and particularly the empowerment of women; as well as traditional aid to the health and education sectors.

In the last decade Italy has concentrated its modest resources on involvement in areas whose development and stability is of direct interest to it (reconciliation and stability in the Balkans) or those where it feels it has an historical responsibility (the Horn of Africa), and on Italian participation in the global effort to tackle the great challenges (poverty in Africa, foreign debt in the poorest countries).

The three main aims of Italian international aid can be identified by considering the priorities noted above. They are:

1 Political: stability in developing countries means greater security in Italy. Here the slowing of the flow of migrants to the country is crucial, hence the focus on the Balkans and the Mediterranean region.
2 Economic: here integration into the world economy and support for the private sector (particularly small and medium businesses), are considered vital, if developing countries are to find their way out of poverty.
3 Humanitarian: from the moment that emergencies caused by conflicts and catastrophes require the reconstruction of the social fabric and the reduction of poverty, this is the primary objective of development aid policies (Zupi 2001: 240).

The close ties between aid, foreign policy objectives and Italian security are evident from the funding given to humanitarian emergency and reconstruction projects in the countries where the Italian Armed Forces are deployed. The March 2007 decree on the re-financing of Italian missions abroad allocated 40 million Euros for development in Afghanistan and 30 million for Lebanon.

Despite the rhetoric and public announcements that funding for this sector will be increased, the Italian aid budget remains well below average among OECD countries, in tenth place in 2008, or rather 20th, if calculated as a percentage of GDP. Italy contributes only 0.2 per cent of GDP to Overseas Development Aid, and therefore falls far short not only of the 0.7 per cent objective agreed internationally, but also of the average contributed by developed countries (about 0.3 per cent of GDP) (Table 4.4).

Italy's meagre financial commitment to international aid is clearly a strategic error for a country that wishes to be a civilian power, and for which military options remain culturally and politically undesirable. The Italian predilection for multilateral channels is nevertheless still marked. In recent years more than half

Table 4.4 Italian ODA: net disbursement in millions of US dollars (current prices)

Year	ODA	ODA as a percentage of GNI
1990	3,394.96	0.31
1992	4,121.92	0.34
1994	2,704.63	0.27
1996	2,415.52	0.2
1998	2,278.31	0.2
2000	1,376.26	0.13
2002	2,332.13	0.15
2004	2,461.54	0.15
2006	3,641.06	0.2
2008	4,443.59	0.2

Source: OECD 2008

of Italian projects have been carried out in collaboration with multilateral organizations, and Italy is better integrated globally, from this point of view, than most other donor countries.

Particularly since 11 September 2001 (9/11), the issue of migration has definitely escalated from a question of public order to one of security, both in terms of societal security and sheer security. Immigration is a new phenomenon for Italy. During the 1990s the flow of immigrants increased, in response to the 'migration crises' produced by the political turmoil in Albania (1991 and 1997), the Balkan wars of the mid-1990s, and, above all, Kosovo (1999) (ISPI 2003: 17). This increase is detailed in Table 4.5, showing the numbers of residence permits granted to foreigners in the years 1996–2007.

The 1990s also saw an increase in asylum requests from people fleeing conflict, political unrest and human rights violations in various parts of the world. About 2,000 asylum requests were made in 1997, 11,000 in 1998 and more than 33,000 in 1999. Although this increase is significant in absolute terms, it is much less so in comparison with the other main European countries.

At present there are almost 38,000 refugees and in 2007 about 14,000 asylum requests were made. The numbers of both refugees and asylum requests for Italy are very low, absolutely and relatively, when compared with other European countries. Germany has about 580,000 refugees, the UK almost 300,000 and Holland and France 85,000 and 150,000, respectively.[7]

Although the importance of immigration to sustain the economy of a country with one of the lowest birth rates in the world and a rapidly ageing population is recognized, the issue has been gradually securitized, to the point where the subject, combined with that of security, has been one of the main campaign issues in recent elections. This led to a transformation of the migrational flows from a simple matter

Table 4.5 Residence permits issued 1996–2007

1996	729,159
1997	986,020
1998	1,022,896
1999	1,090,820
2000	1,340,655
2001	1,379,749
2002	1,448,392
2003	1,503,286
2004	2,227,567
2005	2,245,548
2006	2,286,024
2007	2,414,972

Source: ISTAT 2009

of public order to a crucial element among the new challenges to international security (Aliboni 2002: 104).[8]

Despite the importance of the issue, Italian policies around migration and the reception of migrants are still heavily flawed and often inefficient, as demonstrated by the lack, uniquely in the European Union, of a coherent law on the right to asylum.

Protection

In recent years, Italy has invested significantly in protection policies, both at the national level and in cooperation with European and international partners. The country's engagement has nevertheless been diversified according to specific issues of concern, and above all on the level of securitization that the issue has reached. Over time a clear trend has emerged of a growing sense of insecurity. From this follows the steady growth in demands for reassurance and protection: in Italy the number of police per 100,000 inhabitants is among the highest in the industrialized world.

In 2007, almost 3 million crimes, 492 per 10,000 inhabitants, were reported to the judiciary by the various police forces, 5.8 per cent more than in the previous year. This increase was part of a long-term trend: there had been a 20.2 per cent increase in recorded crime over the previous decade. In the period between 1997 and 2003 homicide rates decreased by 17.5 per cent, while robberies increased by 26.9 per cent and thefts by 5.2 per cent (mainly over the last three years) (Table 4.6).

According to data from the Ministry of Justice, on 30 June 2008 the Italian prison

Table 4.6 Crimes reported to the judiciary by the police 1997–2007

Type of crime	Murder	Robbery	Theft	Total
1997	863	32,896	1,401,471	2,440,754
1998	876	37,782	1,478,221	2,425,748
1999	805	39,401	1,480,775	2,373,966
2000	746	37,762	1,367,216	2,205,782
2001	704	38,056	1,303,356	2,163,826
2002	639	40,006	1,305,245	2,231,550
2003	712	41,747	1,328,350	2,456,887
2004	714	46,265	1,466,582	2,417,716
2005	601	45,953	1,503,712	2,579,124
2006	621	50,270	1,585,201	2,771,490
2007	627	51,210	1,636,656	2,933,146
% variation for period 1997–2003	−7.5	+26.9	−5.2	+0.7
% variation for period 2004–7	−12.2	+10.7	+11.6	+21.3

Source: Censis 2009: 695

population was 55,057 – 20.2 per cent more than that of the previous year; 37.4 per cent of prisoners were foreign (Moroccan, Romanian, Albanian, Tunisian and Algerian, in that order) and an overwhelming majority were male (95.6 per cent).

Organized crime. For decades the fight against organized crime has been considered a top security priority for the country, given how widespread the phenomenon is, how deeply rooted, particularly in some southern regions, and given its all too frequent lethal fusion with political power. The phenomenon also has an international dimension, with numerous links between Italian organizations and transnational networks.

The most important criminal organizations are: the infamous Sicilian Cosa Nostra, the Ndrangheta in Calabria, the great web of gangsters and 'paramafiosi' in Campania commonly known as the 'Camorra', and, from the 1990s, the Sacra Corona Unita of Puglia. The so-called 'new mafia', of foreign origin (Russian, Albanian and others) are quickly catching up with their Italian counterparts. They control a large part of the sex and drug trades in the centre and north of Italy (Paoli 2003).

Like organized crime, corruption is an extremely worrying phenomenon. It is so common, and so deeply rooted, that Italy is an anomaly among Western democracies. In Transparency International's 2008 report, Italy comes 55th out of 180 countries, in terms of the levels of perceived corruption in the country, and is now 20th out of the 27 EU countries (Censis 2009: 663).

Terrorist activities. Furthermore, Italy is engaged in the fight against terrorism, both at home and internationally. The significance of international terrorism became all too apparent after the 9/11 attack on the Twin Towers and the Pentagon; it is now unquestionably a genuinely global issue. Italy seems to be particularly exposed to possible terrorist attack, since the country is militarily engaged in all the principal theatres of the global struggle against terrorism (particularly Afghanistan), and could therefore suffer an act of retaliation. Moreover, some of the main Christian symbols, potential targets for Islamic *jihadis*, are located in Italy. In the Department of Security Related Information report for 2008, international terrorism was described as 'a high level threat to Italian security, both abroad and at home'. The risk represented by so-called 'lone terrorists' (people with no links to any organization who operate alone as *jihadis*, finding ideological inspiration and technical know-how on the internet) is considered to be particularly high.

In 2001 the crime of 'association with international terrorism' was introduced into Italy's penal code in an effort to confront the threat of terrorism. A new Special Committee for financial security was created within the Interior Ministry in order to curb the use of the Italian financial system for terrorist purposes. In 2005, a series of measures were passed to increase the powers of the authorities charged with public security. These measures applied both to prevention of terrorism and intelligence gathering, and to crime control. Alongside these internal measures, Italy has embarked on a series of multilateral initiatives in the field of international cooperation with the UN, G8, EU and NATO. In the UN context, Italy supports the activities of the Counter Terrorism Committee, established after 9/11. According to the Ministry of Foreign Affairs, Italy has ratified 12 of the 13 International Conventions against terrorism. The Convention on the Suppression of Acts of Nuclear Terrorism, adopted by the General Assembly in April 2005, was signed by Italy in September 2005 and its ratification is in progress. In addition, Italy contributes significantly to the Sanctions Committee against Al-Qaeda and the Taleban. Since 2002, Italy has presented eight proposals to the Committee for the registration of 85 subjects on the list of terrorist individuals and organizations. Only the US has made more registration proposals.[9]

In the G8 context, Italy is involved in two anti-terrorist committees: the Rome-Lione group, established with the merger, in 2002, of the Lione Group (which had been charged with fighting organized crime), and the Rome Group, created by the Italian government in the fight against terrorism. The second body – called CTAG (Counter Terrorism Action Group) – is tasked with providing technical assistance to Third World countries unable to address terrorist threats unaided. In the EU context, Italy is involved in the Plan of Action against Terrorism, adopted by the European Council on 28 September 2001. Finally, as far as NATO is concerned, Italy participates in the package of initiatives – known as Defence against Terrorism – agreed in 2006 to fight terrorism.

Health protection. Health threats are not perceived as real security threats by either the political elite or the general public. Nonetheless, especially after the anthrax attacks in the US, Italy has strengthened measures to face potential biological or chemical attacks. These measures include three main areas of intervention:

emergency management, reconnaissance of available resources, and the elaboration and diffusion of the national defence plan in the health sector. In 2004, the Ministry of Health established a National Centre for the Prevention and Control of Disease (CCM), whose task is the coordination of surveillance and prevention activities for the Ministry and the regions. According to its constitution, the CCM's remit is not only prevention, but also the coordination of emergency response: prompt reactions both to 'extraordinary' events (terrorist attacks, the spreading of new transmissible biological agents, accidental releases of chemical and infective agents, pandemic flu, etc.) and to 'recurrent' events (food poisoning, hospital infections, etc.). Thus the role of the CCM is to guarantee a rapid reaction to potential non-conventional threats to the country's security, involving the use of toxins and biological agents.

Environment. Italy supports international environmental regimes and is party to the Kyoto Protocol. At institutional level Italy has a Ministry for Environmental Affairs, although it is not considered a key player in national policy-making. Italy has made strong declarations in support of environmental protection, but actual performance is rather weak because of the economic costs linked to the implementation of 'green' regulations. Recently, environmental issues are seen as linked to organized crime activities, as in the case of illegal waste disposal.

Compellence

As explained, Italy's national security culture has significantly slowed the development and modernization of the Armed Forces. Although it would like to be considered a medium-great power, like France or the UK, Italy is therefore still unable to muster a military with a force-projection capacity equal to that of France or the UK.

Since the end of WWII, the main case of Italian involvement in a compellence operation has been the war against Iraq in 1991, in which it deployed eight Tornado fighters. This intervention highlighted all the structural shortcomings of the country's military capability, stretched to its limits by the prolonged bombardment of Iraqi targets and the harsh debates, both among politicians and within the general public. Another important compellence mission was the participation in NATO's bombing campaign during the Kosovo War.

In the post-Cold War period, the Italian Armed Forces have undergone profound changes: from defenders of the national territory to international peacekeepers and, in some cases, peace-enforcers and participants in nation-building. The problem of inadequate resources for defence has been a constant (Table 4.7), characterized by excessive waste and insufficient funding for research and development and the purchase of new equipment.

The transformation of the Armed Forces from a static army assigned to territorial defence to a flexible and professional instrument capable of intervening in distant crisis zones was accompanied by an attempt to increase the percentage of the defence budget invested in research and modernization. After 9/11, expenditure on the modernization of various weapon systems increased, and then stalled in 2005–6, due to the country's economic and financial difficulties. The

Table 4.7 Italian defence expenditure

	1990–94	1995–99	2000–4	2005	2006	2007
Share of GDP	2.0	1.9	2.0	1.9	1.8	1.8
Rate of change in defence spending	–0.5	–0.7	–1.7	–8.1	–10.5	–3.5
Distribution of defence expenditures:						
Personnel	63.6%	71.8%	73.1%	77.1%	81.9%	79.6%
Equipment	16.3%	12.9%	12.3%	09.1%	07.2%	10.9%
Infrastructure	2.4%	0.8%	0.9%	0.8%	0.6%	1.0%
Other	17.7%	14.3%	13.5%	13.0%	10.3%	8.5%
Defence spending per capita	N/A	N/A	343	322	287	276

Source: NATO 2007

modernization efforts re-started in 2007–8 with an increase in investment expenditure relative to that on personnel (which, however, continued to account for the bulk of the country's defence budget).

A better understanding of the ongoing transformation of the Italian military can be gained from an analysis of the weapon systems purchased during that period and their allocation to the three Armed Forces (Army, Air Force and Navy). In 2002, the Army purchased 600 armoured vehicles, 60 NH90 helicopters, 482 self-defence missile systems, 201 tracked vehicles, and 70 Howitzers for the ground artillery. In the same year, the Navy began the construction of a new aircraft carrier, which entered into service in 2009, two anti-aircraft frigates and two new-generation submarines, in co-production with Germany.

In the Air Force, the programmes to modernize the operational capacities of existing vehicles and the development of the new air-to-air missiles (METEOR programme) continued. A key modernization programme is that of the Eurofighter in cooperation with Germany, Spain and the UK.[10]

In successive years, the allocation of military expenditure continued to favour investment and modernization. After the slowdown in 2005–6, the post-9/11 trend towards higher spending continued in 2007–8. Resources were directed, in particular, to cooperation with European partners in R&D, in a common effort to reduce the many operational shortcomings caused by the Revolution in Military Affairs. This led to a focus on high-tech sectors like digitalization programmes for ground components; the development of passive defence against WMD attacks; and the purchase of traditional equipment: artillery units, armoured vehicles and missile-support systems.

In short, the transformation of the Armed Forces in the early twenty-first century is characterized by an effort – albeit constrained by the budget – to achieve a more modern military which emphasizes the technological component over the human dimension, in line with similar trends in other countries. At the same time, the areas of military expenditure (an aircraft carrier, helicopters, new generation fighters), and the transition from conscript to professional Armed Forces, underline the country's willingness to acquire a force-projection capacity.

Despite this change in direction of a more assertive security policy, Italian Armed Forces are mainly used in multilateral peace-support operations (PSOs), based on an awareness that to face the threats of regional instability and 'new wars' and to avoid the complete collapse of failing states (for instance Afghanistan and Iraq), it is necessary to intervene by sending troops to the areas in crisis, to guarantee the conditions necessary to allow peace and order, stabilization and reconstruction and, even more ambitiously, the democratization of the target country. The international actions of the Italian Armed Forces fit perfectly within the definition of PSOs established by NATO, which defines them as:

> 'multi-functional operations, conducted impartially, normally in support of an internationally recognized organization such as the UN or the Organization for Security and Cooperation in Europe (OSCE), involving military forces and diplomatic and humanitarian agencies. PSOs are designed to achieve a long-term political settlement or other specified conditions. They include peacekeeping and peace-enforcement as well as conflict-prevention, peace-making, peace-building and humanitarian relief'.[11]

The key elements of the Italian approach to peace-support operations are:[12]

- the proportionate use of human and material resources;
- the flexibility of the decision-making process in military planning on the ground; while fully respecting the chain of command and rules of engagement (ROE);
- the adaptability of the decision-making mechanism to the needs of the context
- the ability to mediate and negotiate to promote dialogue among the parties in conflict;
- the increasing importance of civilian-military cooperation (CIMIC) and of the role of civilians.

Italian peacekeeping contingents are constantly in demand. Their mandates are precisely limited by national caveats (within an internationally agreed framework) on their rules of engagement.

Since the early 1990s, Italy has played a growing role in military assurance missions. As of July 2008, Italian military forces are deployed in 30 missions in 19 countries (plus one 'geographical area'), with a total of 8,938 soldiers.[13] In absolute terms, Italy is the eighth largest troop contributor to UN peacekeeping and ranks sixth among contributors to the UN's peacekeeping budget, with a share of 5.08 per cent.[14] As of July 2008, Italian troops are deployed on eight of the 16 missions led by the United Nations Department of Peacekeeping Operations: UNAMID, MINURSO, MINUSTAH UNFICYP, UNIFIL, UNMIK, UNMOGIP

Table 4.8 Italian participation in current UN operations

Name	Location	Italian personnel
MINURSO (UN Mission for the Referendum in Western Sahara)	Morocco	5
UNFICYP (UN Peacekeeping Force in Cyprus)	Cyprus	4
UNMOGIP (UN Military Observer Group in India and Pakistan)	India-Pakistan	7
UNAMID	Sudan	28
UNFIL	Lebanon	2,470
MFO (Multinational Force and Observers)	Egypt	78
UNTSO	Israel	7
Total personnel contribution		2,599

Source: Ministry of Defence (accessed 27 April 2009)

and UNTSO. Italy, with 2,800 soldiers, is the main contributor of troops to UNIFIL, the UN mission in Lebanon (Table 4.8).

Italy is also very active in the ambit of the ESDP. Italy has always been a pro-European country, in favour also of further integration in the area of foreign policy decision-making.[15] Italy strongly supported the creation of the ESDP, although it has always been careful not to undermine NATO or relations with the US. Both the Italian public and the elite support increased EU involvement in the shared management of international problems, as evidenced in every survey carried out.[16] The country contributes, as do the other big European powers, up to four brigades (12,500–14,500 troops), 19 naval units and 18 aircraft to the ESDP.[17] Italy also takes part in the European Battlegroups project (one 'alpine' with Hungary and Slovenia and one 'maritime' with Spain, Greece and Portugal). Italy is the largest contributor to ESDP operations on the ground, as shown below (Table 4.9).[18]

Besides the ESDP, Italy contributes substantially to various European multinational standing contingents such as: EUROMARFOR (285 personnel), EUROFOR (European Operational Rapid Force) and MLF (Multinational Land Force).

Italy's most significant contribution, in both quantitative and qualitative terms, is made under the aegis of NATO. Italy is a loyal NATO member and always refers to the organization when making decisions about security and defence matters. As Table 4.10 shows, Italy has taken part in all NATO's most important missions in the Balkans and Afghanistan.

Italy is heavily involved in the NATO mission to Afghanistan, ISAF, and particularly in Herat province, where it is entrusted with the Regional Command West (RC-W) and the leadership of the Provincial Reconstruction Team (PRT) of Herat (where 1,400 of the 2,400 Italian soldiers are deployed). The strategic objective of the Italian presence in Herat is to 'assist the local leadership to extend its authority in order to facilitate the development of a safe, stable environment in the province

Table 4.9 Italian participation in ESDP military operations

Name	Location	Italian personnel
CONCORDIA	Macedonia	27
EUFOR Althea	Bosnia-Herzegovina	882
EUFOR DR Congo	DRC	56
EUSEC	DRC	4
(EU support to) AMIS	Sudan	6
EUFOR Tchad/RCA	Chad	105
EU NAVAR	Somalia	*225
Total personnel contribution to EU operations		1,305

Source: Ministry of Defence (accessed 14 April 2009); see also: http://www.fscpo.unict.it/adism/adism. htm (accessed 16 April 2009)

Note:
* Embarked on Maestrale frigate

Table 4.10 Italian participation in NATO missions as of 1 July 2008

Name	Location	Italian personnel
IFOR	Balkans	2,000
SFOR	Balkans	2,000
XFOR	Balkans	1,000
KFOR	Balkans	2,200
TFH	Balkans	1,000
TFF	Balkans	100
OAH	Balkans	42
ISAF	Afghanistan	1,950
NTM-I	Iraq	44
Total Italian personnel contribution to NATO operations		10,336

Source: ADISM DATASET, http://www.fscpo.unict.it/adism/dataItaly.pdf (accessed 22 April 2009)

and encourage reconstruction'.[19] Italian task forces operate under stringent rules of engagement which limit the Italian contingents' freedom of action and ability to use force. The Prodi government, a patchwork of parties from both the centre and the far-left, and therefore inevitably weak, was unable to do much to resolve this ambiguity. Berlusconi's government has substantially changed the remit of the Italian mission to Afghanistan, providing it with more, and more offensive, systems and eliminating the most stringent caveats.

Conclusions

The 'civilian power' nature of Italian security culture does not foster a process of securitization of threats and a militarized approach to their management. Italian security culture creates preferences for accommodation strategies and the country's participation in multilateral initiatives.

The Italian security culture, and the actual behaviour which follows from it, seem to be compatible with a system of global security and to be in a position to make an important contribution to the maintenance of the system.

Italy's strengths within the global security system are that: 1) the Italian security culture is profoundly multilateralist and hence comfortable cooperating with others (in particular within the UN, EU and NATO frameworks); 2) Italy is an ambitious and extrovert security-actor, keen to play an active and visible role on the international security scene and afraid to be excluded from the 'great power' system; and 3) in the last 15 years, Italy has gained important expertise, skills and a reputation in PSOs, which are by their very nature multilateral undertakings. This sort of mission, once considered a marginal security activity, has gradually become one of the main methods used to achieve stability in the international system.

However, Italy is hampered in its global cooperation efforts by: 1) its weak military tradition, which means, for instance, that Italy has a very low threshold of casualty acceptance; 2) the fact that its limited military capabilities are already stretched to the limits by the country's engagements abroad; 3) a problem of technical interoperability in high-tech warfare given the condition of the country's military equipment; 4) the excessive influence of domestic politics which means that Italy cannot always be relied on to fulfil its international commitments; and 5) financial constraints on defence spending.

In the final analysis, Italy's strategic behaviour seems to suffer from a sort of 'capability-expectations gap' (Hill 1993). On the one hand, the country wants to play an international role on a par with the other great nations, and to take part in all the important international diplomatic negotiations, never failing to contribute somehow to the main multilateral interventions. The country continues to be torn between a perception of itself as the last of the great powers, or the first of the small ones. It is ambitious and is struggling – although often in an ambivalent, incoherent and compromised fashion – to raise its international status. On the other hand, this activism, and Italy's consequent visibility internationally, do not always seem to be supported by coherent aims or by a strong, cross-party political will. Even at the time of writing, there is often no correspondence between the country's international involvements and the economic resources allotted to them.

The idea of being present, at any cost, or rather an obsession with not being present, frequently prompts the making of extemporary, incoherent choices, or choices out of synch with available resources. The obvious overstretching of the Italian Armed Forces, engaged in too many international missions, is an example as much of this tendency as it is of the inadequacy of the development aid budget. If the country wants to fulfil its ambitions to be a global security-player it cannot continue to spend significantly less than the other medium-large powers with whom it wants to be ranked, and it will have to break its taboo on participation in high-intensity conflict.

Notes

1 This section largely draws from Foradori and Rosa (2007).
2 *Intervento del presidente della Repubblica, Giorgio Napolitano, nell'incontro con la delegazione della Commissione politica dell'Assemblea parlamentare della Nato, 03.04.2007.* Available online at: http://www.quirinale.it/Discorsi/Discorso.asp?id = 32712 (accessed 16 September 2008).
3 On this point, see Johnston (1995).
4 Although UN missions usually combine military and civilian personnel, the majority of personnel involved have military associations. It is for this reason that Italian contributions to UN missions will be listed in the Compellence section.
5 See http://www.cooperazioneallosviluppo.esteri.it/pdgcs/italiano/Cooperazione/intro.html (accessed 1 April 2009). Author's translation.
6 In 2005, Italian aid to developing countries was divided as follows: Sub-Saharan Africa (42 per cent); Middle East and North Africa (24 per cent); Asia (14 per cent); Latin America (12 per cent); Balkan Europe (8 per cent).
7 See UNHCR at http://www.unhcr.it/news/dir/57/statistiche.html (accessed 9 April 2009).
8 The Italian government responded to this challenge by passing law 189/02 in August 2002, after a lively parliamentary debate. The law reformed Italian legislation on immigration controls. 'As regards expulsions, it could be argued that law 189/02 sought to align Italian expulsion procedures with those of the most restrictive European countries' (Sciortino 2003: 100).
9 See http://www.esteri.it/MAE/IT/Politica_Estera/Temi_Globali/Lotta_Terrorismo/ (accessed 1 April 2009).
10 See *Nota aggiuntiva allo stato di previsione per la Difesa* (2002). Available online at: http://www.difesa.it (accessed 16 April 2009).
11 Allied Joint Publication-3.4.1 (AJP-3.4.1), NATO Peace Support Operations (2001), ch. 2, para. 0202.
12 See http://www.cespi.it/WP/wp19-ENG.pdf (accessed 18 April 2009).
13 Source: Ministry of Defence: http://www.difesa.it/Operazioni+Militari/missioni_attività_internazionali; ADISM: http://www.fscpo.unict.it/adism/adism.htm (accessed 3 May 2009).
14 In 2008 Italy contributed 83 million Euros to the UN's core budget, 246 million to peacekeeping operations and 12 million to the International Tribunal. Source: Italian Ministry of Foreign Affairs: http://www.esteri.it/MAE/IT/Politica_Estera/Organizzazioni_Internazionali/ONU/ (accessed 12 April 2009).
15 See Bonvicini (1983; 1996); Foradori and Rosa (2004; 2007).
16 See Rosa (2003).
17 Source: Ministry of Defence: http://www.difesa.it/Approfondimenti/Archivio Approfondimenti/Semestre+UE/Il+contributo+italiano+alla+Difesa+Europea.htm (accessed 3 May 2009).
18 Cf. http://www.esteri.it/ita/0_1_01.asp?id = 1995
19 See http://www.cooperazioneallosviluppo.esteri.it/pdgcs/italiano/Speciali/Herat/Intro.htm (accessed 11 April 2009).

References

Aliboni, R. (2008) 'Upgrading Political Responses in the Mediterranean', *The International Spectator*, 2: 103–12.

Aprile, S. and Marco, M.S. (2005) 'Civil-military Relations in PSOs: The Italian Experience, CIMIC and Future Perspectives', *CeSPI Working Papers*, 19.

Bonvicini, G. (1983) 'Italy: An Integrationist Perpective', in Hill, C. (ed.) *National Foreign Policy and European Political Cooperation*, London: Allen and Unwin.

——(1996) 'Regional Reassertion: The Dilemmas of Italy', in Hill, C. (ed.) *The Actors in Europe's Foreign Policy*, London: Routledge.

Caligaris, L. and Santoro, C.M. (1986) *Obiettivo difesa*, Bologna: Il Mulino.

Carabinieri (2009) 'Principali missioni all'estero' [Afghanistan, Bosnia, Chad, Cyprus, DRC, Iraq, Kosovo, Lebanon], Available online at: http://www.carabinieri.it/Internet/Arma/Oggi/Missioni/Oggi/Approfondimenti/default.htm (accessed 15 January 2010).

Censis (2009) *Rapporto sulla situazione sociale del paese 2008*, Milano: Franco Angeli.

Cornelli, R. (2003) 'Le forze di polizia: situazione attuale e prospettive di riforma', in Barbagli, M. (ed.) *Rapporto sulla criminalità in Italia*, Bologna: Il Mulino, 257–575.

Foradori, P and Rosa, P. (2004) 'Italy and the Politics of European Defence: Playing by the Logic of Multilevel Networks', *Modern Italy*, 9(2): 217–33.

Foradori, P. and Rosa, P. (2007) 'New Ambitions and Old Deficiencies: Italy's Security Policy in the XXI Century', in Kirchner, E. and Sperling. J. (eds) *Global Security Governance: Competing Perceptions of Security in the 21st Century*, London: Routledge.

Hill, C. (1993) 'The Capability-Expectations Gap, or Conceptualising Europe's International Role', *Journal of Common Market Studies*, 31(3): 306–28.

ISPI (2003) 'Geopolitica dell'Italia nel dopo guerra fredda', *Relazioni internazionali*, XI, 13: 16–17.

Johnston, A.I. (1995) 'Thinking about Security Culture', *International Security*, 19: 32–64.

Kier, E. (1996) 'Culture and French Military Doctrine before World War II', in Katzenstein, P. (ed.) *The Culture of National Security*, New York: Columbia University Press.

Marta, L., Pirozzi, N. and Ronzitti, N. (2008) 'Le missioni italiane all'estero: Afghanistan e Libano', in Colombo, A. and Ronzitti, N. (eds) *L'Italia e la politica internazionale*, Bologna: Il Mulino, 117–31.

Ministry of Defence (undated) *Missioni/attività internazionali*. Available online at: http://www.difesa.it/Operazioni+Militari/missioni_attività_internazionali (accessed 16 April 2009).

NATO (2007) *NATO-Russia Compendium of Financial and Economic Data relating to Defence*. Available online at: http://www.nato.int/docu/pr/2007/p07–141.pdf (accessed 16 April 2009).

Paoli, L. (2003) 'Il crimine organizzato', in Barbagli, M. (ed.) *Rapporto sulla criminalità in Italia*, Bologna: Il Mulino, 275–301.

Perani, G. and Pianta, M. (1992) 'L'acquisto di armamenti in Italia', in De Cecco, M. and Pianta, M. (eds) *Amministrazione militare e spesa per armamenti in Europa*, Bologna: Il Mulino.

Rosa, P. (2003) 'L'europeizzazione della politica estera: tra sovranazionalismo e transgovernativismo', in Fabbrini, S. (ed.) *L'europeizzazione dell'Italia*, Roma-Bari: Laterza.

Sciortino, G. (2003) 'Le politiche di controllo migratorio in Europa e in Italia', *Ottavo Rapporto sulle migrazioni 2002*, Franco Angeli, 91–103.

Zupi, M. (2001) 'Evoluzione nella politica italiana di cooperazione allo sviluppo', in Bruni, F. and Ronzitti, N. (eds) *L'Italia e la politica internazionale*, Bologna: Il Mulino, 239–63.

5 United Kingdom

How much continuity? How much change?

Martin A. Smith[1]

In analysing the nature of the British security culture, attention in this chapter will focus on specific aspects of each of our four policies of governance where, it is argued, official priorities have most clearly become apparent. In discussing these, the principal focus will be on the period from 1997 and the policies and approaches pursued by successive Labour governments under Tony Blair and Gordon Brown. Before embarking upon these discussions, however, it is necessary to consider what may be called the UK's 'established' or 'traditional' security culture. This will constitute the benchmark against which post-1997 developments will be measured in order to ascertain whether the UK is becoming a post-Westphalian state in terms of its security culture evolution.

The British security culture

A clear public statement of Britain's traditional security culture was given in March 2007 by Air Chief Marshal Sir Jock Stirrup, Chief of Defence Staff. Significantly, Stirrup used the present tense. This suggested that, for him at least, the picture he painted continued to describe reality:

> From our perspective we have looked at our experiences of the last five, six or seven years, which have clearly demonstrated the need for military capabilities across the full spectrum of operations, from high end war fighting to peace operations and everything in between. ... If we take the UK's position in the world as one of its leading economies, as one of the five permanent members of the [UN] Security Council, a leading member of the world's most successful military alliance – NATO, the European Union (EU) and so on – then it seems to us that the UK is going to want and needs to play a substantial role in delivering the right degree of global stability in that extremely challenging environment, and that is going to need the right level of investment.
>
> (Defence Committee 2007: 4–5).

It is hardly surprising that a state's principal military adviser should view security in essentially military terms. The discussions here will in part examine whether and to what extent this view is held more widely in the contemporary UK.

A second important element of the British security culture has often found expression in the phrase 'punching above its weight in the world'. This was coined by Douglas Hurd, the then Foreign Secretary, in 1993 (Open Politics 2008). More recently a subtle but significant change has been observable in its official usage. Officials have tended to speak less of the UK punching *above* its weight in world affairs and more about it punching *at* its weight (Meyer 2005: 69; Evans 2008), based on the international assets noted by Stirrup. The idea of the UK punching at its weight is at least implicit in such foreign policy models as the 'global hub' suggested by Gordon Brown's Foreign Secretary, David Miliband (Miliband 2008).

A third key component – this one linking aspiration and capability – has been the bilateral relationship with the US. This has been most apparent in the area of compellence. In a review of the UK's military policy published at the end of 2003, it was stated plainly that 'the most demanding expeditionary operations, involving intervention against state adversaries, can only plausibly be conducted if US forces are engaged, either leading a coalition or in NATO' (Ministry of Defence 2003: 8). This encapsulates the foundation of current British military policy.

The extent to which British security priorities remain militarized can be assessed in the first instance by considering the financial resources committed to the four central government departments with relevant responsibilities. In the UK these are the Department for International Development (DfID), which takes the lead on overseas aid; the Foreign and Commonwealth Office (FCO), responsible for international relations and diplomacy; the Home Office, which is the lead department dealing with terrorist incidents in the UK; and the Ministry of Defence (MoD), which is responsible for executing British military policy.

An initial reading of the data in Table 5.1 shows the extent to which the annual budget for the MoD has outweighed those funds allocated to the other three departments. Over the five-year period 2003–8, the British government consistently devoted around two-thirds of its total 'security' budget to the MoD. Having said this, it is notable that the most consistent growth in expenditure has been in DfID's budget. This reflects the political priority given by the Blair and Brown governments to overseas aid and development. Indeed DfID did not exist as a separate government department before Tony Blair's first election victory in May 1997; its subsequent creation was one of his government's first acts.

Greater political priority and institutional innovation does not necessarily mean

Table 5.1 Annual UK 'security' spending by government department 2003–8 (£ millions)

	2003–4	*2004–5*	*2005–6*	*2006–7*	*2007–8*
DfID	3,447	3,645	4,107	4,206	5,354
FCO	1,511	1,710	1,877	1,827	1,581
Home Office	7,914	7,977	8,298	8,343	9,214
MoD	31,376	31,316	33,462	33,491	32,579

Source: Ministry of the Treasury 2008

that development issues have been securitized. In UK discourse – both in the official arena and more widely – the distinction continues to be made between 'security' and 'development', with the former regarded as the preserve of the military (Picciotto 2006; Waldman 2008). This reflects the tenacity of traditional notions, even in an era when the UK's armed forces have increasingly been working alongside various aid agencies on operations.

Policies of assurance

When the fact of the UK's permanent status on the UN Security Council is coupled with the extent to which the demand for UN peacekeeping and other post-conflict stabilization operations has increased since the end of the Cold War, it might be expected that the UK would be playing a leading role in such operations. In reality, the number of British personnel deployed on UN missions in 2008, for example, is consistent with the low level of UK commitment to UN missions over a number of years. This data suggests that governments have not seen the success of most UN peace operations as mattering very much to the UK. The two exceptions are Cyprus and Kosovo which, of the 11 missions in which the UK participates, account respectively for 76 per cent and 17 per cent of the total UK commitment to UN peacekeeping missions (United Nations 2008). This level of commitment can be explained by the extent of the ongoing military commitment to these areas. More generally, this level of commitment is indicative of the extent to which, officially at least, punching 'above' the country's assumed weight has been replaced by a more relaxed stance based on the premise that the UK is punching acceptably at its weight in international affairs.

A consistent feature of British foreign policy since 1975 has been the low priority generally accorded to the CSCE/OSCE. In the contemporary context, this is reflected in the small numbers of UK personnel deployed on OSCE missions (see Table 5.2), even in important regions such as the Balkans. The data demonstrates that this low level of commitment has been consistent across both time and space, despite significantly increased demand for OSCE field deployments since the end of the Cold War and the partial operationalization of the institution in the early 1990s. Overall, British governments have been content to follow the American lead on OSCE matters. From time to time it has been actively supported as a useful means of advancing particular foreign policy objectives, such as the holding of acceptably free and fair elections in Ukraine in 2004. For much of the time, however, the OSCE has been largely ignored.

A similar story, finally, can be told about EU operations (see Table 5.3). The reluctance of successive British governments to engage seriously with projects designed to endow the EU with any significant military capability is noteworthy here. It is true that Tony Blair led a high-profile political initiative in 1998–99 with French President Jacques Chirac, calling for the EU to develop such a capability. Nonetheless, a decade on from the formal launch of the European Security and Defence Policy (ESDP), the British position has remained at best ambivalent and its actual involvement limited.

Table 5.2 UK personnel contributions to OSCE field missions 2000–9

OSCE Mission	Dates	UK personnel	% share of total
Albania	2003–9	17	10.00
Bosnia-Herzegovina	2000–9	24	5.76
Croatia	2006–7	3	4.92
Dushanbe (Tajikistan)	2006–9	3	10.71
Georgia	2002–9	22	6.03
Kosovo	2005–9	44	5.55
Moldova	2001–9	7	8.86
Montenegro	2006–7	2	7.14
Serbia and Montenegro	2001–5	10	9.90
Serbia	2006–9	14	11.76
Skopje (Macedonia)	2005–9	24	8.19

Source: SIPRI 2009

Table 5.3 UK personnel contributions to EU peacekeeping and stabilization operations 2003–7

	2003	2004	2005	2006	2007
Concordia (Macedonia)	3 (0.9%)				
Aceh Monitoring Mission (Indonesia)			11 (9%)	5 (18.5%)	
EUFOR Althea (Bosnia-Herzegovina)		669 (11.5%)	706 (12.5%)	573 (11%)	21 (1%)
EUPM Bosnia-Herzegovina		64 (13.5%)	23 (12%)	17 (10%)	21 (11.5%)
EUBAM Rafah (Gaza/Egypt)			3 (4%)	2 (3%)	3 (4%)
EURST (Georgia)				1 (12%)	1 (10%)
EUBAM Moldova and Ukraine					1 (1.5%)
EUPT Kosovo				4 (13%)	5 (14%)

Sources: Missiroli (2003); SIPRI 2009

In operational terms, NATO remains the multilateral institution of choice. It is revealing that the only EU operations to show more than a token commitment are those in Bosnia. Both operations were transferred from NATO to the EU at the end of 2004. Even here, a significant decline in the level of British commitment is observable thereafter. The major British operational commitments have been deployed either as part of NATO (Afghanistan and Kosovo) or a US-led 'coalition of the willing' (Iraq). In 2008, the UK deployed over 13,000 military personnel to ongoing operations in Afghanistan and Iraq. It also made a contribution to the NATO Kosovo Force of around 150 troops, temporarily reinforced by a further 300 after the February 2008 Kosovar declaration of independence (Military Balance 2008: 161–2).

In addition, Britain devoted a larger number of military personnel to the training of Commonwealth national armies in states such as Sierra Leone and Kenya than to UN, OSCE or EU operations. This suggests that, despite often being denigrated as a security actor of negligible importance, the Commonwealth is more significant for the UK in this respect than the UN, OSCE or EU.

An attempt at improved civil-military cooperation has been made, consistent with the operational conflation of security and development strategies. A new doctrinal concept, floated by the MoD in 2006, is the 'Comprehensive Approach'; it was designed to facilitate operational cooperation across relevant government departments. The Comprehensive Approach is based on identifying 'commonly understood principles and collaborative processes that enhance the likelihood of favourable and enduring outcomes within a particular situation' (Ministry of Defence 2006: 5). There has not been much evidence of this in practice, however. The attitude of DfID and FCO officials to the Comprehensive Approach has been marked by suspicion, in part because the concept originated from within the MoD rather than being the result of a genuinely cross-departmental deliberative process. There have been striking examples of non-cooperation – or even non-contact – between officials from these two ministries and British military forces. In 2006 for example, a parliamentary committee found that in Sierra Leone British army officers were not even aware of the existence of a senior DfID official with responsibility for the region (International Development Committee 2006: 33).

Cultural differences between DfID and the MoD were made plain in the former's response to questioning by the same committee about its prospective support for the innocuous-sounding objective of 'winning hearts and minds' on stabilization operations. DfID stated that 'objectives for projects do not include "winning hearts and minds"', which it saw as 'a military concept normally associated with force protection' (Department for International Development 2006: 121). DfID officials frequently cite the terms of the International Development Act of 2002, which frames the department's mandate as contributing to a reduction in poverty rather than post-conflict stabilization *per se* (International Development Act 2002). This both reflects and reinforces the traditional approach of regarding security and development as separated – if not wholly separate – issues. Although some reports suggest that institutional coordination on operations has been improving (National

Audit Office 2008: 25), bringing about significant changes in departmental cultures will be an uncertain, long-haul process.

Policies of prevention

The view that security and development are divergent and can only be integrated in occasional circumstances (Ministry for Peace 2006: 184–5; Waldman 2008: 3, 12, 24) has also influenced the UK contribution to the task of conflict prevention, particularly with regard to overseas aid.

Overseas aid. The headline figures for the growth of Official Development Assistance (ODA), since DfID was established as a separate government depart-ment, are impressive. Based on the rates of growth evident in Table 5.4, Gordon Brown was justified in telling the House of Commons in March 2008 that the UK's overall aid spending was on track to quadruple between 1997 and 2011 (BBC 2008). The Blair and Brown governments earned generally good marks, even from the sometimes-critical NGO sector, for the progressive nature of their aid polices and pledges (Joint NGO Briefing Paper 2005). In the context of the discussions here however, what is interesting is evidence of discrepancies between ODA priorities and key 'security' commitments. There are striking discrepancies between the UK's principal stabilization and reconstruction priorities and those of its development ministry, perhaps most clearly with regard to Iraq. Despite being the predominant political and military focus, Iraq received at most only about one-third of the ODA given to India – one of the world's emerging great powers – during the period 2004–7. In 2006–7 Iraq received only £11 million more in UK aid than China, which had once again achieved the world's fastest annual rate of economic growth. DfID's figures also show that aid to Sudan has been a constant

Table 5.4 Total UK ODA net spending 1997–2006

	Spending (USD millions)
1997	3,433
1998	3,864
1999	3,426
2000	4,501
2001	4,566
2002	4,929
2003	6,262
2004	7,905
2005	10,772
2006	12,459

Source: OECD 2008

development priority for the UK, although the British contribution to assurance operations in Sudan has been minimal (Department for International Development 2008). Between 2004 and 2007, at least half of the DfID top 20 aid recipients were Commonwealth members. The British approach does implicitly acknowledge a link between development and security in the Commonwealth context. The UK often pursues a two-pronged approach to aiding these states, with ODA on the one hand and military advice and training on the other.

The headline figure for OECD aid provides a sense of the UK's overall preference for disbursing aid through bilateral channels (government-to-government and via NGOs) rather than through multilateral organizations and institutions (see Table 5.5). Yet data produced by the UK's National Audit Office (NAO) in 2008 paints a more nuanced picture. The NAO conducted a detailed analysis of four of DfID's aid programmes – in Afghanistan, the Democratic Republic of Congo, Nepal and Sudan. The NAO's data suggests that the UK approach to disbursing aid has been essentially pragmatic and situation-dependent. For example, a fundamental objective of the UK and NATO in Afghanistan has been to build the capacity of the Afghan government. It is hardly surprising, therefore, that over three-quarters of UK ODA to Afghanistan should have been channelled through that government, with UN agencies playing only a negligible role. The situation is effectively reversed in the case of Sudan. Here, UN agencies channel over half of UK ODA, with the Sudanese government playing no direct role. This reflects the scale of the UN presence on the ground and the British government's view that the Sudanese government has itself been a major contributor to instability and the regional humanitarian crisis, especially in the Darfur region (National Audit Office 2008).

Migration. During the first decade of the new millennium, migration became an issue of increasing popular and political salience and controversy in the UK. Partly this has reflected growing public awareness of (and opposition to, in certain sections of the media) the consequences of EU enlargements embracing the former Warsaw Pact states in Central, Eastern and Southeastern Europe. Enlargement entailed granting citizens in these new member states the right of free movement to the UK, a right that helps explain the growth in the total numbers of migrants

Table 5.5 UK aid disbursement priorities 2004–7 (USD millions)

	2004	2005	2006	2007
ODA	7,904.7	10,771.7	12,459.0	9,920.7
Bilateral aid	5,360.7	81,68.5	8,717.6	5,190.1
Grants	5,262.3	8,250.3	8,809.5	6,167.0
Technical cooperation	751.1	844.8	860.1	1,208.4
Humanitarian aid	522.7	628.4	834.6	521.1
Multilateral aid	2,544.0	2,603.2	3,741.4	4,730.6

Source: OECD 2009

Table 5.6 Migration inflows to the UK 2000–6

	2000	2001	2002	2003	2004	2005	2006
Total migration inflow (thousands)	478.7	479.5	512.8	508.1	586.0	562.9	590.8
Asylum seekers (thousands)	91.6	84.5	95.9	53.6	36.5	26.5	23.4

Source: Office of National Statistics 2008

Table 5.7 Inflows of asylum seekers to the UK by nationality 2000–5

	2000	2001	2002	2003	2004	2005
Iran	5,610	3,415	2,630	3,495	3,990	3,505
Pakistan	3,165	2,860	2,405	3,145	3,030	2,290
Somalia	5,020	6,465	6,540	7,195	3,295	2,105
Eritrea	0	620	1,180	1,070	1,265	1,900
China	4,000	2,390	3,675	3,495	2,410	1,775
Afghanistan	5,555	9,000	7,205	2,590	1,605	1,775
Iraq	7,475	6,705	14,570	4,290	1,880	1,595
Zimbabwe	1,010	2,115	7,655	4,020	2,520	1,390
DRC	1,030	1,395	2,215	1,920	1,825	1,390
Nigeria	835	870	1,125	1,110	1,210	1,230
India	2,120	1,850	1,865	2,410	1,485	1,000
Sudan	415	390	655	1,050	1,445	990
Turkey	3,990	3,700	2,835	2,990	1,590	950
Sri Lanka	6,395	5,510	3,130	810	400	480
Bangladesh	795	500	720	820	550	465
Others	32,900	23,585	25,730	19,637	12,123	8,000
Total	80,315	71,370	84,135	60,047	40,623	30,840

Source: OECD 2009

from 2004 – the year of the EU's 'big bang' eastern enlargement (see Table 5.6).

Most controversy, however, has been generated by the issue of asylum seekers. The figures for the total number of asylum seekers in Table 5.7 show that their numbers were indeed growing in the early 2000s, but that they fell substantially year-on-year thereafter. It is likely that the decline occurred in part at least as a result of changes in asylum legislation coupled with enhanced enforcement mechanisms and procedures. These had been introduced largely in response to the issue's increased domestic political salience (Home Office 2007). Despite these measures, there has been no obvious diminution in the asylum-seeker issue as a source of political controversy. Indeed the British National Party, an anti-immigrant and pro-repatriation political party, has begun to win seats regularly in local and regional elections, largely on the back of vociferous campaigns against current asylum laws.

Migration and asylum have thus become important and seemingly established political issues in the UK, but are they primarily security issues? Unease about them has undoubtedly been stimulated by the widely perceived deterioration in the international security environment since 11 September 2001 (9/11). The United Nations High Commissioner for Refugees (UNHCR) has suggested a link between the scale and incidence of international security breakdowns and the total number of refugees and asylum seekers (UNHCR 2007). The case for such a link might seem intuitively obvious and it appears to be strengthened by the OECD statistics in Table 5.7, which suggests a clear connection between numbers of asylum seekers and areas of significant conflict and insecurity (including human rights abuses). With this in mind it is notable that, with occasional exceptions (Borger 2008), consideration of migration as a security issue has *not* been a prominent feature of the domestic UK discourse. The debates surrounding it have been fired primarily by racial and economic, rather than security, factors. These reflect traditional British concerns. Stretching back to the officially sanctioned waves of migration to the UK from Commonwealth countries in the 1940s and 1950s, successive governments and much of wider British society have traditionally seen immigration as an economic issue, sometimes charged with a racial dimension.

Policies of protection

In the protection area, two issues have been especially prominent. Both of them can be traced back in large part to the impact of the events of 9/11 and the Labour government's response, albeit one directly and the other derivatively. The two relevant issues are terrorism and organized crime.

Terrorism. The terrorist challenge to the UK has been officially identified as resulting primarily from criminal activity rather than acts of war, as in the US (at least under the Bush administration). The 2008 National Security Strategy unveiled by the Brown government stated that 'while terrorism represents a threat to all our communities, and an attack on our values and our way of life, it does not at present amount to a strategic threat', that is, a threat to the British state and society *per se* (Cabinet Office 2008: 11). Elsewhere, in what could be seen as implicit criticism of the Bush administration's approach, the document stated that 'we need to respond [to terrorism] robustly, bringing those involved to justice while defending our shared values, *and resisting the provocation to over-react*' [emphasis added] (Cabinet Office 2008: 28).

The official view of what can be achieved by domestic counter-terrorism efforts has been relatively modest. In 2006 the Blair government published its counter-terrorism strategy, known in official shorthand as CONTEST. It began by stating that its aim was to 'reduce the risk from international terrorism, so that people can go about their daily lives freely and with confidence' (CONTEST 2006: 1). The objective was therefore one of *containing* terrorism and its effects rather than attempting to eliminate either altogether.

With these points in mind, it is perhaps not surprising that increases in resources for agencies at the forefront of tackling terrorism have been relatively modest. Since 9/11 and the attacks on the London transport network on 7 July 2005, both the Blair and Brown governments emphasized the importance of effective police work and intelligence in countering terrorism. Yet neither the intelligence agencies nor the police have seen dramatic increases in their budgets. Scepticism is in order with regard to official claims that 'resources dedicated to counter-terrorism and intelligence ... have more than doubled' (Cabinet Office 2008: 27). The Security Service's own figures suggest that the intelligence agencies' collective resource budget in particular did little more than keep pace with the rate of inflation in the period following the 7 July attacks (see Table 5.8).

A similar point can be made with regard to central government grants to regional police forces (the police are organized on the basis of regional and county forces in the UK). The data in Table 5.9 relate to a selection of English police forces covering London, major provincial conurbations (Greater Manchester and West Yorkshire), regions with smaller but still significant population centres (Leicestershire and

Table 5.8 Spending on UK intelligence agencies 2004–8 (£ millions)

	2004–5	2005–6	2006–7	2007–8
Resource budget	1,156.8	1,156.4	1,266	1,324
Capital budget	156.9	204.9	214	229
Total	1,313.7	1,361.3	1,480	1,553

Source: MI5 2008

Table 5.9 Central government grant to selected regional police forces in England 2000–11 (£ millions)

	2000–1	2007–8	2008–9	2009–10	2010–11
Metropolitan Police (Greater London)	955.6	1,081.4	1,108.0	1,138.3	1,169.4
Greater Manchester	195.0	231.9	240.5	246.7	253.2
West Yorkshire	149.8	175.2	183.3	188.5	193.9
Leicestershire	53.2	65.0	66.8	68.6	70.4
Surrey	52.5	66.3	67.9	69.7	71.5
Cumbria	31.4	32.5	33.4	34.2	35.0
Devon and Cornwall	90.4	107.5	110.2	113.5	117.0

Source: The Home Office 2008

Surrey) and essentially rural forces (Cumbria and Devon and Cornwall). The pattern is one of only modest increases in budgetary support from central government. This is the case even with regard to London, notwithstanding arguments that the UK's overall counter-terrorism effort has been predominantly – and perhaps excessively – London-focused (Hewitt 2008: ch. 4). It is also the case with regard to regional forces responsible for policing major cities with significant Muslim populations such as Leeds, Manchester and Leicester, among whom militant Islamist groups might be seeking to radicalize and recruit.

Neither 9/11 nor 7 July led to major structural reforms in the way in which the policing agencies tackle the terrorist problem. In September 2008 Andy Hayman, recently retired as head of counter-terrorism at Scotland Yard, argued in *The Times* that 'the way that the counter-terrorism effort in Britain is organised is a mess'. The main focus of Hayman's criticism was on the fact that policing in the UK still has no genuinely national counter-terrorism capacity. Instead, prerogatives remain essentially with the heads of nearly 50 regional and specialist police forces (Hayman 2008).

The contemporary British approach to terrorism should be seen in the context of a historical tradition more than a century long – dating back to armed attacks in London by militant Irish republicans in the mid-nineteenth century (Hewitt 2008: ch. 1). Arguably stretching back even further has been the antecedent tradition of policing by consent, which in turn helps explain why the UK has retained local police forces and also why British police are still routinely unarmed. There is also a tradition asserting civil supremacy over the Armed Forces, which can be traced back to at least the seventeenth century. It was reinforced by the experiences of successive British governments in combating terrorism during the 'Troubles' in Northern Ireland after 1969. Even when it appeared as if the level of violence was in danger of escalating out of hand in the early 1970s, British governments remained committed to the constitutional position that the role of the Army in Northern Ireland was to render 'military aid to the civil power'. This meant that the police always remained the lead agency in combating the terrorist threat.

All told, a distinctly British counter-terrorist culture has evolved over a long period of time. It contributes to our understanding of why the UK has refrained from making significant attempts to promote international coordination and cooperation against terrorism. There has been little appreciation that multilateral approaches in this area are likely to add anything significant to the established national approach.

Organized crime. Organized crime has been posited as a security issue for the UK mainly because of its alleged links to terrorism (Mabey 2007: 34) and – through human trafficking – the number of asylum seekers entering the country. It has been officially conceptualized in a similar manner to terrorism: as a source of 'damage … to individuals, communities, society, and the UK as a whole' (SOCA 2008: 6). The main recent innovation in the UK approach to tackling organized crime has been the creation of the Serious Organised Crime Agency (SOCA) by the Home Office in 2006. According to SOCA's figures, drugs and human trafficking/immigration fraud have consistently taken up more than half its efforts and resources, with the interdiction of drugs its foremost priority. SOCA figures for the quantity of drugs impounded in the first two years of its existence were in many respects impressive (SOCA 2008: 31). Nevertheless, when assessing any new level of seriousness with which organized crime is being tackled by UK authorities, the lack of substantial increases in central government funding of the police should be recalled and reference also made to the relatively small size of SOCA's budget. The latter was reported to be £400 million in 2008 (O'Neill 2008). This can be set against SOCA's own estimate of the costs of organized crime to the UK of 'at least £20bn a year and probably significantly more' (SOCA 2008: 8).

Although interdicting drug trafficking is SOCA's main priority and reflects estimates that illegal drug use costs the UK £24 billion every year in policing, health and social costs (Mabey 2007: 34), the Royal Navy no longer regards overseas drug interdiction patrols as an operational priority. Counter-drugs operations had been identified as a specific 'military task' in the first full-scale post-Cold War defence review in 1998 (Ministry of Defence 1998: 6/14), but this operational priority has since been scaled back. In March 2007, Sir Jock Stirrup stated that 'those particular tasks we do out of spare capacity, we do not build and resource force structure to do those tasks' (Defence Committee 2007: 14). This assessment suggested that, although drugs continued to be regarded as a significant social problem in the UK, they were if anything coming to be seen as less of a security priority than they had been in the late 1990s. Overall, and despite the creation of SOCA, there is still no definitive sense that organized crime has moved up the official priority list in terms of sustained political commitment and significant allocation of resources.

Policies of compellence

As noted earlier, the UK has continued to spend more on the Armed Forces than any other single aspect of its 'security' resources. Significant defence cuts were made following the end of the Cold War and the impact of these was felt throughout the 1990s. Relatively speaking however, the percentage share of GDP and amount spent per capita on the military budget have continued to place the UK near the top of NATO league tables. It is also in this area that the three core features of traditional British security culture – an emphasis on the military instrument, commitment to 'punching' at a significant level in the international arena, and the importance of the strategic 'special' relationship with the US – are most clearly evident (see Table 5.10).

Compared to many of its NATO allies, the UK has tended to spend relatively less on military personnel and somewhat more on defence equipment. Historical factors help us to understand this. Since the eighteenth century, the British Armed Forces have been surprisingly small in number, given the country's significant overseas commitments. During its imperial heyday, British governments relied primarily on the projection capabilities of the Royal Navy – rather than expensive overseas garrisons – to protect the country's overseas interests. Imperial territories were, where possible, garrisoned mainly by indigenous troops. Following World War II, the UK reverted comparably quickly to its familiar pattern of maintaining

Table 5.10 UK defence spending 1990–2007 (%)

	1990–94	1995–99	2000–4	2005	2006	2007
Share of GDP	3.7	2.7	2.4	2.5	2.5	2.3
Rate of change in defence spending	–4.2	–1.6	+0.9	+12.1	+2.8	–4.7
Distribution of defence expenditures:						
Personnel	42.2	39.4	39.4	41.6	40.4	41.2
Equipment	21.0	24.8	23.8	23.1	21.2	24.2
Infrastructure	5.2	5.2	1.4	0.4	2.5	1.5
Other	30.5	30.5	35.1	34.9	35.8	33.1
Defence spending per capita (USD)	841	605	608	678	693	657

Source: NATO 2007

a relatively small army, with the phasing out of conscription in the late 1950s and early 1960s. It was in the minority in NATO in opting for all-volunteer armed forces for most of the Cold War.

During the twentieth century, emphasis was increasingly placed on important equipment projects in lieu of numbers. Official interest in the UK being seen to be punching at its weight in the world helps to explain the endurance of three major prestige 'legacy projects' in British defence equipment policy in the post-Cold War era: the Eurofighter/Typhoon aircraft, two new large aircraft carriers, and the Trident strategic nuclear missile system (with a recently approved follow-on). Although each of these projects has been criticized for being more appropriate in the Cold War context, they have survived under both Conservative and Labour governments. This has been despite the view that the UK does not – and in the foreseeable future will not – face a military threat from another state or group of states 'either with nuclear weapons or other weapons of mass destruction, or with conventional forces' (Cabinet Office 2008: 15).

From 1997 a shift towards a more expeditionary military strategy and capability, which was already underway, was reinforced by Tony Blair's public commitment to the idea of the UK acting as a 'force for good in the world'. This heightened latent tensions with enduring equipment priorities based around the major legacy projects. The latter are seen by critics to be of little relevance to expeditionary requirements for relatively light forces based on substantial numbers of infantry soldiers capable of swift and appropriately protected movement in-theatre (Dunne *et al.* 2007; Garden and Ramsbotham 2004; Jenkins 2008; Norton-Taylor 2008).

There has in fact been a decline in the numbers of infantry units in the British army since the Cold War's end. It would be unfair to blame this solely on the MoD's financial priorities. The Ministry has argued with some justification that the various rounds of regimental amalgamation, which have taken place since 1990, have been necessitated in part by demographic and economic factors. Various regiments have found it increasingly difficult to hit manning targets, given smaller overall numbers of potential recruits and increasing competition from civilian employers. Having said that, reports of poor or absent equipment, poor accommodation for service families and many combat and support units exceeding the MoD's own guidelines for operational deployments will certainly have played a role in putting some people off a military career (Defence Committee 2008). As far as the Royal Navy is concerned, as noted earlier, the priority attached to the nuclear and carrier forces has not diminished since the end of the Cold War. In terms of expeditionary capability, a major deficiency in the current force structure is the Royal Navy's small number of landing craft suitable for carrying troops and helicopters. The number of landing craft has barely increased over this period.

The UK has maintained a broad and disparate array of military commitments. These fall into six main categories: 'hot' operations, such as Afghanistan and Iraq; less intense and demanding post-conflict stabilization missions in Kosovo and Bosnia; ongoing deployments under NATO auspices in Germany; military training and support in countries like Sierra Leone, Nepal and Kenya; imperial legacy commitments and deployments in, for example, Cyprus, the Falkland Islands and Gibraltar; and ongoing military contacts and cooperation with allies such as Brunei and Saudi Arabia.

The US and NATO have remained the key priorities for the UK. All of the major operations involving the use of coercive armed force that the UK has conducted since the end of the Cold War have either been through NATO or else undertaken as part of a US-led coalition. This forms a powerful incentive to maintain a 'full spectrum' military capability. As one analyst puts it:

> A fundamental proposition of Britain's present defence policy is that *British military expeditionary capability should be sufficient in scale and quality to allow British forces to conduct largely autonomous operations at the operational level that are important enough to the overall outcome that the UK government has influence at the strategic level over the US in planning and execution of the operations.* This requirement can be met by a 'balanced' force at the operational level containing ground, air and maritime elements. [emphasis in the original]
>
> (Codner 2007: 19–20).

Military support to Commonwealth states has absorbed a much more limited share of resources. Nevertheless this has been important politically, not least because it gives the UK influence and a presence in a variety of regions and on a genuinely global basis. With the partial exception of *la Francophonie*, the Commonwealth is a unique international arrangement and its importance in underpinning successive governments' sense of the UK's role in the world should not be underestimated.

The nuclear component, finally, is widely seen as representing a leading international 'status symbol' for the UK. Notwithstanding official denials, there is a common view that this has been an important factor in persuading all governments since 1945 to maintain a British nuclear weapons capability (Ritchie 2008). Since the early 1960s, the UK has procured the backbone of its nuclear force – successively Polaris and Trident missiles – from the US. Cooperation in this area has therefore come to represent one of the most high-profile and significant aspects of Anglo-American relations.

Conclusion: the contemporary British security culture

Table 5.11 summarizes key elements of the UK approach with regard to the four areas of security governance.

Overall, *assurance* issues have received the least focus and commitment. The British contribution to UN, OSCE and EU operations has usually been limited or even token in nature. The few exceptions can be explained with reference to UK/NATO military interests in particular states or regions. Despite (or perhaps because of) the UK's guaranteed seat on the UN Security Council, British governments have failed to give any significant priority to UN assurance missions. There is little official sense that the UK's international status depends to any significant degree on its being seen as a leading contributor in the multilateral assurance field. Both the OSCE and the EU have remained marginalized actors and there is little to support any argument that UK policy is being Europeanized.

In terms of *prevention*, the most significant development has been the increase in the UK's ODA effort under the Labour governments of Tony Blair and Gordon Brown. This has been characterized by a pragmatic approach to choosing appropriate channels to distribute aid. Multilateral, national and local agencies have all been used and the specific mix has depended significantly on the situation on the ground. Crucially for the discussions here, 'development' and 'security' have remained essentially separate-tracked in official British discourse. ODA is often not officially seen as an important tool of *security* policy, which remains focused on the military dimension.

It is hardly surprising that preventing and countering terrorism has been the main concern for the UK in the *protection* area. The British government's response has been predominantly national in its orientation, with little official

Table 5.11 Aspects of the UK approach to security governance

	Assurance	*Prevention*	*Protection*	*Compellence*
Patterns of interaction	Limited	Pragmatic	Limited	Atlanticist
Institutional choice(s)	UN, OSCE and EU	National, UN, international financial institutions, NGOs	National	NATO, US-led coalitions
Degree of securitization	Low	Low	Medium	High

interest in promoting greater institutional cooperation through, for example, the EU. Domestically, traditional societal norms have continued to govern the role and organization of the police and the armed forces. Terrorism is still officially viewed as primarily a criminal challenge. Thus the degree of securitization here is graded only as medium.

With regard to the category of *compellence*, UK security policy has remained military based. This is the area in which British governments have been most inclined to act multilaterally, albeit in a limited way. The institutions or coalitions in question have been restricted to those led by the US and in which British governments have effectively been able to portray the UK as acting as second-in-command.

The UK remains essentially a Westphalian state. The discussions here suggest that there have been occasional glimpses of post-Westphalian elements, with regard to the new emphasis on ODA for example. Thus far, however, these have remained sufficiently limited and *ad hoc* as to mitigate against the view that a new security culture *per se* is emerging.

Note

1 The views expressed here are personal and should not be taken to represent the views or opinions of the British Government, Ministry of Defence or the Royal Military Academy Sandhurst. The author is grateful to David Brown and Mark Webber for their helpful comments on earlier drafts of this chapter.

References

BBC (2008) 'Brown Security Statement', London: BBC. Available online at: http://news.bbc.co.uk/go/pr/fr/-/1/hi/uk_politics/7304999.stm (accessed 19 March 2008).

Borger, J. (2008) 'Conflicts fuelled by climate change causing new refugee crisis, warns UN', *The Guardian*, 17 June.

Cabinet Office (2008) *The National Security Strategy of the United Kingdom: Security in an Interdependent World*, London: The Cabinet Office.

Codner, M. (2007) 'British Defence Policy – Rebuilding National Consensus', *RUSI Journal*, 152(2): 18–22.

CONTEST (2006) *Countering International Terrorism: The United Kingdom's Strategy*, London: The Stationery Office.

Defence Committee (2007) *UK Defence: Commitments and Resources. Uncorrected Transcript of Oral Evidence*, London: House of Commons Select Committee on Defence.

—— (2008) *Recruiting and Retaining Armed Forces Personnel*, London: House of Commons Select Committee on Defence.

Department for International Development (2006) *Written Evidence: Memorandum Submitted by the Department for International Development on behalf of HMG*, London: House of Commons International Development Committee.

—— (2008) *Statistics on International Development 2007*, London: Department for International Development.

Dunne, P., Perlo-Freeman, S. and Ingram, P. (2007) *The Real Cost behind Trident Replacement and the Carriers*, London: British American Security Information Council.

Evans, M. (2008) 'Defence chiefs have last-minute doubts about £4bn carriers', *The Times*, 17 May.

Garden, T. and Ramsbotham, D. (2004) 'About Face: The British Armed Forces – Which Way to Turn?', *RUSI Journal*, 149(2): 10–15.

Hayman, A. (2008) 'Police politics are stalling our war on terror', *The Times*, 10 September.

Hewitt, S. (2008) *The British War on Terror*, London: Continuum.

Home Office (2007) *Enforcing the Rules*, London: Home Office.

—— (2008) 'Central Government Grants to Selected Regional Police Forces in England'. Available online at: http://police.homeoffice.gov.uk/finance-and-business-planning/index.html/ (accessed 19 July 2008).

International Development Act (2002). Available online at: http://www.opsi.gov.uk/acts/acts2002/ukpga_20020001_en_1 (accessed 14 July 2008).

International Development Committee (2006) *Conflict and Development: Peacebuilding and Post-conflict Reconstruction*, London: House of Commons International Development Committee.

Jenkins, S. (2008) 'Lovely new aircraft carrier, sir, but we're fighting in the desert', *The Sunday Times*, 24 February.

Joint NGO Briefing Paper (2005) *EU Heroes and Villains*, ActionAid, Eurodad and Oxfam.

Mabey, N. (2007) 'Security Trends and Threat Misperceptions', in Cornish, P. (ed.) *Britain and Security*, London: The Smith Institute.

Meyer, C. (2005) *DC Confidential*, London: Weidenfeld & Nicolson.

MI5 (2008) 'The Security Service – MI5'. Available online at: http://www.mi5.gov.uk/output/Page76.html (accessed 19 July 2008).

Miliband, D. (2008) 'Foreword to the FCO's Departmental Report 2007–8'. Available online at: http://www.fco.gov.uk/en/departmental-report/introduction/foreignsec foreword/ (accessed 2 August 2008).

Military Balance (2008) *The Military Balance 2008*, London: International Institute for Strategic Studies.

Ministry for Peace (2006) *Written Evidence: Memorandum Submitted by Ministry for Peace*, London: House of Commons International Development Committee.

Ministry of Defence (1998) *The Strategic Defence Review: Supporting Essays*, London: Ministry of Defence.

—— (2003) *Delivering Security in a Changing World*, London: Ministry of Defence.

—— (2006) *The Comprehensive Approach*, Shrivenham, Wiltshire: Joint Doctrine and Concepts Centre, Ministry of Defence.

Ministry of the Treasury (2008) *Public Expenditure Statistical Analyses 2007–08*, London: HM Treasury. Available online at: http://www.hm-treasury.gov.uk/media/2/7/Budget_2008_budgeting_tables.xls (accessed 12 July 2008).

Missiroli, Antonio (2003) *Euros for ESDP: Financing EU Operations*, Paris: EUISS.

National Audit Office (2008) *Department for International Development: Operating in Insecure Environments*, London: The Stationery Office.

NATO (2007) *NATO-Russia Compendium of Financial and Economic Data Relating to Defence*, Brussels: NATO.

Norton-Taylor, R. (2008) 'Selling our soldiers short', *The Guardian*, 3 July.

OECD (2008) *Official Development Assistance 1950–2007*, Paris: OECD. Available online at: http://www.oecd.org/dac/stats (accessed 12 July 2008).

—— (2009) 'Asylum Statistics', Paris: OECD. Available online at: http://www.oecd.org/dataoecd/26/41/39332370.xls (accessed 1 March 2009).

Office of National Statistics (2008) *Total International Migration Time Series 1991 to 2006*,

(London: Office for National Statistics). Available online at: http://www.statistics.gov. uk/STATBASE/Product.asp?vlnk = 15053 (accessed 12 July 2008).

O'Neill, S. (2008) 'Whatever happened to the fight against the Mr Bigs?', *The Times*, 29 April.

Open Politics (2008) 'UK's World Role: Punching above Our Weight', London: BBC. Available online at: http://news.bbc.co.uk/hi/english/static/in_depth/uk_politics/2001/ open_politics/foreign_policy/uks_world_role.stm (accessed 8 July 2008).

Picciotto, R. (2006) *Oral Evidence: Taken before the International Development Committee on Tuesday 2 May 2006*, London: House of Commons International Development Committee.

Ritchie, N. (2008) *Trident and British Identity: Letting go of Nuclear Weapons*, Bradford: University of Bradford Department of Peace Studies.

SOCA (2008) *Serious Organised Crime Agency Annual Plan 2008/09*, London: Serious Organised Crime Agency.

SIPRI (2009) 'Database on Peace Operations'. Available online at: http://conflict.sipri.org/ SIPRI_Internet/index.php4 (accessed 27 February 2009).

United Nations (2008) *UN Missions Summary Detailed by Country 31 May 2008*, New York: United Nations.

UNHCR (2007) *2007 Global Trends: Refugees, Asylum-seekers, Returnees, Internally Displaced and Stateless Persons*, Geneva: UNHCR. Available online at: http://www. unhcr.org/statistics/STATISTICS/4852366f2.pdf (accessed 17 July 2008).

Waldman, M. (2008) *Falling Short: Aid Effectiveness in Afghanistan*, Kabul: Agency Coordinating Body for Afghan Relief.

6 European Union

Moving towards a European security culture?

Emil J. Kirchner

When compared to the speed of previous developments in European Union security policy there has been a tremendous expansion of activities since 1999, comprising both institutional innovations and engagements on the ground. Following the decision by EU member states to engage in a peace-enforcement exercise in Kosovo and the announcement of a European Security Policy (ESDP) with a standing military force in 1999, a number of important steps have been taken to promote EU security policy. Of particular importance has been the introduction of the European Security Strategy (ESS) in 2003. Although the ESS is primarily a statement of intent, it has been relatively quickly joined by the steady flow of ESDP missions to various global regions, the formation of a European Defence Agency, the introduction of so-called Battlegroups, and the establishment of policy-making instruments, such as the Political and Security Committee and the Situation Centre. However, the emphasis given in the ESS is more on preventive engagement, non-military instruments and persuasive action than on peace-making exercises, military instruments and coercive methods. It also commits itself to multilateral efforts and effectiveness. Some see the ESS as confirming the characterization of the EU as civilianized security community (Harnisch and Maull 2001), or suggest it signifies that national strategic cultures converge towards 'higher preparedness to use coercive means and accept risks, lower thresholds for the authorization of force, and a higher acceptance of the European Union as the legitimate vehicle for conduct of defence policies' (Meyer 2005: 525–26).

It will be assumed in this chapter that there is an emerging European security culture, not one which will replace the security cultures of its constituent parts, but rather which prevails on a parallel level. Such a parallel security culture could be conceived of primarily as the incremental institutionalization of those ideas, norms and values that are sufficiently shared at the national level (Meyer 2005: 7). This set of ideas, norms and values can be captured with reference to four characteristics: the view of the external environment; European identity; instrumental preferences; and interaction patterns. An important element in the incremental institutionalization of the ideas, norms and values is the ESS. The ESS marks important changes in threat perception by EU member states, a more pro-active engagement in regional or international conflict prevention and resolution, and a distinct move towards a post-Westphalian system.[1] A second assumption is that the emerging security culture has an impact on how EU security and defence policy will be conducted, or how instruments and resources will be used in the process. To explore this potential impact, an assessment will be made as to whether EU financial expenditures (military and non-military expenditures) and the allocation of civilian or military personnel for security actions are being made in accordance with the objectives of the ESS. The stipulated ESS aims and identified threats will be used as a guideline for the assessment of defence expenditures and security personnel. In addition, to account for the spectrum of EU security activities, and hence the scope of aims identified in the ESS, four EU security dimensions will be selected for this examination. These are policies of prevention (dealing with root causes of conflict), policies of assurance (measures taken in post-conflict situations), policies of compellence (peace-making and peace-enforcement interventions) and policies of protection (internal security).[2]

This chapter will first examine the ESS in the light of the post-Westphalian state order; it will then examine empirically the four security dimensions, and conclude with a summary of the major findings.

The European Union as security actor

The 'dynamic density' of the European state system has fostered a collective European identity that has cultural, political, economic and geographic components. The evolution of a *Schicksalsgemeinschaft* (a community bound together by a common fate) implies that a threat to any society or state or the regional system of governance is easily translated into threats against all, albeit with different levels of intensity and concern. The vulnerability derived from the structural and cultural interpenetration of these states in combination with the evolution of a collective identity within Europe has produced an effort to enforce a club *acquis* on all the states that constitute 'Europe'. The geographic redefinition of Europe in the 1990s removed a barrier to the containment of economic or political disturbances originating within East, Central or Southern Europe or projected from the Eurasian periphery. The wealthy European states, particularly those who are members of the EU, made a rhetorical and political commitment to aid the transition to democracy and the market in Central and Eastern Europe. That commitment produced a *de facto* membership in the Western 'club' even when it was clear that many of those states could not be safely assimilated into the institutional arrangements that brought peace and prosperity to the states of Western Europe. By the end of the twentieth century, all the states that can reasonably be assumed to occupy a part of Europe have claimed or have been extended the explicit or implicit right to 'belong' to either NATO or the EU or both. This largely acknowledged membership right has produced a paradox: rather than the EU or NATO serving as a 'firewall' between the stable and unstable states of Eurasia, the expansion of either institution has forced the Western European states to fashion policies addressing the sources of instability within Europe as well as monitoring the network of diffusion mechanisms linking Europe with its periphery. The interlinkage of security interests between the two is, as noted above, explicitly recognized in the European Neighbourhood Policy (ENP).

A great deal of this EU collective action logic is both recognized and officially explicated as policy in the ESS. Although heavily influenced by the Bush security doctrine of 2002 and the fallout of disagreements among member states over how to relate to the Iraq conflict in the spring of 2003, the ESS reflects wider EU security concerns such as the need to respond to 'neighbours who are engaged in violent conflict, weak states where organized crime flourishes, and dysfunctional societies' (European Council 2006: 8). Pointing to these differences, the ESS acknowledges and illuminates the Westphalian/post-Westphalian dichotomy by setting itself apart from its neighbours and other parts of the world. Moreover, it suggests that 'no single country is able to tackle today's complex problems on its own' (Solana 2003: 1) and that 'we are stronger when we act together' (Solana 2003: 13). Hence 'the EU considers itself a collective of European countries ... committed to dealing peacefully with disputes and cooperation through common institutions' (Solana 2003: 1). One of its core functions is to express a European security identity (Becher 2004). Moreover, the ESS is about more than how to react to and behave in security and defence situations, and represents a strategy for external action.

Threats perceived by the EU, as articulated in the ESS, only partially concentrate on 'hard' security. Only one of the five key threats identified falls into this category, namely proliferation of weapons of mass destruction (WMD). Three of the other threats identified – terrorism, regional conflicts and state failure – have 'hard' security edges, such as poverty and migratory movements. Organized crime is the fifth key threat given in the ESS. Military force cannot usually cope in a substantial manner with organized crime, making it a 'soft' security threat. It is in this context that the ESS stresses that 'none of the new threats is purely military; nor can any be tackled by purely military means' (Solana 2003: 9). In order to relate to external threats, the EU utilizes economic and political means, military operations and the mandate of multilateral institutions. It attaches great importance to effective multilateralism, with a strong UN at its heart. It also acts in response to mandates and UN-sanctioned military engagements in conformity with the notion of multilateralism.

As stated above, it will be assumed in this chapter that the ESS has an impact on the way the EU conducts its foreign and security policy. However, caution is required as this impact of the European security culture will take the form more of 'shaping' rather than 'determining' such a policy. Two working hypotheses appear relevant in this context:

- H_1: *European security culture accounts for the securitization of threats and the preferred instruments relied upon to meet them.*
- H_2: *European security culture produces preferences for specific forms of security governance systems that, in turn, facilitate or inhibit international cooperation.*

In support of these hypotheses, there are indications that official French, German, Italian and British views on threat perception (type of key threats, agency of threats, target of threat and geographical source of threat) and preferred responses to threats (interaction patterns and institutional preferences for meeting threats) have a high degree of convergence among themselves and largely correspond to those expressed in the ESS (Kirchner 2007). However, further empirical work is required in terms of resources committed by the EU for security purposes, which is the task of this chapter. The pursuance of this task will be explored through the application of four EU security dimensions: policies of prevention, assurance, protection and compellence.

Policies of assurance

As the number of major conflicts, mostly of an intrastate nature, has increased in the post-Cold War period (Wallersteen and Sollenberg 2001), efforts to rebuild states and nations through outside intervention have become regular features in countries such as Afghanistan, the Democratic Republic of Congo and Iraq, to name but a few. As the challenges in post-war Iraq and Afghanistan show, one of the most important missions in conflict-ridden societies is the stabilization of local situations. While peacekeeping operations and police missions are important elements in the rebuilding of states and nations, civilian efforts are essential for stabilizing war-torn states and societies.[3] Essentially, assurance policies are non-coercive instruments applied in the building of civic institutions, civil societies and the creation of conditions for the promotion of democratic societies playing by EU rules.

A number of features of EU assurance policies can be identified. First, since 1999, the EU has undertaken special responsibilities in the state and nation-building efforts of the Western Balkan nations through two channels. One is the Stability and Association Policy (SAP) which emphasizes regional cooperation, democratization, capacity-building and trade liberalization, both with the EU and intra-regional, and which provides a trajectory for EU membership. It also stipulated full cooperation with the International Criminal Tribunal for the former Yugoslavia (ICTY) in The Hague, sought guarantees for the rights of refugees to return to their homeland, and a full commitment to the fight against corruption and organized crime. The other channel is through its role in, as well as financial contribution to, the Stability Pact for South Eastern Europe. This Pact heightens the emphasis for the countries of Southeastern Europe to demonstrate regional cooperation, good neighbourly relations and a functioning economic and security framework.

Second, since 2003, the EU has introduced a number of so-called civilian ESDP missions in Europe, Africa and Asia. These serve in such capacities as training police forces in post-conflict areas (Police Missions), training judges, legal personnel and civil servants (Rule of Law Missions), or monitoring border controls (Border Missions). As Table 6.1 shows, there has been a steady growth of such ESDP civilian missions since their inception in 2003. EU countries also undertake

Table 6.1 Overview of ESDP civilian missions

ESDP Mission	Country	Mission duration	Assigned Task	Staff
EUPM	Bosnia-Herzegovina	1.1.2003–31.12.2009	Police Mission	*182
EUPOL Proxima	Macedonia	15.12.2003–14.12.2004	Police Mission	170
EUJUST Themis	Georgia	16.7.2004–14.7.2005	Rule of Law Mission	10
EUPOL Kinshasa	DR Congo	8.6.2005–15.7.2007	Police Mission	37
EUSEC	DR Congo	1.7.2005–30.6.2009	Security Sector Reform	*40
EUJUST LEX	Brussels/Iraq	1.7.2005–30.6.2009	Training Iraqi officials outside Iraq	*25
AMIS II Assistance	Dafur, Sudan	18.7.2005–31.12.2007	Support for the African Union mission in Darfur	31
Aceh Monitoring	Aceh, Indonesia	15.9.2005–15.12.2006	Monitoring the peace agreement	146
EU BAM Rafah	Palestinian Territories	15.11.2005–15.11.2009	Monitoring the Rafah border (Gaza/Egypt)	*27
EU BAM Moldova/	Moldova/Ukraine	30.11.2005–30.11.2009	Monitoring the Moldova/Ukraine border	*220
EUPAT	Macedonia	15.12.2005–15.6.2006	Assist with police reform	30
EUPOL COPPS	Palestinian Territories	1.1.2006–31.12.2010	Police Mission	*31
EUPT Kosovo	Kosovo	10.4.2006–31.3.2008	Planning team > Rule of Law Mission	100
EUPOL AFG	Afghanistan	15.6.2007–15.6.2010	Police Mission	*230
EUPOL Congo	DR Congo	1.7.2007–30.6.2009	Follow-up to EUPOL Kinshasa	*53
EULEX	Kosovo	8.12.2008–8.12.2010	Rule of Law Mission	*1,900
EU SSR	Guinea-Bissau	1.6.2008–30.11.09	Security Sector Reform	*19
EUMM	Georgia	1.10.08–30.11.09	Monitoring the peace agreement	*266

Source: Council of the European Union (undated)

Note:
* Marks the mission strength as of January 2009. The figures of completed ESDP missions reflect 'end of mission' numbers, again as reported in January 2009

Table 6.2 Percentage of EU member states' contributions to OSCE field operations

Year	2001	2002	2003	2004	2005	2006	2007	2008
	69.43	70.7	66.03	66.03	70.9	70.64	71.78	71.78

Source: SIPRI 2008

similar missions under OSCE and UN auspices. An overview of OSCE missions is provided in Table 6.2.

Third, to complement EU Civilian Crisis Management measures, in 2004 a number of EU countries established the European Gendarmerie Force (EUROGENDFOR). The force is about 3,200 strong, with a rapid version element of approximately 800 gendarmes, and will have an initial reaction capability of 30 days.

Fourth, the EU appoints Special Representatives (EUSRs) to promote EU policies and interests in troubled regions and countries and to play an active role in efforts to consolidate peace, stability and the rule of law. They support the work of the High Representative of the Union for Foreign Affairs and Security for the Common Foreign and Security Policy (CFSP), in the regions concerned. The 11 EUSRs in office in 2009 cover the following regions: Afghanistan, the African Great Lakes Region, the African Union, Bosnia and Herzegovina, Central Asia, Kosovo, the former Yugoslav Republic of Macedonia, the Middle East, Moldova, the South Caucasus and Sudan. Some EUSRs are resident in their country or region of activity while others are working on a travelling basis from Brussels.

To ensure that the desired assurance policies have some success, the EU has provided appropriate motives or incentive structures, together with a comprehensive policy approach and workable enforcement mechanisms. EU assurance policy efforts are financed by various means. The SAP for the Western Balkans falls under the Instrument for Pre-Accession Assistance (IPA), which replaced the former Community Assistance for Reconstruction, Development and Stabilisation (CARDS). Besides the IPA, the Instrument for Stability (IFS), formerly the Rapid Reaction Mechanism (RRM); the European Initiative for Democracy and Human Rights (EIDHR); and the European Community Humanitarian Office (ECHO) fund also serve assurance policy purposes. (For a listing of these funds see Table 6.3). ESDP missions are partly financed (seed money) by the CFSP budget and partly (operational costs) by the participating member states of the missions. OSCE and UN civilian missions are paid directly by the participating EU member states. Contributions to the Stability Pact for South Eastern Europe are divided between EC contributions and member state contributions (see Table 6.4).

EU assurance policy is not so much a question of succeeding where states have failed, but one where the collective effort has been able to achieve more than those of individual states. The commitment to a comprehensive programme like the SAP would have been difficult, if not impossible, for individual member states. Similarly, civilian ESDP can be more effectively carried out when done collectively rather than by individual states. The growing number and geographic spread (half are outside the European continent) of civilian ESDP missions, since their

Table 6.3 Budgets for EU policies of assurance and prevention

Instrument	Duration of budget	Total (Euro billions)
EDF	2008–13	22,682
DCI	2007–13	16,897
ENPI	2007–13	11,181
IPA	2007–10	5,740
ECHO	2008–13	4,881
EIDHR	2007–13	1,104
IFS	2009–11	0.225

Sources: EDF: http://europa.eu/scadplus/leg/en/lvb/r12102.htm (accessed 28 May 2009); DCI: http://ec.europa.eu/europeaid/what/delivering-aid/funding-instruments/documents/dci_en.pdf (accessed 28 May 2009); ENPI: http://www.euroresources.org/guide_to_population_assistance/european_community/enpi_1.html (accessed 28 May 2009); IPA: http://europa.eu/scadplus/leg/en/lvb/e50020.htm (accessed 28 May 2009); ECHO: http://ec.europa.eu/echo/files/funding/budget/finances_2008_2013.pdf (accessed 28 May 2009); EIDHR: http://www.euroresources.org/guide_to_population_assistance/european_community/eidhr.html (accessed 28 May 2009); IFS: Commission of the European Communities 2009

Table 6.4 Stability Pact allocations: total assistance by donors 2001–5 (Euro millions)

Donor	Total grants	Total loans	Final total
EU member states + EC budget	12,728.56	943.80	13,672.36
Non-EU countries	3,228.08	225.49	3,453.57
International financial institutions	91.40	15,772.51	15,863.91
Total	16,048.04	16,941.80	32,989.84

Source: European Commission/World Bank, Office for South East Europe 2007: 90. Cited in Kirchner and Sperling 2007: 90

inception in 2003, give testimony to this fact. They reflect the emphasis given in the ESS on assisting states in post-conflict situations or in the process of peace-building. However, given the rising number of fully or partly intrastate conflicts, post-conflict engagement requires greater EU resources and material commitment, in the shape of deployable gendarmerie, policing and civilian capabilities (Ashdown and Robertson 2009).

Policies of prevention

The rise of the EU as a security actor is connected with the fact that the threat spectrum has broadened. New categories of threat have emerged in the post-Cold War period, marked by such phenomena as intrastate conflicts, terrorist attacks, and the proliferation of WMD. Security is no longer limited to the task of territorial defence and the use of military force to do so. Owing to the inability to effectively control national borders, to deter terrorist attacks or to respond effectively to environmental or health threats, the overlap between internal and external security is growing. Thus, enlargement of the EU, association agreements, the Schengen Convention, and the volume and diversity of travel/migration reflect in part the interdependence of the EU's external environment and the realization of its milieu goals. In turn, these milieu issues have made conflict prevention a critical aspect of security governance in Europe today and have made it a cornerstone of the ESS's stress on 'preventive engagement'. They have also highlighted that what the EU was already doing in the field of conflict prevention came to be considered as important for security.

Policies of conflict prevention seek to prevent the occurrence of a major conflict or, once started, try to prevent it from spreading. The instruments used consist of financial and technical assistance, economic cooperation in the form of trade or association agreements, the promise of EU membership, nation-building efforts, and support of internal democratization. The support of nation-building and democratization efforts is conditioned on tangible evidence that reforms have indeed taken place and been implemented by the recipients.

Three areas of EU prevention policy can be identified. One is the wider European geographic area, where the emphasis is either on enlargement of the EU, or the stability of the neighbouring countries of the Union. The latter are covered by the ENP, which covers 16 East European and Mediterranean states.

The second relates to the 'root causes of conflict', particularly as they manifest themselves in 'failed' or 'failing states' in various part of the globe. The ESS calls for 'early, rapid and, when necessary robust intervention' and is willing to support 'preventive engagement that could avoid more serious problems in the future' (Solana 2003: 11). With regard to early intervention, development policy and other cooperation programmes are identified by the Commission as providing 'the most powerful instruments at the Community's disposal for treating the root cause of conflict' (European Commission 2001: 4). These run under so-called Partnership Agreements, like Lomé/Cotonou, comprising 78 African, Caribbean and Pacific (ACP) states; Association agreements such as with ASEAN, Chile and Mexico; Cooperation Agreements like with Mercosur, the Andean Community and Central America; or Economic Partnership Agreements, e.g. the Gulf Cooperation Council. Some of these efforts to deal with root causes of conflict are complemented by EU humanitarian assistance, or assisted by the crisis-management facilities IFS, the EIDHR, and the ECHO programme. It is fair to say that ECHO, IFS and EIDHR have a more general application both with regard to prevention policy, including their geographic use, and with regard to assurance policies in post-conflict situations.

To prevent the proliferation of WMD and to respond to specific crisis situations is a third area of EU prevention engagement. The so-called EU-3 engagement by France, Germany and the UK to prevent an expansion of the nuclear energy programme in Iran is a case in point. Besides recognizing the importance of political, diplomatic and economic pressures, it also advocates greater use of the carrots of

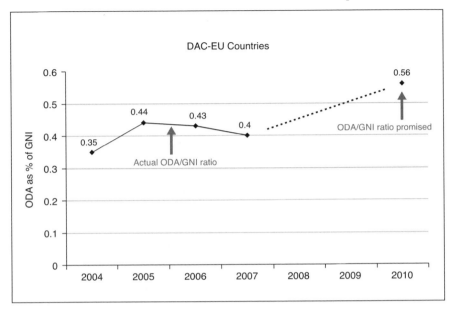

Figure 6.1 EU countries' contribution to ODA/DAC

Source: OECD:DAC (2008)

economic inducements and the stick of sanctions to encourage better governance. The EU undertakes mediation exercises in situations of conflict, which can take various forms. In some instances the EU acts collectively and autonomously, e.g. the offer to act as 'third-party mechanism' in any future negotiation and talks between the Israel and the Palestinian Authority (European Council 2001). Mediation efforts are undertaken by the High Representative of the Union for Foreign Affairs and Security, such as in Macedonia in 2001 and in the Ukraine in 2004. Complementary tasks are performed by the European anti-terrorism coordinator. The EU also often links with UN, OSCE or NATO efforts to resolve potential conflict or actual conflict situations.

Financial assistance is provided through a number of mechanisms. EU enlargement policy and ENP are covered by the IPA and the European Neighbourhood Policy Instrument (ENPI) respectively. EU development policy is carried out by the European Development Fund (EDF),[4] supporting the 78 ACP countries, and the Development Cooperation Instrument (DCI), which provides assistance to South Africa, and 47 developing countries in Latin America, Asia and Central Asia, and the Middle East (only those countries not covered by the ENPI or the EDF).[5] An overview of the budgets of these instruments plus those of ECHO, IFS and EIDHR is provided in Table 6.3. In addition to these instruments, both EU member states and the European Community[6] contribute to the Development Assistance Cooperation (DAC) of the OECD. For the trend of EU member state contributions to the DAC see Figure 6.1. Under the Gleneagles commitment frame, the EU has pledged to reach 0.7 per cent of ODA/GNI by 2015 with a new interim collective target of 0.56 per cent by 2010. The EU intends to nearly double its ODA contributions between 2004 and 2010 from 34.5 billion Euros to 67 billion Euros. The combined contributions by EU member states and the EU to UN aid and development programmes (38 per cent of the UN regular budget) make the EU the world's largest donor of aid and development assistance.

Thus EU collective behaviour can be observed in development and cooperation policy, and the ENP. There is sufficient agreement among EU member states that collective action in development and cooperation policy is needed to contribute to international peace and stability; that EU values and experience can act as a model for emulation in developing countries; that joint efforts between EU member states and Community programmes are necessary; and that the Commission should play a lead role in streamlining the activities in this sector. As a consequence, there are both long-standing and well-entrenched collective behavioural characteristics (i.e. the Community method) guiding this policy area. In turn, through a range of financial and technical assistance, economic cooperation in the form of trade or association agreements, or enlargement provisions and nation-building and democratization efforts, the EU has helped to shape the behaviour of problem countries (Hill and Smith 2005: 402). Similarly, in order to combat security threats emanating from unstable neighbouring states, terrorism, organized crime, failing states and the proliferation of WMD (Solana 2003), the EU enrolled in certain collective security initiatives, such as the ENP. By emphasizing the need for preventive action, the ESS has thus been instrumental in securitizing new threats and has given rise to the use of specific instruments such as ENP. Moreover, the need to protect EU freedom of goods and services and with it the existence of porous borders has made the EU abandon strict adherence to the Westphalian dictum of territorial defence in favour of milieu security goals. It has also made the EU pay more attention to the link between policies of prevention and policies of protection.

Policies of protection

Europe's evolution towards a post-Westphalianism, in conjunction with the rise of malevolent sovereign-free actors operating outside and targeting Europe, no longer warrants or suffers the conceptual disassociation of internal and external security requirements. European states, particularly the member states of the EU, have experienced a progressive loss of sovereign control over national territory, a development aggravated by the EU's enlargement and association processes, the signing of trade and cooperation treaties (drawing the states of the former Soviet Union into the EU's economic and social orbit), the rising diversity and volume of interactions between the EU and the states along its periphery, and the implementation of the Schengen *acquis* within most of the EU.

The Amsterdam Treaty established the goal of a European area of freedom, security and justice as the core objective of EU protection policies. Internal security requires member states to harmonize their institutional and legal infrastructures and covers a wide spectrum of issues, including narcotics trafficking, organized crime, epidemiological surveillance, the policing of external borders, and infrastructure security. Progress on EU cooperation has been slow on these issues.

While the number of asylum applications to EU countries has decreased since 2002, there has been a steady increase of foreign population into the EU between 1990 and 2004 (see Tables 6.5 and 6.6). The growing irrelevance of political-territorial boundaries within Europe makes it increasingly difficult to control the flow of people, goods and ideas. Thus, the very success of the European project has sharply limited the effective exercise of sovereign prerogatives and eroded the sovereignty principle; it has also occasioned the growing vulnerability of society to a broad spectrum of threats.

Besides establishing in the Treaty of Amsterdam the goal of a European area of freedom, security and justice as a core objective of EU protection policies, the EU has targeted two general threats to internal security: organized crime and terrorism. Both organized crime and terrorism present a security threat when the activities of transnational crime organizations or terrorist groups perpetrate illicit

Table 6.5 Asylum applications

	EU 15	EU 25
1996	227,802	
1997	242,774	
1998	295,506	
1999	352,222	
2000		403,372
2001		411,731
2002		400,489
2003		335,879
2004		276,675
2005		234,675
2006		197,410

Source: Eurostat yearbook 2006–7

Table 6.6 Inflows of foreign population by nationality

	1990–94	1995–99	2000–4	2005
OECD total	16,393,500	14,064,200	22,237,600	4,867,790
EU total	6,366,540	6,562,430	11,941,600	2,595,580
EU total (%)	39.38	46.44	53.57	53.25

Source: http://www.oecd.org/dataoecd/26/41/39332370.xls (accessed 28 May 2009)

acts, weakening the political, social or economic integrity of a state. As Table 6.7 shows, the number of individuals tried for terrorism charges increased fourfold between 2005 and 2006 in eight EU member states. The EU members recognize that these two threats to internal security require joint action. An elaborate set of policy principles now defines the balance between member states' and EU prerogatives. Successive action plans and framework decisions identify EU-wide policy objectives. In addition to the problem of terrorism and organized crime, the EU has sought to increase its competence in allied areas of internal security: border control (FRONTEX), money laundering, computer and information network security, and health security. Moreover, the EU has strengthened existing coordinating mechanisms at the supranational level, created new institutional avenues for member state cooperation, and carved out special competencies that necessarily impinge upon the sovereign prerogatives of its members. Progress has been made towards achieving the overall goal of a single area of justice through the mutual recognition of judicial decisions, which includes the establishment of the European Arrest Warrant and uniform surrender procedures. The European Union Judicial Cooperation Unit (Eurojust) has assumed an important role within the EU, primarily as a mechanism for exchanging information and linking cases in different jurisdictions towards meeting the threat posed by organized crime. The introduction of the European Police Office (EUROPOL) has promoted cooperation among member states' police authorities. As shown in Table 6.8, both the budgets and the activities have seen steep increases between 2000 and 2005. Internal security requires member states to harmonize their institutional and legal infrastructures and covers a wide spectrum of issues, including narcotics trafficking, terrorism, organized crime, epidemiological surveillance, the policing of external borders, and infrastructure security. The

Table 6.7 Number of individuals tried for terrorism charges (in selected EU countries) 2005 and 2006

Member state	2005	2006	Total
Belgium	0	24	24
France	0	21	21
Germany	0	16	16
Italy	7	0	7
Spain	51	154	205
Sweden	2	3	5
The Netherlands	1	20	21
UK	1	3	4
Total	63	240	303

Source: http://www.europol.europa.eu/publications/EU_Terrorism_Situation_and_Trend_Report_TE-SAT/TESAT2008.pdf (accessed 28 May 2009)

Table 6.8 Europol and Eurojust budgets activities 2000–7

	2000	2001	2002	2003	2004	2005	2006	2007
EUROPOL								
Budget (in million)	28.5	36.6	53.2	57.8	58.8	63.4	63.5	67.9
Number of cases referred	1,919	2,267	3,442	5,388	6,388	6,761	7,246	7,618
Number of operational messages exchanged	35,366	45,093	70,079	96,860	155,050	183,526	210,268	260,463
EUROJUST*								
Number of coordinating meetings		15	20	26	52	73	91	91
Bilateral cases referred		116	144	222	272	N/A	813	956
Multilateral		68	58	78	109	N/A	272	237
Total of Eurojust cases referred		185	202	300	381	588	1,085	1,093

Sources: Europol: http://www.europol.europa.eu/publications/Annual_Reports/Annual%20Report/Annual%20Report%202007.pdf (accessed 3 August 2009); Eurojust: Pro-Eurojust: http://www.eurojust.europa.eu/press_annual_report_2008.htm (accessed 3 August 2009)

Note:
* The Eurojust budget was 24.8 million Euros in 2008

sharing of information among member states on these issues and the unfettered support of the free flow of people, goods and ideas represent a vital ingredient for the effective working of policies of protection. Yet, there has been a limited willingness of member states to surrender sovereign policing or judicial prerogatives even when confronted with the spectre of terrorists acquiring chemical, biological, radiological or nuclear (CBRN) materials or devices. The necessity of joint action to meet internal security threats is unquestioned by the governing elites, yet governments are unable to cede sovereignty in this policy domain because national electorates remain attached to national political and legal cultures.

Policies of compellence

Defence policy differs from conflict prevention measures and assurance policies in one fundamental respect: whereas conflict prevention and assurance policies require the 'hidden' expenditure of material resources or civilian personnel engagement, policies of compellence – peace enforcement, peacekeeping and peace-making – carry a high political cost owing to the potential loss of life. For this reason alone, the EU has engaged in policies of compellence sparingly, limited to a relatively small number of peace-enforcement and peacekeeping missions (see Table 6.9). In addition to the transparent costs of these policies and the attending domestic political costs of failure, historical circumstances condition the EU's

Table 6.9 Overview of ESDP military missions

ESDP Mission	Country	Mission duration	Assigned task	Staff
EUFOR Concordia	Macedonia	31.3.2003–15.12.2003	Peace support	400
Artemis	DR Congo	12.6.2003–1.9.2003	Peace support for MONUC	1,800
EUFOR Althea	Bosnia-Herzegovina	2.12.2004–1.3.2009	Peace support	7,000 (initially) 2,500 (Jan. 2009)
EUFOR DR Congo	DR Congo	30.7.2006–30.11. 2006	Peace support for MONUC	2,300
EUFOR Tchad/RCA	Chad and RCA	28.1.2008	Military operation to improve security in the region	3,400
EU NAVAR Atlanta	Somalia	1.12.08–30.11.09	Military naval operation against piracy	1,500 serving around 20 vessels and aircraft

Source: Council of the European Union (undated)

inability to move towards greater defence integration. The failure of the European Defence Community (EDC) was a decisive factor for the eventual demarcation by the original six member states to pursue territorial security within NATO and economic security within the confines of the Treaties of Paris and Rome (see Hanrieder 1978; Eilstrup-Sangiovanni *et al.* 2005; Laffan 2000: 38–39), resulting in the creation within the EU of a 'civilian security culture'. This 'civilian security culture' had two effects: it minimized the pressure for greater defence cooperation since it was not seen as particularly relevant to the security tasks facing the EU; and it reinforced the willingness to rely on NATO (and the US) to supply the military requirements of security.

Nonetheless, the EU has made progress since the 1990s, and especially since 1999, towards creating effective formal and informal authority structures facilitating security structures and has championed the idea of European defence policy while tolerating the bilateral and unilateral arrangements between overlapping sets of member states (Rosenau 2000; Smith 2003). More particularly, EU efforts include a strengthening of its military capacity through the establishment of a Rapid Reaction Force with a standing force of between 60,000 and 100,000, 13 Battle Groups, and a European Defence Agency. Importantly, it has also introduced the ESS, which explicitly refers to the use of military force as a legitimate option to tackle security threats (not only attacks) and adopts a global perspective, thus signalling the intention to pursue security and defence pro-actively. The progress towards greater defence cooperation and its institutionalization can be attributed to the emergence of a common European interest that itself is abetted by the development of a common identity; partly in response to the perceived threats emanating from upheavals in the Western Balkans and partly in opposition to the US (Wendt 1994; Nuttal 1992; Jepperson *et al.* 1996). The fallout from September 11, the Madrid and London terrorist bombings, and the invasion of Iraq have together eroded the emerging consensus on military cooperation and integration. The ESS presented a consensus view on the need for the EU to take greater responsibility for regional and global security, but the military component did not play a particularly prominent role. The Strategy, which reaffirmed the importance of the Petersberg Tasks, did not commit the member states to redressing the broad spectrum of capabilities shortfalls that hindered joint peace enforcement or peacekeeping operations in regions acknowledged as critical to European stability and security (the Balkans, the Caucasus and Mediterranean Basin). Moreover, the ESS's emphasis on 'preventive engagement' signifies a preference for positive civilian rather than coercive military measures. There is also no equivalent to NATO's Article 5 in regard to territorial defence, and uncertainties remain as to how military forces and capabilities (including civilian aspects) will be fully coordinated by the EU (Missiroli 2004: 60).

Although limited in numbers and specific assignments, the peace-enforcement and peacekeeping exercises have been instructive, especially with regard to peacekeeping tasks. The peace-enforcement exercises have demonstrated both that joint EU-NATO operations (e.g. Macedonia 2001) can be successful and that the EU can carry out autonomous missions (e.g. the Democratic Republic of

Congo). With regard to peacekeeping, a cumulative effect can be noticed between the rather small force (400) used in Macedonia and the much larger one in Bosnia (7,000), as well as in the duration of the operations involved (e.g. the engagement of EUFOR Althea in Bosnia since 2004). Besides the ESDP military missions, EU member states made significant contributions to NATO-led (45 per cent to ISAF in Afghanistan and 82 per cent to KFOR in Kosovo) and UN-led (62 per cent) peacekeeping operations in 2008. However, significant shortcomings remain in terms of EU security and defence commitments, the streamlining of national armed forces, and the investment in high technological equipment. The EU spends less than half of the US defence budget, but has a greater proportion of military-force personnel than the US. Moreover, the inability to streamline different national forces and command structures affects the interoperability and military capacity of the EU, especially in such areas as air and sea power and surveillance. Overall, while EU member states have military personnel of around 2 million, only about 10 per cent of these are deployable. While EU member state forces in operation total 70–80,000,[7] ESDP military missions comprise a mere 10,000 Armed Forces. In contrast to personnel budgets, the EU spent less on equipment allocation and infrastructure measures than the US. For further details on EU force strength and defence expenditure (see Table 6.10).

The ESS recommends 'more resources for defence and less duplication, as well as an improvement of crisis management capability, shared intelligence, and enlargement of the spectrum of missions, beyond the "Petersberg tasks"' (ESS 2004: 13). However, the ESS is tacit on how military means could achieve Europe's political ends (Vennesson 2007: 25). This connects with a number of shortcomings

Table 6.10 EU countries' defence expenditures (in Euros) and force strength (2005–7)

	2005*	2006**	2007**
Total military personnel	1,855,517	1,940,112,000	1,836,882
Total civilian personnel	468,836	484,827,000	457,392
Total defence expenditure	193 billion	201 billion	204 billion
Defence expenditure as % of GDP	1.81%	1.78%	1.69%
Defence expenditure per capita	425	412	417
Defence spending per soldier	103,974	103,602	103,602
Investment (equipment procurement and R&D) per soldier	19,057	20,002	22,795

Sources: European Defence Agency, National Defence Expenditures in 2006 and 2007; European-United States Defence Expenditures in 2007; European Defence Expenditure in 2005; and European-United State Defence Expenditure in 2005. All available at: http://www.eda.europa.eu/defencefacts/ (accessed 23 July 2009)

Notes:
* Refers to EU-24 countries and excludes Denmark
** Refers to EU-26 countries and excludes Denmark

in military hardware and planning. There is a need to increase 'the number of battlegroups on standby at any one time, to expand the size of support units such as logisticians, engineers, helicopter squadrons, medics and intelligence teams' (Ashdown and Robertson 2009). Another remaining troublesome issue is the extent to which the EU should pursue autonomous ESDP actions or missions and/or link with NATO. A central concern here is the extent to which the EU should have an independent planning cell or continue to rely upon the EU civil-military planning cell established in 2003. This existing cell, while technically independent from NATO, will only be used as a last resort and will not develop into fully-fledged headquarters (Giegerich 2007: 44). Finally, it remains to be seen to what extent the European Defence Agency can help member states to reach their capabilities targets, e.g. bring on stream the Airbus transport aircraft A400M.

Conclusion

EU follow-up measures and the EU allocation of resources and material are in line with the emphasis given in the ESS to tackle threats by preventive civilian means and in accordance with the notion of a post-Westphalian security culture. These measures and allocations give support to the hypothesis that the embryonic European security culture accounts for the securitization of threats and the preferred instruments relied upon to meet them. Furthermore, the large EU commitments to multilateral aid and development programmes and to UN-mandated ESDP missions signify a strong orientation towards multilateralism and give credence to the second hypothesis posed in this chapter, namely that the embryonic European security culture produces preferences for specific forms of security governance systems that, in turn, facilitate or inhibit international cooperation.

The ESS is operating on two levels simultaneously: it is codifying a security culture *acquis* and is also a component in validating national security culture discourses in the form of ideas, values and norms (Howorth 2004; Whitman 2006). The latter process can to some extent be observed in France. As noted by Irondelle and Besancenot in this volume, France has undergone a certain Europeanization on matters of security and defence; conflict prevention items have been securitized and even militarized (e.g. migration), and there has been a transition towards a post-Westphalian world, especially in areas with strong financial constraints. However, they also note that when threats are securitized, they tend not to be as militarized, nor are they tackled by strictly preventive civilian means, as they would be in a clear-cut post-Westphalian security culture.

While a European security and defence culture is not yet a reality, and while national security cultures within Europe remain divergent in certain areas, there is a growing awareness that the EU member states share similar security interests. The sharing of these interests has given rise to the emergence of an embryonic European security culture which coexists in parallel with the national security cultures. This embryonic security culture, enshrined in the logic of the ESS, reflects the civilianized trait of the EU. The strategy discounts the probability of 'large scale aggression' against EU member states, but identifies a specific range of threats that do not necessarily call for large-scale investments in power projection capabilities or the need to acquire them (Solana 2003: 2–5). In fact, the ESS expressed the belief that 'none of these new threats is purely military, nor can any be tackled by purely military means', and that these threats were best addressed with policies of prevention and assurance, both of which rely almost exclusively on the civilian instruments of statecraft (European Commission 2003: 6–7).

With the accent on preventive engagement, the ESS seeks to target the sources of instability in societies and the causes of failed or failing states; it points to a demilitarized conception of security and sees the relative utility of military force as secondary. This demilitarized security strategy also reflects the tenacity of the sovereignty principle in defence affairs. EU prerogatives have always relied on the delegation of member state authority, but the delegation of authority in security matters is generally incomplete, uneven in application and, in many instances, non-binding. Member state contributions to EU security governance consequently vary across the four security dimensions of assurance, prevention, protection and compellence, with greater collective engagement in policies of prevention and assurance. States remain largely unwilling to pool their resources (troops and materials) or authority over the use of military force to pursue policies of compellence (peace-making and peace enforcement). Yet, it is also the case that the ESS has legtimized the use of military force as an instrument for tackling security threats outside EU territory – an option the EU has availed itself of on six occasions between 2003 and 2008. These actions provide evidence of the growing engagement of the EU in security and defence matters, its strength as a collective actor, and its development of a common identity. The commitment to a solidarity clause[8] in the Lisbon Treaty will further elevate the cohesion and strength of EU actions in his field.

Notes

1 For an elaborate treatment of the post-Westphalian concept see Sperling (2008).
2 For an earlier development and application of these four security dimensions see Kirchner (2006) and Kirchner and Sperling (2007).
3 Carl Bildt (2005) makes a similar point when he notes that: 'hard power can certainly bring down regimes, as Iraq demonstrated, but in order to build new regimes, soft power is largely required'. For a more elaborate treatment of the need to create effective civil society structures and state institutions see Paris (2004).
4 The EDF is the main instrument for Community aid going to the ACP countries, but it does not come under the general Community budget, as it is funded by member states, covered by unique financial rules, and managed by a specific committee. The EDF started in 1959, and is presently in its tenth funding period; there was an increase in funds from 13,800 billion Euros for the ninth EDF to 22,682 billion Euros for the tenth.
5 However, the DCI supports the restructuring of sugar production in 18 ACP countries.
6 The EC share to ODA/DAC (in USD) was 7.17 billion in 2003, 8.70 billion in 2004, 10.2 billion in 2006 and 11.7 billion in 2007.
7 A significant proportion is made up of NATO-led operations in Kosovo and Afghanistan, and UN-led peacekeeping operations.
8 The text of this clause reads: 'If a Member State is the victim of armed aggression on its territory, the other Member States shall have towards it an obligation of aid and

assistance by all the means in their power in accordance with Article 51 of the United Nations Charter. This shall not prejudice the specific character of the security and defence policy of certain Member States.' See http://europa.eu/lisbon_treaty/full_text/index_en.htm (accessed 20 May 2009).

References

Ashdown, P. and Robertson, G. (2009) 'The Cold War is over. We must move on, fast', *The Times*, 30 June.

Becher, K. (2004) 'Has-Been, Wannabe, or Leader: Europe's Role in the World after the 2003 European Security Strategy', *European Security*, 13(4): 345–59.

Bildt, C. (2005) 'Europe must keep its soft power', *Financial Times*, 1 June. Available online at: http://www.christusrex.org/www1/news/ft-6-1-05b.html (accessed 28 October 2006).

Commission of the European Communities (2009) 'The Instrument for Stability: Multi-annual Indicative Programme 2009–11', C(2009)2641, Brussels, 8 April. Available online at: http://www.reliefweb.int/rw/RWFiles2009.nsf/FilesByRWDocUnidFilename/SNAA-7TW575-full_report.pdf/$File/full_report.pdf (accessed 24 August 2009).

Council of the European Union (undated) 'ESDP Operations'. Available online at: http://www.consilium.europa.eu/cms3_fo/showPage.asp?id = 1458&lang = EN (accessed 19 January 2009).

Eilstrup-Sangiovanni, E., Verdier, D. and Verdier, M. (2005) 'European Integration as a Solution to War', *European Journal of International Relations*, 11, 99–135.

EUROPA (undated) 'Treaty of Lisbon: Taking Europe into the 21st Century'. Available online at: http://europa.eu/lisbon_treaty/full_text/index_en.htm (accessed 20 May 2009).

European Commission (2001) 'Communication from the Commission on Conflict Prevention', COM(2001)211 final, Brussels, 11 April.

European Council (2001), Laeken European Council, 14 and 15 December 2001, 'Presidency Conclusions' in M. Rutten (ed.) *From Nice to Laeken. European Defence Core Documents, Vol. II, Chaillot Paper*, 47, Paris: Institute for Security Studies.

—— (2003) *A Secure Europe in a Better World: European Security Strategy*. Available online at: http://www.consilium.europa.eu/showPage.asp?id = 266&lang = en&mode = g (accessed 20 May 2009).

European Union External Relations (undated) 'The Common Foreign and Security Policy'. Available online at: http://europa.eu.int/scadplus/leg/en/lvb/r0001.htm (accessed 12 May 2009).

Eurostat Yearbook 2006–2007. Available online at: http://epp.eurostat.ec.europa.eu (accessed 18 January 2010).

Giegerich, B. (2007) 'European Positions and American Responses: ESDP-NATO Compatibility', in Casarini, N. and Musu, C. (eds) *European Foreign Policy in an Evolving International System*, London: Palgrave.

Hanrieder, W.F. (1978) 'Dissolving International Politics', *American Political Science Review*, 4: 1280–81.

Harnisch S. and H. Maull (2001) 'Introduction', in Harnisch, S. and Maull, H. (eds), *Germany as a Civilian Power? The Foreign Policy of the Berlin Republic*, Manchester: Manchester University Press.

Hill, C. and Smith. M. (2005) 'Acting for Europe: Reassessing the European Union's Place in International Relations', in Hill, C. and Smith, M. (eds) *International Relations and the European Union*, Oxford: Oxford University Press, 388–404.

Howorth, J. (2004) 'Discourse, Ideas, and Epistemic Communities in European Security and Defence Policy', *West European Politics*, 27(2), 211–34.

Jepperson, R., Wendt, A. and Katzenstein, P.J. (1996) 'Norms, Identity, Culture and National Security', in Katzenstein, P.J. (ed.) *The Culture of National Security: Norms and Identity in World Politics*, New York: Columbia University Press.

Kirchner, E.J. (2006) 'The Challenge of European Security Governance', *Journal of Common Market Studies*, 44(5): 947–68.

—— (2007) 'Regional and Global Security: Changing Threats and Institutional Responses', in Kirchner, E.J. and Sperling, J. (eds) *Global Security Governance: Competing Perceptions of Security in the 21st Century*, Abingdon, UK: Routledge.

Kirchner, E.J. and Sperling, J. (2007) *EU Security Governance*, Manchester: Manchester University Press.

Laffan, B., O'Donnell, R. and Smith, M. (2000) *Europe's Experimental Union: Rethinking Integration*, London: Routledge.

Meyer, C. (2005) 'Convergence towards a European Strategic Culture? A Constructivist Framework for Explaining Changing European Norms', *European Journal of International Relations*, 11(4): 523–49.

Missiroli, A. (2004) 'The EU and its Changing Neighbourhood: Stabilization, Integration and Partnership', in Dannreuther, R. (ed.) *European Union Foreign and Security Policy: Towards a Neighbourhood Strategy*, London: Routledge.

Nuttal, S. (1992) *European Political Cooperation*, Oxford: Clarendon.

OECD:DAC (2008) *Aid Targets Slipping out of Reach?* Paris: OECD. Available online at: http://www.oecd.org/dataoecd/47/25/41724314.pdf (accessed 22 March 2010).

Office for South East Europe (European Commission/World Bank), (2007) 'Financial Flows to South East Europe', *Continued High Assistance Flows to South East Europe*, 9 June 2005. Available online at: http://www.iucn.org/about/union/secretariat/offices/europe/resources/see_bulletin/ (accessed 24 March 2010).

Paris, R. (2004) *At War's End: Building Peace after Civil Conflict*, Cambridge: Cambridge University Press.

Rosenau, J. (2000) 'Change, Complexity, and Governance in Globalizing Space', in Pierre, J. (ed.) *Debating Governance*, Oxford: Oxford University Press.

Rynning, S. (2003) 'A Fragmented External Role: The EU, Defence Policy and New Atlanticism', in Knodt, M. and Princen, S. (eds) *Understanding the European Union's External Relations*, Abingdon, UK: Routledge.

SIPRI (2008). Available online at: http://conflict.sipri.org/SIPRI_Internet/index.php4 (accessed 8 January 2009).

Smith, M.E. (2003) 'The Framing of European Foreign and Security Policy: Towards a Post-modern Policy Framework?', *Journal of European Public Policy*, 10(4), 556–75.

Solana, Javier (2003) 'A Secure Europe in Better World: European Security Strategy', Brussels: The European Union Institute for Security Studies. Available online at: http://www.iss.europa.eu/uploads/media/solanae.pdf (accessed 3 October 2009).

Sperling, J. (2008) 'State Attributes and System Properties: Security Multilateralism in Central Asia, Southeast Asia, the Atlantic and Europe', in Bourantonis, D., Ifantis, K. and Tsakonas, P. (eds) *Multilateralism and Security Institutions in an Era of Globalization*, Abingdon, UK: Routledge.

Vennesson, P. (2007) 'Europe's Grand Strategy: The Search for a Postmodern Realism', in Casarini, N. and Musu, C. (eds) *European Foreign Policy in an Evolving International System*, London: Palgrave.

Wallersteen, P. and Sollenberg, M. (2001) 'Armed Conflict, 1989–2000', *Journal of Peace Research*, 38(5): 629–44.

Wendt, A. (1994) 'Collective Identity Formation and the International State', *American Political Science Review*, 88(2): 384–96.

Whitman, R. (2006) 'Road Map for a Route March? (De-)civilianizing through the EU's Security Strategy', *European Foreign Affairs Review*, 11(1): 1–15.

Part II
North America

7   Canada
Facing up to regional security challenges

Osvaldo Croci

This chapter examines the evolution of Canadian security policies since the end of the Cold War and assesses the Canadian contribution to global/regional security governance. Following the analytic framework developed by Duffield (1998: 13–39), this chapter considers Canadian national security policy to result from Canadian political elites' perceptions of three major variables: 1) type of international system; 2) national capacity; and 3) national security culture. Its focus is primarily on the role of the last of these variables and more precisely on assessing how changes in security policies might be related to changes in security culture. The chapter is divided into five sections. The first provides an overview of Canada's security culture after the end of the Cold War, identifies Canada's core national security interests and perceived threats and sketches the type of security policy mix one could expect the Canadian government to have adopted on the basis of these variables. The next four sections examine the evolution of Canadian security policies in four functional policy domains: prevention, assurance, protection and compellence. The conclusion evaluates Canada's contribution to global and regional security governance, and advances a hypothesis concerning the relationship between security culture and security choices.

Canadian security culture, interests and perceived threats

Security culture

Security culture consists of four core elements: view of the international environment, national identity, instrumental preferences, and interaction preferences. Canadians view the international political environment basically through 'liberal-internationalist' lenses, i.e. they believe that international peace and order rest more on the active promotion of international rules and institutions than on deterrence or the balance of power. This attitude is evidenced, among other things, by the fact that Canadian elites use the term 'international community' much more often than 'international system'.[1]

The political values Canadians regard as fundamental include an attachment to liberal democracy, respect for the rule of law, defence of human rights and civil liberties, and a belief in pluralism. The latter is understood not simply as the respect

Table 7.1 Canadian security culture

Core elements	Description of core elements
View of the international environment	Basic 'liberal-internationalist' view, i.e. belief that the promotion of international rules and institutions leads to a more orderly and peaceful world (international society)
National identity	Defined primarily in opposition to the US; attachment to pluralism, vocation for mediation and peacekeeping
Instrumental preferences	Preference for soft power and civilian instruments
Interaction preferences	Preference for multilateralism but awareness of the need to maintain good bilateral relations with the US

for, but also as the proud embracing of, diversity and differences as exemplified for instance by the concept of multiculturalism which Canadians regard not simply as a policy but as a key component of their identity. These values are of course common to all liberal democracies, the US included, but Canadians claim that they have 'moulded them into a particular constellation' (Canada 2005a: 4). Such a claim allows Canadians to cast the US as the 'other' against which they define their 'imagined community' (Thompson 2003: 18).

Concerning the instruments to use when acting on the international scene, Canadians privilege the use of soft power. As starkly stated in the 2005 International Policy Statement, 'in no circumstances is violence an acceptable means for seeking to effect political change, either from within or without' (Canada 2005a: 4). Canadians also believe that because of the diversity of their society they have learned how 'to resolve disputes peacefully' through 'effective and principled compromises' and that such experiences 'can be useful for engaging with other societies around the globe' (Canada 2005a: 4). Consequently, they believe that they are eminently suitable to act as international mediators and peacekeepers.

Finally, Canadians prefer to act multilaterally within global or regional international organizations. However, they are also aware that a great deal of attention must be paid to bilateral relations with their southern neighbour on whose market they depend for their prosperity and on whose military capabilities they would have to depend in the event of any serious threat to the North American continent.[2] Table 7.1 provides a brief summary of the core elements of Canadian security culture.

Security interests

Since the end of World War II, Canadian governments have defined Canada's core security interests as: protecting the homeland and providing emergency assistance in the event of natural disasters or other threats to domestic peace; defending the North American continent in cooperation with the US; supporting allies through NATO; and contributing to international security and stability by participating in UN operations. What varied from one government to the other was the relative importance paid to each of those interests and the relative attention paid to security and defence issues in general. Thus, if under Prime Minister Lester Pearson (1963–68) 'contribution to the UN collective security' was Canada's first security priority, under Pierre Trudeau (1968–79) the most important issue became ensuring Canada's status as 'an independent political entity', while international commitments were downgraded to contributing 'to select UN peacekeeping operations'. Under Brian Mulroney (1984–93) new tensions in the Cold War initially led to plans to rebuild Canadian military capacity, which had deteriorated under Trudeau, in order to contribute adequately to collective deterrence of the Soviet Union both through bilateral cooperation with the US and multilateral cooperation through NATO. In the end, however, all came to nought because of the need to reduce budget deficits, which took precedence over defence spending with the end of the Cold War. Under Jean Chrétien (1993–2003), the Canadian government continued with its policy of fiscal austerity and considered – but in the end rejected – the option of steering Canadian Forces away from combat capabilities and turning them into mere providers of peacekeeping and humanitarian aid. The Canadian Forces had to learn how to make do with less and remained a multipurpose force ready to engage also, if necessary, in compellence operations within the multilateral frameworks of the North American Air (later Aerospace) Defence Command (NORAD), NATO and the UN.[3]

The events of 11 September 2001 (9/11) led the Canadian government to change the rank order of Canada's core security interests once more. As described in the 2004 National Security Paper, they now were: 'protecting Canada and Canadians at home and abroad; ensuring Canada [was] not a base for threats to its *allies* [emphasis added]; and contributing to international security' (Canada 2004: 5–6). Indeed, after 9/11, given the widespread perception in the US that Canada was the favourite gateway of terrorists into North America, the Canadian government adopted policies that would reassure the US about the security of its northern border. Not to upset Canadians' sensibilities about national sovereignty, the government chose to refer to its new security measures as meant to reassure not the US but its 'allies' in general. In the same vein, it referred to increased security cooperation with the US as evidence of its 'commitment to North American security', which it defined as 'an important means of enhancing Canadian security' (Canada 2004: 5).

Perceived threats

Until the end of the Cold War, the Soviet Union was perceived as representing the major threat to Canada. With the end of the Cold War, the Canadian government, as mentioned in its 1994 Defence White Paper, felt that 'direct threats to Canada's territory [had] diminished' and that now it had to face primarily indirect threats such as 'regional and ethnic conflict, weapons proliferation, global overpopulation and environmental degradation' (Sokolsky 1995: 9). Interestingly, the Canadian Security Intelligence Service (CSIS) in its annual reports identified terrorism and the proliferation of WMD as the main threats to Canada. The perception that terrorism represented a significant new threat was also reflected in the amount of resources CSIS was devoting to counter it: in 1984, when CSIS was created, the ratio of resources dedicated to counter-terrorism and counter-intelligence functions were 20 to 80 per cent in favour of counter-intelligence; in 1993, this ratio had become 56 to 44 per cent in favour of counter-terrorism (CSIS 1993). In its 1998 report, moreover, CSIS mentioned what it described as a new 'disturbing trend', namely terrorism's new 'religious or messianic' character (CSIS 1998). Briefly, when Islamic terrorists struck the twin towers in New York, CSIS had consistently ranked terrorism as the greatest threat Canada faced for a number of years and continued to do so afterwards (e.g. CSIS 2003). The Canadian government, however, did not publicly focus on terrorism as a serious threat to Canada until the publication of its 2004 National Security Paper. Even then, terrorism was mentioned together with other threats, namely proliferation of WMD, failed and failing states, foreign espionage, natural disasters, critical infrastructure vulnerability, organized crime and pandemics (Canada 2004: 6–8). Additionally, as reflected in its title, *Securing an Open Society*, and clearly stated in the foreword by Prime Minister Paul Martin, the Paper focused the readers' attention not on the government's adopted or intended policies but on the fact that it was addressing the new threats 'in a way that fully reflect[ed] and support[ed] key Canadian values of democracy, human rights, respect for the rule of law and pluralism' (Canada 2004: iii). The Paper seemed to suggest, in other words, that things were done differently in Ottawa than in Washington.

The 2005 International Policy Statement, while admitting that 'the fluid nature of the international security environment ma[de] it difficult to predict the precise threats that [Canada] might face', stated that 'nevertheless, in order to concentrate [its] efforts in areas where Canada c[ould] make a difference, the Government ha[d] decided to focus on failed and failing states' (Canada 2005b: 5). The Statement then proceeded to justify such a choice by arguing that, first, the human suffering generated by the inability of governments 'to provide security and other basic services and to protect essential human rights' is 'an affront to Canadian values'; second, the 'refugee flows' failed states generate 'threaten the stability of their neighbours' and 'plant the seed of threats to regional and global security'; and last, they become 'potential breeding grounds or safe havens for terrorism and organized crime' (Canada 2005b: 5–6). The Statement also suggested that terrorism represents primarily an indirect threat to Canada, i.e. terrorist attacks in other parts of the world could have significant negative consequence on international peace and the international economy (Canada 2005a: 12). The worst scenario identified was 'a major terrorist incident within one of [Canada's] continental partners', which 'could have direct and potentially devastating consequences for the movement of people and commerce within the North American space' (Canada 2005a: 7). Although mentioning 'continental partners', it is obvious that what the Canadian government fears is an attack on US territory and not one in Mexico. Finally, the Statement recognizes the proliferation of WMD as posing another indirect threat by undermining the international arms control regime and hence international order and increasing the chances that some WMD might fall into the hands of terrorist groups (Canada 2005a: 15; see also Canada 2005b: 6). Table 7.2

Table 7.2 Canadian government's threat perceptions after September 11

Type of key threats	Failed and failing states, terrorism, and proliferation of WMD, all conceived primarily as indirect threats
Agency of threats	Terrorist groups taking advantage of failed states and WMD
Target of threats	The economy, civilians and Canadian core values
Source of threats	Wherever failed states are located (Middle East, Asia, Africa)

provides a brief summary of the main post-9/11 threats perceived by the Canadian government.

Which security policies does security culture predict?

If national security culture affects the choice of national security policies, which policies should one expect the Canadian government to have adopted after the end of the Cold War? During the years of bipolar confrontation, the US could but consider Canadian security as its own. Consequently, the Canadian government could take care of its security needs through membership in NATO and bilateral agreements with the US such as NORAD, and concentrate on promoting Canada's image of international mediator and peacekeeper. The end of bipolarity and the consequent relaxation of systemic constraints should have increased Canada's ability to chart its own distinct course on the international scene and concentrate on 'prevention' and 'assurance' policies which call for the use of soft, persuasive instruments for institution-building and conflict resolution. The pursuit of these policies should have acquired even more urgency after 9/11 given that they can be regarded as being at the core of any approach towards failing or failed states and as having therefore also a preventive character with respect to terrorism. Canadian security culture also suggests the eschewing of 'compellence' policies with the exception of participation in multilateral operations with a UN or NATO mandate. Finally, one should also expect the 9/11 events to have led the Canadian government to reinforce existing, as well as adopt new, 'protection' policies, i.e. measures dealing with domestic security.

Policies of prevention

The term 'prevention' denotes policies aimed at preventing conflict by fostering democratization. Consequently, this section analyses Canadian provision of international economic aid, promotion of 'human security' and contributions to electoral observation missions.

Given that a relationship exists between economic development and democratization (e.g. Inglehart and Welzel 2009), 'official development assistance' (ODA), designed to assist in economic development, fosters democratization and hence can be seen as forming the core of 'prevention' policies. The Canadian government has even suggested a link between economic development and security by

Table 7.3 Canadian ODA spending (CAD billions and as a percentage of GNI)

Period	Bilateral	Multilateral	Total	ODA/GNI (%)
1991–95	2.0	1.0	3.0	0.43
1996–2000	1.78	0.85	3.63	0.29
2001–5	2.46	1.04	3.5	0.28
2006	N/A	N/A	4.6	0.3
2007	N/A	N/A	4.1	0.28
2008	N/A	N/A	4.4	0.3

Sources: CIDA 2008: 7; Pistor 2007: 2; Tomlinson 2008

Note: The year refers to the first part of the fiscal year; thus 2006, for instance, refers to the April 2006–March 2007 fiscal year

quoting approvingly from the 2004 report of the UN High Level Panel on Threats, Challenges and Change, that 'development has to be the first line of defence for a collective security system that takes prevention seriously' (quoted in Canada 2005c: 1). Table 7.3 presents Canadian bilateral and multilateral ODA in CAD billions since 1990 and as a percentage of Gross National Income (GNI).

The amount of Canadian ODA delivered bilaterally after 1990 has been about double the amount delivered through multilateral institutions. About three-quarters of Canadian bilateral ODA is channelled though the Canadian International Development Agency (CIDA). Almost all of the balance is disbursed through the Department of Foreign Affairs and International Trade (DFAIT), the Department of Finance (mostly debt relief), and the International Development Research Centre (IDRC), a crown corporation created in 1970 to support research capacities in developing countries.

Canada still falls well below the UN target of 0.7 per cent of GNI set in 1969 by a UN commission chaired by former Canadian Prime Minister Lester B. Pearson. The relatively strong economic growth Canada has experienced since 2000 understates the real increase in Canadian ODA, which has almost doubled since 2004 when compared with the second half of the 1990s. The House of Commons Standing Committee on Foreign Affairs and International Trade has repeatedly called on the government to commit itself to reach the 0.7 per cent target, but this target is unlikely to be met anytime soon.[4] This shortfall probably reflects objective constraints such as the current economic recession as well as the fact that Canadian public support for aid is, as put by Thérien and Lloyd (2000: 29) 'a mile wide [but] an inch deep'. During the period of fiscal austerity in the 1990s, for instance, a large majority of the Canadian public supported the general principle of develop-ment assistance but only a small majority favoured an increase in the aid budget (Tomlin *et al.* 2008: 173; see also Potter 2002).

Another characteristic of Canadian ODA is that it has traditionally been widely dispersed with only a few countries receiving more than CAD 10 million annually.

To strengthen aid effectiveness, in its 2002 Policy Statement, CIDA announced that in the future it would provide aid only to countries with 'a high level of poverty as measured by income per capita and a commitment to development effectiveness' and concentrate it on sectors such as health, especially the fight against HIV/AIDS, basic education, governance, and private sector development (CIDA 2002: 11–12, 6). The countries meeting CIDA's new standards were later identified as Bangladesh, Bolivia, Ethiopia, Ghana, Honduras, Mali, Mozambique, Senegal and Tanzania (Tomlin *et al.* 2008: 196). Six of these nine were countries in Africa, the continent to which the Canadian government had made a special aid pledge at the G8 summit Canada hosted in Kananaskis in 2002. Three years later, however, the government recognized that CIDA's 2002 objectives had yet to be met (Canada 2005c: 6). After 2002 the countries CIDA had identified as priority recipients began to slide down the list of Canadian ODA top recipients to the point that in 2004 and 2005 (the last year for which CIDA's *Statistical Report on ODA* is available) none of them appeared in the top three. The top three recipients of Canadian ODA in those two years, all receiving about CAD 100 million, were instead Afghanistan and Haiti (two countries in which Canada had military forces deployed) as well as Indonesia in 2004 (mostly due to the emergency funds made available for tsunami relief) and Iraq in 2005. The latter received the extraordinary amount of CAD 467 million, most of which, however, consisted of bilateral debt relief.[5] To conclude, it would appear that, at least for the moment, CIDA's objectives have been overtaken by events, as it were. Since 2003, in other words, Canadian ODA has been redirected to countries representing a 'security problem'. This fact provides some evidence, albeit not very strong, that Canadian ODA might be undergoing a 'securitization' process.[6]

At least one of the initiatives the Canadian government has taken under its so-called 'human security agenda' can be regarded as contributing, indirectly at least, to democratization and hence as part of its 'prevention' policies. The Canadian government played a leading role in the convening of the International Commission on Intervention and State Sovereignty. In its 2001 report, *The Responsibility to Protect*, the Commission reworked the concept of state sovereignty to include the responsibility to protect civilians, thereby providing a new legal and ethical basis for 'humanitarian interventions'.[7]

Canada has also taken initiatives that support democratic developments abroad in a more direct manner. Thus, in 1988, the Canadian government set up the International Centre for Human Rights and Democratic Development, later renamed Rights and Democracy (R&D) in 1988. R&D was conceived as 'an independent, free-standing body working closely with Canadian human rights groups and non-governmental organizations' (House of Commons 1987: 30–31) and was located in Montreal as opposed to Ottawa, underscoring its independence from the government. To distinguish R&D from US efforts in the area of democracy promotion (Schmitz 2004: 14–15), the government also took great care to avoid giving the impression that the new agency was designed to export Western values. Thus, R&D claims that its mandate is 'to encourage and support the universal values of human rights and the promotion of democratic institutions and practices around the world' and at the same time it points out that it understands 'human and democratic rights' as those 'defined in the United Nations' International Bill of Human Rights'.[8] R&D's independence, however, has come at a price, namely the relatively small core funding provided by the government, which until 2005 always amounted to slightly less than CAD 5 million. It then increased to CAD 7.37 million in 2006, CAD 8.63 million in 2007 and CAD 9.03 million in 2008.[9] Its pattern of disbursement shows a preference for width over depth: over the ten-year period 1991–2000 the agency disbursed CAD 8.6 million in 337 democratic development projects in almost 50 different countries (Schmitz 2004: 17).

In 2004, the Canadian government established within CIDA the so-called Canada Corps, renamed Office for Democratic Governance (ODG) in October 2006. ODG's aim is 'to promote freedom and democracy, human rights, the rule of law and open and accountable public institutions in developing countries'.[10] One of the main tasks of ODG has been participating in elections-observation missions thus complementing the work of Elections Canada, an independent, non-partisan agency reporting directly to Parliament, which between 1990 and 2004 was involved in over 300 missions to evaluate, assist or observe elections in emerging democracies and developing countries (Schmitz 2004: 24). Since 2004, however, ODG has been more active than Elections Canada and has sent observers to 15 different elections in 13 different countries.[11] Most of these missions have been multilateral. Thus, Canada has contributed a small number of observers (usually fewer than 30) to nine missions of the Organization for Security and Cooperation in Europe (OSCE), all of them in countries of the former Soviet Union plus Serbia, and three missions of the European Union in Aceh (Indonesia), Lebanon and the Democratic Republic of Congo.[12] In at least four cases, however, Canada has played a more central role. Thus, in May 2005, besides contributing ten observers to the EU mission in Lebanon, Canada also sent its own independent mission (11 observers) to oversee the first round of the election in Beirut. In January 2006, it sent its own mission (56 observers) to oversee the West Bank and Gaza legislative elections. Even more importantly, in 2005, Elections Canada took the initiative of establishing the International Mission for Iraqi Elections (IMIE) and the International Mission for Monitoring Haitian Elections (IMMHE). IMIE oversaw the 2005–6 elections for the Transitional National Assembly, provincial governor elections, Constitutional Referendum, and Council of Representative elections while IMMHE, to which Canada contributed 106 observers, oversaw the 2006 local, regional, legislative and presidential elections.

Canada also actively promotes democratic civil-military relations. Most of the work in this field takes place in the erstwhile member states of the defunct Warsaw Pact and the former Soviet Union and is conducted multilaterally through the OSCE. Canada has led or participated in over 300 missions established under the provisions of the 1990 Treaty on Conventional Forces in Europe (Operations Verify and Reduction) and over 90 under the Vienna Document (Operation Question). Some unilateral activities are conducted by Directorate of Military Training Assistance Programme (DMTAP), which offers courses on civil-military relations (the principles and practice of democratic civil control of the military) and peace-support operations training (instructing candidates in the duties of a UN military observer and providing theoretical knowledge of issues surrounding peace-support operations). DMTAP's overall annual budget amounts to approximately CAD 17 million, which also in this case is allocated among a rather high number (68 to be precise) of active MTAP member countries.

Policies of assurance

Some Canadian observers have recently argued that the most recent Canadian governments have betrayed the country's vocation and tradition as global peace-keeper. Steven Staples (2006: 9), for instance, has argued that 'today Canada's total contribution of troops to UN peacekeeping missions could fit on a single school bus: 56 soldiers, out of 66,786 international troops serving in UN peacekeeping operations, which means that Canada now ranks a dismal 52nd out of 97 contrib-uting countries' (see also Charbonneau and Cox 2008; Rudderham 2008). To put Staples' remarks into context a number of observations must be made. Since the end of the Cold War, the term 'peacekeeping' has been used, improperly one should add, to describe a wide range of operations ranging from attempts to prevent or quell civil wars, to combat operations against terrorists and other rogue elements, as well as complex operations designed to build or rebuild civil societies and state apparatuses. More often than not, moreover, these 'peace-support' operations, as they are sometimes and more appropriately called, are authorized under Chapter VII (instead of Chapter VI, as was the case with traditional 'peacekeeping') of the UN charter and imply therefore the use of force. Staples does use the term 'peacekeeping' to describe this wider range of operations, but disregards another characteristic of these operations, namely that an increasing number of them are authorized by international organizations other than the UN, such as the OSCE, the EU, the African Union (AU), NATO, and even the Commonwealth. In some cases, they are even launched upon the initiative of one or more 'willing' states (e.g. IMATT in Sierra Leone established by the UK). Furthermore, even in the case of operations authorized by the UN, an increasing number of them are devolved or contracted out, as it were, to other organizations. The soldiers in the field, in other words, do not wear the blue helmets of the UN but are under the military command of other organizations (e.g. the ISAF in Afghanistan, which is a UN-authorized NATO operation). Staples' computation takes into consideration only Canadian military personnel participating in UN-authorized and UN-led missions. Not surprisingly his conclusions grossly underestimate the Canadian contribution to these types of operations and hence to global security. Figure 7.1 shows the number of Canadian military personnel participating in international operations between 1980 and 2004.

As Figure 7.1 shows, the number of military personnel Canada has contributed to international operations since the end of the Cold War has been higher than the number contributed during the last decade of the Cold War: an average of about 2,700 soldiers deployed at any given time as compared to an average of about 1,100. After the end of the Cold War, however, Canada has ceased to participate

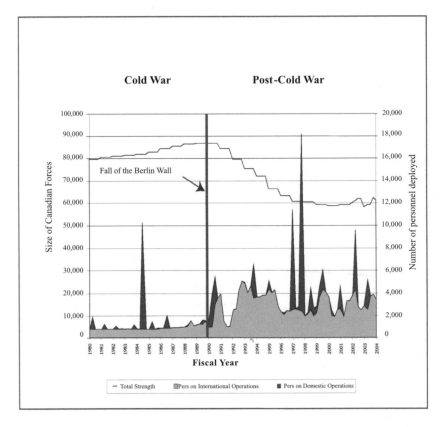

Figure 7.1 Personnel operational tempo to overall strength 1980–2004, increasing demand vs falling capacity

Source: Canada (2005b: 7)

in all UN-led missions and is contributing a relatively small number of personnel to those in which it does participate. In February 2009, for instance, the UN had 16 ongoing missions but Canada was present in only ten of them and was providing only a total of 171 military, police and civilian personnel, more than half of which (98 to be precise) were deployed in Haiti (MINUSTAH).[13] At the same time, however, Canada has participated in almost all non-UN-led missions, including all those led by NATO, and has more often than not contributed a high number of personnel, both military and civilian. Such a shift, however, is neither surprising nor makes Canada an exception among Western countries. During the age of 'traditional peacekeeping' only a few countries (Canada, Ireland, Australia, Sweden, Austria and India in particular) contributed most of the personnel. With the end of the Cold War, the number of troop-contributing countries increased substantially because of the participation of developing countries and the permanent members of the UN Security Council. In January 2006, for instance, there were 107 countries contributing 71,811 military and police personnel to UN-led missions.[14] As a result,

Table 7.4 Incremental cost of Canadian peace-support missions 1989–2009
(CAD millions)

Fiscal year	Europe	Asia	Mid. East	Africa	Americas	Total/Year
1989–90			13.1	9.5		22.6
1990–91		0.1	14.3	0.6	6.4	21.4
1991–92	1.0	3.1	152.4	1.3	1.2	159.0
1992–93	101.0	4.0	25.0	124.5	0.9	255.4
1993–94	166.0	7.0	11.0	44.0	3.0	231.0
1994–95	143.0	1.0	7.0	53.0	7.0	211.0
1995–96	176.0		9.0	13.0	20.0	218.0
1996–97	76.2	0.4	8.4	15.1	47.0	147.1
1997–98	92.7	0.3	12.8		32.5	138.3
1998–99	119.7	0.3	12.8	2.8	13.3	148.9
1999–2000	340.0	33.1	12.0	3.2	1.9	390.2
2000–1	220.0	2.0	15.7	28.5	0.1	266.3
2001–2	169.7	190.8	12.7	18.8		392.0
2002–3	181.3	233.6	9.3	1.4		425.6
2003–4	180.8	625.9	9.5	4.7	9.0	829.9
2004–5	49.4	313.9	4.0	1.2	27.8	396.3
2005–6	22.9	431.3	3.9	52.0	9.0	519.1
2006–7	18.1	813.7	5.9	5.4	0.8	843.9
2007–8	8.6	1,086.0	1.0	25.6	0.6	1,121.80
2008–9	13.1	1,084.0	1.5	52.4	0.7	1,151.70
Total/Region	2,079.50	4,830.50	341.3	457.0	181.2	7,889.50

Sources: Fetterly 2006 and Department of National Defence 2006–9

Note: The figures for 2008–9 are estimates

all Western countries, and not only Canada, are contributing fewer personnel to UN-led missions. In May 2006, for instance, the 26 members of NATO contributed collectively 2,173 military personnel to UN-led missions corresponding to 3.4 per cent of the total (Robinson 2006: 4).

Another way to gauge Canadian contribution to global security governance is to examine how much money Canada spends on peace-support missions. Table 7.4 shows the total incremental costs of Canadian peace-support missions by region since the end of the Cold War.[15]

The incremental cost of Canadian peace-support operations has been almost steadily on the rise since the end of the Cold War, with the major increases occurring during the first Gulf War, NATO's intervention in the Kosovo dispute, and participation in the Operation Enduring Freedom and ISAF missions to Afghanistan.[16] Table 7.4 also shows that Canadian efforts have concentrated, in increasing order of importance, in the Americas (almost all the costs having been incurred in various missions to Haiti), the Middle East (the Gulf War accounting for more than half the incremental costs in this region), Europe (or perhaps more precisely the former Yugoslavia throughout the 1990s and the early 2000s), Africa (especially Somalia in 1992–93 and most recently Sudan) and finally Asia where almost all the money has been spent on the mission to Afghanistan and the contribution to Combined Task Force (CTF) 150.[17] Indeed, Afghanistan has accounted for about 80 per cent of all Canadian incremental costs since 2001. The fact that the non-UN missions have been the most costly is not surprising since such missions have usually included compellence tasks and have involved a higher number of personnel as well as required the use of more sophisticated military hardware.

Critics can certainly question the wisdom of the Canadian decision to devote the greatest bulk of its military and developmental assistance resources to the civil, political and economic reconstruction of Afghanistan but there is no evidence to support the claim that Canada has abandoned peacekeeping, at least when the term is understood in its current as opposed to traditional sense. As Figure 7.1 and Table 7.4 show, since the end of the Cold War Canada has increased – dramatically in terms of incremental costs – its contribution to global security governance through 'peace-support' operations. At the same time, however, it has restricted the geographic scope of its missions for at least two reasons. First, as mentioned, 'peace-support' operations demand a greater number of personnel and are more complex and dangerous than traditional peacekeeping (suffice to say that at the end of August 2009, 127 Canadian soldiers plus one diplomat and two aid workers had been killed in Afghanistan).[18] Second, as shown in Figure 7.1, the Canadian army found itself understaffed precisely when the demand for international operations began to increase. Beginning in 1991, the number of Canadian Forces personnel began to decline steadily from around 80,000 and had reached a low of 60,000 by 1997 where they remained until after 2001. At the same time, the average number of troops deployed in international operations rose from about 1,100 (between 1980 and 1990) to about 2,700, but with peaks of over 4,000. Pressure on the Canadian Forces was further increased by the need to respond to domestic emergencies such as the ice storm that hit Quebec and Ontario in January 1998, which required the deployment of some 18,000 soldiers (Canada 2005b: 7). Faced with an increasing 'operational tempo'[19] and unable to meet fully its commitments to both organizations, the Canadian government chose to give priority to NATO operations over those led by the UN, the latter being well staffed by personnel from developing countries. Both the Canadian mission to Afghanistan and participation in CTF 150 involve close military cooperation with the US and require a capability for participating in medium- to high-intensity combat operations.

Increasing public criticism of Canadian participation in ISAF led the government to establish an Independent Panel in 2007 to make recommendations on Canada's future role in Afghanistan. As expected, the Panel recommended the continuation of the mission, judging it to be in line with Canada's traditional multilateral approach to international security as well as its values. First, Canadian soldiers, diplomats and aid workers are in Afghanistan 'in support of the UN, contributing to the UN's capacity to respond to threats to peace and security and to foster better futures in the world's developing countries'. Second, they are there because 'Afghanistan is chiefly ... a NATO endeavour (26 out of 39 ISAF partners are NATO members)' and 'NATO is the UN's instrument for stabilizing a durable peace in Afghanistan'. Last but not least, they are there to promote and protect 'human security in fragile states' (Independent Panel on Canada's Future in Afghanistan 2008: 20–22). The report carefully avoided stating that Canada is in Afghanistan also to support the US and skirted the fact that a core component of the ISAF missions is to compel the Taleban to stop fighting so that the country can be stabilized and reconstructed. The report also obfuscated the fact that when the Canadian forces redeployed from Kabul in the summer of 2005 to head a Provincial Reconstruction Team (PRT) in Khandahar, this region was far from having been stabilized and was not yet under ISAF jurisdiction (this would only happen a year later), but under the control of US Operation Enduring Freedom (OEF) in which, according to the report, Canada participated only between February and July 2002. The report simply stated, in a rather sibylline way, that 'in 2005 Canada chose, *for whatever reason* [emphasis added], to assume leadership of a PRT in Kandahar City and the security obligations that went with it' (Independent Panel on Canada's Future in Afghanistan 2008: 11, 23). The government has been equally cautious in its public pronouncements concerning Canadian participation in CTF 150. Even if it is undoubtedly a Canadian contribution to global security governance, the Canadian government presents it as little more than a training exercise, emphasizing the fact that participation helps 'keep Canada's navy relevant, responsive, and effective in the new security environment'.[20]

Policies of protection

Protection policies encompass four general issue areas: terrorism, organized crime, health and the environment. The only issue area in which the Canadian government has been particularly active, either by amending existing policies or developing new ones, is that of terrorism.[21] Most of the initiatives, moreover, reflected not so much an increased perception of threat as a heightened perceived need to reassure the US about the security of its northern border in the wake of 9/11.

In December 2001, the Canadian and US governments announced the so-called 'Smart Border' initiative which consisted of a number of measures aimed at enhancing border security (the US concern) while at the same time guaranteeing the quick flow of people and goods (the Canadian objective). Concerning people, the measures included the issuance of travel cards (called NEXUS) aimed at expediting the flow of low-risk travellers, the sharing of basic air passenger information, the adoption of biometric identifiers, the issuance of permanent resident cards to all Canadian landed immigrants, the coordination of visa policy, and the signing of a 'safe third country agreement' with the US to prevent 'asylum shopping', i.e. to oblige refugee claimants to make their claim in the first safe country they reach. Although much criticized, the agreement has had no impact on the number of refugees taken into Canada.

Concerning goods, the main measures were the removal of customs inspection activities away from the border both to improve security and relieve congestion, and the establishment of FAST (Free and Secure Trade), a programme designed to expedite the movement across the border of shipments by low-risk companies.[22] Some of the measures adopted under the 'Smart Border' initiative are jointly managed. Thus, joint units assess information on incoming air passengers, joint customs teams inspect containers at the port of arrival in North America, and Integrated Border Enforcement Teams (IBETs), made up of personnel from different levels of law enforcement agencies from both countries, inspect the border between different ports of entry to interdict trafficking, smuggling, and other criminal activities.

While willing to heighten bilateral cooperation in border security on an *ad hoc* basis, the Canadian government has steered clear of the idea of institutionalizing regional cooperation through the creation of a so-called 'continental security perimeter' which would imply the harmonization of most security policies. The project is supported by business (Coalition for Security and Trade-efficient Borders 2005) but opposed by nationalist intellectual elites, mostly linked to the Canadian Labour Congress, the New Democratic Party and the Liberal Party. They maintain that any form of security integration with the US would undermine Canadian national distinction, or, as argued by one of them, pose an 'explicit threat ... to the expression of distinctive Canadian values on defence, international affairs, and immigration and refugees issues' (Jackson 2003: 26). Under these circumstances, to assuage US security concerns, the Chrétien Liberal government adopted the *ad hoc*, and mainly technical, policies of cooperation contained in the 'Smart Border' initiative, set up a temporary (2002–6) Binational Planning Group tasked with developing detailed bi-national maritime, land and civil support contingency plans in the event of emergency circumstances (e.g. terrorist attacks or natural disasters), but eschewed any permanent, comprehensive plan, perceiving it as politically damaging. Publicly, moreover, the government presented the 'Smart Border' measures, some of which had indeed been in the policy pipeline for a long time, as aimed primarily at facilitating trade rather than being a response to the new security environment. The minority Conservative government that came to power in 2006 has so far stayed clear of the issue of a 'continental security perimeter'.

Canadian governments' reluctance to take steps that could be interpreted as a close alignment with US positions is best evidenced by the Martin Liberal government decision in May 2005 not to take part in the Ballistic Missile Defence Programme (BMDP). Since Canada continues to be a member of NORAD, the main task of which is to detect incoming threats from the north, the decision not to be part of the BMDP results in Canada not participating in decision-making about how to deal with an incoming rogue missile. The decision to stay out of the BMDP does not affect Canadian security except for the fact that it gives responsibility for it fully to the US. Thus, in the name of Canadian sovereignty, the government prefers to be publicly seen as not adhering to a controversial US programme even if the consequences of its decision are the renunciation of a seat at the table and hence the relinquishment of sovereignty.[23]

Another protection policy taken by the Canadian government in the wake of 9/11 was the Anti-Terrorism Act (ATA). Introduced in the House of Commons on 15 October 2001 and proclaimed in force on 24 December the same year, ATA, which the government presented as designed 'to create a balance between the need to protect the security of Canadians and the protection of their rights and freedom', amends the Criminal Code by making it a crime to belong to, fund, or otherwise help a terrorist organization – all activities that take place before a terrorist event can occur.[24] It also provides new investigative tools (mainly easier access to electronic surveillance) to law enforcement and national security agencies, first and foremost CSIS. Investigating possible terrorist threats to Canada and Canadians is the primary, albeit not exclusive, focus of CSIS (2008: 9). As shown in Table 7.5, since 2001 its budget has almost doubled while the number of its employees has increased by 20 per cent, rising from 2,091 to 2,529.[25]

While CSIS's main duty is investigation, 'offensive and defensive measures taken to prevent, deter, pre-empt and respond to terrorism' are the main task of the Canadian Special Operations Forces Command (CANSOFCOM), which was set up in 2006 as part of a restructuring of the Canadian Forces.[26] Not much is known about CANSOFCOM activities at home or abroad but there is no doubt

Table 7.5 Canadian Security Intelligence Services: full-time equivalent employees and financial resources

Year	Employees	Resources (CAD millions)
1998	2,000	171
1999	2,061	179
2000	2,091	196
2001	2,097	248
2002	2,290	256
2003	2,327	268
2004	2,357	278
2005	2,400	349
2006	2,449	356
2007	2,529	389

Source: CSIS 2008: 28, 30

Note: The year refers to the first half of the fiscal year, hence 2007 stands for 2007–8

that terrorism is perceived and treated mainly as an intelligence and policing rather than military problem.

Finally, the Public Safety Act, originally introduced in the House of Commons in November 2001 and passed in May 2004, amended various federal laws to strengthen civil aviation and marine security, as well as to facilitate the sharing of law enforcement and national security information between federal departments and agencies and between Canada and its partners internationally, particularly the US. It should also be noted that the Canadian government has made an effort to rationalize the working of various departments and agencies dealing with security through the creation, in December 2003, of the Department of Public Safety and Emergency Preparedness. Its main responsibility is to provide policy leadership and ensure coordination across all federal departments and agencies responsible for national security and the safety of Canadians.

Policies of compellence

At the beginning of World War II, military historian C.P. Stacey noted that 'Canada's history is marked by an alternation of long periods when the national defences are utterly neglected with short violent interludes, arising out of sudden foreign complications, when the country wakes up to the inadequacy of the defences and tries to make up for earlier inactivity by measures taken in the teeth of the crisis' (Stacey 1940: 53). The post-9/11 period is one of those 'interludes' during which Canada has scrambled to make up for its earlier inactivity. As shown in Table 7.6, after the end of the Cold War, Canadian defence expenditures declined steadily, in real terms by roughly 30 per cent (Canada 2008b: 11). This trend was reversed in 2001 but the increases were minimal and did not affect the percentage of GDP devoted to defence.[27] In 2006, the Liberal government decided to inject CAD 5.3 billion into the defence budget over five years and to increase the budget baseline by CAD 8 billion starting in 2011. Two years later, the Conservative government committed to increase the defence budget by 2 per cent per year starting in 2011 and bring annual expenditures to some CAD 30 billion by 2027. This promise means that Canada will spend a total of about CAD 490 billion over the next 20 years to be allocated as follows: 51 per cent to personnel (up from an average of about 46 per cent in the last two decades since the government plans to increase the number of regular forces to 70,000 and the reserve to 30,000), 12 per cent to equipment, 8 per cent to infrastructure, and 29 per cent to readiness, i.e. spare parts, maintenance and training (Canada 2008b: 4, 12). Some of the new equipment (e.g. four strategic lift aircraft C-17 Globemasters, 17 tactical lift aircraft C-130J Hercules and 16 medium-to-heavy lift helicopters CH-47F Chinook) aims at strengthening the readiness of the Canadian Expeditionary Force Command (CEFCOM) to deploy forces and its ability to sustain operations in the field. CEFCOM was set up in 2006 and given the responsibility of deploying 'task forces around the world to carry out military operations ranging from humanitarian aid through peace support to combat'.[28] The fact that the Canadian government has been busy upgrading its military readiness does not mean that it envisages

Table 7.6 Canadian defence expenditures 1985–2008

Year	Total (CAD millions)	% GDP	Average % GDP
1985	10,332	2.1*	4.5 (3.1)*
1990	13,473	1.8*	3.5 (2.5)*
1995	12,457	1.3*	2.7 (2.1)*
2000	12,314	1.2	2.6 (2.1)
2001	13,191	1.2	2.6 (2.0)
2002	13,379	1.2	2.7 (2.0)
2003	14,064	1.2	2.7 (2.0)
2004	14,951	1.2	2.8 (1.9)
2005	16,001	1.2	2.8 (1.9)
2006	17,066	1.2	2.8 (1.8)
2007	19,255	1.3	2.7 (1.7)
2008	21,026	1.3	2.6 (1.7)

Sources: NATO 1980–2003; NATO 2009

Note: The average refers to all NATO countries while the number in parentheses refers to all NATO countries less Canada and the US, i.e. the European members of NATO. Percentages marked with an asterisk (*) are five-year averages (1985–9, 1990–4 and 1995–9)

an increase in the number or type of compellence interventions it will undertake abroad. All these measures were necessary simply to sustain Canada's current missions.[29] These are likely to continue to be of the same type as those in which Canada has engaged since the end of World War II, i.e. undertaken by coalitions acting with the authorization of multilateral institutions, more precisely the UN as in the Korean war, the Gulf War and Afghanistan, or NATO as in Kosovo. The use of compellence, in other words, is envisaged primarily, if not exclusively, within the context of 'peace-support' operations, as confirmed by the Canadian Forces' recent adoption of new doctrinal concepts such as the 'three-block war' and the 3-D (diplomacy, defence and development) approach. The first refers to the fact that in 'peace-support' operations the military has to be ready to undertake a variety of tasks practically at the same time and in the same place. Thus it might have to protect the delivery of humanitarian aid in one city block, manage stabilization operations in the next block, and fight rogue elements in the third block. The 3-D approach highlights the fact that most 'peace-support' missions call for the coordinated work of the Department of National Defence, the Department of Foreign Affairs and the Canadian International Development Agency because they have three objectives to fulfil: to provide security, rebuild civil and political institutions, and deliver economic aid (Canada 2005b: 8; see also Tomlin *et al.* 2008: 151).

Another area in which Canada has been planning to increase its military presence is the Arctic, allegedly in order to assert its sovereignty. Owing to global warming, the Northwest Passage, which Canada claims to be part of its internal waters but most states regard as an international strait, might soon become accessible to commercial shipping (McRae 2007). Even if a dispute between Canada and Denmark over Hans Island (a barren knoll between Ellesmere Island and Greenland) made the headlines in August 2005, clashes over the Arctic are unlikely. Nobody, after all, challenges Canadian sovereignty over the Arctic Archipelago. Yet, Canada intends to give itself the ability to 'put footprints in the snow' (Humphreys 2004: A1), that is to show that it is present and acts in the Arctic as in the rest of the country. To this end, in 2007, the government announced its intention of building up to eight Arctic offshore patrol ships, scheduled military exercises, and stepped up land patrols in the area. It also launched 'Project Polar Epsilon' (to provide all-weather day and night observation of Canada's Arctic and ocean approaches through information gathered from Canada's RADARSAT-2 satellite) and the 'Northern Watch project' (designed to do the same but through a combination of both surface and underwater sensors collecting data at navigation choke points where marine traffic passes through), as well as a programme to map the Arctic seabed to strengthen Canada's claim to its underwater resources.[30] The military aspects of the Canadian effort to demonstrate its presence in the Arctic are not evidence that Canada envisages the use of compellence policies in this area. The dispute over the state of the Northwest Passage has been pragmatically but adequately addressed through the 1970 'Arctic Waters Pollution Prevention Act', which extended Canadian jurisdiction out to 100 miles from the coast. Although the official purpose of the Act was to prevent pollution, essentially it enabled Canada to assert its authority to control shipping in the Passage. In December 2008, moreover, the Canadian government availed itself of Art. 234 of the 1982 Convention on the Law of the Sea to introduce legislation extending the provisions of the Act from 100 to 200 nautical miles.[31] In line with its security culture, the government intends instead to work with other Arctic stakeholders, within the Arctic Council and other international organizations, to develop an Arctic regime capable of promoting the sustainable development of the region and the security of its aboriginal inhabitants (Canada 2008c).

Conclusion

Canada perceives itself as a post-Westphalian state actively contributing to the construction of a rule-governed international community. Canada's foreign policy actions are, for the most part, perfectly congruent with its self-image and security culture. The country, in other words, plays a constructive and, often, innovative and leading, role within international organizations whether global and general (the UN) or more regional and specific (e.g. NATO or the Arctic Council). Canada, however, is also willing to circumvent such organizations when their functioning hampers the achievement of goals the country deems important (e.g. the unilateral extension of the territorial sea to 12 miles in 1970 and of its economic zone to 200 miles in 1977, or the convening of the anti-personnel landmine conference in

Ottawa in 1996 outside the UN framework). The eagerness to work within multi-lateral fora does not mean, however, that Canada is always able, or even willing, to deliver on the engagements assumed. Domestic political and economic constraints, limited national capacity (both economic and military), as well as unforeseen contingencies, can hamper action. Thus, Canada has never met the UN target for ODA of 0.7 per cent of GNI and has recently redirected the bulk of its ODA from target countries, selected on the basis of need and potential for development, to a small number of countries in which it has made military commitments. Likewise, albeit a signatory of the Kyoto Protocol, Canada has yet to take any action to reduce emissions to the level it agreed, largely because of the opposition of business groups, one provincial government and, more generally, energy concerns. Peace-support operations have acquired more urgency in the wake of 9/11 but Canada has been unable to increase the number of its missions because of limited and, until recently, decreasing military capacity. At the same time, it has redirected its efforts away from UN and towards NATO missions, all of which have a more marked compellence component and are more explicitly linked to international security issues. In conclusion, it can be said that the post-9/11 threat environment has not changed the way Canada thinks and talks of itself – what one could call the rhetoric of national identity and security culture – but has nevertheless obliged the government to alter some of its policies to adjust to the new situation. This has been done underhandedly in order not to give the impression that Canada was acting in unison with the US or, even worse, doing its bidding. Of course, given geographic realities, Canada has little choice but to cooperate in security matters with the US. When international tensions are high, as was the case during the Cold War, Canadian cooperation with the US can also be strategic and long-lived (e.g. NORAD). In general, however, Canadian governments prefer to act in an *ad hoc* manner and are reluctant to enter into permanent and highly institutionalized security arrangements as demonstrated by the refusal to consider a 'continental security perimeter' or participate in the BMDP, even if the latter was simply a logical addition to NORAD. Ironically then, Canadian identity and security culture represent an obstacle to security cooperation – at least on issues that that are politically charged but do not jeopardize the security of the country – precisely where it is most needed, that is, at the regional level. In these cases, reluctance to cooperate simply prevents Canada from having an input in decisions concerning North American defence and thus ends up undermining rather than strengthening Canadian sovereignty. When governments think that cooperation with the US is absolutely necessary, as in wartime or emergencies, they pursue it and deal with the obstacle of security culture semantically, i.e. they underline the aspects of their choices which are consonant with Canadian security culture and obfuscate those that are not.

The Canadian case provides evidence to refine Duffield's framework (1998: 13–39) concerning the relationship between security culture and security policy. Duffield defines security culture as a 'set of ideas relevant to security policy that are widely shared within a society or by its political elites'. Yet, he does not offer any insight into the relationship between society and political elites apart from suggesting that in democracies one can assume that the security culture of society as a whole and that of its political elites cannot be totally at odds with one another, or at least not for very long (Duffield 1998: 22, 34). He admits, moreover, that his framework is better suited to explain security policy 'in times of relative peace rather than wartime or crisis behaviour' and to predict 'general and sustained patterns and trends in national security policy rather than specific decisions and actions' (Duffield 1998: 15). Consequently, 'security culture' might not be as important a variable when it comes to explaining specific security decisions as opposed to long-term trends, especially if such decisions are taken 'as the result of dramatic events' (Duffield 1998: 23). The Canadian case suggests that political elites (the term refers not only to elected politicians but also to civil servants) are responsible for defining security interests, identifying what might threaten them and choosing how to respond to those threats. In a democracy, political elites have to justify, or sell if one prefers, their choices to the electorate. Over time, the justifications offered by political elites for their security choices firm up, as it were, and become 'national security culture' equally shared by elites and the public at large. This is likely to be the case as long as no major changes occur in the international environment. When 'dramatic events' occur, however, political elites, perhaps because of their greater knowledge and expertise, are prompter than the public at large to call into question their cultural predispositions and make changes in national security policy to adjust to the situation. In these cases, the security culture of society as a whole acts as a constraint on the actions of the elites. Such a constraint will not prevent political elites from making choices they consider necessary but will affect the way they justify, or sell, the new policies to the electorate. Elites will emphasize those aspects suggesting continuity and downplay those representing change. It can therefore be concluded that, in the wake of 'dramatic events', national security culture has a lesser impact on the formulation of national security policy than in ordinary times or, to put it differently, changes in national security culture following 'dramatic events' begin at the level of political elites and then, over time, depending on the aftermath of those events and the outcome of the new security policies, either trickle down to society as a whole or fade away.

Notes

1 See Canada (2004; 2005a; 2005b; 2005c).
2 Canada's trade with the US accounts for 53 per cent of Canadian GDP, 80 per cent of Canada's exports and over 50 per cent of its imports. Canada, in return, accounts for 22.2 per cent of US exports and 16.5 per cent of its imports. The US and Canada are each country's preferred destinations for capital: US FDI in Canada was worth more than USD 241 billion (approximately 65 per cent of total FDI), while Canadian FDI in the United States was close to USD 197 billion in 2006 (DFAIT 2009).
3 Tomlin *et al.* (2008: 132–77).
4 In 2002 the Liberal government committed itself to increase the ODA budget by 8 per cent per annum with a view to reaching the 0.7 per cent target by 2010 (Tomlin *et al.* 2008: 175). In its 2008 budget, the current Conservative government promised to increase ODA spending to CAD 5 billion by 2010–11 (Canada 2008a: 22).
5 CIDA (annual). In its budget plan for 2008–9, the government provides increased aid

for reconstruction and development to Afghanistan – increased by CAD 100 million for a total of CAD 280 million – which places Afghanistan at the top of the Canadian ODA recipient list (Canada 2008a: 22).

6　This hypothesis is in part corroborated by the fact that in 2005 the fourth top recipient of Canadian ODA was Pakistan (CAD 88 million), although about half of the amount was humanitarian assistance in response to the October 2005 earthquake.

7　The other two 'human security' initiatives taken by Canada were the key role played in the so-called 'Ottawa process' that led to the Ottawa Treaty on anti-personnel landmines (1997) and the contribution given to the development of the Rome Statute (1998) establishing the International Criminal Court.

8　R&D (undated). The CIDA states that it 'does not seek to export particular Canadian institutions or practices; rather, [it] seeks to work carefully and sensitively with those in developing countries who are best placed to achieve positive change' (CIDA 1996: 4).

9　R&D (undated b).

10　ODG (undated a).

11　The data come from the ODG (undated b) and Elections Canada (undated).

12　The only exception is the 2004 OSCE mission to the Ukraine, which included 463 Canadian observers.

13　See UN (undated) and UN (2009).

14　UN (2006).

15　Incremental cost is defined as 'the cost to the Department of National Defence which is over and above the amount that would have been spent for personnel and equipment if they had not been deployed on the task. It is derived from the "full" cost (not reported in the table) by subtracting wages, equipment depreciation, attrition, and other costs that otherwise would have been spent on exercises or absorbed as part of normal activities' (Fetterly 2006: 53).

16　The decrease in incremental costs in 2004–5 reflects a temporary decrease in the number of troops in Bosnia and Afghanistan needed to give them an operational pause.

17　First created as part of Operation Enduring Freedom, CTF 150 is a multilateral force patrolling the waters from the straits of Hormuz to the Suez Canal to protect commercial ships from pirate attacks. In its first four deployments Canada contributed one warship (about 250 naval and air personnel). In its most recent deployment (April–October 2008), when the CTF was under Canadian command, Canada contributed two warships and a supply refuelling ship (850 naval and air personnel).

18　CBC News (undated).

19　The term 'operational tempo' refers to the number and size as well as length and complexity of missions undertaken by a military force relative to its strength.

20　Department of National Defence (undated a).

21　Besides the activities concerning terrorism there have been only two other protection initiatives worthy of note: the creation in 2004 of the Public Health Agency of Canada in the wake of the 2002–3 SARS near-pandemic scare; and the tabling, in October 2006, of the Clean Air's Act designed to reduce greenhouse emissions levels.

22　More details can be found in DFAIT (2003).

23　For a systematic treatment of this paradox in Canadian-US relations, see Rempel (2006).

24　Department of Justice (2008). The official statement that ATA was designed 'to create a balance between the need to protect the security of Canadians and the protection of their rights and freedom' seems to suggest that such a balance does not exist in similar legislation introduced in the US.

25　It should be pointed out however that CSIS's budget underwent a major decline during the period of fiscal austerity that began in 1994. At its apex, in 1992–3, for instance, it had 2,760 full time employees and a budget of CAD 244 million (CSIS 2002).

26　CANSOFCOM (undated).

27　It should be noted that the Canadian trend was mirrored in virtually all NATO members.

28 CEFCOM (undated). CEFCOM is complemented by the already mentioned CANSOFCOM (active in counter-terrorism operations), Canada Command (responsible for all routine and contingency operations at home and in continental North America), and Canadian Operational Support Command (CANOSCOM), charged with delivering operational support to missions at home and abroad.

29 Because Canada lacked a strategic airlift capability, it joined the NATO consortium (SALIS) that in 2006 chartered six Ukrainian and Russian Antonov An-124-100 strategic airlift aircraft (NATO undated). The need of additional heavy lift helicopters in Afghanistan led Canada to borrow two Mi-17 helicopters from Poland in April 2008 (Chase 2008).

30 Davis (2005). Canada hopes to demonstrate that the so-called Lomonosof Ridge, which extends under the Arctic sea, originates from the Canadian continental shelf. If successful, in accordance with the UN Convention on the Law of the Sea, Canada could extend its jurisdiction beyond the continental shelf to the under-sea ridge itself (McCarthy 2008).

31 Canwest News Service (2008). On Art. 234, see McRae (2007: 9).

References

Canada (2004) Privy Council Office, *Securing an Open Society: Canada's National Security Policy*, Ottawa. Available online at: http://www.pco-bcp.gc.ca/docs/information/publications/natsec-secnat/natsec-secnat-eng.pdf (accessed 18 January 2010).

—— (2005a) *Canada's International Policy Statement. A Role of Pride and Influence in the World: Overview*. Ottawa. Available online at: http://merln.ndu.edu/whitepapers/Canada_2005.pdf (accessed 20 January 2009).

—— (2005b) *Canada's International Policy Statement. A Role of Pride and Influence in the World: Defence*. Ottawa. Available online at: http://merln.ndu.edu/whitepapers/Canada_Defence_2005.pdf (accessed 20 January 2009).

—— (2005c) *Canada's International Policy Statement. A Role of Pride and Influence in the World: Development*. Ottawa. Available online at: http://www.acdi-cida.gc.ca/ips-development (accessed 20 January 2009).

—— (2008a) Department of Finance, *Responsible Leadership, The Budget Plan 2008*, Ottawa, 26 February. Available online at: http://www.budget.gc.ca/2008/pdf/plan-eng.pdf (accessed 18 January 2010).

—— (2008b) National Defence, *Canada First Defence Strategy*. Available online at: http://www.forces.gc.ca/site/focus/first-premier/June18_0910_CFDS_english_low-res.pdf (accessed 15 January 2009).

—— (2008c) Foreign Affairs and International Trade Canada, *The Northern Dimension of Canada's Foreign Policy*. Available online at: http://www.international.gc.ca/polar-polaire/ndfp-vnpe2.aspx (accessed 18 January 2010).

CANSOFCOM (undated) 'CANSOFCOM core tasks'. Available online at: http://www.cansofcom.forces.gc.ca/gi-ig/cct-tbc-eng.asp (accessed 2 September 2009).

Canwest News Service (2008) 'New bill extends Canada's sovereignty in Arctic', December 4. Available online at: http://byers.typepad.com/arctic/2008/12/new-bill-extends-canadas-sovereignty-in-arctic.html#more (accessed 18 January 2010).

CBC News (undated) 'Afghanistan. In the line of duty: Canadian casualties'. Available online at: http://www.cbc.ca/news/background/afghanistan/casualties/list.html (accessed 21 August 2009).

CEFCOM (undated) 'The CEFCOM mission statement'. Available online at: http://www.

comfec-cefcom.forces.gc.ca/pa-ap/about-notre/index-eng.asp (accessed 18 January 2010).

Charbonneau, B. and Cox, W.S. (2008) 'Global Order, US Hegemony and Military Integration: The Canadian-American Defense Relationship', *International Political Sociology*, 2(4): 305–21.

Chase, S. (2008) 'Harper thanks Poles for lending helicopters', *Globe and Mail*, 5 April: A12.

CIDA (annual) *Statistical Report on Official Development Assistance, Fiscal Years 2002–2003, 2003–2004, 2004–2005, 2005–2006*, Gatineau. Available online at: http://www.acdi-cida.gc.ca/CIDAWEB/acdicida.nsf/En/JUD-4128122-G4W (accessed 5 March 2009).

CIDA (2002) *Canada Making a Difference in the World: A Policy Statement on Strengthening Aid Effectiveness*, Hull. Available online at: http://www.acdi-cida.gc.ca/INET/IMAGES. NSF/vLUImages/pdf/$file/SAE-ENG.pdf (accessed 18 January 2010).

—— (1996) *Government of Canada Policy for CIDA on Human Rights, Democratization and Good Governance*, Hull. Available online at: http://www.acdi-cida.gc.ca/inet/images.nsf/vLUImages/HRDG2/$file/HRDG-Policy-e.pdf (accessed 3 February 2009).

Coalition for Security and Trade-efficient Borders (2005) *Rethinking Our Borders: A New North-American Partnership*. Available online at: http://www.cme-mec.ca/pdf/Coalition_Report0705_Final.pdf (accessed 18 January 2010).

CSIS (1993) *Public Report 1993*. Available online at: http://www.csis-scrs.gc.ca/pblctns/nnlrprt/1993/rprt1993-eng.asp (accessed 21 February 2009).

—— (1998) *Public Report 1998*. Available online at: http://www.csis-scrs.gc.ca/pblctns/nnlrprt/1998/rprt1998-eng.asp (accessed 21 February 2009).

—— (2002) *Public Report 2002*. Available online at: http://www.csis-scrs.gc.ca/pblctns/nnlrprt/2002/rprt2002-eng.asp (accessed 21 February 2009).

—— (2003) *Public Report 2003*. Available online at: http://www.csis-scrs.gc.ca/pblctns/nnlrprt/2003/rprt2003-eng.asp (accessed 21 February 2009).

—— 2008) *Public Report 2007–2008*. Available online at: http://www.csis-scrs.gc.ca/pblctns/nnlrprt/2007/PublicReport0708_Eng.pdf (accessed 18 January 2010).

Davis, K. (2005) 'Project Polar Epsilon: Canada's Security and Surveillance Enhancement'. *The Maple Leaf / La feuille d'érable*, 8 (26) (13 July), 7. Available online at http://www.forces.gc.ca/site/Commun/ml-fe/vol_8/vol8_26/826_full.pdf (accessed 27 January 2010).

—— (2008) 'Northern Watch: A Window into Canadian Arctic Surveillance'. Available online at: http://www.drdc-rddc.gc.ca/news-nouvelles/spotlight-pleinfeux/index-eng.asp (accessed 27 January 2010).

Department of Justice (2008) 'The Anti-terrorism Act: Context and Rationale'. Available online at: http://justice.gc.ca/eng/antiter/act-loi/contex.html (accessed 2 September 2009).

DFAIT (Canadian Department of Foreign Affairs and International Trade) (2003) 'The Canada-US Smart Border Declaration. Action Plan for Creating a Secure and Smart Border'. Available online at: http://www.dfait-maeci.gc.ca/anti-terrorism/actionplan-en.asp (accessed 1 September 2009).

—— (2009). Available online at: http://www.canadainternational.gc.ca/washington/commerce_can/trade_partnership-partenariat_commerce.aspx?lang = eng (accessed 20 January 2009).

Department of National Defence (undated) 'Operation Altair'. Available online at: http://www.comfec-cefcom.forces.gc.ca/pa-ap/ops/altair/index-eng.asp (accessed 2 September 2009).

——— (2006–9) *Report on Plans and Priorities, 2006–7*. Available online at: http://www. tbs-sct.gc.ca/rpp/index-eng.asp (accessed 22 January 2009).

Duffield, J.S. (1998) *World Power Forsaken. Political Culture, International Institutions and German Security Policy after Unification*, Stanford: Stanford University Press.

Elections Canada (undated). Available online at: http://www.elections.ca/intro.asp?section = int&document = index&lang = e (accessed 10 March 2009).

Fetterly, R. (2006) 'The cost of peacekeeping: Canada', *The Economics of Peace and Security Journal*, 1(2): 46–53.

House of Commons (1987) Standing Committee on External Affairs and International Trade, *For Whose Benefit?*, Ottawa.

Humphreys, A. (2004) 'Canada's troops to reclaim Arctic: Five-year plan to put footprints in the snow and assert northern sovereignty', *National Post*, 25 March: A1.

Independent Panel on Canada's Future in Afghanistan (2008) *Final Report*, Ottawa: Minister of Public Works and Government Services. Available online at: http://dsp-psd.communication.gc.ca/collection_2008/dfait-maeci/FR5-20-1-2008E.pdf (accessed 18 January 2010).

Inglehart, R. and C. Welzel (2009) 'How Development Leads to Democracy: What We Know about Modernization', *Foreign Affairs*, 88(2): 33–48.

Jackson, A. (2003) 'Why the "Big Idea" Is a Bad Idea', *Policy Options*, 24(4) (April): 26–28.

McCarthy, S. (2008) 'Ottawa plans huge claim to resource-rich Arctic seabed', *Globe and Mail*, 27 May: A4.

McRae, D. (2007) 'Arctic Sovereignty? What Is at Stake?', *Behind the Headlines*, 64(1): 1–23.

NATO (undated) 'Strategic Airlift Interim Solution'. Available online at: http://www.nato. int/cps/en/natolive/topics_50106.htm (accessed 1 March 2009).

——— (1980–2003) Public Diplomacy Division, 'Defence Expenditures of NATO Countries'. Available online at: http://www.nato.int/docu/pr/2003/p03–146e.htm (accessed 27 August 2009).

——— (2009) 'Financial and Economic Data Relating to NATO Defence', PR/CP 009, 19 February. Available online at: http://www.nato.int/docu/pr/2009/p09–009.pdf (accessed 27 August 2009).

ODG (Office for Democratic Governance) (undated a). Available online at: http://www. acdi-cida.gc.ca/CIDAWEB/acdicida.nsf/En/NIC-54102116-JUN (accessed 10 February 2009).

——— (undated b). Available online at: http://www.acdi-cida.gc.ca/CIDAWEB/acdicida.nsf/ En/JUD-41273226-FJT (accessed 10 March 2009).

Pistor, M. (2007) 'Official Development Assistance Spending', Ottawa: Parliamentary Information and Research Services. Available online at: http://www.parl.gc.ca/information/ library/PRBpubs/prb0710-e.pdf (accessed 3 February 2009).

Potter, E. (2002) 'Le Canada et le monde. Continuité et évolution de l'opinion publique au sujet de l'aide, de la sécurité et du commerce international, 1993–2002', *Études internationales*, 33(4): 697–722.

Rempel, R. (2006) *Dreamland: How Canada's Pretend Foreign Policy Has Undermined Sovereignty*, Montréal-Kingston: Breakout Educational Network and School of Policy Studies, Queen's University.

R&D (Rights and Democracy) (undated a). 'Who We Are'. Available online at: http://www. dd-rd.ca/site/who_we_are/index.php?lang = en (accessed 11 March 2009).

——— (undated b) 'Feature Publications'. Available online at: http://www.dd-rd.ca/site/ publications/index.php?subsection = annual&lang = en (accessed 10 February 2009).

Robinson, B. (2006) 'Boots on the Ground: Canadian Military Operations in Afghanistan and UN Peacekeeping Missions', Ottawa: Polaris Institute. Available online at: http://www.polarisinstitute.org/files/Boots%20per%20cent20on%20per%20cent20the%20per%20cent20ground.pdf (accessed 27 January 2010).

Rudderham, M.A. (2008) 'Canada and United Nations Peace Operations', *International Journal*, 63(2): 359–84.

Schmitz, G.J. (2004) 'The Role of International Democracy Promotion in Canada's Foreign Policy', *IRPP Policy Matters*, 5(10). Available online at: http://www.irpp.org/pm/archive/pmvol5no10.pdf (accessed 18 January 2010).

Sokolsky, J.J. (1995) *Canada: Getting It Right This Time. The 1994 Defence White Paper*, Carlisle: US Army War College, Strategic Studies Institute. Available online at: http://www.strategicstudiesinstitute.army.mil/pubs/display.cfm?pubID=43 (accessed 27 January 2010).

Stacey, C.P. (1940) *The Military Problems of Canada: A Survey of Defence Policies and Strategic Conditions Past and Present*. Toronto: The Ryerson Press.

Staples, S. (2006) *Marching Orders. How Canada Abandoned Peacekeeping and Why the UN Needs Us Now More than Ever*, a report commissioned by the Council of Canadians, Ottawa, October. Available online at: http://www.canadians.org/documents/Marching_Orders_06.pdf (accessed 18 January 2010).

Thérien J.-P. and Lloyd, C. (2000) 'Development Assistance on the Brink', *Third World Quarterly*, 21(1): 21–38.

Thompson, J.H. (2003) 'Playing by the New Washington Rules: The US-Canadian Relationship, 1994–2003', *American Review of Canadian Studies*, 33(1): 5–26.

Tomlin, B.W., Hillmer, N. and Hampson, F.O. (2008) *Canada's International Policies: Agendas, Alternatives, and Politics*, Don Mills: Oxford University Press.

Tomlinson, B. (2008) 'Donors Fail to Deliver on Promises Revealed in DAC Preliminary 2007 ODA Numbers', Canada's Coalition to End Global Poverty, Briefing Note. Available online at: http://www.ccic.ca/_files/en/what_we_do_/002_aid_2008-04-4_prelim_dac_oda_numbers.pdf (accessed 27 January 2010).

UN (undated) 'UN Peacekeeping, Current Operations'. Available online at: http://www.un.org/Depts/dpko/dpko/currentops.shtml#africa (accessed 20 May 2009).

—— (2006) 'Ranking of Military and Police Contributions to UN Operations', 31 January. Available online at: http://www.un.org/Depts/dpko/dpko/contributors/2006/jan06_2.pdf (accessed 20 May 2009).

—— (2009) 'UN Mission's Summary detailed by Country', 28 February. Available online at: http://www.un.org/Depts/dpko/dpko/contributors/2009/feb09_3.pdf (accessed 20 May 2009).

8 Mexico
Current and future security challenges

Roberto Dominguez

Historical analysis of the Mexican security culture unveils a country deeply hurt both by the expansion of the US in the nineteenth century and by the rule of its own authoritarian regimes in the second half of the twentieth century (Domínguez and Fernandez de Castro 2001). The combination of these elements delineated a security culture which was permeated by international distrust and domestic intolerance. Although some of those scars remain in the collective memory, the Mexican security culture has undergone a remarkable transformation in the past 20 years. The association with the US is now seen as an opportunity rather than a threat, even as there is a consensus among the elite that democracy strengthens rather than weakens the political system. Nonetheless, the security culture still faces numerous challenges and obstacles, some of which surpass the capacity of the Mexican government to address them suitably and proficiently.

Against this background of steady transformations, this chapter argues that a convergence of domestic and external factors has securitized and desecuritized a range of threats in the past 50 years. Just as in the 1950s opposition groups were viewed as enemies of the state, today that place has been taken by organized crime. The Mexican government has relied upon a variety of instruments to confront existential threats. By applying the security governance framework, the following questions are posed here: What is the nature of the threats Mexico is facing in the twenty-first century? Are the traditional Westphalian security instruments appropriate to the current threats posed to Mexico? Is the Mexican security culture ready to engage in mechanisms of deeper cooperation to make safer both Mexico in particular and North America in general? Working towards answering these questions, the first section of this chapter presents an overview of the main transformations in the security culture in Mexico in the past 50 years. The four subsequent sections examine the policies of assurance, compellence, prevention and protection in Mexico.

Development of the Mexican security culture: trapped in the Westphalian values

The conceptual analysis of the Copenhagen School is useful to explain the evolution of the security culture in Mexico. The transformation of the Mexican security culture over the past five decades reflects a pattern of securitization and desecuritization of threats (Buzan *et al.* 1998; Fierke 2007). This evolution is clearly divided into four periods. The first lasted from the end of World War II to the late 1970s. While economic growth, social peace and stable borders made a national debate on security unnecessary, the government primarily equated the concept of security with control of dissident groups and relied upon intelligence activities and force to do so. Monitoring the activities of opposition leaders and co-optation were strategies of the governmental apparatus to subtly manage political dissidence. Likewise, when the government felt threatened by public demonstrations, military force was used, notably the suppression of student protests in 1968 and 1971.

The second period was initiated in the early 1980s. The historical context facilitated the broadening and externalizing of the concept of security as a result of two main events during this period. The first was a reaction to the Central American conflicts; the other was the discovery of new oil reserves that created in the governing elite the illusion that the time had come to project Mexican power abroad, particularly in Central America. These developments initiated a process of securitization that identified external threats to Mexican security. The Miguel de la Madrid administration (1982–8), for example, attempted to define the concept of national security for the first time in the National Development Plan; the broad and rhetorical official definition included integral elements of national security such as the economic development of the nation, the maintenance of liberty, peace and social justice, and the primary function of the armed forces as guarantors of national security.

The third period, distinguished by the convergence of domestic and external factors which took place in the late 1980s, produced the simultaneous processes of securitization (organized crime) and desecuritization (political opposition). Internally, the political system crumbled in the electoral fraud of 1988. This watershed in Mexican political culture opened a new chapter in the Mexican security culture. Slowly but steadily, a plurality of actors demanded more accountability and transparency from the security forces. Concurrently, the organized crime and drug cartels gradually scaled to the top of the government's security concerns and displaced organized domestic political opposition as the main internal threat to the Mexican state. Externally, the end of the Cold War motivated the Salinas de Gortari administration (1988–94) to negotiate the North American Free Trade Agreement (NAFTA), which was intended to reinforce the opening of the political system and to mark the formal transition of an inward-oriented and protectionist economic model to an outward-oriented open economy. The National Development Plan of the Salinas de Gortari Administration stated that one objective of Mexican security was to act decisively to avoid any action which could threaten national security. Likewise, the same document included drug trafficking as the main threat to security (Bagley and Aguayo 1993: 140–90).

The fourth period started with the inauguration of the Vicente Fox administration (2000–6), the first government from an opposition party in seven decades. The Mexican transition to democracy endowed Fox with unprecedented legitimacy to carry out reform of the state and the national security apparatus. Within the new government, the post of the national security adviser was created, whose main responsibility was to coordinate a long-term perspective on national security, national sovereignty, preservation of the rule of law, and democratic governability. Despite high expectations for real change, the transformations were partial. Unfortunately the Fox administration was unable to inhibit the spread of organized crime, which has since amassed unprecedented power and has become the most important item on the national security agenda under the current administration of President Felipe Calderón (2006–12) (Rodríguez Sumano 2007: 8). Therefore, the challenge for Mexican security in the second decade of the twenty-first century is to map more efficiently the coordination of its security apparatuses and to conceive a long-term plan to address regional security challenges in North America. Today, most of the security challenges such as drug trafficking, migration or environmental degradation are transnational in nature and require regional cooperation. Thus far, regional cooperation remains piecemeal at best and has prevented the development of comprehensive regional strategies to meet these threats.

Policies of assurance

The non-intervention principle has been one of the main pillars of Mexican foreign policy. As an approach, it was seen as quite useful during the decades of Institutionalized Revolutionary Party (PRI) rule in Mexico, because it acted as a shield against criticisms pointing to the absence of democracy within the country. Therefore, Mexico's participation in UN missions in post-conflict areas was not foreseen as part of the national agenda. To date, Mexico's only participation in a post-conflict operation has been with UN Observers Mission in El Salvador (ONUSAL), which was established under Security Council Resolution 693 (1991) on 20 May 1991. While the ONUSAL mission focused on human rights and deployed military and police contingents, the Mexican contribution to the operation was limited to the participation of a small group of police officers.

In 2000, the Fox administration examined the possibility of partaking in UN peacekeeping operations. The initial responses from Congress and the public were negative and reflected the fact that the non-intervention principle remains an essential part of the Mexican security and political cultures. The enduring strength of this principle was further underscored in the way the Mexican government dealt with the 11 September 2001 attacks, the invasion of Iraq, and the more general debate surrounding Mexican participation in peacekeeping operations. While Mexico's then foreign secretary, Jorge Castañeda, defended the right of the US to avenge the 9/11 attacks and believed that Mexico 'should not hold back its support' for the US, the Mexican Congress was fearful that such support – particularly in Iraq – would directly involve Mexico in the war against terrorism (Roett 2005: 156–7). As a result, any debate about peacekeeping operations was peremptorily deleted from the congressional agenda. Mexican society remained divided on this issue; in a 2006 public opinion poll, only 49 per cent of the respondents would have supported Mexican participation (COMEXI 2006: 15).

The Mexican government has limited plans for aiding in foreign economic reconstruction owing to internal economic restrictions of the overall Mexican budget. The last significant contribution took place in the early 1990s, when Mexico made contributions to El Salvador's reconstruction. Since then, the Mexican government has not employed systematic policies in this area. Rather, the government has made symbolic contributions; for instance, after the 2006 war between Israel and Hezbollah, the Mexican government donated an ambulance to the Lebanese Red Cross.

A second area in which the Mexican government has intervened in post-conflict situations with economic or financial aid was in the case of the Guatemalan migration to Southern Mexico in the early 1980s. In this regard, the United Nations High Commissioner for Refugees (UNHCR) opened an office in 1983 to support Mexico's efforts to help thousands of Guatemalan refugees, many of whom became either Mexican citizens or returned to Guatemala. This policy eventually decreased the number of Guatemalan refugees in Mexico from 34,569 in 1996 to 3,229 in 2005 (Echandi 2007). Noticeably, while the vast majority of the original refugee population was from Guatemala, today, the largest number of refugees originates from El Salvador (UNHCR 2008a). In 2008, the Mexican government contributed USD 101,479 to UNHCR. Mexico's funding to UNHCR has remained constant in terms of total contribution (USD 100,000) since 1994, with the exception of 1996 when Mexico contributed USD 200,000 (UNHCR 2008b).

While war has been absent in Central America for more than a decade, the reconstruction and development of the region has been of interest to the Mexican government. Accordingly, the Fox administration laid out a broad vision for the economic and social development of the region and, in 2001, proposed the Puebla-Panama Plan (PPP) for regional development in Southern Mexico and Central America. In 2006, Colombia also joined the Plan (Roett 2005: 166). With regard to the concrete initiatives generated by this programme, during the 2008 Summit of the PPP, the heads of state agreed to create a housing programme for Central America with the aim of building 50,000 houses for USD 33 million (Presidency of the Republic 2008a).

Additionally, the Mexican government also assists with economic reconstruction in areas which have been struck by natural disasters. During 2007, Mexico sent a humanitarian mission and aid amounting to USD 2 million to Bolivia to help it overcome the damage of the March floods. Likewise, Mexico's unprecedented offer of aid in the aftermath of Hurricane Katrina, combined with America's unprecedented acceptance of the aid, brought the first deployment of troops from the Mexican Army into Texas since the US-Mexican War of 1846–8. The disaster aid to victims of Hurricane Katrina included assistance ranging from 195 Army troops to 162 tons of food, clothing and medicine and two ambulances with mobile surgical units (De Córdoba 2005).

Policies of prevention

Mexico was traditionally disinclined to include the spread of democracy as an element of foreign policy owing to its own rigid political system, which was both a corporatist regime in the 1940s and an authoritarian government in the 1980s. During these periods, the US did not pressure Mexico to democratize; it benefited from the stability provided by the PRI's seven-decade rule. Based on declassified US government documents (Doyle 2003),[1] conversations between Presidents Richard Nixon (1969–74) and Luis Echeverría (1970–6) indicate that Mexico was an ally in the Cold War period and it was believed to be advantageous for the US government if it did 'not disturb its neighbor' (Mazza 2001).

However, electoral fraud in 1988 forced the government to create new institutions in order to bring openness to the Mexican political system. Bottom-up actors in the civil society emerged and the government was forced to develop credible institutions that effectively respected its citizens' votes. Two institutions were of paramount importance, namely the Federal Electoral Institute, which was responsible for ensuring the organization, transparency, and legality of elections, and the Electoral Tribunal, which was responsible for resolving election-related conflicts at all municipal, state and Federal levels of government (Chavez 2006: 313). The domestic democratization process in Mexico had an impact on foreign policy as well. This relationship between Mexican foreign policy and democratization can be divided into three phases. The first phase was from the Mexican Revolution until the early 1990s, in which democracy promotion abroad was a rhetorical device overshadowed by the non-intervention principle. The second period is characterized by two main policies of President Ernesto Zedillo's government. Zedillo was actively interested in presenting Mexico as a country on the road to democratization. To do so, he actually criticized Cuba for resisting the democratic tide and developed contacts with Cuban opposition groups. At this time, the Mexican government accepted the inclusion of the democracy clause in the Global Agreement with the European Union (EU), which had aroused a debate in Mexico as a violation of the non-intervention principle in foreign policy.

The third period started immediately after the electoral process in July 2000, when the ruling PRI was defeated in the national elections. The incoming government, led by Vicente Fox, saw itself freed from the burden of a flawed electoral democracy and became more assertive with regard to the role of democracy in foreign policy. The main target of democratization was once again Castro's regime. Several diplomatic disagreements between Mexico and Cuba in 2002 made clear that Cuba had become a liability for Mexico's policy of economic integration with the US. With Soviet support withdrawn, Cuba posed little potential threat to domestic political stability in Mexico. Even Mexican leftists had begun to express cautious disapproval of Castro.

With respect to civil-military relations, Mexico has been the exception in Latin America. For almost a century, the military sector has abided by the rule of law and has complied with civilian power. Nonetheless, the role of the military has varied over time. From the 1920s to the 1940s, the Secretariat of National Defense was the source of presidential leadership, given the historical control exercised by revolutionary generals. Since the 1950s, however, the heads of the executive branch have been civilians and the Secretariat of Interior has replaced the Secretariat of National Defense as both a source of presidential leadership and as a major voice in policy decisions (Ai Camp 2007: 178–79). Unlike the great powers, the military's primary responsibility has focused on domestic national security; the military has acted to maintain electoral peace, settled contentious strikes and, since the late 1980s, carried out anti-narcotics raids and repressed incipient guerrilla movements (Ai Camp 2007: 141).

Since President Fox's administration, the government has given the military a broader role in national security. In 2000, the President appointed a senior military officer to the traditionally civilian post of Attorney General. Likewise, the secretariats of the Army and Navy have brought about structural changes aimed at improving efficiency. As the drug cartels have amassed more power and the government has steadily lost control over public security, the Armed Forces have increased their role in the anti-drug mission (Ai Camp 2007: 144). This later task has been heavily endorsed by public opinion. Within the military sector, however, criticism remains regarding the increased police functions assumed by the military, because it overexposes the Armed Forces – particularly at the lower levels – to powerful temptations of corruption from the drug traffickers.

With regard to forestalling international conflicts via negotiated settlements, Mexico has cautiously promoted negotiated peace settlements in a few cases. Mexico actively participated with the Contadora Group in the mediation of the conflicts in Central America during the 1980s. Then in the 1990s, Mexico was a key player for a peace agreement in El Salvador; it also used its good offices to assist negotiations between the Colombian government and guerrilla groups. In this new century, Mexico has withdrawn itself as a location for peace settlements. Even in the case of the Colombian conflict, for example, Mexico closed down the offices of an insurgent movement in Mexico City.

Unlike the discrete use of diplomacy in conflict prevention, migration is of the utmost relevance for Mexican society. Mexico is as an exporter and transit country for economic migrants. Its geographic proximity to the US labour market has made the US an attractive destination for more than 18 million Mexicans. Likewise, the shared border of 3,200 kilometres is a great attraction for citizens from Central and South America, who use Mexico as a bridge to the American dream. With this in mind, there are three main security-migration complexes that can be identified. The first pertains to the role that Mexican immigrants in the US play in the Mexican economy; the second is the securitization of immigration policies in the US; and the third is the problem of organized crime in Mexico, particularly with regard to transit migrants from Central America.

Mexico is by far the most significant emigration country within the OECD (OECD 2006). Almost 500,000 undocumented Mexicans emigrate to the US every year with most of them crossing the border to seek employment in agriculture and the construction and service industries. The number of Mexican emigrants, as a percentage of the Mexican population, has grown from 4 to 11 per cent between the early 1980s and 2005 (Fitzgerald 2006: 171–91). In response, US local, state and federal governments have launched policy initiatives including the building of higher walls along the border, expanding guest worker programmes, and even deporting undocumented workers (Escobar and Martin 2006: 10). Particularly in

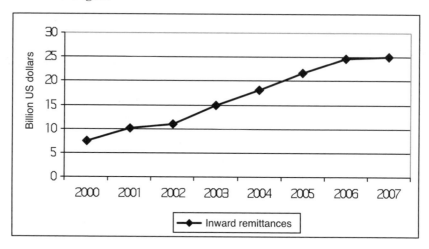

Figure 8.1 Remittances to Mexico
Source: World Bank (2008)

the context of the current recession in the US economy and in the aftermath of the
9/11 attacks, negative views towards immigration have gained greater prominence
in the US.

From the Mexican perspective, the economic impact of a massive deportation
of Mexicans or even higher unemployment rates would reduce the significant
annual remittances to Mexico, which amounted to USD 25 billion in 2007 (see
Figure 8.1). As most of the remittances are used for consumption, the Mexican
government has developed programmes to institutionalize the emigrants' ties to
Mexico. They have organized emigrants to invest in their communities through the
3 for 1 programme, where each dollar invested by a migrant organization locally
is matched by an additional dollar by both the local and federal governments. This
programme has expanded fourfold in the past five years and its procedures have
been modified to allow for more projects.

The second element to consider is the securitization of immigration in the US
agenda. While the prospects of comprehensive migration reform seem unlikely
in the near future, an alternative solution, with the recent construction of a fence
between both countries, attempts to slow undocumented migration. As of December
2008, a pedestrian fence of 370 miles and a vehicle fence of 300 miles were completed along the southwest border of the US (US Department of Homeland Security
2008). The US has also expanded the border patrol from 6,000 officers in 1996 to
18,000 at the time of writing, an increase representing the largest expansion of a
US agency in history. Likewise, in January 2008, Homeland Security Secretary,
Michael Chertoff, stated that, consistent with the recommendations of the 9/11
Commission, the US government would end the process of accepting oral declarations of citizenship at land and sea ports and would begin the process of strictly
regulating the kinds of documents accepted at land and ports of entry (Chertoff
and Mukasey 2008: 1–4).

At the regional level, far from being a solid regional security complex, Canada, Mexico and the US have established the Security and Prosperity Partnership, in order to increase border security. In its first stages, agencies from the three countries are harmonizing risk assessment mechanisms, exchanging information, and establishing protocols to facilitate detection of fraud and smuggling. Under the United States–Mexico Voluntary Repatriation Program, more than 35,000 persons were returned to their home in a secure, legal and humanitarian way in 2006 alone.

The third component is the securitization of migration policies in Mexico. Since 2000, the National Migration Institute (NMI) has been in charge of coordinating the protection of migrants, particularly with the creation of the Beta Groups. These groups attempt to save the lives of migrants in what are seen as 'dangerous zones'. Originally organized to deal with migrants in the northern regions of Mexico, the Beta groups have increased their presence along the southern border and have steadily expanded in size to 16 groups. In 2007, they rescued 6,091 migrants in dangerous situations. It was in this context that the NMI was legally recognized as an institutional body of the Mexican National Security Council in 2005.

While the number of immigrants to Mexico is quite small, the government has developed policies to prevent irregular legal situations with regard to non-citizens residing in Mexico. In 2000, the numbers of immigrants within Mexico accounted for only 0.5 per cent of the country's total population; a large majority of the migrants come from the US (69 per cent), followed by Central America (9 per cent) and South America (5.9 per cent) (United Nations 2006a). In order to prevent an increasing number of illegal residents, the Mexican government has initiated programmes to normalize the immigration process for foreigners living in Mexico. From 2002 to 2007, just under 18,000 foreigners normalized their legal immigration situations in Mexico (Instituto Nacional de Migración 2007: 2–4).

Policies of protection

Protection policies encompass a variety of areas, ranging from health to organized crime, terrorism and environmental degradation. Acts of terrorism in Mexico have been traditionally related to either guerrilla movements or drug-related events. Since 9/11, however, the US has strongly influenced the counter-terrorist initiatives of the Mexican government with its demands to keep the North American region safe.

Mexico's slow reaction to the securitization of terrorism in the US reflects the history of terrorism in Mexico. During the 1970s, guerrilla movements were active and regularly fought with the Mexican government, primarily in the southern mountain region. While in the 1980s these movements remained latent, the 1990s saw isolated terrorist acts carried out by both the Popular Revolution Army and the Revolutionary Army of the Insurgent People. Since the early 2000s, with a rising number of victims from drug-related incidents, Mexican drug trafficking groups have similarly resorted to terrorist activities. Thus, some actions, presumably targeted at other drug trafficking groups, have unfortunately affected innocent citizens. On 15 September 2008, the public was outraged when a drug trafficking group hurled two grenades into a crowd of innocent people on Independence Day in the state of Michoacán. Eight people were killed and more than 100 people were injured.

In order to provide the Mexican government with legal instruments to combat terrorism, Congress has passed several laws. For instance, the Federal Organized Crime Act allows for the interception of private communications, the doubling of pre-trial detention periods, and the infiltration of agents into criminal groups. Likewise, Mexico's Health Act imposes severe penalties on anyone using pathogenic agents without the requisite licenses. In June 2007, President Calderón signed legislation outlawing terrorist-financing and associated money laundering. The new law established international terrorism and terror-financing as serious criminal offences, as called for in UN Security Council Resolution 1373 (2001), and allows for prison sentences up to 40 years (US Department of State 2007a). However, the reforms to the Mexican Penal Code provoked controversies in Congress. While the opposition supported the modifications of financing and money laundering, it was critical of the political pressure applied by the US to make such legal changes. They further argued that the reform of Article 139 of the Federal Penal Code could be used to repress social movements on the grounds of terrorism.[2]

At the international level, the Mexican government sought to link domestic and international counter-terrorist initiatives in May 2007 by establishing the High Level Specialized Committee (HLSC). The aim of this committee is to foster international collaboration in order to deal with terrorism, disarmament and international security. In particular, this committee is in charge of implementing three important UN Security Council Resolutions on terrorism: 1373 (2001), 1540 (2004) and 1624 (2005).

At the regional level, the reordering of the US foreign policy agenda after 9/11 clashed with the chief priorities of the Mexican government, primarily because Mexico maintained a different conceptualization of security. In 2002, Mexico abandoned the Rio Treaty on the grounds that the chief threats to the region were not military, but social and economic. Likewise, Mexico resented Washington's focus on drugs and terrorism, and its refusal to include a new, post-9/11 immigration agreement; to loosen import restrictions on agricultural products; or to legalize the status of the estimated three million undocumented Mexican workers in the US. In October 2003, Mexico's foreign secretary publicly accused the US of seeking to militarize the Organization of American States (OAS) (Taylor 2004: 36–37).

In the area of information-sharing on counter-terrorism, Mexico and the US signed an arrangement for the exchange of terrorist-screening information. Likewise, both governments have agreed to share biometric data, on a case-by-case basis, for comparison in the Integrated Automated Fingerprint Identification system (AIFI). And since mid-2006, there have been negotiations for the installation of specialized equipment as a way to screen cargo containers for nuclear or other radioactive materials.

Contrary to the response to terrorism, Mexico has become assertive in implementing policies and leading initiatives to combat organized crime. Since his inauguration in 2006, President Calderón has emphasized Mexico's need to protect

Table 8.1 Crime statistics for Mexico 1998–2007

	1998	1999	2000	2001	2002	2003	2004	2005	2006	2007
Arrests										
Robbery	57,678	56,388	53,800	58,974	62,504	64,335	72,927	69,929	70,118	73,979
Homicide	6,977	6,554	6,634	6,520	6,662	6,617	6,775	6,815	6,359	6,615
Fraud	5,071	5,303	4,692	4,916	4,789	5,254	5,894	5,207	4,905	4,787
Weapons violations	15,864	15,191	12,616	14,991	15,826	14,657	15,047	15,611	15,189	15,754
Drug-related	10,818	12,298	9,567	11,214	12,064	13,507	13,895	16,095	16,290	16,874
Other*	85,324	89,160	92,236	92,562	101,982	101,912	102,705	100,501	95,579	94,052
Total arrests	**188,698**	**185,684**	**183,977**	**192,614**	**198,777**	**207,247**	**211,650**	**214,153**	**208,369**	**212,051**
Convictions										
Robbery	47,675	48,924	46,321	48,024	48,996	53,181	57,563	59,677	58,822	62,317
Homicide	5,599	5,970	5,979	6,132	6,115	6,259	6,214	6,449	6,230	6,123
Fraud	2,446	2,218	2,146	2,001	1,904	1,971	2,097	2,077	1,972	1,901
Weapons violations	14,639	14,298	12,156	14,454	14,934	15,583	15,528	15,279	14,642	15,310
Drug-related	8,638	8,287	9,567	9,746	9,765	10,601	12,240	12,916	14,437	14,666
Other	65,449	69,608	68,561	74,328	70,551	72,157	72,743	71,722	66,986	63,786
Total convictions	**140,312**	**143,255**	**141,725**	**147,813**	**152,260**	**158,801**	**166,397**	**168,218**	**162,989**	**163,910**

Source: Presidency of the Republic 2008c

Note:
* Includes, *inter alia*, injuries, material damages, rape and dispossession

the rule of law from organized crime. In recent times, the increasing activities of criminal organizations have become a major concern for Mexican society. Under the conditions of recurrent economic crisis and rampant corruption among the police, there has been a rapid increase in the crime rate since the mid-1990s. The number of crimes has increased from 188,696 in 1998 to 212,051 in 2007 (see Table 8.1). However, this number undoubtedly falls short of the actual number of crimes owing to the public's lack of trust in the police and fear of drug traffickers. By 2002, 47 per cent of Mexicans claimed that they lived in an unsafe state; and several protests of more than 250,000 citizens have taken place in silent marches around the capital (Ai Camp 2007: 59).

One crime that has continually outraged the population is kidnapping, which occurs frequently. The precise number of kidnappings is difficult to determine since the majority of them are not reported to the authorities. It is estimated that only 1 in 8 kidnapping victims are business executives or members of the elite, while the rest are ordinary citizens (Ellingwood 2008). On the other hand, crime related to drug trafficking has increased not only in number, but in terms of violence. By June 2007 the number of drug-related deaths had surpassed those in 2006, with 2,100 murders. Concurrently, violence reached peak levels in 2006, when decapitations became common and cartels distributed videos documenting these gruesome deaths as 'narco messages' to threaten rival cartels or government officials. While the majority of violence is between cartels, police officers and journalists have also been targeted. This spillover of violence as well as the pervasive corruption in law enforcement agencies prompted new federal action to reverse both (Hanson 2007).

The comprehensive approach to public security began with the establishment in 1996 of the National Public Security System (NPSS) under the management of the Interior Secretariat. This system pursued better collaborative efforts among police groups. As a result, it raised public security to the status of state policy, and it also for the first time gave the Mexican military a role in decision-making and policy-making in important domestic public security matters (Ai Camp 2007: 141). This system also encompasses the Public Security Secretariat, the National Defence Secretariat, the Navy Secretariat and the Federal Public Attorney. Its budget, which has grown exponentially from USD 200 million in 1997 to USD 2.4 billion in 2008, has tripled per capita expenditures on internal security (see Table 8.2).

In Mexico, the police force has been characterized by a multiplicity of police bodies, the lack of cooperation among them, clashing jurisdictions, and widespread corruption. Several institutional changes have been carried out in response to the growing levels of crime and drug-related violence. While there is no predominant national police force, recent reforms indicate that the actions against organized crime are in the hands of two main police bodies, the Federal Agency of Investigations (FAI) and the Federal Preventive Police (FPP) (Reames 2003: 2–3). The FAI, created in November 2001, replaced the notoriously corrupt Federal Judicial Police. Contrary to the reactive approach of its predecessor, the FAI aims to be a more professional body. As part of the Office of the Federal Attorney General, it performs intelligence-gathering and conducts investigations to combat

Table 8.2 Spending per capita on public security (USD)

1997	1998	1999	2000	2001	2002	2003	2004	2005	2006	2007
38.41	41.79	49.74	54.56	71.42	80.18	86.24	128.69	91.1	99.6	108.52

Source: Center of Research for Development 2008

Table 8.3 Drug trafficking and drug-related crime in Mexico 1997–2007

	2007	2006	2005	2004	2003	2002	2001	2000	1999	1998	1997
Seizures											
Cocaine HCl (MT)	48	21	30	27	21	12	30	18	33	22	34
Cannabis (MT)	2,174	1,849	1,786	2,208	2,248	1,633	1,839	1,619	1,459	1,062	1,038
Opium gum (kg)	292	75	275	464	198	310	516	270	800	150	340
Heroin (kg)	298	351	459	302	306	282	269	268	258	120	115
Methamphetamine (kg)	899	621	979	951	751	457	400	555	358	96	39
Arrests/Detentions											
Nationals	19,120	11,493	19,076	18,763	8,822	6,930	9,784	N/A	10,261	10,034	10,572
Foreigners	264	86	146	180	163	125	189	N/A	203	255	170
Total	19,384	11,579	19,222	18,943	8,985	7,055	9,973	N/A	10,464	10,289	10,742

Source: US Department of State 2007a

crime. Overall, it has seen modest growth in its membership, from 3,583 in 2001 to 5,996 in 2008. The FPP was created in 1999 to prevent and combat crime throughout the country. With an increasing budget, it has combined and reorganized police departments from major agencies, such as those of migration, treasury and highways. Since its creation, the number of members in the FPP has increased from 10,241 in 2001 to 24,478 in 2008 (Presidency of the Republic 2008b: 62).

In October 2008, as a response to increasing crime rates and violence in Mexico, Congress began discussing a reform package on public security, sponsored by President Calderón. The most important reform is set to take place in the National Public Security System which aims to improve coordination between the federal, state and municipal governments, to create a single system of criminal information, and to adopt a system evaluating and certifying the reliability of all the members of the public security institutions. Likewise, there is also an ongoing debate in the Mexican Congress about the creation of the United Forces for Federal Support (CFAF), which would merge the two chief police bodies, the FPP and the FAI. This proposal has found resistance from several sectors of society and within Congress as well. Members of the FAI have even gone as far as to protest publicly on the streets, arguing that their professionalization and working conditions are superior to those of the FPP.

The reforms to improve police force efficiency have been insufficient to combat the power of the drug cartels. The resources in the war against drugs amount to USD 2.5 billion annually and President Calderón has deployed roughly 30,000 troops to work with the federal police in nine states, including Michoacán, Guerrero and the so-called Golden Triangle of Sinaloa, Durango and Chihuahua. These troops destroy drug crops, gather intelligence, conduct raids, interrogate suspects and seize contraband. In 2005, as a result of these actions, the Mexican government had destroyed 85 per cent of the cannabis under cultivation and dismantled some 34 meth labs (up from ten in 2002) (United Nations 2006b). Likewise, the number of seizures and arrests has dramatically increased in the past decade (see Table 8.3).

In order to make the police and military more reliable with regard to drug trafficking, the Mexican government has increased the salaries of the Army by 40.9 per cent and the Navy by 57.5 per cent since 2006 (Presidency of the Republic 2008b). Many cities and states have also announced pay raises for their police forces, amounting to as much as 40 per cent, to dissuade the police from joining the 'narcos'. Likewise, since 2007, the office of Public Security Secretary replaced 284 federal police commanders and ordered federal and state officers to undergo training courses with US, Canadian and European experts (Padgett 2007: 28–31). The ongoing public security campaign has reduced the legal impunity that drug cartels have traditionally enjoyed in Mexico, but it has come at a high cost. Mexico suffered approximately 2,650 drug-related killings in 2007 and 2,120 in 2006.

Despite the high levels of violence, the Mexican public supports the use of the Armed Forces to combat drug cartels. According to a June 2007 poll in the newspaper *Reforma*, 83 per cent of Mexicans back the use of military force (*Reforma* 2007). However, a May 2007 report from the National Human Rights Commission documented serious human rights violations by the Army in the state of Michoacán. Likewise, Jorge Castaneda, a former Mexican Foreign Minister, states that Calderón's plan may ultimately only have the effect of pushing the drug lords to another state and will not necessarily eradicate them.

The US is key to any analysis of Mexico's fight against drug trafficking. About 90 per cent of the cocaine that enters the US is trafficked through Mexico; Mexico is also the US's largest foreign supplier of marijuana. Additionally, a 2007 report indicated that 99 per cent of all methamphetamine produced in the country is exported to the US (United Nations 2008). In this regard, cooperation plays a crucial role, especially in terms of extradition. Mexico has increased the number of drug lords extradited to the US from 68 in 2006 to 98 in 2007 (Thomson and Dombey 2008). On the other hand, Mexico had received USD 40 million annually for anti-drug efforts from the US, a sum far less than the annual USD 600 million received by Colombia (Hanson 2007). However, in light of the growing threat of drug lords, both countries launched the Merida Initiative in 2007; the US has pledged to provide USD 500 million annually – including USD 306 million for counter-narcotics, counter-terrorism and border security; USD 100 million for institution-building and implementing the rule of law; and USD 56 million for public security and law enforcement (Lugar 2007). As a result, in October 2007, the Bush administration asked the US Congress to approve USD 1.4 billion over the next three years to help the Mexican government fight drug traffickers.

In addition to drug trafficking, two more issues are relevant for the regional security agenda. The first is the trafficking of guns into Mexico. Mexican authorities estimate that more than 90 per cent of the weapons that they confiscate were originally purchased in the US. While United States-Mexican cooperation to combat arms sales has improved, gun laws in bordering states like Arizona, New Mexico and Texas do not limit the number of handguns and assault weapons one can purchase, making it easier for weapons to flow south of the American border (Engel 2007).

The second concern is the expansion of Central American gangs into Mexico and the US, particularly the so-called Maras. In 2007 fiscal year, the US Immigration and Customs Enforcement arrested 3,302 gang members and their associates as part of Operation Community Shield (ICE 2008). In the case of Mexico, this has meant the increased presence of soldiers, police officers and naval patrols, and the creation of immigration checkpoints near Mexico's porous southern border. The purpose of increased security at Mexico's border is to prevent the flows of illegal immigrants, drugs and guns entering Mexico from Central America. Following the events of 11 September 2001, the US has increasingly pressured Mexico to act on this front (Roett 2005: 160–61).

Aspects of public health and the environment have been securitized, but in a more limited fashion. Mexico has not securitized the outbreak of natural pandemics but, on a regional level, Mexico, the US and Canada have worked to mitigate the impact of pandemics. The three countries have outlined a collaborative approach in the *North American Plan for Avian and Pandemic Influenza*. At the March 2006 Security and Prosperity Partnership meeting in Cancun, the leaders of the three countries committed their nations to developing a comprehensive, coordinated and science-based approach to prepare for and manage avian and pandemic influenza. This approach is based on four pillars of emergency management: prevention and mitigation, preparedness, response and recovery. Canada, Mexico and the US also established a senior-level Coordinating Body on Avian and Pandemic Influenza to facilitate effective planning and preparedness within North America for a possible outbreak (US Department of State 2007b). In this context, the Mexican government created a laboratory to produce vaccines in the event of emergencies, particularly for influenza and hepatitis A and B. The infrastructure of this programme was developed under the government Biological Laboratories Program in 2007 (Presidency of the Republic 2008b: 329).

Cooperation among the three North American members in this policy area is still at an early stage of development. In November 2007, however, a declaration was signed in order to improve the emergency response and preparedness in health security, border health, pandemic influenza and bioterrorism (US Department of Health and Human Services 2007). Additionally, in order to make consumer goods safer, the US and Mexico signed an agreement to provide advance notifications when consumer goods violate safety standards or pose a danger to consumers. Canada and the US signed a similar agreement in June 2007.

With respect to the environment, the first 2007 *State of the Nation Report* asserts that the environment is a topic of national security owing to the evidence of global warming manifested in droughts, severe storms and hurricanes (Presidency of the Republic 2007). However, the Mexican government has not translated such concerns into concrete policies and those policies in play are still in the early stages of development. One area where the depletion of resources has crystallized the potential for security and diplomatic conflict is water scarcity, particularly in Northern Mexico. Since 1944, the US and Mexico have shared the waters of the Rio Grande and Conchos River under treaty provisions. After two different periods of drought (1988–91 and 1993–97), Mexico began to withhold water deliveries to the US. After a short period of diplomatic disputes, Mexico paid the accumulated water debt to the US (Rosson *et al.* 2003: 3–5). These droughts demonstrated the need to improve irrigation systems in Mexico, but thus far there is no evidence that consistent policies have been implemented to address this potential threat to Mexican–American amity and security cooperation.

Policies of compellence

There is no evidence that Mexico has engaged or ever will engage in military operations abroad. However, under the auspices of the OAS and the UN, Mexico has participated in four peacekeeping operations with civilian staff. The UN missions include the UN Verification Mission in Guatemala in 1994 and the UN operation in Timor Leste during 2005. More recently, operations have also been conducted under the legal authority of the OAS: Mexico participated in the 2004 OAS Special Mission for Strengthening Democracy in Haiti and the Mission to Support the Peace Process in Colombia.

During the period of unbroken PRI governments, Mexico consistently disavowed the use of military force to solve international problems. This resulted in a doctrine in which the Armed Forces focused more on the preservation of internal order (Díez and Nicholls 2006: 32). In the 1990s, in light of the growing threat of drug trafficking, the Armed Forces increased their presence in civil institutions, taking on the traditional responsibilities of law enforcement. Although the Armed Forces focused primarily on domestic security, the external component has been important as well. In 2001, President Fox argued that the 1947 Inter-American Reciprocal Assistance Treaty, also known as the Rio Treaty, had become obsolete with the end of the Cold War, and that his government, after consulting other Latin American nations, would withdraw from it in 2002. Speaking at the OAS on 8 September 2001, President Fox stated that communism was no longer the main threat to the region, and urged the organization to begin working on the development of new regional strategies that would take on 'the threats that stalk us, including extreme poverty, human rights abuses, environmental degradation, and natural disasters' (Roett 2005: 166). However, the effort to bury the Rio Treaty was overshadowed on 11 September 2001, when, as a token of support for the US, the OAS decided to invoke the treaty. Mexico, still part of the Rio Treaty, had no other choice but to support the resolution, although Mexico expressed reservations (Roett 2005: 166–67).

While the hemispheric military doctrines of Mexico and the US have diverged, the bilateral military relationship has been reinforced since 2001. Information-sharing and military cooperation have taken place on different levels, particularly since the revamping of US military structures. Mexico is considered an area of responsibility for the US Northern Command (NORTHCOM). Formed in October 2002 and operational since October 2003, NORTHCOM's international role has been to build and sustain relationships, and to acquire the capabilities necessary to deter, detect, prevent and defeat current emerging threats in all domains (USNORTHCOM 2008). The relationship does not include the stationing of US troops on Mexican soil, the transfer of modern military hardware to Mexico, or the Mexican commitment of troops to Iraq and Afghanistan. However, it has led to the Mexican adoption of US standards and practices in terms of security procedures and to widespread intelligence-sharing (IISS 2008). While military cooperation with the US is quite important, Mexico's diplomatic position on the use of military force remains firmly anchored to the traditional principle of non-intervention. This position was reiterated again in early 2003 when, as a member of the UN Security Council, Mexico refused to support the US initiative to attack Iraq. This decision alienated the Bush White House and forestalled a meaningful bilateral dialogue at the highest level for the remaining term of Fox administration (Roett 2005: 167).[3]

While the armed forces have taken on newer roles, such as combating drug trafficking, this has not led to a significant increase in government on defence spending. Total government expenditure on the military has remained stable for the past two decades, consuming between 0.4 and 0.5 per cent of national GDP. The main variation took place in 1996, when expenditure reached 0.6 per cent of GDP, with the emergence of guerrilla groups in the states of Chiapas and Guerrero (CIA 2008). Mexican military expenditures as a share of GDP are comparable to countries such as the Bahamas, Gambia, Georgia and Laos, but more importantly are in line with the Latin American average of 0.54 per cent of GDP. In order to combat drug cartels, however, the Mexican military has undergone a process of modernization. Despite important investments in new equipment over the past few years, including the procurement of helicopters and light aircraft, the public still believes that the military lacks the necessary resources to combat drug traffickers successfully.

Conclusion

The examination of the Mexican policies of security governance provides the foundation for a comprehensive understanding of the Mexican security culture. The assessment of the security culture reveals a government working emphatically on combating organized crime, a priority captured by the massive allocation of resources to that task. However, the security culture has gradually evolved in the past 20 years by broadening the concept of security, whereby more public policies have included a security component.

Several obstacles have hampered the role of the Mexican state as provider of the collective goal of security. Foremost is the weakness of the Mexican government to effectively implement the rule of law. However, from the perspective of the security governance framework, a deeper obstacle is that most of the officially recognized threats are regional or international in nature. Thus, the four policy domains possess a common feature: each is approached from a Westphalian orientation towards the external environment. In the area of foreign policy, debates are developing over the viability of the non-interference principle given the external and internal security context facing the Mexican government. Nonetheless, Mexico has become more, rather than less, cautious towards participating and implementing international assurance and compellence policies. When issues related to democracy promotion and peacekeeping operations are raised, Mexico relies upon the principle of non-interference and refrains from active participation in several international fora.

Unlike the EU where a post-Westphalian security culture prevails, Mexico is part of the North American region where Westphalian values still dominate. However, increasing levels of cooperation between Mexico and the US have been realized in several areas, particularly combating organized crime, drug trafficking and terrorism. Some initiatives, such as the Security and Prosperity Partnership or the Merida Initiative, suggest a different direction in Mexican security policy: deeper cooperation without the construction of regional institutions of governance. Mexico has thus preserved the key Westphalian preoccupation with national sovereignty. Consequently, levels of cooperation with its neighbours remain low and regional actors to address collective threats are largely absent. This characteristic is most evident where the use of force is an issue; Mexico adamantly defends the non-intervention principle. In other instances, Mexico has modified its Westphalian preoccupation with sovereignty and has opened channels for deeper cooperation, a development that would have been proscribed by the Mexican security culture as recently as a decade ago. This change has occurred in those policy areas where there is a shared understanding of common regional threats, such as the actions of drug trafficking groups. This transformation of Mexico's Westphalian security culture is ongoing. Mexican political elites and publics will continue to reconsider those tenets of the country's security culture that pose a barrier to the safety of its citizens and the stability of the region.

Notes

The author wishes to thank Emil Kirchner, James Sperling, Han Dorussen and Sebastian Harnisch for helpful comments on the previous drafts of this chapter and Apoorva Shridar, Borana Hajnaj and Olympia Banerjee for their assistance in the research.

1 Doyle (2003: 4) argues: 'Echeverría spent much of his time discussing communism's threat to the region. Latin America was in imminent danger, he told Nixon, beset by poverty and unemployment and bombarded by Soviet propaganda touting Fidel Castro's Cuba as the answer to the hemisphere's problems. The solution, he insisted, was private capital. Echeverría urged Nixon to promote American business investments in Mexico and the region.'
2 As of January 2009, it was expected that an amended Article 139 would avert any use of authoritarian measures against social movements.
3 An important turning point came with the November 2003 resignation of the Mexican ambassador to the UN, Adolfo Aguilar Zinser, who, as a defender of Mexico's independent foreign policy, was viewed by the White House as a negative element in the relations between Mexico City and Washington.

References

Ai Camp, R. (2007) *Politics in Mexico: The Democratic Consolidation* (5th edn), Oxford: Oxford University Press.

Bagley, B.M. and Aguayo Quezada, S. (eds) (1993) *México: In Search of Security*, Miami: North-South Center, University of Miami.

Buzan, B., Waever, O. and de Wilde, J. (1998) *Security: A New Framework for Analysis*, Boulder, CO: Lynne Rienner.

Center of Research for Development (2008) *Seguridad Ciudadana, Justicia Penal y Derechos Humanos*. Available online at: http://www.cidac.org/en/index.php (accessed 23 November 2009).

Chavez, A.H. (2006) *Mexico: A Brief History*, Berkeley: University of California Press.

Chertoff, M. and Attorney General Mukasey (2008) *Briefing on Immigration Enforcement and Border Security Efforts*, 22 February.

CIA (Central Intelligence Agency) (2008) 'Mexico: Military'. Updated 20 March 2008. Online. Available online at: https://www.cia.gov/library/publications/the-world-factbook/geos/mx.html (accessed 8 April 2008).

COMEXI (Consejo Mexicano de Asuntos Internacionales) (2006) *Mexico and the World 2006*. Available online at: http://mexicoyelmundo.cide.edu/2006/repmexeng.htm (accessed 21 November 2008).

De Córdoba, J. (2005) 'Mexico's Historic Aid Mission', *Wall Street Journal*, 13 September.

Díez, J. and Nicholls, I. (2006) *The Mexican Armed Forced in Transition*, Washington, DC: Strategic Studies Institute.

Domínguez, J.I. and Fernandez de Castro, R. (2001) *The United States and Mexico: Between Partnership and Conflict*, New York: Routledge.

Doyle, K. (2003) 'The Nixon Tapes: Secret Recordings from the Nixon White House on Luis Echeverría and Much Much More', *The National Security Archive*, 18 August. Available online at: http://www.gwu.edu/~nsrachiv/NSAEBB/NSAEBB95/index2.htm (accessed 3 April 2008).

Echandi, M. (2007) 'Mexico marks 25 years of collaboration with UNHCR', *UNHCR News*. Available online at: http://www.unhcr.org/news/NEWS/4889ec4e4.html (accessed 20 April 2008).

Ellingwood, K. (2008) 'Fear of Kidnappings grips Mexico', *Los Angeles Times*, 1 September.

Engel, E.L. (2007) 'US Security Assistance to Mexico', Hearing before the House Foreign Affairs Committee, United States House of Representatives, 25 October Available online at: http://foreignaffairs.house.gov/hearing_notice.asp?id=915 (accessed 6 April 2008).

Escobar Latapí, A. and Martin, S. (2006) 'Mexico – US Migration Management: A Binational Approach', Research Paper, *Institute for the Study of International Migration*.

Fierke, K. (2007) *Critical Approaches to International Security*, Oxford: Polity Press.

Fitzgerald, D. (2006) 'Mexico', Focus Migration Country Profile 14, Hamburg Institute of International Economics, August.

Hanson, S. (2007) 'Mexico's Drug War', *Backgrounder*, Council of Foreign Relations, 28 June. Available online at: http://www.cfr.org/publication/13689/mexicos_drug_war.html (accessed 3 April 2008).

ICE (US Immigration and Customs Enforcement) (2008) *2007 Annual Report*. Available online at: http://www.ice.gov/about/index.htm (accessed 15 November 2008).

Instituto Nacional de Migración (2007) *Boletín Nº 338/07*, México Df, 27 December.

IISS (International Institute of Strategic Studies) (2008) *The Military Balance 2007*, London.

Lugar, R.G. (2007) 'Combating Drug Trade in Mexico and Central America', Hearing before the Senate Foreign Relations Committee, United States Senate, 15 November.

Mazza, J. (2001) *Don't Disturb the Neighbors: The United States and Democracy in Mexico, 1980–1995*, New York: Routledge.

OECD (Organization of Economic and Cooperation Development) (2006) 'Policy Note, Mexico and International Migration', Directorate for Employment, Labor and Social Affairs, September.

Olson, E.L. (2007) *Six Key Issues in United States Mexico Security Cooperation*, Washington, DC: Wilson Center.

Padgett, T. (2007) 'The War Next Door', *Time*, 170(8), 20 August.

Presidency of the Republic (2007) *Primer Informe de Gobierno*. Available online at: http://www.informe.gob.mx (accessed December 2009).

—— (2008a) *Declaración de Villahermosa. Consolidan Presidentes Proyecto de Integración y Desarrollo de Mesoamérica*, 28 June.

—— (2008b) *Segundo Informe de Gobierno*. Available online at: http://www.informe.gob.mx (accessed 20 November 2008).

—— (2008c) *Second Presidential State of the Nation Report. Statistical Annex*. Available online at: http://segundo.informe.gob.mx/ (accessed 3 March 2009).

Reames, B. (2003) 'Police Forces in Mexico: A Profile', Working Paper Series USMEX, Center for Mexican Studies.

Reforma (2007) *Encuesta Mensual*, Mexico, June. Available online at: http://www.reforma.com/ (accessed 18 September 2008).

Rodríguez Sumano, A. (2007) 'Mexico's Insecurity in North America', *Homeland Security Affairs*, Supplement No. 1.

Roett, R. (2005) 'Mexico and the Western Hemisphere', in Crandall, R., Paz, G. and Roett, R. (eds) *Mexico's Democracy at Work: Political and Economic Dynamics*, Boulder, CO: Lynne Rienner Publishers.

Rosson, C.P., Hobbs, A. and Adcock, F. (2003) 'The US/Mexico Water Dispute: Impacts of Increased Irrigation in Chihuahua, Mexico', paper presented at the Southern Agricultural Economics Association Annual Meeting, Alabama, 1–5 February.

Taylor, P. (ed.) (2004) 'Latin American Security Challenges: A Collaborative Inquiry from North and South', *Naval War College Newport Paper 21*.

Thomson, A. and Dombey, D. (2008) 'Deaths rise as Mexico drug gangs return fire', *Financial Times*, 18 March.

UNHCR (2008a) 'Global Report 2007'. Available online at: http://www.unhcr.org/gr07/index. html (accessed 20 November 2008).

—— (2008b) 'Government of Mexico – UNHCR Donor Profile and Donor History'. Available online at: http://www.unhcr.org/partners/PARTNERS/3b9f631658.html (accessed 20 November 2008).

United Nations (2008) *World Drug Report 2007*. Available online at: http://www.unodc.org/unodc/en/data-and analysis/WDR-2007.html (accessed 30 October 2008).

—— (2006a) 'Presentation of the Report of Mexico to the Committee on the Protection of the Rights of Migrants', 31 October.

—— (2006b) *World Drug Report 2005*. Available online at: http://www.unodc.org/ unodc/en/data-and analysis/WDR 2005.html (accessed 20 October 2008).

US Department of Health and Human Services (2007) *Declaration among the Department of Health and Human Services of the United States of America, the Department of Health of Canada, the Public Agency of Canada, and the Ministry of Health of the United States of Mexico*, Washington, DC, 1 November.

US Department of Homeland Security (2008) 'Southwest Border Fence'. Available online at: http://www.dhs.gov/xprevprot/programs/border-fence-southwest.shtm (accessed 25 July 2008).

US Department of State (2007a) *Country Reports on Terrorism*. Available online at: http://www.state.gov/s/ct/rls/crt/2007 (accessed 10 April 2008).

—— (2007b) 'North American Plan for Avian and Pandemic Influenza'. Available online at: http://www.state.gov/g/avianflu/91242.htm (accessed 7 November 2008).

USNORTHCOM (United States Northern Command) (2008) 'About USNORTHCOM'. Available online at: http://www.northcom.mil/About/index.html (accessed 3 November 2008).

World Bank (2008) *Migration and Remittances Fact Book 2008*, Washington, DC: World Bank, March.

9   United States

A full spectrum contributor to governance?

James Sperling

The American impact on the global and regional systems of security governance would be difficult to overstate. The US remains singular in its possession of a military capable of global power projection and simultaneous multi-theatre combat operations. Its economic capacity and financial resources are similarly unparalleled. Yet the Bush Administration's wars in Afghanistan and Iraq, in combination with the global, economic and financial crises of 2008–9, have progressively reduced American power and influence in the international system, making America more, rather than less, dependent upon cooperation with its allies and competitors to meet the threats and challenges to American security.

It appears increasingly unlikely that the net impact of the American occupation in Iraq will be greater stability in the Persian Gulf region, the elimination of the terrorist threat posed by those aligned with Al-Qaeda, or a more pliable Iran.[1] Many American allies, particularly France and Germany, and domestic opponents, notably the current occupant of the White House, President Barack Obama, viewed the Iraq War as a diversion from the more immediate and important task of defeating Al-Qaeda and the Taliban in Afghanistan. The intramural conflicts between the NATO allies over the relative importance and wisdom of both Operation Iraqi Freedom (OIF) and Operation Enduring Freedom (OEF) engendered a heated transatlantic debate over the relative American and European contributions to global security governance. American recriminations against some European allies over the appropriate policy responses to the global terrorist threat was captured most famously by Robert Kagan's assessment that Americans are from Mars and Europeans from Venus: the US relies upon the 'hard' elements of power to vanquish existential security threats, whereas the Europeans are instead preoccupied with the task of addressing the origins of those threats with the 'soft' elements of power (Kagan 2003). These instrumental preferences were not located in alternative (or even complementary) understandings of the long-term requirements of global order, but instead in the European inability to project military force. This caricature not only grossly underestimates the military role played by Europeans in regional and global governance, but underestimates the American reliance upon the 'soft' elements of power and policies addressing the underlying causes of disorder, including terrorism.

The disjunction between elements of the American security culture, the changing nature of the threat environment, and the increasingly complex requirements of regional and global security governance have produced an American security policy paradox. Although the Bush administration militarized American foreign policy in the aftermath of 11 September 2001 and relied upon a policy rationale that justified American security policy initiatives in language consistent with the Westphalian logic of territorial security ('defence of the homeland'), there was nonetheless a broad spectrum of complementary policy initiatives and objectives that effectively recognized the rising salience of post-Westphalian vulnerabilities for the US, a heavy reliance upon the 'soft' elements of power, and even a belated recognition of the importance of multilateral cooperation. The Obama administration has not deviated significantly from the security policies put in place by his predecessors, particularly with respect to the requirements of internal security or the continuing importance of eradicating safe havens for the Taliban and Al-Qaeda in Afghanistan and Pakistan. The unmistakeable continuity between the instruments and purposes of American security policy surviving the transition from the Bush to Obama administrations raises two important questions: Does the American security culture explain that continuity? Is the United States a full-spectrum contributor to global governance?

The American national security culture

The American security culture has preserved the confluence of security and defence, a confluence made necessary by the exigencies of the Cold War and embraced in the aftermath of September 11. Consequently, the discourse consistent with the American national security culture relies upon the idioms of power and influence, retains the state-centric preoccupations of defence and deterrence, and highlights the importance of the 'hard' elements of power in public justifications of American security policies and expenditures across the security domains of assurance, prevention, protection and compellence. The national security culture has produced a legitimizing discourse that has prevented a conjunction between the threats identified by national foreign policy elites and the policies required to alleviate them.

The American foreign policy elite embraces a worldview conjoining a Kantian optimism about the possibility of perpetual peace and prosperity to a Hobbesian pessimism about human nature and the dynamics of the international system. For any number of plausible reasons – cultural, theological or sociological – Americans require a palpable existential threat to conduct a purposeful security policy; there appear to be no permanent interests independent of the threat posed by a malevolent 'other'. This worldview largely explains the often parochial or even solipsistic definition of interest and unwillingness to treat differences of interest as just that, a difference of interest rather than as evidence of an ally's (or adversary's) moral deficiency or ethical failing. Likewise, placing the US in mortal combat with a well-defined enemy limits the tolerance for an American foreign policy presented in shades of grey rather than in black and white. And despite the subtlety of successive administrations' analyses of the threats posed to the US, this worldview places a cognitive constraint on how security (and threats to security) should be understood and remedied.

The American security culture is essentially Westphalian with respect to identity. The US retains an 'egoist' definition of the national interest supported by the stature of the US as the world's most important country in the second half of the twentieth century and the continual process of renewing what it means to be American internally. Internal fragility and external power reinforce the 'national' in the national interest. Moreover, there has been an historical tendency in the US to conflate the interests of the US with the interests of the world (Carr 1938; Osgood 1952; Hixson 2009). A critical part of the American identity is the continual process of identifying or creating an 'other' against which the US defines itself: fascism and communism in the twentieth century; and an 'Islamic' one after September 11.[2] That process of identity formation, however, also required a countervailing strategy of creating a 'we' possessing a common interest in order to meet common threats. This partial denationalization of the American identity has found fullest expression in the notion of the 'transatlantic community' concretized with the NATO alliance.

The US has increasingly relied upon the exercise of 'soft power' to ameliorate the underlying sources of threat between 1990 and 2010, particularly those targeting the 'domestic homeland'. An increasingly larger share of the federal budget was dedicated to policy initiatives enhancing the capabilities of American law enforcement to monitor and prevent terrorist activity. Additional attention and budgetary resources were devoted to understanding and addressing the underlying sources of conflict and instability in regions breeding terrorism. Although each administration recognized that, after 1989, many of the threats to American security could not be adequately remedied or deterred by military force alone, each administration nonetheless placed a relatively greater emphasis on the military rather than the economic or diplomatic elements of power. This development reflected the importance of military power in ending the civil wars in the former Yugoslavia and the profound trauma of September 11 that effectively remilitarized American foreign policy. As non-state actors increasingly exploited the vulnerabilities of American society, an increased reliance was placed on the police powers of the state internally. Yet the military idiom remained paramount in defining the responses to external threats, state and non-state alike.

Multilateralism has been the rhetorical foundation of the American foreign and security policy agenda since the end of World War II. In the aftermath of that war, the US was a key sponsor of the institutionalized multilateral frameworks that have supported global or regional systems of collective security (the UN, NATO and OSCE) and economic order (notably, the Bretton Woods institutions). The US is a relatively dependable multilateral actor in the domain of foreign economic policy, behaviour no doubt driven in large part by material interests. But the US has approached macroeconomic crises, particularly, as presenting a collective threat to global economic stability and welfare that require a multilateral solution. American behaviour in the security realm, however, has not been reflexively or even dependably multilateral. Many of America's security relations take place within an exclusively bilateral framework (China, Israel, Japan) or are bilateralized within a multilateral framework (e.g. with the UK or Germany in NATO, the Russian Federation in the NATO-Russia Council). NATO and ANZUS have represented the multilateral exception rather than rule for American security policy; there has been a marked tendency to 'go it alone' when allied cooperation has not been forthcoming or America finds itself isolated diplomatically. More generally, the American preference for multilateral, bilateral or unilateral responses to international crises or challenges varies from administration to administration and issue area to issue area, although the American penchant for unilateralism found its most extreme post-Cold War expression in the Bush administration's policy of seeking 'coalitions of the willing' and purposely eschewing NATO, notably in Afghanistan.[3]

The US security culture is animated by a Westphalian discourse, although its content shares some post-Westphalian elements (see Table 9.1). What kinds of security policies should this security culture produce? The three hypotheses presented in the Introduction to this volume address three interrelated issues: the process of securitization and instrumental preferences; the impact of a security culture on the mitigation or exacerbation of collective action problems; and the range of security governance systems consistent with the national security culture. Consistent with the structural characteristics of the American state, particularly its perforated sovereignty and difficulty of acting as an effective gatekeeper between internal and external flows, we should expect the United States to have securitized issues heretofore placed in the domain of 'domestic' welfare or 'international development'. This process of securitization, however, has been justified and elaborated within a Westphalian discourse. The US has similarly understood that the new threat agenda requires collective action, but the persistence of a national rather than collective definition of interest (and identity) should limit or make conditional multilateral responses to security threats, even when acknowledged rhetorically as common or collective. The structural role of the US as the guarantor of global order requires

Table 9.1 US national security culture

Worldview of external environment	Paradox of Kantian optimism combined with Hobbesian expectations. See world as hostile and threatening. Threats are always existential and ideological: fascism, communism, 'radical Islam'. Or threat posed by a great power with interests inimical to the US (Soviet Union prior to 1989 and China since then). US requires a hostile 'other' to frame its understanding of the external world
National identity	National and parochial; yet some sense of 'community' within transatlantic area
Instrumental preferences	US administrations have relied on military as well as civilian instruments. There is an embedded assumption that military instruments are the most efficacious and appropriate
Interaction preferences	Interaction pattern dependent upon the threat faced. There has been a willingness to avoid institutionalized multilateral frameworks and operate either unilaterally or in *ad hoc* coalitions of the willing which allow the US greatest freedom of action

its participation in a broad range of security governance systems, ranging from a balance of power in the Asia-Pacific to the fused security community found in the European Union.[4] The explanatory power of the American national security culture is limited owing to the unavoidable global engagement of the US: there can be no *a priori* preference for one security governance system over another. But the American security culture does suggest an elective affinity for concerts among regional or great powers which squares the American preference for maintaining the greatest possible degree of freedom in the execution of its foreign policy and the recognition that some security challenges require a multilateral solution.

Threats to American security, 1990–2009

The George H.W. Bush administration's final *National Security Strategy* (NSS) (1993) identified four major threats to the US: nuclear proliferation stemming from unsecured nuclear materials in the former Soviet Union (FSU), particularly in Ukraine and Kazakhstan; a generic concern with terrorism; the nexus between narcotics and transnational organized crime; and an undefined challenge to American military-strategic dominance. The Clinton administration published two NSSs, the first in 1995 and the second in 1999 (White House 1995, 1999). Each identified a relatively stable set of security threats: the Iranian, Iraqi, North Korean or another rogue state's acquisition of nuclear weapons; the proliferation threat of unsecured nuclear materials and sites in the Russian Federation; missile technology proliferation, particularly its acquisition by Iran and North Korea; terrorism, including specific references to Al-Qaeda and Osama bin Laden. In the 1999 NSS, the Clinton administration directed attention towards a number of non-traditional security threats: cyber-vandalism and information warfare; the proliferation of dangerous technologies; environmental degradation (irreparable damage to regional ecosystems); public health (epidemics); and narcotics trafficking (White House 1999; Oakley 1998).

President George W. Bush issued his first NSS in 2002 and his second in 2006 (White House 2002a, 2006). Both documents focused upon Islamic terrorist groups and their acquisition of chemical, biological, radiological and nuclear (CBRN) devices and upon the acquisition of nuclear, biological and chemical (NBC) weapons by Iran, Iraq and North Korea, the so-called 'Axis of Evil'. While many of these concerns can be traced back to the Clinton administration, the 2002 NSS was clearly preoccupied with the threat posed by 'radical Islam', which eventually mutated into a Sunni jihadist or extremist movement (Tenet 2004; Loy 2005). The decision to evict the Taliban from Afghanistan and remove Saddam Hussein from power in Iraq militarized the terrorist threat and American foreign policy more generally. The 2006 NSS, which described the 'War on Terror' as a fight 'against terrorists and against their murderous ideology' (White House 2006: 1), adopted and then modified the Cold War syllogism once applied to communism: democracy was 'the opposite of terrorist tyranny' and terrorism anywhere threatened it everywhere (White House 2006: 11).

During his campaign for the presidency, Barack Obama promised a renewed

American multilateralism, a timely end to the American occupation in Iraq, and a redirected focus on the insurgency in Afghanistan that had spread into western Pakistan. Yet in the first months of his administration, the domestic and foreign policy agendas were dominated by the fall-out and response to the global macroeconomic and financial crisis and his desire to reform of the American health system. The administration has not yet produced a comprehensive statement on national security policy in the form of a NSS, but various policy statements and initiatives suggest that the Obama administration has identified four major sources of security threat to the US: nuclear proliferation (White House 2009a); inadequate cyber-security (White House 2009b); political-military failure in Afghanistan and Pakistan (White House 2009c); and the porousness of the Mexican-American border (White House 2009d).

The August 2009 *National Intelligence Strategy* (NIS) is the Obama administration's first comprehensive foreign and security policy statement. In the NIS, the administration identified four states posing a present or putative threat to US security: Iran, North Korea, China and the Russian Federation. And it identified three categories of non-state actors: violent extremist groups, insurgents and transnational criminal organizations. What is remarkable about this classification of non-state actors is the substitution of 'violent extremist groups' for 'terrorist groups' found in earlier NSSs, but also a sharp distinction between those groups and insurgents, and between insurgents (particularly in Afghanistan and Pakistan) that share or are indifferent to the Al-Qaeda agenda. The NIS also identified the administration's four key security tasks as combating 'violent extremism', countering WMD proliferation, enhancing cyber-security, and continuing current combat operations in Iraq, Afghanistan and Pakistan (White House 2009a: 6–10).

There has been a remarkable degree of continuity in the definition and agents of threat between 1990 and 2009, despite marked differences in ideological orientation or presidential attitude towards the nature of America's engagement in the outside world. The Bush and Clinton administrations were preoccupied with managing the aftermath of the end of the Cold War. Both administrations relied upon a twin strategy of integrating those erstwhile European adversaries into the transatlantic system of security governance and ensuring that the Western forms of economic and political governance flourished in Central and Eastern Europe as well as the republics of the former Soviet Union. This aspiration was conjoined to a fear that China would emerge as a peer competitor, a renascent Russian Federation could still emerge as a geopolitical adversary in Central Asia, the proliferation of WMD would be unstoppable, and terrorism would pose an intractable threat to American society and physical infrastructure. The post-September 11 environment did not eliminate those concerns, but they were eclipsed by the 'war against terrorism' carried over into the Obama administration, albeit under a different name and with a new emphasis on the nature and objectives of effective counter-insurgency warfare (Obama 2009a; White House 2009c; ISAF 2009). These security concerns have been addressed across the four policy domains of security governance – assurance, prevention, protection and compellence – and have drawn upon the full spectrum of policy instruments.

Policies of assurance

The US has made major investments in post-conflict economic and political stabilization in states and regions where it has been a direct (Iraq and Afghanistan) or indirect (the Balkans) participant to the conflict. After 2001, the vast majority of US expenditures on post-conflict stabilization programmes have demonstrated a fidelity to former Secretary of State Colin Powell's aphorism, 'Once you break it, you are going to own it', more commonly referred to as the 'Pottery Barn rule' (Powell 2007; Woodward 2004: 50). The State Department's international affairs budget, financial and personnel commitments to UN and OSCE missions, and contributions to multilateral trust funds dedicated to the task of post-conflict stabilization capture the general thrust of American contributions to post-conflict stabilization. The ongoing stabilization efforts in Iraq and Afghanistan, however, provide a more focused basis for assessing the American contribution to post-conflict stabilization. Two dimensions of these efforts are relevant for assessing the nature of American assurance policies: the absolute and relative resource shares dedicated to post-conflict stabilization; and the balance between bilateralism and multilateralism.

Global assurance

The US contributes to global assurance in two respects: first, a significant share of the US State Department's international affairs budget is dedicated to the task of post-conflict stabilization; and second, the US is a major contributor to the two major international organizations responsible for post-conflict states and regions, the UN and OSCE. Approximately USD 30.19 billion (or 19 per cent) of the international affairs budget has been devoted the task of post-conflict stabilization between 2001 and 2010. The major categories of expenditure have been peace-keeping (USD 16.52 billion), migration and refugee assistance (USD 10.43 billion) and aid to the post-conflict states of the Balkans (USD 2.46 billion). Of the SEED (Support for East European Democracy) funds distributed to the republics of the former Yugoslavia, USD 4.12 billion (or 64 per cent of the total SEED budget) went to the four post-conflict states: Bosnia-Herzegovina, Croatia, Kosovo and Serbia (see Table 9.2).

Since 2001, the US has played an important role in OSCE post-conflict stabilization missions. It has met its financial obligations to the organization (standard scale assessment of 11.5 per cent of OSCE budget and 14 per cent of OSCE budget for large-scale operations).[5] The US has contributed 12.5 per cent of the personnel to the post-2001 OSCE missions, ranging from a high of almost 18 per cent (Mission to Serbia and Montenegro) to providing no personnel at all (Assistance Group in Chechnya) (OSCE 2008a, 2008b). The American contribution to the UN is much more problematic and difficult to assess. The US ranks 70th in the number of personnel provided for UN peacekeeping missions (UN 2009c); the US share of personnel has steadily declined from an already anaemic 2.28 per cent in 2001 to a negligible 0.34 per cent in 2008. Yet, US personnel are currently participating in six of the 19 current UN peacekeeping missions and have participated in 15

Table 9.2 Assurance programmes, International Affairs budget 2001–10 (USD millions)

	2001	2002	2003	2004	2005	2006	2007	2008	2009ᵉ	2010ʳ	Total	Share (%)
SEED Act (post-conflict Europe)*	448	332	242	237	208	197	194	216	197	190	2,461	8.15
Peace-keeping operations	127	375	214	124	548	173	223	261	395	296	2,736	9.06
UN peacekeeping	846	825	636	795	1,258	1,152	1,447	2,064	2,504	2,260	13,787	45.67
Migration and refugee assistance	704	820	888	811	914	813	888	1,414	1,618	1,555	10,425	34.53
Demining	40	43	49	49	59	55	51	67	75	74	562	1.86
Small arms destruction	2	3	3	3	7	9	16	45	47	82	217	0.72
Total	2,167	2,398	2,032	2,019	2,994	2,399	2,819	4,067	4,836	4,457	30,188	

Source: US Department of State (annual)

Notes:
* Bosnia-Herzegovina, Croatia, Kosovo, Serbia
ᵉ Estimate
ʳ Request

Table 9.3 Contributions and arrears to UN 2001–8 (%)

	Peacekeeping contributions		Peacekeeping arrears		Regular budget arrears	
	Personnel	Financial	Arrears	Assessment	Arrears	Assessment
2001	2.28	49.19	46.75	28.13	69	22
2002	1.63	29.39	50.09	27.35	62	22
2003	1.55	23.91	63.93	26.93	61	22
2004	1.00	31.82	34.02	26.69	68	22
2005	0.66	24.51	34.39	26.49	76	22
2006	0.52	16.99	43.94	26.69	80	22
2007	0.37	22.22	47.61	26.08	92	22
2008	0.34	16.52	34.71	25.96	92	22

Sources: Browne 2006; Schaefer 2007; Global Policy Forum 2009; UN General Assembly 2008; UNDPKO 2009a, 2009b

of 22 peacekeeping missions between 2001 and 2009. Of the three categories of participants in any UN mission – police, military observers and troops—the US has favoured sending police (ranging from 277 to 844), then military observers (ranging from 235 to 26 over the same period) and, lastly, troops (no more than ten to any single mission) over the period under consideration. The US progressively shirked its financial responsibilities to the UN between 2001 and 2008: at the beginning of the period the US covered approximately 49 per cent of the costs of peacekeeping missions, but by 2008 the US share had declined to 16.5 per cent of the total cost. This contribution fell short not only of the UN assessment (28.31 per cent to 25.96 per cent between 2001 and 2010), but the congressionally-mandated 25 per cent-share ceiling. The US has also been responsible for the lion's share of member-state arrears to both the peacekeeping budget (ranging from a high of 64 per cent in 2003 to a low of 34 per cent in 2004) and the regular budget (peaking at 92 per cent in 2008) (see Table 9.3). The 2010 Obama administration budget made provisions for retiring US arrears to the UN, marking a significant departure from the hostility of the Bush administration and a Republican controlled Congress.[6]

Regional assurance: Afghanistan and Iraq

The invasions and occupations of Iraq and Afghanistan, both of which were a reaction to the events of September 11, enjoyed broad support in the international community, but Operation Iraqi Freedom (OIF) did not enjoy a UN mandate or the support of some major NATO allies, and was an American-led 'coalition of the willing', while the International Security and Assistance Force (ISAF) mission in Afghanistan not only enjoyed a UN mandate, but was also a NATO mission. The multilateral aid facilities and bilateral contributions to Afghanistan and Iraq jointly provide a measure of the American fidelity to the 'Pottery Barn rule'.

The multilateral funding agencies established for the express purpose of providing for the political stabilization of Afghanistan are consistent with successive UN mandates for ISAF and US policy objectives, particularly those found in the Obama administration's April 2009 strategy for Afghanistan and Pakistan and the August 2009 ISAF memorandum outlining the requirements of an integrated civilian-military counter-insurgency strategy (White House 2009; ISAF 2009: 1–1). Two trust funds were established at the 2004 Berlin Agreement to finance the ISAF stabilization and reconstruction mandate, the Afghan Reconstruction Trust Fund (ARTF) and the Law and Order Trust Fund (LOTFA) (International Afghanistan Conference 2004). The 2006 Afghanistan Compact created a third multilateral financing mechanism, the Counter-Narcotics Trust Fund (CNTF), a response to the threat posed by the narcotics trade to the authority of the central Afghan government (London Conference on Afghanistan 2006: annex 1). These multilateral funds, established to support reconstruction and institution-building in Afghanistan, are supplemented by bilateral Official Development Assistance (ODA).

Similarly, the international community established the International Reconstruction Fund Facility for Iraq (IRFFI) in 2004, explicitly defined as a multi-donor trust fund for a post-conflict environment (UN and World Bank 2003: 2). The IRFFI consists of two funds, the World Bank Iraq Trust Fund (WBITF) and the UN Development Group Iraq Trust Fund (UNDGITF). The WBITF funds civil society capacity-building, sectoral infrastructure improvements and structural policy reforms, while the UNDGITF provides technical assistance across a wide range of policy areas, including human development, economic infrastructure, the protection of human rights, rule of law and food security (UN and World Bank 2003). The International Compact with Iraq (May 2007) subsequently aligned the Iraqi National Development Strategy with the IRFFI programmes for a five-year period (UN 2008: 11). Perhaps unsurprisingly, the funding and developmental categories of the IRFFI parallel those of the American bilateral aid programme for stabilizing Iraq, the Iraq Relief and Reconstruction Fund (IRRF).

The US provides the largest share of the programme finance for the stabilization and reconstruction of Afghanistan and Iraq, tasks identified as essential to regional and global order by the international community (UN Security Council 2001, 2003, 2005, 2007). The US provided 82 per cent of bilateral aid between 2002 and 2008, although it only accounted for 25 per cent of the multilateral aid donated to the trust funds. Overall, the US provides just over 50 per cent of the total aid to Afghanistan. The American index of effort (aid share divided by GDP share) exceeds unity for total and bilateral aid (1.23 and 1.87, respectively), while the index of effort for contributions to the multilateral trust funds is 0.47 (see Table 9.4).[7]

The US budgeted over USD 17 billion for the stabilization of Iraq between 2003 and 2008. Almost half of the aid has been dedicated to economic infrastructure, particularly the electric sector (49 per cent), water and sanitation (23 per cent) and oil infrastructure (20 per cent), with the remainder distributed to repairing the transportation and telecommunications networks. The second largest IRRF expenditure category has been security and law enforcement, with a 28 per cent

Table 9.4 Bilateral and multilateral development assistance to Afghanistan and Iraq, 2002–8

	Multilateral contributions					Bilateral contributions (ODA)		Total contribution	
Afghanistan	ARFT (%)	LOFTA (%)	CNFT (%)	Share (%)	Index of effort*	Share (%)	Index of effort	Share (%)	Index of effort
NATO Europe	69.27	18.78	77.38	59.79	1.15	14.28	0.27	37.75	0.58
US	14.59	65.44	21.00	24.76	0.47	82.01	1.87	53.73	1.23
Canada	16.15	15.76	1.47	15.43	1.88	3.75	0.92	8.52	2.05
Iraq	WBITF (%)	UNDGITF (%)							
NATO Europe**	89.82	92.31		91.67	1.76	32.25	0.62	34.23	0.66
US	1.61	0.56		0.83	0.02	66.12	1.51	64.05	1.46
Canada	8.57	7.13		7.50	1.83	1.54	0.38	1.72	0.42

Sources: World Bank 2008, 2009; UNDP Afghanistan 2008a, 2008 b; OECD 2009

Notes:
* Contribution/NATO GNI share
** Includes contributions of European Commission for multilateral funds only

share (evenly split between police and armed forces). Those programmes listed under the rubric of justice and public safety infrastructure account for 13 per cent of total IRRF funds, of which 60 per cent are dedicated to democracy-building, judicial security, prosecuting crimes against humanity, and rule of law. The two remaining categories, human security and private sector development, account for just over 10 per cent of the IRRF budget. Almost 43 per cent of the private sector budget is devoted to debt forgiveness, while just half of the budget for human security is devoted to refugee and migration assistance (US Department of State 2007). These spending priorities are not misaligned with those identified by the international community. Moreover, the US has provided over 62 per cent of the total aid to the stabilization of Iraq (an effort index of 1.46) and over 66 per cent of the bilateral aid to Iraq (an effort index of 1.51), but less than 1 per cent of the multilateral aid (an effort index of 0.02).

Comparing American financial contributions to the stabilization and reconstruction of Afghanistan and Iraq provides a partial test of the American preference for bilateral or multilateral cooperation, an assumption resting upon the dissimilar legal and diplomatic contexts of OIF and OEF. This difference should have produced a greater level of effort by the NATO allies in Afghanistan, thereby producing a lower American index of effort. It did not. The US has over-contributed financial resources to stabilization and reconstruction of Iraq and Afghanistan; it has expended funds in a manner consistent with the expectations of the international community, but remains largely unwilling to channel those resources through multilateral funding authorities.

Policies of prevention

The Bush administration, recognizing the importance of facilitating the transition to democracy in Central and Eastern Europe with the end of the Cold War, adopted the non-military instruments of statecraft as a critical component of the American national security strategy. This appreciation was linked to the idea that market-oriented democracies were more likely to share the values and interests of the US. Similarly, the administration supported efforts in the Senate to ensure the continuing stability of the Russian Federation and the other successor republics to the Soviet Union, not only to prevent domestic political destabilization that could potentially threaten regional stability inside and outside Europe, but to ensure the orderly transfer of the Soviet nuclear arsenal to the Russian Federation. The Clinton administration similarly realized that peace in Europe was contingent upon continent-wide political and economic stability, and understood that direct and indirect security threats were diffused throughout the international system (White House 1999: 29). The Clinton administration's willing embrace of policies of prevention recognized that the security threats facing the US had changed qualitatively; security threats were no longer solely military in nature and were increasingly transnational phenomena, particularly terrorism and organized crime.

Although the administration of George W. Bush initially rejected nation-building as a realistic or appropriate goal for American foreign policy, the post-September

11 international context transformed nation-building into a centrepiece of the 'War on Terrorism'. The administration fully securitized bilateral economic assistance in the 2002 NSS: there was not only a greater emphasis on bilateral aid as an instrument for conflict prevention (US Department of State 2003: 9), but it also 'for the first time elevated development as the third component of US national security, alongside defence and diplomacy' (US Department of State 2007: 11). Bilateral aid was treated after September 11 as an important instrument for supporting countries 'on the front lines in the War on Terrorism', ameliorating the sources of domestic instability in other geopolitical regions critical to American security, and maintaining American leadership in promoting democracy and global governance (US Department of State 2007: 11–12).

The Obama administration has not deviated significantly from its predecessor, at least with respect to the centrality of bilateral aid in the American security strategy. The role of bilateral economic assistance was clearly divided between the tasks of supporting the administration's revised strategies for Iraq and for Afghanistan and Pakistan, and ensuring US leadership on key global development issues, particularly those that contribute to 'sustainable development and accountable governance' (US Department of State annual-a, FY 2010: xvi). Bilateral economic assistance has lost none of its substantive significance as an instrument for combating terrorism in the Obama administration; the administration even claimed that it hoped to revitalize 'the role of foreign assistance as a cornerstone of US foreign policy' (US Department of State annual-a, FY 2010: xx). Aid directed to Eurasia and Europe, for example, was designed not only to stabilize the Balkan region, but to facilitate 'the critical participation of European friends and allies in US security operations in Afghanistan, Iraq, and around the world' (US Department of State annual-a, FY 2010: xviii).

Political and economic stabilization

US programmes have supported either the expansion or consolidation of democracy and the market, and those that support the mitigation or prevention of communicable diseases (see Table 9.5). The Obama administration is continuing the Bush administration's major investment in global health, particularly the effort to slow the spread of HIV/AIDS and improve children's health. The share of these two programmes has risen from 28 per cent to 58 per cent of total expenditures between 2004 and 2010. The bulk of other US bilateral assistance is dedicated to two programmes, Development Assistance and the Economic Support Fund (ESF), accounting for 13 per cent and 32 per cent of total aid disbursements, respectively, over the period 2001 to 2010. The ESF targeted terrorism during the Bush administration, delivering assistance to 'front-line states and building new relationships as the campaign against global terror widens' (US Department of State annual-a, FY 2004: 13; see also US Department of State annual-a, FY 2009: 26). The distribution of ESF funds shifted dramatically over the course of the Bush administration: in 2003, almost 56 per cent of the ESF aid was devoted to Egypt, Israel and the West Bank, but in 2007, almost 67 per cent of aid went to the Near East[8] (25 per

Table 9.5 Political and economic stabilization programmes 2001–10 (USD millions)

	2001	2002	2003	2004	2005	2006	2007	2008	2009ᵉ	2010ʳ	Total	Share (%)
Democracy and the market												
SEED Act (pre-conflict Europe)*	228	289	280	193	185	160	80	68	73	103	1,659	1.27
FREEDOM Act (FSU)	808	958	755	585	626	509	432	397	604	469	6,143	4.70
Transition initiatives			62	55	49	40	40	47	50	126	469	0.36
Development assistance	1,274	1,178	1,480	1,364	1,448	1,808	1,508	1,624	2,038	2,734	16,456	12.59
Economic Support Fund	2,315	3,289	4,802	3,288	3,915	2,616	432	5,362	7,018	6,504	39,541	30.26
Democracy Fund							94	238	116		448	0.34
Stabilization												
Regional Stability and Humanitarian Assistance		46	10	10	10	10	7	13	13	8	127	0.10
International Disaster and Famine Assistance	299	422	432	544	575	361	361	670	750	880	5,294	4.05
Health programmes												
Child survival and Global Health Programs Fund	1,051	1,468	1,940	1,824	1,562	1,591	1,740	6,498	7,189	7,595	32,458	24.84
HIV/AIDS				488	1,374	1,975	5,121	5,981	6,490	6,655	28,084	21.49
Total	5,975	7,650	9,761	8,351	9,744	9,070	9,815	20,898	24,341	25,074	130,679	

Source: US Department of State (annual-a)

Notes:
* Albania, Bulgaria, Romania, Macedonia, Montenegro, regional programmes
ᵉ Estimate
ʳ Request

cent) and Southeast Asia (42 per cent). The Obama administration acknowledged that the ultimate purpose of ESF aid remained 'countering terrorism and extremist ideology', but put a 'civilian' face on the long-term purposes of the aid – good governance and economic development (US Department of State annual-a, FY 2010: 38). The Obama administration continued the Bush administration's pattern of ESF expenditures in 2009–10: 50 per cent is destined for Southeast Asia and 26 per cent to the Near East.

The disbursement of US ODA, according to the OECD classification system, provides yet another window into the pattern and purposes of US aid. A cursory examination of Table 9.6 reveals two important trends in US ODA over the period 1995 to 2007. First, the American share of total OECD ODA has climbed from just under 16 per cent to almost 27 per cent. Over the same time period, the American share of OECD GNP has remained fairly steady at approximately 35 per cent. Arguably, the US has assumed an increasingly larger share of the global aid burden, although still less than its GDP share would indicate, and has done so owing to the securitization of preventive aid to combat terrorism and the threat that regional instability could adversely affect American (or allied) interests. The distribution of American aid within ODA aid categories has shifted towards supporting the development of social and economic infrastructures (from 56 per cent of aid in 1995–99 to 75 per cent of aid in 2007). American aid, however, remains primarily bilateral in nature (during the period 2000–7 over 85 per cent of aid was bilateral), provides little debt relief and no support to non-governmental organizations, and supplies a disproportionately greater share of humanitarian relief (45 per cent of the OECD total).

Non-proliferation

The non-proliferation of weapons of mass destruction (WMD) is the second major policy dimension of American prevention policies. American non-proliferation policies have had three major components: the Nunn-Lugar cooperative threat reduction programmes that have spanned the entire proliferation spectrum (chemical, nuclear and biological) vis-à-vis the Russian Federation and former republics of the Soviet Union; participation in multilateral efforts to prevent the acquisition of WMD by non-state actors, particularly Al-Qaeda-aligned terrorist groups; and efforts to prevent the acquisition of a nuclear weapons capability by a small number of states with suspected or confirmed nuclear weapons ambitions (particularly Iraq, Iran and North Korea).

Successive post-Cold War American administrations have been dedicated to stopping or reversing the Iraqi, Iranian and North Korean acquisition of a nuclear weapons capability. American diplomatic initiatives, economic sanctions and threatened military action during the Clinton and Bush administrations did not succeed in stopping or reversing the nuclear ambitions of Iran and North Korea, despite periodic and short-lived diplomatic agreements with either. The American-led invasion of Iraq in 2003 ended Saddam Hussein's already suspended effort to acquire a nuclear weapons capability. But President Obama apparently entered

Table 9.6 US Official Development Assistance

	1995–9		2000–4		2005		2006		2007	
	% of US ODA	% of all ODA	% of US ODA	% of all ODA	% of US ODA	% of all ODA	% of US ODA	% of all ODA	% of US ODA	% of all ODA
Social infrastructure and services	31.42	16.58	40.77	32.93	42.16	39.64	44.09	32.71	51.40	33.80
Economic infrastructure and services	10.54	7.86	9.83	19.32	8.83	23.42	13.42	29.41	12.63	26.47
Production sectors	7.60	11.59	6.20	25.46	6.00	32.38	5.18	27.22	6.60	29.00
Multisector/cross-cutting	6.68	16.51	9.05	33.19	3.92	18.20	6.73	28.84	4.69	17.71
Subtotal	56.24	13.08	65.86	29.10	60.90	33.08	69.42	31.16	75.31	30.25
Commodity aid/general programme assistance	12.03	31.56	11.56	60.58	4.05	43.65	5.40	36.73	3.77	22.10
Debt relief	1.68	3.52	4.74	9.47	14.78	15.83	6.94	7.70	0.42	1.06
Humanitarian aid	13.23	39.94	10.40	47.40	14.26	49.65	11.43	41.52	12.76	45.11
Administrative costs of donors	8.08	23.40	5.39	25.92	4.09	29.34	4.67	28.59	5.64	28.55
NGO support	0.00	0.00	0.00	0.00	0.00	0.00	0.00	0.00	0.00	0.00
Refugees in donor country	1.35	16.54	2.05	22.85	1.91	26.49	2.13	28.34	2.07	26.03
Unallocated	7.39	22.20	neg.	neg.	0.01	0.10	neg.	0.04	0.03	0.53
Total		15.79		27.07		28.79		24.65		26.65

Source: OECD 2009

office determined to 'speak softly and carry a large stick': he affirmed his will-ingness to negotiate with North Korea within the Six-Party process, broke with the previous administration's unwillingness to negotiate directly with Iran, and has kept the military option on the table without drawing undue attention to it. In October 2009, the Obama administration entered into direct negotiations with Iran along with the four other permanent members of the UN Security Council and Germany after the discovery of an undeclared nuclear enrichment facility at Qom. The administration's decision to negotiate, in conjunction with the willingness of the Russians and Chinese to entertain tougher economic sanctions against Iran, appears to have created a diplomatic opportunity for preventing Iranians from acquiring weapons-grade enriched uranium without denying Iran the possibility of enriching uranium for peaceful purposes (*Economist* 2009).

The dissolution of the Soviet Union seriously threatened the integrity of the non-proliferation regime: it not only increased the number of nuclear weapons states overnight, but unsecured weapons storage facilities made possible the acquisition of NBC weapons by state and non-state actors alike on the open market. The post-September 11 fear that nuclear or chemical weapons could fall into the hands of terrorists galvanized the international community and led to the Global Partnership Against the Spread of Weapons and Materials of Mass Destruction. The signato-ries to the initiative, launched at the June 2002 G-8 Kananaskis Summit, pledged USD 17.8 billion to the task of securing nuclear waste, weapons grade materiel and weapons facilities in the former Soviet Union. The US pledged USD 10 bil-lion to the fund or 56 per cent of the total – far in excess of its 35 per cent OECD GDP share.[9]

The goal of protecting the non-proliferation regime continues to resonate with the American security community (US Department of Defense 2008: 14; White House 2009a: 6–7). The two major American non-proliferation programmes – the Cooperative Threat Reduction (Department of Defense) and Defense Nuclear Non-proliferation (Department of Energy) – have jointly expended over USD 17.5 billion between 2002 and 2010. These two funding sources covered a wide range of specific programmes designed to limit the proliferation of NBC weapons to state and non-state actors, funded programmes in Armenia, Azerbaijan, Georgia, Kazakhstan, Kyrgyzstan, Moldova, Russia, Tajikistan, Ukraine and Uzbekistan, and made possible the implementation of the 2002 Moscow Treaty on the elimi-nation of strategic offensive arms and the Strategic Arms Reduction Treaty (see Table 9.7).[10]

Policies of protection

September 11, 2001 did not usher in an era of the undifferentiated securitization of domestic policy domains. The Clinton administration had already securi-tized domestic policies once considered matters of domestic law enforcement: cyber-vandalism and information warfare; the flow of narcotics into the US, porous borders and uncontrolled migration; and public health (pandemics, natu-ral or otherwise) (Oakley 1998). This securitization process, which accelerated

Table 9.7 Non-proliferation: cooperative threat reduction and defence nuclear non-proliferation programmes (USD millions)

	2002	2003	2004	2005	2006	2007	2008	2009ᵉ	2010ʳ	Total	Share (%)
Cooperative threat reduction											
Strategic offensive arms elimination			55	52	49	63	76	80	66	444	2.54
Strategic nuclear arms elimination					1	3	2	6	6	19	0.11
Chemical weapons destruction			210	164	112	47	1			536	3.06
Nuclear weapons storage			48	73	128	92	34	23	15	416	2.37
Nuclear weapons transportation security			23		30	32	41	40	46	214	1.22
Biological threat reduction			67	68	69	72	174	185	152	790	4.51
WMD proliferation prevention initiative			29	36	40	32	59	59	90	348	1.99
Other			16	10	22	29	37	38	26	180	1.03
Subtotal			448	408	455	371	426	433	404	2,946	16.81
Defense nuclear nonproliferation											
Nonproliferation and verification	259	256	228	219	305	265	279	293	311	2,418	13.80
Nonproliferation and international security	83	131	86	143	133	128	132	134	138	1,111	6.34
Nuclear materials protection and cooperation	315	333	228	403	408	597	403	444	530	3,664	20.91
Elimination of weapons-grade plutonium	14	49	81	67	139	231	182	139	24	928	5.30

(continued)

	2002	2003	2004	2005	2006	2007	2008	2009[e]	2010[r]	Total	Share (%)
Fissile materials disposition	252	445	664	619	660	470	642	654	710	5,119	29.21
Global threat reduction initiative			69	7	152	131	120	129	115	725	4.14
Other*	14	92	75	117			72	73	74	518	2.96
Subtotal	1,048	1,308	1,417	1,578	1,798	1,824	1,833	1,869	1,906	14,580	83.19
Total	1,048	1,308	1,865	1,986	2,253	2,195	2,259	2,302	2,310	17,526	

Sources: US Department of Defense (annual); Defense Threat Reduction Agency 2010; Department of Energy (annual): author's calculations

Notes:
* Includes: programme direction, Russian transition initiatives, HEU transparency implementation, offsite recovery and accelerated recovery project
[e] Estimate
[r] Request

post-September 11, reached into virtually every aspect of daily life, ranging from threats to the financial system to terrorist links with organized crime; each shared the common denominator of being connected directly or indirectly to Al-Qaeda and other aligned movements.

Homeland security policies, particularly those targeting border control and the protection of critical infrastructures and key assets, were progressively militarized during the Bush administration. In the 2005 Strategy for Homeland Defense and Civil Support, the Department of Defense claimed a domestic role for itself in the war against terrorism, a role made essential owing to the assessment that the 'global war against terror' transformed US territory into 'an integral part of a global theatre of combat' (US Department of Defense 2005: 1 and 26). Yet the overwhelming share of the initiatives put into place after September 11 were narrowly defined as domestic, although a number of multilateral programmes were put into place, most prominently the Container Security Initiative and the Proliferation Security Initiative to manage the security vulnerabilities arising from the high volume of global shipping, and the Mérida Initiative designed to retard the migration of Mexican drug cartels into the American Southwest (Seelke and Beittel 2009: 1). The Obama administration does not yet appear to be contemplating the reversal of this decade-long securitization process, particularly as it pertains to domestic terrorism, the range of securitized crimes, and the critical task of infrastructure protection, particularly cyberspace.

Terrorism

The 2002 *National Strategy for Homeland Security* identified a CBRN attack on the homeland as the major threat facing the US (Office of Homeland Security 2002: vii; cf. Fingar 2005). America's vulnerability to CBRN terrorism was ascribed to the liabilities facing any open society, long and difficult-to-control borders, unsecured key infrastructures, and an extraordinarily large number of soft, valuable targets (Office of Homeland Security 2002: 7–10). The Obama administration's 2010 budget tracked the policy priorities of the Bush administration, although future spending would reflect recalibrated priorities in a new NSS and *Quadrennial Homeland Security Review*.

Six government departments (Homeland Security, Defense, Health and Human Services, Justice, Energy, and State) expend 94 per cent of the federal budget on terrorism and terrorism-related policy objectives. The Department of Homeland Security accounts for almost 50 per cent of those expenditures, followed by the Department of Defense (27 per cent), with the share of the other four departments ranging from 8 per cent to 2 per cent. Four policy categories are identified in the federal budget as constituting the core policy obligations of homeland security: protecting and disrupting terrorist attacks; protecting the American people, critical infrastructures and key resources; emergency preparedness and response (excluding expenditures on natural disasters); and health security. The first policy category – protecting and disrupting terrorist attacks – absorbs 45 per cent of the federal budget and has four components: intelligence and warning; border and transportation security; domestic counter-terrorism; and international counter-terrorism. Border and transportation security have absorbed just under 34 per cent of the federal budget (and 80 per cent of funds dedicated to the policy category 'protecting against and disrupting terrorist attacks'), while just less than 8 per cent has been dedicated to domestic and international counter-terrorism, and well under 1 per cent has been invested in intelligence and warning (see Table 9.8). The second largest budget item is the protection of critical infrastructure, which consumes approximately 30 per cent of the homeland security budget, and it is the primary responsibility of the Department of Defense (with a 60 per cent budget share). The final two categories, health security and emergency preparedness and response, have accounted for approximately 16 per cent of the federal homeland security budget and have remained relatively flat in nominal terms.

Infrastructure and cyber security

The Clinton administration recognized that the private and public American infrastructures, particularly cyberspace, were vulnerable to malign state and non-state actors. Presidential Decision Directive-63 (PDD-63), issued in 1998, had already recognized the problem of protecting critical infrastructures in the US and led to the creation of the National Infrastructure Protection Center housed in the FBI. The primary menaces to the American infrastructure were identified as: an attack on information networks by vandals, organized crime and terrorists; as a form of foreign espionage; or as a component of an adversary's strategic attack. The critical infrastructures identified were agriculture and the food supply, water, public health, emergency services, the defence industrial base, telecommunications, energy, transportation, banking and finance, chemicals and hazardous materials and shipping. The Clinton administration also implemented the Key Asset Programme to protect critical infrastructures from terrorist attacks. The catalogue of critical infrastructures identified in 1998 included government and private sector telecommunications and information systems, critical sectors of the economy highly dependent upon information technologies (banking and finance), energy distribution networks and transportation systems (Vatis 1999: 1, 2000: 5; Goslin 2000).

September 11 underscored the vulnerability of the American infrastructure. The vulnerabilities attending the public and private sector dependence on cyberspace presented policy-makers with a double-edged threat: first, information warfare could erase the battlefield advantages of net-centric warfare, which was key to the modernization of American armed forces; second, the government and public rely upon cyberspace for every aspect of daily life, and that dependence left society and the state vulnerable to mass disruptions (Department of Justice 2003; Federal Bureau of Investigation 2004). The Bush administration also understood that protecting cyberspace was particularly problematic owing to the absence of defensible boundaries and the relatively low barrier to carrying out a successful attack (White House 2003b: 6–7). In the USA Patriot Act, the Bush administration not only expanded the categories of critical infrastructures, but added to the list national monuments and icons, both considered 'symbolically equated with traditional

Table 9.8 Terrorism (USD millions)

	2003	2004	2005	2006	2007	2008	2009ᵉ	2010ʳ	Total	Share (%)
Protect and disrupt terrorist attacks	17,805	19,461	20,978	23,021	25,063	30,904	31,872	33,048	202,152	42.20
Intelligence and warning	125	242	350	443	671	722	766	858	4177	0.87
Border and transportation	15,171	15,840	16,652	18,042	19,365	25,130	25,713	26,739	162,652	33.96
Domestic counter-terrorism	2,509	3,379	3,976	4,536	5,027	5,052	5,393	5,451	35,323	7.37
International anti-terrorism	96	146	149	136	135	154	182	310	1,308	0.27
Protect American people, critical infrastructures, and key resources	15,322	15,253	25,982	26,507	26,984	27,772	29,220	31,380	198,420	0.00
Protecting critical infrastructures	12,893	12,279	17,836	17,933	18,388	19,492	20,165	22,833	141,819	29.61
Defending against catastrophic threats	2,429	2,974	8,146	8,574	8,596	8,280	9,055	8,929	56,983	11.90
Emergency preparedness and response*	3,873	6,003	5,655	4,992	4,822	5,611	6,718	6,379	44,053	9.20
Health		5,611	3,746	3,808	4,285	4,494	5,157	6,552	33,653	7.03
Infectious diseases		1,654	1,679	1,695	1,810	1,821	1,935	2,007	12,601	2.63
Global health		286	302	380	308	367	309	319	2,271	0.47
Terrorism		1,507	1,623	1,631	1,473	1,577	1,515	1,547	10,873	2.27
Public Health and Social Services Security Fund*		2,164	142	102	694	729	1,398	2,679	9,763	2.04
Other	118	10	44	119	57	187	199	N/A	734	0.15
Total	37,118	46,338	56,405	58,447	61,211	68,968	73,166	77,359	479,012	

Sources: Centers for Disease Control (annual); OMB (annual-a); US Department of Health and Human Services 2009; author's calculations

Notes:
* Biological, radiological, chemical and cyber-security threats to health
ᵉ Estimate
ʳ Request

values and institutions or US political and economic power' (White House 2003a: viii–xii). Despite the acknowledged vulnerability of the American private sector to cyber disruption, the Bush administration reasoned that the resources necessary for protecting the private sector exceeded those available to the government. The Bush administration consequently adopted subsidiarity as a governing principle: the government would assume responsibility for protecting federal networks and information systems, but left the responsibility for monitoring and protecting private and public information systems to the private sector as well as state and local government, respectively (White House 2003b: 11).

The Obama administration rejected this approach in 2009.[11] In the 2009 *Cyberspace Policy Review* (*CPR*), the administration argued that the cyber-security policies of the previous 15 years had failed to address the complexity and seriousness of the threat.[12] The administration identified four major challenges facing the US government in this policy area: the failure of critical infrastructures (e.g. the electricity grid or air traffic control system); the disruption or potential collapse of the global financial system; intellectual property theft; and cyber-warfare (White House 2009b: 1–9; Obama 2009b; cf. Rollins and Henning 2009). The *CPR* also advocated the creation of a 'cybersecurity policy official' reporting directly to the President, serving as a member of the White House staff and formulating policy with the aid of the National Security Council.

The Obama strategy for cyber-security introduced two innovations. First, the strategy insisted that the federal government must assume joint responsibility for protecting not only the cyber-infrastructure of state and local governments, but also (and perhaps more critically) of the private sector. It recognized that 'the public and private sectors' interests are intertwined with a shared responsibility for ensuring a secure, reliable infrastructure' (White House 2009b: iv). Second, the administration underscored the necessity of creating a set of 'acceptable norms regarding territorial jurisdiction, sovereign responsibility, and the use of force' to meet the challenge of cyber-security. And it underscored the need for institutionalizing international cooperation on cyber-security, creating compatible 'legal frameworks and capacity to fight cybercrime', and making progress towards promoting common 'cybersecurity practices and standards' (White House 2009b: 21). Finally, the administration increased the funding for cyber-security to USD 50 million in fiscal year 2010, a fivefold increase over the annual amount budgeted during the Bush administration (US Department of Health and Human Services 2009).

Securitized crimes

The securitization of law and order reflects the trauma of September 11 and the necessity of justifying such expenditures in terms of a national security threat. The 2007 Stewards of the American Dream (SAD), the strategic plan for the period 2007–12, designated three goals for federal law enforcement agencies: prevent terrorism and promote the nation's security (Goal 1); prevent crime and enforce federal laws (Goal 2); and ensure the fair and efficient administration of justice (Goal 3). The Obama administration has not yet amended this strategic orientation;

the Department of Justice budget priorities for fiscal year 2010 are largely consistent with those that came before it. In SAD, the Bush administration claimed that 'terrorism is the most significant national security threat our country faces' and assigned the Department of Justice with the task of preventing, disrupting and defeating 'terrorist operations before attacks occur' (Department of Justice 2007: 17). The Department of Justice adopted a peremptory strategy that elevated counter-terrorism to the first priority of the FBI, despite the creation of a National Security Division (NSD) in 2007 within the Justice Department.[13] Nonetheless, the Justice Department's budget allocation for Goal 1 between 2008 and 2010 amounted to USD 15.10 billion or 18 per cent of the total budget, whereas the budgets for Goals 2 and 3 amounted to 42.39 (51 per cent) and USD 25.92 (31 per cent) respectively.

The FBI designated the suppression of terrorism as its first and foremost priority in its fiscal year (FY) 2010 budgetary request (Goal 1), followed by counter-intelligence and counter-espionage activities, cyber-security and infrastructure protection, and combating (trans)national criminal organizations. Despite the high priority ascribed to the protection of cyberspace and the national infrastructure, there is not a budget line explicitly dedicated to that particular law enforcement task. It is clear, however, that FBI resources are being overwhelmingly directed towards two categories of crime that have become highly securitized after September 11: counter-terrorism and counter-intelligence; and criminal enterprises (see Table 9.9).[14] The size of the FBI budget for these Goal 1 priorities as compared to the relatively low level of budgetary support for complementary international programmes, including the sizeable Andean Counterdrug Initiative, reveals the extent to which counter-terrorism and organized crime are considered primarily as a threat to *national* security rather than as a threat to the regional milieu.

Money laundering, border control and drug trafficking have been long-standing law enforcement concerns in the US, but all three have been securitized in the last decade. A twofold nexus has been established between drug trafficking, money laundering and terrorism: the first links money laundering and financial support for terrorist organizations to threats against American society; and the second connects the growing role of (trans)national criminal enterprises as subcontractors for terrorist organizations or as malign independent agents to the destabilization of governments friendly or aligned with the US. The primary loci for policing money laundering are the Department of the Treasury's Financial Crimes Enforcement Network (FinCEN) and the Office of Terrorism and Financial Intelligence (TFI). The 2007 National Money Laundering Strategy, while underscoring the importance of disrupting the flow of finance to terrorist groups as a major national security challenge, nonetheless primarily targeted drug cartels and individuals seeking personal or corporate gain (US Department of the Treasury 2007: v–vi, 1–12; 2008: 3, 9). Despite the considerable attention paid to terrorist financing networks, terrorist money laundering cases nonetheless account for less than 1 per cent of the total (US Department of the Treasury 2007: appendix A, 25; cf. FinCEN 2008).

Border control became a highly securitized issue after September 11 for the US; it led to joint Canadian-American efforts to monitor the flow of individuals across

Table 9.9 Resources devoted to securitized crimes (USD millions)

	2002	2003	2004	2005	2006	2007	2008	2009	2010	Total	Share (%)
FBI											
National security/intelligence	516	673	680	806	1,053	975	1,199	1,490	1,541	8,933	17.78
Counter-terrorism/-intelligence	988	1,297	1,472	1,913	2,055	2,002	2,880	2,934	3,141	18,682	37.19
Foreign terrorist tracking task force		61	67	23	19	2	2	0	0	174	0.35
Criminal enterprises	1,679	1,740	1,842	2,014	1,897	1,769	2,271	2,292	2,409	17,913	35.66
Interagency law enforcement	448	368	542	553	486	512	506	489	533	4,437	8.83
International law and narcotics programmes											
Corruption	3.6	2.3	3.0	6.75	3.9	6.8	4.0	4.5	N/A	35.85	0.07
Border security and alien smuggling	1.9	1.4	1.2	1.53	0.6	1.3	1.0	1.5	N/A	10.43	0.02
Cybercrime and intellectual property rights	0.7	2.3	2.7	3.30	3.4	3.8	3.5	4.0	N/A	23.7	0.05
Financial crimes and money laundering	1.6	0.8	1.0	3.50	2.5	4.0	3.5	4.0	N/A	20.9	0.04
Total	3,638.8	4,145.8	4,610.9	5,324.08	5,520	5,276	6,870	7,219	7,624	50,229	

Source: US Department of State (annual-b); US Department of State Bureau of International Narcotics and Law Enforcement Affairs 2007; OMB (annual-b); author's calculations

the border without forgoing the benefits of the earlier and laxer border regime (see Croci in this volume). Although the uncontrolled inflow of Mexican migrants has pushed border control to the top of the domestic policy agenda, American security concerns revolve around the growing violence of Mexican drug cartels and American complicity in it, and the challenge those cartels may eventually pose to the Mexican government's power and legitimacy (White House 2009d). The Mérida Initiative, an agreement struck between Presidents Bush and Calderón in March 2007, provided a foundation for deepened US-Mexican law enforcement cooperation to meet those challenges. Between 2008 and 2010, the US will have invested approximately USD 1.8 billion in a border control and law enforcement programme described as serving a 'core US national interest' (Seelke and Beittel 2009: 5; see also Dominguez (Chapter 8) in this volume).

Policies of compellence

The end of the Cold War left the US as a military power without peer and as the only credible guarantor of global order. The US remains the world's uncontested conventional power, capable of projecting power to any point on the compass. This so-called unipolar moment (Layne 2007; Kapstein and Mastanduno 1999) has had at least a two-decades-long half-life and seems likely to continue at least for another. The military misadventure in Iraq has destabilized the Persian Gulf region and heightened Iranian insecurity, no doubt an important factor fuelling the pursuit of a nuclear deterrent. By 2008, the Bush administration accepted the interdependence of American and global security, but nonetheless insisted that the US military be capable of withstanding 'the challenges posed by rogue states and would-be hegemons' (US Department of Defense 2008: 6). That the US retains a clear dominance in conventional warfare is almost self-evident, but the US Defense Department has recognized that the changing nature of the threats posed to the US and the agents of those threats, particularly non-state or substate actors, have made military dominance less salient (US Department of Defense 2008: 4). The continuing role of military compellence in the overall American security calculus is captured by the twofold evolution from 'simple' to 'complex' deterrence, and from conventional defence to irregular or asymmetrical warfare.

Defence capabilities

No country other than the US can project military power and engage in high intensity conflict in several theatres of operations simultaneously and autonomously. The US outspends the rest of the world on military capabilities, however measured. As compared to its NATO allies, the US accounted for almost 75 per cent of NATO weapons acquisitions expenditures and 65 per cent of total NATO defence expenditures in 2008. The US also accounted for just over 55 per cent of the aggregate defence expenditures of the top 10 defence-spending nations and for almost 50 per cent of aggregate global defence expenditure. Moreover, the US spent 5.8 and 10.2 times as much on defence as the two countries frequently referred to a potential peer competitors, China and Russia respectively (Perlo-Freeman 2009; Center for Arms Control and Non-Proliferation 2009).

The global reach of the American military may also be measured by military deployments *outside* the US: there are currently 293,701 members of the American armed forces serving overseas (onshore and afloat), approximately 21 per cent of those serving in the Armed Forces.[15] A comparison of the relative share of global and NATO alliance nuclear or naval capabilities provides another measure of American military dominance and power projection capabilities. The US and the Russian Federation are relatively equally matched with respect to the global share of deployed warheads (48 per cent and 41 per cent, respectively), but the US accounts for 89 per cent of the NATO member state nuclear arsenal, and possesses almost 30 times as many warheads as does China (Carnegie Endowment for Peace 2009).[16] The more important indicator of power projection capabilities, however, may be the number of carrier task forces a nation can muster. The US have ten Nimitz and one Enterprise class aircraft carriers in service that displace 97,000 and 89,600 tons, respectively. Seven other nations (France, Italy, Russia, Spain, India, Brazil and the UK) have a total of nine fixed-wing aircraft carriers in service, the majority of which are STOVL carriers;[17] and only France's *Charles de Gaulle*, Russia's *Admiral Kuznetsov* and Brazil's *NAe São Paulo* exceed 30,000 tons.

The evolution of the international system and the use of force

The task of maintaining global order became increasingly complex after the end of the Cold War. Prior to 1989, the core tasks of the US Department of Defense were the deterrence of the Soviet Union from launching a strategic nuclear attack on American or allied territory or from encroaching on areas considered critical to America's strategic interests, the successful conduct of defensive conventional wars to protect its European and Asian allies, and the projection of power anywhere in the world. When the Cold War ended, the task of global deterrence did not evaporate: the Russian Federation retained a considerable nuclear arsenal and the rise of China was perceived as a potential constraint on future American preroga- tives in the Pacific. The rise of assertive regional powers, particularly in the Persian Gulf region, and the September 11 terrorist attacks on the US led the Department of Defense to identify two additional tasks for American military power in the 2006 *Quadrennial Defense Review*: transnational deterrence (the ability to deter attacks by non-state actors or engage those actors in counter-insurgency warfare) and regional deterrence (the ability to maintain regional stability by retaining the ability to engage in conventional warfare) (US Department of Defense 2006: 38).

Peer competitor

Each post-Cold War administration identified Russia and China as global powers posing quite different threats to the US. The Russian threat mutated and conformed to that country's ongoing political and economic progress or regress. The Russian Federation's integration into the Western security and economic systems, central to removing Russia as a geopolitical threat, remains vulnerable to the vagaries of Russian domestic developments or a renascent imperial impulse. China has been viewed as posing the more traditional threat of a rising, revisionist power. China's sustained weapons modernization programme and the oft-expressed desire to reclaim its historical role in Southeast and Central Asia will inevitably constrain America's unfettered military presence in the Asia-Pacific (Goss 2005; US Department of Defense 2005a). Notably, however, the language of 'peer competitor' has been recently abandoned in favour of a generic concern with the Chinese ability to project power in Asia and beyond (US Department of Defense 2009: I).

Regional deterrence

After 1989, North Korea, the Russian Federation, Indonesia, Iran, Iraq and China were identified as those states representing the greatest threat to American security. Even before President Bush bestowed the moniker 'Axis of Evil' on Iran, Iraq and North Korea in his 2002 State of the Union Address, the Clinton administration viewed these states as presenting the greatest risks to regional stability and the nuclear non-proliferation regime. Iraq was cited for its call to overthrow moderate Arab regimes in the Gulf region and its WMD programmes, while Iranian nuclear ambitions were considered unlikely to evaporate, even in the presence of a moderate government. North Korea emerged as greatest a threat to Northeast Asian stability, particularly peace on the Korean peninsula and the relatively amicable relations between South Korea, Japan and China (Jacoby 2003 and 2005).

Transnational deterrence

The 2005 National Military Strategy concluded that the US military required a force structure capable of defeating 'a wide range of adversaries – from states to non-state actors'. The Strategy formulated a new form of deterrence tailored to the WMD threat that rogue states and terrorists posed. It called for a 'diverse portfolio of capabilities' enabling the US to destroy terrorist networks, effect regime change, 'swiftly defeat' an adversary, or undertake a prolonged occupation that entailed a 'significant investment' of blood and treasure (US Department of Defense 2005b: 3, 12; cf. US Department of Defense 2005b: 7–8). Military pre-emption was a central feature of the new deterrence strategy, but the deterrent also included non-military components: improving data collection and analysis, increasing R&D expenditures to improve responses to WMD threats, deepening bilateral and multilateral cooperation (particularly with respect to intelligence-sharing), eroding ideological support for terrorism, thereby delegitimizing terrorism and its state sponsors, and supporting 'models of moderation in the Muslim world' (US Department of Defense 2005d: 5; White House 2002b: 2).

Transnational deterrence was given its starkest formulation in the Bush Doctrine, which took aim at rogue states and terrorist groups. The Doctrine invoked the principle of pre-emptive attack in response to an imminent threat to the US or simply to forestall or prevent 'hostile acts' (White House 2002a: 15; White House

Table 9.10 NATO troop commitments to KFOR, ISAF and OEF 2008

	KFOR (%)	Burden-sharing index*	ISAF (%)	Burden-sharing index	KFOR/ ISAF/OEF (%)	Burden-sharing index
NATO Europe	88.26	1.69	50.87	0.98	45.12	0.87
US	11.53	0.26	43.97	1.01	51.54	1.18

Source: Sperling and Webber 2009

Note:
* Ratio of contribution to GNI share

2006: 18). The doctrine also downgraded the importance of formal alliances and emphasized the administration's intention to rely upon coalitions of states 'able and willing to promote a balance of power that favors freedom' (White House 2002a: 25; cf. Jervis 2003). The short-lived strategy of pre-emption was implemented in OIF, although the unwillingness to rely upon formal alliances first manifested itself in the case of Afghanistan, where the US initially preferred an American-led OEF to a NATO-led operation to oust the Taliban and destroy Al-Qaeda. The evolution of the counter-insurgency campaign in Afghanistan not only forced the US to rediscover the benefits of multilateralism, but highlighted the not insignificant material contributions of the NATO allies to KFOR and ISAF, the two major NATO operations (see Table 9.10).[18] The American military and political experiences in the Balkans, Iraq and Afghanistan have demonstrated America's continuing dependence upon others to achieve its goals of transnational and regional deterrence, and the blurring of the line between them which has required a consideration of how America will prepare and fight wars in the future. It is just as clear, however, that without American military power the world would enjoy less rather than more order.

Conclusion

The US shares many of the structural vulnerabilities and characteristics of a post-Westphalian state, but nonetheless retains an essentially Westphalian temperament and policy orientation. This survey of American policy across the four governance policy domains generally confirms the three national security culture hypotheses presented in the Introduction to this volume.

The decade-long absence of a dependable post-Cold War 'other' to frame the security debate or identify the source of threat(s) initiated a securitization process reflecting the international system's progressive fragmentation and incalculability as the number of 'unknown unknowns' multiplied (Rumsfeld 2002). This process, which accelerated after the events of September 11, was recast as a reaction to a set of vulnerabilities posed by an imagined 'other' – an Islamist threat to the American way of life. Many of the security threats identified post-September 11 had already found a place on the American security agenda, but the securitization process was militarized, notably in the high-intensity combat operations in the Persian Gulf region and counter-insurgency warfare in Central Asia. Yet, each administration recognized the lessened utility of military force to meet a large class of threats to American security and the necessity of complementary non-military instruments to mitigate the long-term threats facing the US. The reliance of each successive post-Cold War administration on the military instrument cannot be denied, but the reliance upon economic and technological assistance to address the root causes of conflict cannot be discounted, particularly if American expenditures are compared to other major states in the international system, either in absolute or relative terms.

The security threats confronting the US are not contained by national borders, either in effect, source or solution. The threats associated with the governance tasks of assurance and prevention present a problem of collective action insofar as the major states of the system have a major stake in system stability and the financial wherewithal to supply it. The American tendency to define threats in national rather than collective terms has exacerbated rather than minimized the challenge of creating international order and meeting the US' declared security governance objectives. Arguably, the American national security culture imposes the constraint on effective collective action: its egotist rhetoric and definition of interest are dissonant with the intrinsic nature of security threats demanding a collective response. The American unwillingness 'to play with others' manifests itself most clearly in the bilateral execution of its assurance and prevention policies; the definition of multilateralism as states unquestioningly following the American lead, particularly in the domain of compellence; and the low level of salience given to collective efforts that address threats to the 'homeland'.

The American national security culture comports best with those systems of governance abjuring the logic of appropriateness and favouring the logic of consequentiality. As the sole guarantor of global order, the US must and does, for better or worse, participate in a broad spectrum of security arrangements, ranging from the balance of power regulating great power relations in the Asia-Pacific, to the emerging Eurasian concert of powers that brings North America, Europe and the Russian Federation into a common security framework, to the NATO collective defence regime that defines the transatlantic community. In each of these security governance systems, including NATO, sovereign prerogatives remain intact and freely exercised, the binding power of institutional norms ranges from moderate in the transatlantic geopolitical space to virtually non-existent in the Asia-Pacific. The conflation of a strong national identity and preference for bilateral or unilateral action make the US an unsuitable advocate or participant in a regional or global system of governance requiring either the abnegation of sovereignty or voluntary compliance with elaborate normative and legal frameworks.

There can be no doubt that the US is a full-spectrum contributor to global security governance. The US clearly projects power because it has both the capability and obligation to do so as the system leader. It is as clear that the federal government's rising annual budget deficits, the concomitant increase in government debt as a share of GDP, and the growing share of the US budget dedicated to debt service will eventually force a reduction in future expenditures on global and regional security governance.[19] This crowding-out process will be compounded by the asymmetrical distribution of resources between the four domains of governance and the demands of the American security culture. Just as the share of the federal budget allocated to the policies of compellence presently dwarfs those dedicated to the combined budgets of protection, assurance and prevention, the imperatives of the national security culture are more likely to produce deep cuts in budgets dedicated to assurance, prevention and even protection in order to ensure that the US can continue to meet the tasks of 'complex deterrence'. The real question about American governance policy, therefore, is whether the US is making, and in the future will make, the most efficient use of its considerable resources to act effectively upon its Kantian impulses in an incorrigibly Hobbesian world.

Notes

1 Only someone with the narrative skills of Baron von Munchhausen or former Vice-President Dick Cheney could argue otherwise.
2 President Obama has made an effort to change the public discourse. In his Cairo speech, for example, he stated: 'I have come here to seek a new beginning between the United States and Muslims around the world; one based upon mutual interest and mutual respect; and one based upon the truth that America and Islam are not exclusive, and need not be in competition. Instead, they overlap, and share common principles – principles of justice and progress; tolerance and the dignity of all human beings' (Obama 2009c).
3 The Obama administration's *National Intelligence Strategy* (NIS) acknowledged that there exist some 'opportunities for cooperative multilateral action' to meet a range of security challenges (White House 2009a: 3). Yet in his September 2009 UN address, President Obama transformed the qualified endorsement of multilateralism into a virtual categorical imperative: the US required a cooperative relationship with the rest of the world (Morris 2009).
4 A comprehensive typology of security governance systems is found in Sperling (2008).
5 The US' assessment for large-scale operations was 12.4 per cent in 2000, only to rise to 13.57 per cent in 2002 (OSCE 2000, 2001).
6 The US has also refrained from contributing to the UN multilateral trust funds established to stabilize war-torn regions of the world. There are approximately 27 such funds and pilot projects for the Central African Republic, Darfur, the DR Congo, Sudan, Lebanon, Iraq, Rwanda and Sierra Leone, among others. The US has only contributed to two funds (USD 5 million to the UNDG Iraq Trust Fund and USD 35 million to the UN Central Fund for Influenza Action). The US contribution, which amounts to 10 per cent of the total, leaves the US in 11th rank (ahead of Germany, France and Russia, but behind the UK, Japan, Canada and Italy) (UNDP 2009).
7 The US provides 59 per cent of the direct support provided to the Afghan government's core and external budget, a share that represents an effort index of 1.37.
8 The Israeli share declined from 26 per cent to under 5 per cent of total ESF disbursements between 2003 and 2007.
9 Of the other major countries, Russia pledged USD 2 billion (11.2 per cent), Germany USD 1.5 billion (8.43 per cent), Italy USD 1.2 billion (6.74 per cent), Canada USD 804 million (4.5 per cent), France and the UK USD 750 million each (4.21 per cent), and Japan USD 200 million. Twelve other donors, including the EU, pledged approximately USD 560 million (3.15 per cent) (Monterey Institute of International Studies 2008). By way of comparison, The Nunn-Lugar Cooperative Threat Reduction Programme (The Soviet Nuclear Threat Reduction Act of 1991) already dedicated USD 3.14 billion in those tasks between 1991 and 2001 (Woolf 2001: 32).

10 These programmes have financed, *inter alia*, the deactivation of 7,260 nuclear war-heads, the destruction of 671 intercontinental ballistic missiles (ICBM), 119 ICBM mobile launchers, 33 ballistic nuclear missile-carrying submarines and 622 sea-launched ballistic missiles.

They have additionally made possible the construction of 12 biological and epidemi-ological monitoring stations, the upgrading of 12 nuclear weapons storage facilities, and the design and construction of chemical weapons destruction facilities (US Department of Defense 2009: 3).

11 The Bush administration's 2007 Comprehensive National Cybersecurity Initiative (CNCI) sought to integrate the cyber-defensive policies and programmes of law enforcement, (counter)intelligence and the military to address 'the full spectrum of cyber threats from remote network intrusions and insider operations to supply chain vulnerabilities' (White House 2009b: 4). The private sector was left to its own devices and the CNCI remained classified.

12 The urgency of the threat is reflected in the proposed Cybersecurity Act of 2009. The preamble to the Bill claims that 'America's failure to protect cyberspace is one of the most urgent national security problems facing the country' (US Congress 2009: Section 2).

13 The NSD budget has hovered around 1 per cent of that of the FBI and between 1 per cent and 2 per cent of the budget devoted to the goal of preventing terrorism and pro-moting national security (US Department of Justice 2009). Moreover, 70 per cent of NSD employees are attorneys.

14 In the annual budget justifications submitted to Congress, the FBI and DEA highlight their performance in prosecuting those crimes that have been securitized: money laundering, counter-terrorism, computer intrusions, and the dismantling or disrup-tion of national or transnational criminal organizations on the US Attorney General's Consolidated Priority Organization Target List (CPOT) (DEA 2009; FBI 2009). It is difficult to draw any firm conclusions about the success or failure of either the FBI or DEA to achieve the goals set out in SAD owing to sketchy data and the absence of a baseline for measuring progress towards eliminating the absolute number of crimes committed or reducing the absolute number of criminal organizations.

15 By comparison, Britain deploys 39,300 troops overseas, approximately 18 per cent of total British military personnel (208,000); and France deploys 12,000 troops overseas, approximately 5 per cent of total French military personnel (259,050).

16 If non-deployed warheads are taken into account, the balance shifts in favour of the Russian Federation, with 55 per cent of the total warheads versus 42 per cent for the US.

17 STOVL stands for short take-off/vertical landing. Italy and the UK have two STOVL carriers each. Both Japan and Thailand have a helicopter carrier in service.

18 These calculations do not take into account the additional deployments to Afghanistan made in 2009. If considered, it would reduce (increase) the European (American) index of effort. On the changes taking place in the American approach to counter-insurgency warfare, see Obama (2009b), White House (2009c) and ISAF (2009).

19 In 2008, for example, the Department of Defense accounted for 21 per cent of the federal budget, while the net debt service amounted to 8.4 per cent, the Department of Justice approximately 1.6 per cent, and International Affairs 0.96 per cent (OMB 2009).

References

Browne, M.A. (2006) 'United Nations Peacekeeping: Issues for Congress', *CRS Issue Brief for Congress, IB 901031*, Washington, DC: Library of Congress, 5 July.

Carnegie Endowment for Peace (2009) *World Nuclear Arsenals 2009*. Available online at: http://www.carnegieendowment.org/publications/index.cfm?fa = view&id = 22710 (accessed 17 August 2009).

Carr, E.H. (1938) *The Twenty Years' Crisis, 1919–1939: An Introduction to the Study of International Relations*, London: Macmillan.

Center for Arms Control and Non-Proliferation (2009) 'US Military Spending vs. the World'. Available online at: http://www.armscontrolcenter.org/policy/securityspending/ articles/fy09_dod_request_global/ (accessed 17 August 2009).

Centers for Disease Control (annual) *FY [2004–2010] CDC/ATSDR Functional Table, Financial Management Office*. Available online at: http://www.cdc.gov/fmo/ fmofybudget.htm (accessed 5 June 2009).

DEA (Drug Enforcement Administration) (2009) *FY 2010 Performance Budget. Drug Enforcement Agency, Congressional Budget Submission*. Available online at: http://www. usdoj.gov/jmd/2010justification/ (accessed 31 August 2009).

Defense Threat Reduction Agency (2010) *Fiscal Year 2010 Budget Estimate Cooperative Threat Reduction Program*, Washington, DC: DTRA, May.

Economist (2009) 'Diplomacy and Iran: Anything more to declare?', *Economist*, 8651 (3–9 October): 57–58.

Federal Bureau of Investigation (2004) *Strategic Plan, 2004–2009*, Washington, DC: Federal Bureau of Investigation.

—— (2009) *Fiscal Year 2010 FBI Congressional Budget Request, June*. Available online at: http://fas.org/irp/agency/doj/fbi/2010just.pdf (accessed 17 July 2009).

FinCEN (Financial Crimes Enforcement Network) (2008) *Annual Report Fiscal Year 2008*. Available online at: http://www.finCEN.gov (accessed 15 July 2009).

Fingar, T. (2005) 'Statement of Thomas Fingar, Assistant Secretary of State for Intelligence and Research', made before the US Senate Select Committee on Intelligence, hearing on *Security Threats to the United States*, 16 February.

Global Policy Forum (2009) 'Debt of 15 Largest Payers to the Peacekeeping Budget'. Available online at: http://www.globalpolicy.org/tables-and-charts-ql/un-finance-tcql. html (accessed 21 August 2009).

Goslin, T.B. (2000) 'Statement of Major General Thomas B. Goslin, Jr., USAF, Director of Operations, US Space Command', made before US Senate Committee on Armed Services, Subcommittee on Emerging Threats and Capabilities, 1 March. Available online at: http://www.armed-services.senate.gov/hearings/2000/e000301.htm (accessed 30 November 2004).

Goss, P. (2005) 'Global Intelligence Challenges 2005: Meeting Long-Term Challenges with a Long-Term Strategy', testimony before the US Senate Select Committee on Intelligence, hearing on *Security Threats to the United States*, 16 February.

Hixson, W. (2009) *The Myth of American Diplomacy: National Identity and US Foreign Policy*, New Haven: Yale University Press.

International Afghanistan Conference (2004) 'Berlin Declaration', 1 April. Available online at: http://www.ag-afghanistan.de/berlindeclaration.pdf (accessed 30 January 2009).

ISAF (2009) *Commander's Initial Assessment: Commander NATO International Security Assistance Force, Afghanistan, US Forces, Afghanistan*, 30 August. Available online at: http://www.globalsecurity.org/military/library/report/2009/090830-afghan- assessment/090830-afghan-assessment.pdf (accessed 30 September 2009).

Jacoby, L.E. (2003) 'Current and Projected National Security Threats to the United States', statement made before US Senate Select Committee on Intelligence, hearing on *Worldwide Threats to the Security Community*, 11 February. Available online at: http:// web.lexis-nexis.com/congcomp/printdoc (accessed 20 September 2004).

—— (2005) 'Current and Projected National Security Threats to the United States', statement made before US Senate Select Committee on Intelligence, hearing on *The World Wide Threat*, 16 February. Available online at: http://intelligence.senate.gov/0502161/jacoby.pdf (accessed 30 June 2005).

Jervis, R.J. (2003) 'Understanding the Bush Doctrine', *Political Science Quarterly*, 118 (3): 365–88.

Kagan, R. (2003) *Of Paradise and Power: America and Europe in the New World Order*, New York: Alfred A. Knopf.

Kapstein, E.B. and Mastanduno, M. (eds) (1999) *Unipolar Politics*. New York: Columbia University Press.

Layne, Christopher (2007) *The Peace of Illusions: American Grand Strategy from 1940 to the Present*. Ithaca, NY: Cornell University Press.

London Conference on Afghanistan (2006) *The Afghanistan Compact*, 31 January–1 February: annex 1. Available online at: http://www.nato.int/isaf/docu/epub/pdf/afghanistan_compact.pdf (accessed 30 January 2009).

Loy, J. (2005) 'Statement of Jim Loy, Deputy Secretary of Homeland Security', made before US Senate Select Committee on Intelligence, hearing on *The World Wide Threat*, 16 February.

Monterey Institute of International Studies (2008) 'Collection of resources on activities under the G8 Global Partnership Against the Spread of Weapons and Materials of Mass Destruction'. Available online at: http://cns.miis.edu/global_partnership/funding.htm (accessed 31 July 2009).

Morris, H. (2009) 'Obama: co-operate on global problems', *Financial Times*, 24 September.

NATO (2009) 'Financial and Economic Data Relating to NATO Defense', *Communiqué PR/CP(2009)009*, 19 February.

Oakley, P.E. (1998) 'Statement by Assistant Secretary of State for Intelligence and Research, Phyllis E. Oakley', made before the US Senate Select Committee on Intelligence, hearing on *Current and Projected National Security Threats to the United States*, 28 January. Available online at: http://www.web.lexis-nexis.com/congcomp/printdoc (accessed 28 September 2004).

Obama, B. (2009a) 'Remarks by the President on a New Strategy for Afghanistan and Pakistan', Washington, DC: White House, 27 March.

—— (2009b) 'Remarks by the President on Securing our Nation's Cyber Infrastructure', Washington, DC: White House, 29 May.

—— (2009c) 'Text: Obama's Speech in Cairo', *The New York Times*, 4 June. Available online at: http://www.nytimes.com/2009/06/04/us/politics/04obama.text.html (accessed 1 October 2009).

OECD (2009) *Aid Statistics*, Paris: OECD. Available online at: http://www.oecd.org/depar tment/0,3355,en_2649_34447_1_1_1_1_1,00.html (accessed 20 June 2009).

Office of Homeland Security (2002) *National Strategy for Homeland Security*, Washington, DC: White House.

OMB (Office of Management and Budget) (annual) 'Homeland Security Funding Analysis', *Analytical Perspectives. Budget of the US Government, Fiscal Year [2004–10]*, Washington, DC: GPO.

—— (2009) 'Historical Tables: Table 3.1, Outlays by Superfunction and Function'. Available online at: http://www.whitehouse.gov/omb/budget/fy2010/assets/hist03z2.xls (accessed 17 October 2009).

OSCE (2000) *Decision No. 398 Interim Financing Arrangement for the Scale of*

Contributions for Large OSCE Missions, 314th Plenary Meeting, PC Journal No. 314, Agenda item 8(a), PC.DEC/398, 14 December.

—— (2001) *Decision No. 408 Scale for Large OSCE Missions and Projects/Corrected reissue*, 330th Plenary Meeting, PC Journal No. 330, Agenda item 2, PC.DEC/408/Corr.1, 5 April.

—— (2008a) *Updated Survey of OSCE Field Operations*, SEC.GAL/182/09, 30 September.

—— (2008b) *Decision No. 850 Scales of Contributions for 2008 and 2009*, 713th Plenary Meeting, PC Journal No. 713, Agenda item 3, PC.DEC/850, 15 May.

Osgood, R.E. (1952) *Ideals and Self-Interest in American Foreign Policy*, Chicago: University of Chicago Press.

Perlo-Freeman, S. (2009) 'NATO Military Expenditure by Category', in SIPRI (ed.) *SIPRI Yearbook 2008: Armaments, Disarmament and International Security*, Oxford: Oxford University Press.

Powell, C. (2007) 'Ideas and Consequences', *The Atlantic* (October). Available online at: http://www.theatlantic.com/doc/200710/aspen-ideas-festival# (accessed 30 September 2009).

Rollins, J. and A.C. Henning (2009) *Comprehensive National Cybersecurity Initiative: Legal Authorities and Policy Considerations*, Washington, DC: Congressional Research Service, 10 March.

Rumsfeld, D.H. (2002) 'DoD Newsbriefing: Secretary Rumsfeld and Gen. Myers'. Available online at: http://www.defenselink.mil/transcripts/transcript.aspx?transcriptid = 2636 (accessed 17 October 2009).

Schaefer, B.D. (2007) 'Keep the Cap on US Contributions to UN Peacekeeping', *Backgrounder*, No. 2067 (September): 1–20. Available online at: http://www.heritage.org/Research/InternationalOrganizations/bg2067.cfm (accessed 10 January 2009).

Seelke, C.R. and Beittel, J.S. (2009) *Mérida Initiative for Mexico and Central America: Funding and Policy Issues*, Washington, DC: Congressional Research Service, June.

SIPRI (2009) *Global Military Expenditure Set New Record in 2008*. Available online at: http://www.sipri.org/media/media/pressreleases/8june_yearbook_launch (accessed 17 August 2009).

Sperling, J. (2008) 'State Attributes and System Properties: Security Multilateralism in Central Asia, Southeast Asia, the Atlantic and Europe', in Bourantonis, D., Ifantis, K. and Tsakonas, P. (eds) *Multilateralism and Security Institutions in an Era of Globalization*, Abingdon, UK: Routledge.

Sperling, J. and Webber, M. (2009) 'NATO: from Kosovo to Kabul', *International Affairs*, 85: 491–512.

Tenet, G.J. (2004) *DCI's Worldwide Threat Briefing. The Worldwide Threat 2004: Challenges in a Changing Global Context*, 24 February. Available online at: http://www.usiraqprocon.org/pdf/tenet0204.pdf (accessed 21 January 2005).

UN (2008) *The International Compact with Iraq. A New Beginning Annual Review May 2007–April 2008*. Available online at: http://www.sweden.gov.se/content/1/c6/10/36/08/dfdaeead.pdf (accessed 29 September 2009).

UN and World Bank (2003) *International Reconstruction Fund Facility For Iraq Terms of Reference*, 11 December. Available online at: http://www.irffi.org/WBSITE/EXTERNAL/IRFFI/0,contentMDK:20479525~isCURL:Y~menuPK:497605~pagePK:64168627~piPK:64167475~theSitePK:491458,00.html (accessed 30 September 2009).

UNDP Afghanistan (United Nations Development Program) (2008a) *Counter Narcotics Trust Fund (CNTF) Quarterly Project Report, 3rd Quarter*, New York: United Nations.

—— (2008b), *Law and Order Trust Fund for Afghanistan (LOTFA-Phase V)*, New York: United Nations.

—— (2009) *Donor Contributions to UNDP-Administered MDTFs as of 30 June 2009*, New York: United Nations. Available online at: www.undp.org/mdtf (accessed 7 July 2009).

UNDPKO (Department of Peacekeeping Operations) (2009a) 'Past Operations'. Available online at: http://www.un.org/Depts/dpko/dpko/pastops.shtml (accessed 15 January 2009).

—— (2009b) 'Current Operations'. Available online at: http://www.un.org/Depts/dpko/dpko/currentops.shtml (accessed 15 January 2009).

—— (2009c) 'Ranking of Military and Police Contributions to UN Operations'. Available online at: http://www.un.org/Depts/dpko/dpko/contributors/2009/aug09_2.pdf (accessed 1 October 2009).

UN General Assembly (2008) *Approved Resources for Peacekeeping Operations for the Period from 1 July 2007 to 30 June 2008*, A/C.5/62/23.

UN Security Council (2001) UNSCR Resolution 1386, S/RES/1386 (2001).

—— (2003) UNSCR Resolution 1510, S/RES/1510 (2003).

—— (2005) UNSCR Resolution 1623, S/RES/1623 (2005).

—— (2007) UNSCR Resolution 1770, S/RES/1770 (2007).

US Congress (2009) *Cybersecurity Act of 2009. S 773*, 111th Congress, 1st Session, Washington, DC: GPO, 1 April.

US Department of Defense (annual) *Cooperative Threat Reduction. Annual Report to the Congress, Fiscal Year [2006, 2007, 2009]*, Washington, DC: US Department of Defense.

—— (2005a) *Annual Report to Congress: The Military Power of the People's Republic of China, 2005*, Washington, DC: Office of the Secretary of Defense.

—— (2005b) The National Defense Strategy of the United States of America, Washington, DC: Office of the Secretary of Defense.

—— (2005c) 'Strategy for Homeland Defense and Civil Support', Washington, DC: Office of the Secretary of Defense.

—— (2006) *Quadrennial Defense Review 2006*. Washington, DC: GPO.

—— (2008) National Defense Strategy, Washington, DC: Office of Secretary of Defense, June.

US Department of Energy (annual) *FY [2005–2010] Congressional Budget Request Budget Highlights*, Washington, DC: Department of Energy.

US Department of Health and Human Services (2009) *Public Health and Social Services Emergency Fund. FY 2010 Budget in Brief*. Available online at: http://www.hhs.gov/asrt/ob/docbudget/2010phssef.pdf (accessed 25 September).

US Department of Justice (2003) *FY 2003–2008 Strategic Plan, US Department of Justice*. Available online at: http://www.justice.gov/jmd/mps/strategic2003–8/pdf.html (accessed 28 October 2004).

—— (2007) *Stewards of the American Dream. FY 2007–2012 Strategic Plan*. Available online at: http://www.usdoj.gov/jmd/mps/strategic2007–12/strategic_plan20072012.pdf (accessed 29 June 2009).

—— (2009) *FY 2010 Budget and Performance Summary*, Available online at: http://www.usdoj.gov/jmd/2010summary/ (accessed 25 September 2009).

US Department of State (annual-a) *Summary and Highlights. International Affairs Function 150. Fiscal Year [2003–2010] Budget Request*, Washington, DC: US Department of State.

—— (annual-b) *Global Programs International Narcotics and Law Enforcement: FY [2004–2007] Budget Justification, June*. Available online at: http://www.state.gov/p/inl/rls/rpt/cbj/ (accessed 15 August 2009).

208   *J. Sperling*

—— (2007) *January 2005 Section 2207 Report on Iraq Relief and Reconstruction*. Available online at: http://2001–9.state.gov/s/d/rm/rls/2207/jan2005/pdf/index.htm (accessed 7 September 2009).

—— Bureau of International Narcotics and Law Enforcement Affairs (2007) *Regional and Global Programs: International Narcotics and Law Enforcement: FY 2008 Program and Budget Guide*, 18 September. Available online at: http://www.state.gov/p/inl/rls/rpt/pbg/93288.htm (accessed 15 August 2009).

US Department of the Treasury (2007) *2007 Money Laundering Strategy*. Washington, DC: GPO.

Vatis, M.A. (1999) 'Statement of Michael A. Vatis, Director, National Infrastructure Protection Center, Federal Bureau of Investigation', made before US Senate Committee on Armed Services, Subcommittee on Emerging Threats and Capabilities, 16 March, Available online at: http://www.armed-services.senate.gov/hearings/1999/e990316.htm (accessed 30 November 2004).

—— (2000) 'Statement of Michael A. Vatis, Deputy Assistant Director and Chief, National Infrastructure Protection Center, Federal Bureau of Investigation', US Senate Committee on Armed Services, Subcommittee on Emerging Threats and Capabilities.

White House (1993) *The National Security Strategy of the United States, 1993*, Washington, DC: White House.

—— (1995) *A National Security Strategy of Engagement and Enlargement*, Washington, DC: White House.

—— (1999) *A National Security Strategy for a New Century*, Washington, DC: White House.

—— (2002a) *The National Security Strategy of the United States of America*, Washington, DC: White House.

—— (2002b) *National Strategy to Combat Weapons of Mass Destruction*, Washington, DC: White House.

—— (2003a) *The National Strategy for the Physical Protection of Critical Infrastructures and Key Assets*, Washington, DC: White House.

—— (2003b) *The National Strategy to Secure Cyberspace*, Washington, DC: White House.

—— (2006) *The National Security Strategy of the United States of America*, Washington, DC: White House.

—— (2009a) *The National Intelligence Strategy of the United States of America*, August, Washington, DC: White House, August.

—— (2009b) *Cyberspace Policy Review. Assuring a Trusted and Resilient Information and Communication Infrastructure*, Washington, DC: White House, May.

—— (2009c) *White Paper of the Interagency Policy Group's Report on US Policy toward Afghanistan and Pakistan*, Washington, DC: White House, 27 March.

—— (2009d) 'Administration Officials Announce US-Mexico Border Security Policy: A Comprehensive Response and Commitment', Washington, DC: White House, 24 March.

Woodward, B. (2004) *Plan of Attack*, New York: Simon and Shuster.

Woolf, A.F. (2001) 'Nunn-Lugar Cooperative Threat Reduction Programs: Issues for Congress', *CRS Report for Congress, 97–1027F*, 23 March.

World Bank (2008) *Afghanistan Reconstruction and Trust Fund, Annual Report to Donors for the Afghan Fiscal Year 1386*. Available online at: http://siteresources. worldbank.org/SOUTHASIAEXT/Resources/223546-1202156192201/4638255-1205807817685/4787643-1205807893828/1386AnnualReport.pdf (accessed 10 January 2009).

—— (2009) *International Reconstruction Fund Facility for Iraq. Donor Commitments to the World Bank Iraq Trust Fund and United Nations Development Group Iraq Trust Fund*. Available online at: http://siteresources.worldbank.org/IRFFI/Resources/WBUNDGITFDonorCommitmentsMarch2009.pdf (accessed 15 September 2009).

Part III
Eurasia

10 China

Power, complementarity and reflexivity

Anthony Coates

Official statements emanating from Beijing over the past two decades reflect a widening in the scope of China's strategic discourse. Traditional security issues in conventional military terms have clearly been added to by the identification of social, economic and environmental threats, with Chinese interests today ranging between such diverse issue-areas as Sino-Western engagement, terrorism, health and development. Indeed, Beijing now faces opportunities and challenges far more varied than those of just two or three decades ago: some the culmination of national policies, such as 'socialism with Chinese characteristics' (*juyou Zhongguo tese de shehuizheyi*); others affected by global contexts, such as regionalization or the global response to the terrorist attacks of 11 September 2001. In this context, given its growing political, military and economic clout in the post-Cold War era, China has become more adaptable and flexible in terms of strategic behaviour. Over the past decade, for instance, Chinese participation in UN peacekeeping operations (UNPKO) has increased significantly; in 2001, China co-founded the multilateral Shanghai Cooperation Organization (SCO) with Central Asian states over mutual security and developmental concerns; and, in 2003, China acquired partner status to the Association of Southeast Asian Nations (ASEAN) on the basis of substantial regional economic ties. China today has undoubtedly changed considerably from the insular and enigmatic power witnessed during the Cold War.

Even so, the state-centric or Westphalian conception attributed to China still applies rather well. For instance, key strategic contingencies remain a possible military conflict over Taiwan, as well as throughout East Asia via Beijing's patron-client relationship with the regime in North Korea. Yet, just as these Cold War relics persist, so too do more historical ones. Concessions to European powers and subjugation by Japan in the nineteenth and early twentieth centuries still scar the Chinese psyche, compounded by a modernist, popular nationalism and millennia of imperial culture (Callahan 2004: 214). With a keen eye on its past, then, China's worldview and strategic approach retain sovereignty and non-interference in the affairs of other states at the core. Moreover, as an autocratic state still dominated by the Communist Party of China (CPC), ensuring political control and social stability is as important now as it was in the dynastic eras and early post-revolutionary period. Beijing's instrumental and interactive preferences thus draw upon strong, traditional conceptions of statehood and autonomy, shaped by the Party's inherent conservatism and paternalistic tendencies (Scobell 2002: 12).

The apparent shift to even limited multilateralism, however, suggests significant changes in Beijing's strategic approach. Several contexts pertain here. First, China's substantial economic growth over the past two decades has translated into vastly increased state capacity. Since the Deng era reforms in 1978, for instance, official government revenue and expenditure has increased almost fortyfold (National Bureau of Statistics 2008). Though domestic problems of socio-economic inequality are increasingly apparent, growth has significantly increased China's 'comprehensive national power' (*quanmian guoli*). Second, an expanding matrix of national interests has emerged, born as much from shifting internal politics, such as stronger liberal elements in the CPC, as from changes in domestic interests and material needs (Zheng 2005). Third, global dynamics have considerably affected Chinese security considerations. While the international struggle against fundamentalist terrorism post-9/11 is a significant context, so too are those of increasing world resource and energy demands and market volatility. Of course, rapid growth and exogenous shocks are not unique to the Chinese experience. What is distinctive in China's case is how these combine with the cognitive issues of the country's evolving self-image and cultural inheritance. Just as thinking about the use of force can affect the actual use of force and vice versa, so culture really matters in assessing China's worldview and strategic preferences (Dellios 1997: 8–9).

Assessing China: some caveats

Unfortunately, there are several sets of problems in assessing Chinese security culture and security governance. Significant problems exist, firstly, with respect to the availability and utility of official data concerning the policy areas of security governance as defined earlier in this book. Though Beijing releases official data annually, these are limited and use metrics that are awkward for the proposed framework. For example, while the category of protection focuses on policing and crime, official statistics are sparse and explicit policy details lacking (see Tables 10.1 and 10.2). Though data suggests a modicum of decentralization, given the shifting ratio of central/local police expenditure, Beijing does not issue particulars concerning policing strategy. Moreover, the apparent shift is somewhat marginalized by the bigger picture of considerable increases in overall government expenditure, underpinned by national economic growth. Similarly, reportage of bodily injury and larceny (which have apparently risen since 1995) and of homicides, rape, trafficking and fraud (decreased) lack details or independent verification. Indeed, given that only these classes of crime are publicly listed and have all apparently decreased as a share of total reported crimes, a large and increasingly significant number of crimes remain unpublished.

Such analytical difficulties apply not just within the proposed categories of security governance, but are problematic for the categorizations in themselves. For example, though judicial, police and militia expenditures used to be disaggregated, data for recent years is aggregated: local militia and police are known

Table 10.1 Government expenditure, public security and policing (USDm)

Year	Government budget	National defence					Public security organs					People's Armed Police (PAP)				
		Total	Central	(%)	Local	(%)	Total	Central	(%)	Local	(%)	Total	Central	(%)	Local	(%)
1997	134,809.08	8,851.40					5,960.45					819.21				
1998	157,653.43	8,913.30					7,612.73					1,527.60				
1999	192,539.98	11,422.89					8,847.60					1,509.93				
2000	231,942.90	13,205.26					10,424.25					1,934.69				
2001	275,977.67	17,293.41					12,645.79					2,590.04				
2002	321,975.99	24,933.59	24,686.26	(99.0)	247.32	(1.0)	16,082.92	881.99	(5.5)	15,200.94	(94.5)	3,612.19	3,307.48	(91.6)	304.72	(8.4)
2003	359,889.27	27,854.90	27,525.23	(98.8)	329.67	(1.2)	18,999.42	1,032.80	(5.4)	17,966.61	(94.6)	3,857.47	3,503.56	(90.8)	353.90	(9.2)
2004	415,908.59	32,120.15	31,711.35	(98.7)	408.80	(1.3)	22,601.68	1,196.32	(5.3)	21,405.36	(94.7)	4,191.51	3,739.94	(89.2)	451.58	(10.8)
2005	495,382.09	36,134.42	35,726.64	(98.9)	407.78	(1.1)	27,052.19	1,296.92	(4.8)	25,755.28	(95.2)	4,772.30	4,172.68	(87.4)	599.62	(12.6)
2006	590,171.86	43,498.95	43,031.16	(98.9)	467.78	(1.1)	31,743.76	1,440.73	(4.5)	30,303.03	(95.5)	5,665.24	4,896.55	(86.4)	768.69	(13.6)

Source: Adapted from National Bureau of Statistics 2008

Note: No official data for above categories prior to 1997 and Central/Local distinction not made prior to 2002. 'National defence' does not refer to the PLA budget, but militia-related expenditures, such as recruitment, construction and (absent details) aspects of national military R&D. State internal security and intelligence agencies are thought to come under 'public security', as are public judicial/prosecutorial costs

Table 10.2 Criminal cases reported to public security organs (category as share of total reported, %)

Year	Homicide Cases (%)	Injury Cases (%)	Rape Cases (%)	Human trafficking Cases (%)	Larceny Cases (%)	Smuggling Cases (%)	Money fraud Cases (%)	Total	Resolved (%)
1995	27,356 (1.69)	72,259 (4.46)	41,823 (2.58)	10,670 (0.66)	1,132,789 (69.88)	1,119 (0.07)	5,237 (0.32)	1,621,003	N/A
1996	25,411 (1.59)	68,992 (4.31)	42,820 (2.68)	8,290 (0.52)	1,043,982 (65.22)	1,147 (0.07)	5,128 (0.32)	1,600,716	79.9
1997	26,070 (1.62)	69,071 (4.28)	40,699 (2.52)	6,425 (0.40)	1,058,110 (65.57)	1,133 (0.07)	5,422 (0.34)	1,613,629	72.6
1998	27,670 (1.39)	80,862 (4.07)	40,967 (2.06)	6,513 (0.33)	1,296,988 (65.30)	2,301 (0.12)	6,654 (0.34)	1,986,068	63.7
1999	27,426 (1.22)	92,772 (4.12)	39,435 (1.75)	7,257 (0.32)	1,447,390 (64.35)	1,205 (0.05)	10,047 (0.45)	2,249,319	N/A
2000	28,429 (0.78)	120,778 (3.32)	35,819 (0.98)	23,163 (0.64)	2,373,696 (65.26)	1,993 (0.05)	15,863 (0.44)	3,637,307	N/A
2001	27,501 (0.62)	138,100 (3.10)	40,600 (0.91)	7,008 (0.16)	2,924,512 (65.61)	1,784 (0.04)	5,780 (0.13)	4,457,579	N/A
2002	26,276 (0.61)	141,825 (3.27)	38,209 (0.88)	5,684 (0.13)	2,861,727 (65.98)	1,149 (0.03)	5,238 (0.12)	4,337,036	N/A

(continued)

Year	Homicide Cases (%)	Injury Cases (%)	Rape Cases (%)	Human trafficking Cases (%)	Larceny Cases (%)	Smuggling Cases (%)	Money fraud Cases (%)	Total	Resolved (%)
2003	24,393 (0.56)	145,485 (3.31)	40,088 (0.91)	3,721 (0.08)	2,940,598 (66.92)	1,178 (0.03)	3,151 (0.07)	4,393,893	41.9
2004	24,711 (0.52)	148,623 (?)	36,175 (0.77)	3,343 (0.07)	3,212,822 (68.10)	955 (0.02)	2,315 (0.05)	4,718,122	N/A
2005	20,770 (0.45)	155,056 (?)	33,710 (0.73)	2,884 (0.06)	3,158,763 (67.95)	925 (0.02)	1,858 (0.04)	4,648,401	45.1
2006	17,936 (0.39)	160,964 (?)	35,352 (0.76)	2,659 (0.06)	3,143,863 (67.56)	974 (0.02)	1,784 (0.04)	4,653,265	N/A

Source: Adapted from National Bureau of Statistics 2008

Note: Case resolution data for 1995, 1999–2002, 2004, 2006 not given. The relatively high number of human trafficking cases in 2000 resulted from a large joint counter-trafficking operation between China, Vietnam and the International Labour Organization (ILO). Similarly, anti-racketeering, corruption and counterfeiting operations were conducted between 1998–2001 to use training and facilities provided for the People's Liberation Army/Navy and Air Force (PLA/N/AF) under 'National Defence' spending; 'Armed Police Troops' expenditure pertains to the paramilitary People's Armed Police Force (PAPF), but not local militias or the special infrastructure police protecting national transportation and resource assets; and spending on internal security forces is counted together with that of the civil and criminal courts under 'Public Security Agency, Procurator Agency, Court and Judicial Agency' (National Bureau of Statistics 2008; IISS 2007, 2008). Only a partial assessment of China in terms of security governance, supplemented by third-party estimates, is thus possible.

Furthermore, it would be overly simplistic to assess Chinese security culture without some consideration of underlying philosophies and etymological distinctions. For instance, in terms of worldview and instrumental preferences, the conceptual Westphalian state is zero-sum competitive, relying on coercion to achieve strategic goals. China might be characterized as such, having used force several times: against a US-led coalition in Korea in 1950, India in 1962 and Vietnam in 1979. Yet China has not engaged in militarized conflict more recently, while those historical actions might also be considered 'defensive' in both Chinese and Western strategic discourses: 'active defence' (*jiji fangyou*); 'counter-attack' (*ziwei fanji*); 'just war' (*yizhan*); and 'pre-emptive' war (*xian xia shou wei qiang*) (Huang 1997; Scobell 2002).

Similarly, the ominous tones often adopted by critics concerned with China's ascent neglect crucial differences between conceptions of 'forceful' (*badao*) and 'benevolent' hegemony (*wangdao*). While the former evokes Occidental notions of rationality and power politics, *wangdao* is an ancient facet of Chinese statecraft obtained via 'moral feeling' (*jen*) and 'proper conduct' (*li*). The product of these is 'virtuous governance' (*jen-li* or *xian guanzhi*), a categorical imperative applicable in all contexts of human interaction, whether personal, familial or governmental. This logic not only informs Chinese strategic behaviour, but is a universalizable normative expectation of other actors too. Though clearly state-centric, it is necessary to note that Chinese security culture thus entails complementarity over opposition: 'Harmonious non-action' (*wen*) and 'martial power' (*wu*) are not contradictory, just as the proverbial *yin* and *yang* are not to be confused as the negation of each other. Although conflict and use of force in the Chinese worldview are thereby 'undesirables', constituting a failure of harmony, this does not preclude the occasional need for coercion where civility (*hiexie xitong*) fails. Complementarity is often neglected in translation and its implications – such as Beijing's frequent reference to 'principles of peaceful co-existence' – are typically viewed through the somewhat partial, sceptical lens of Western 'rationality'.

Finally, assessing substantial changes to Chinese security policy-making and capabilities over the past two decades simply outruns this chapter's scope. With such caveats in mind, assessing China in terms of security culture and security governance would be better served by focusing on four key developments: participation in UN peacekeeping operations (UNPKO); a relatively new 'soft power' approach to official developmental assistance (ODA); engagement in regional security arrangements; and advances in military capabilities and strategy. In each setting, Beijing's interactive and instrumental preferences are clearly founded on a worldview in which state sovereignty is fundamental and inviolable. The Westphalian/post-Westphalian distinction, however, is slightly obscured in China's case due to contextual differences such as those mentioned. Although states are perceived as sovereign and autonomous entities, complementarity and reflexivity in the Chinese worldview in fact *dis*courage unilateralism and *en*courage cooperation. Beijing can thus respect and engage with the EU, for example, since the latter is a legal, supranational entity binding European states; but only so long as China's own modalities of sovereignty and autonomy are respected in the reflexive context of agreed-upon international laws and conventions.

Assurance: 'responsible world power'

With its considerable economic growth in recent years, China's prescribed financial burden for UNPKO has risen accordingly from 0.92 per cent of the budget (1982–95), to 0.99 per cent (1996–2000), to 2.67 percent (2001–7). Currently at 3.16 per cent, China's assessed contribution remains lower than that of the three largest contributors, the US (22 per cent), Japan (16.6 per cent) and Germany (8.6 per cent), and actual contributions are in reality closer to 2 per cent (Gill and Huang 2009: 6). China's troop contributions to UNPKO, however, are often greater than those of other Permanent Security Council members. Since 1990, a total of 12,721 Chinese personnel have been deployed with UNPKO. In 2008, China was the 13th largest troop contributor, with 1,949 peacekeepers, military observers and police deployed to 11 different UN missions worldwide (see Table 10.3). Indeed, since becoming a 'Class A' member of the UN Standby Arrangements System (UNSAS) in 2002, China has maintained a PLA engineering battalion, standard medical team and two transport companies at readiness for UNPKO. Several other national measures have helped China realize its growing commitments. Non-combat PLA units receive standardized UN training in their respective military regions, while military observers are formally instructed in UNPKO at the Nanjing International Relations Academy. A Peacekeeping Affairs Office was created within the Ministry of National Defence in the late 1990s, followed by the establishment of the China Peacekeeping/Civilian Police Training Centre (CPCTC) in 2000 in Langfang City, just outside of Beijing. Frequently used by China and neighbouring Southeast Asian states for joint training and military/police exchanges, the latter will be soon be supplemented by a new centralized PLA Peacekeeper Training Facility in Huairou, another Beijing suburb (IOSC 2009).

Yet Chinese UNPKO participation is a fairly recent development. Indeed, since membership in 1971, Chinese engagement in the UN overall might be classed as passive. Unlike the other Permanent Members of the Security Council, China has rarely obstructed the passage of UN Resolutions, using its veto power only six times and preferring to express dissent through 'critical abstention'. In fact, China's reluctance throughout much of the 1970s and 1980s for UN action reflected a lack of interest and capacity as much as wilful adherence to the principle of non-intervention. Substantial political expertise was for a long time focused instead upon national

Table 10.3a Contributions to ongoing UNPKO, People's Republic of China (by UNPKO start date, as of August 2008)

Mission	Where	Function	Total personnel to date			Financial contributions, 2007 (USDm)			Fatalities to date		
			PRC	UN All	% PRC	PRC	UN All	% PRC	PRC	UN	% PRC
UNFICYP*	Cyprus	PK	0	10,604	0.00	0.36	15.47	2.33	0	178	0
UNDOF*	Middle East	PK/MILOB	0	9,698	0.00	0.64	16.64	3.85	0	43	0
UNTSO	N/A	MILOB	80	2,300	3.48				1	49	2.04
MINURSO	W. Sahara	PK	288	3,431	8.39	1.25	51.95	2.41	0	15	0
UNOMIG	Georgia	PK	0	2,034	0.00	0.30	13.33	2.25	0	11	0
MONUC	DR Congo	PK	698	97,364	0.72	13.22	143.46	9.22	1	127	0.79
UNAMA	Afghanistan	PB/ReConst	2	1,779	0.11				0	>100	0
UNMIL	Liberia	PK	1,222	71,524	1.71	6.45	201.70	3.20	2	112	1.79
UNOCI	Côte d'Ivoire	PK	5	36,846	0.01	8.72	286.71	3.04	0	46	0
UNMIK	Kosovo	PK	55	12,344	0.45	10.20	107.22	9.51	0	11	0
MINUSTAH	Haiti	PK/RC	514	44,440	1.16	6.07	152.48	3.98	0	35	0
UNMIS	Sudan	PK/RC	501	40,727	1.23	13.63	282.96	4.82	0	36	0
UNIFIL*	Lebanon	PK/MILOB	190	54,904	0.35	8.39	302.60	2.77	0	276	0
UNMIT	Timor-Leste	PK/RC	4	5,056	0.08		141.64		0	3	0

Note:
* PRC contributions to UNFICYP, UNDOF and UNIFIL since 1990; PRC PK/MILOB participation in UNIFIL since 2006

Table 10.3b Contributions to completed UNPKO, People's Republic of China (chronological order by start date)

Mission	Where	Function	Total personnel to date			Financial contributions (USDm)			Fatalities to date		
			PRC	UN All	% PRC	PRC	UN All	% PRC	PRC	UN	% PRC
UNIKOM	Iraq-Kuwait	MILOB	164	11,474	1.43	0.26	6.14	4.25	1	128	1
UNAMIC	Cambodia	PK/PB	897	>22,000	3.90		41.77		3	82	4
ONUMOZ	Mozambique	MILOB	20	>9,000	0.22				0	26	0
UNOMIL	Liberia	PK	33	>1,500	2.13				0	0	0
UNOMSIL	Sierra Leone	PK	39	67,095	0.06	2.42	31.29	7.74	0	192	0
UNMISET	East Timor	PK/RC	210	2,816	7.46	1.56	22.91	6.79	0	21	0
UNMEE	Ethiopia/Eritrea	MILOB/PK	45	10,618	0.42	1.43	52.28	2.74	0	20	0
UNMIBH	Bosnia	PK	20	13,110	0.15				0	12	0
ONUB	Burundi	PK	6	13,206	0.05	1.73	61.79	2.79	0	24	0

Sources: Adapted from UNDPKO 2008 and He 2007

development and the resolution of bilateral issues, such as Sino-US relations, promoting Third World partnerships and managing international aid links (He 2007: 16–18). Furthermore, material capacity was stunted by the socio-economic failures of Maoist 'national self-sufficiency' and the Cultural Revolution, as well as the need to stave off Soviet encroachments on China's northernmost borders. Despite international pressures for an 'opening-up' of China in the 1980s, Beijing mostly saw the UN as a stage for superpower squabbling and wanted neither to appear to take sides nor to risk national autonomy and development (Choedon 2005: 40).

By the early 1990s, several other factors further inhibited participation. Beijing's handling of the Tiananmen Square incident of 4 June 1989 drew much international criticism. This was compounded by the demise of the Soviet Union, which saw a 'China threat' discourse emerge in the West to replace old Cold War rhetoric – the suspicions of Washington policy hawks particularly exacerbated by China's inherent secretiveness. Another problem, at least in Beijing's eyes, was that the 'One China' accord with leading world powers was being undermined by a resurgence of international support for Taiwanese independence. Hence, despite China first venturing into UNPKO during this period, its efforts then were extremely limited: 20 civilian officials to the United Nations Transition Assistance Group (UNTAG) in 1989; five military observers to the United Nations Truce Supervision Organization (UNTSO) in 1990; and engineering support to the UN Transitional Administration in Cambodia in 1992–93. Indeed, through the mid-1990s, China appeared to have been painted into a corner. Throughout the Security Council's frequent deliberations on the UN Mission to Haiti (UNMIH), Haiti's traditional support for Taiwan's inclusion in the UN led China to use procedural objections to voice disapproval of tangential issues concerning national sovereignty, rather than UNMIH *per se*. This served only to damage Beijing's credibility and reputation further.

Beijing eventually realized that its stance on UN participation was untenable and would only worsen China's post-Tiananmen isolation, undermining the global links necessary for sustaining national development (Pang 2005: 91–3). The only feasible solution to this strategic failure was to change tack, embrace UN participation and cultivate an image of a 'responsible world power'; and UNPKO provided China its clearest path (He 2007: 69). Beijing thus took several important steps through the mid to late 1990s, including committal to the UNSAS framework, extension of UNTSO and UNTAC contributions, and deploying hundreds of military observers to various missions, such as UNIKOM, ONUMOZ and UNOMIL. In retrospect, on witnessing NATO's intervention in Kosovo in 1999, this change in tack came to make all the more sense. Objecting to the lack of explicit thresholds for peace enforcement and portraying NATO action as belligerence, Beijing exploited the opportunity to redress China's image abroad as a pacific nation supportive of international law (undoubtedly helped by NATO's bombing of the Chinese embassy in Belgrade). Later, US-led military actions in Afghanistan (2001) and Iraq (2003) provided additional contrasts, while China's UNPKO contributions ever since, as with troop and materiel support in 2006 for the UN Interim Force in Lebanon (UNIFIL), also helped Beijing cultivate this image.

Continued growth and greater encouragement from other world powers may yet see greater Chinese UNPKO participation. Yet material incapacity still restricts Chinese participation somewhat to engineering and medical supports. While these are important, more substantial logistical involvement and high-end peacekeeping by China, such as the rapid deployment of comprehensive, flexible and sustainable peacekeeping forces, will also depend upon Beijing's interpretation of justifiable intervention. As its UNIFIL deployments show, China is not averse to sending combat troops into conflict zones; but firm support for peace enforcement remains unlikely, despite official Chinese remarks on the need for 'faster, more robust [UN] responses in future' after reflecting on UNPKO experiences in Sub-Saharan Africa especially (Gill and Huang 2009: 5). Whereas peacekeeping entails acceptance of and consent for international action under Chapter VII of the UN Charter, forcible intervention or even explicit thresholds for this are incompatible with Beijing's worldview and, more particularly, its read on the situation concerning Taiwan. Indeed, in light of recent actions by other leading world powers, China's active, albeit conservative, stance on UNPKO rather improves its own status while delegitimizing that of its peers on the Security Council. For China, the UN's legal foundations demand that international action requires international mooting: Beijing's emphasis of UN multilateralism as a means of 'democratizing' international relations thus limits intervention in principle and in fact simultaneously reinforces China's image, its logic of complementarity and sovereign inviolability.

Prevention: South–South developmental assistance

Beijing's approach to developmental aid reflects a similar logic to the above. Historically an aid recipient, economic growth has seen China become an increasingly significant donor. Although China does not publish detailed aid statistics (and, not being an OECD member, is not tracked by the OECD Development Assistance Committee), estimates suggest that total Chinese ODA in 2006–7 ranged between USD 1.5 and 2 billion. Building on its Non-Aligned Movement ties from the Cold War, Chinese ODA makes up a substantial portion of the 5 per cent of world ODA contributions from non-OECD countries (OECD 2009: 38). Crucially, China's approach to developmental assistance continues to be informed by eight principles first espoused by Premier Zhou Enlai in 1964, including some by now familiar maxims: the inviolability of state sovereignty, 'equality and mutual benefit' and a commitment to 'never attaching conditions'. Indeed, China's somewhat testing, but nevertheless successful, experience as an aid recipient with both the Asian Development Bank (ADB) and International Bank for Reconstruction and Development (IBRD) has reinforced Beijing's thinking that ODA should focus upon technical and financial aspects (Chin and Frolic 2007: 2–4).

Particularly noteworthy is Beijing's focus on developmental assistance to African countries, for which total Chinese public and private financing in 2006 reached USD 8.2 billion (Alden 2007: 7). This focus is reflected in the structure of the Ministry of Commerce's Department of Aid to Foreign Countries (DAFC) that manages Chinese ODA. Of the seven regional DAFC bureaus, Africa has four, together handling around 40 per cent of Beijing's ODA budget (MOFCOM

2008a). Significantly, China's historical tendency for bilateralism in South–South relations has developed into weak multilateralism concerning Africa (Alden 2007: 2). In 2000, Beijing established the Forum on China-Africa Cooperation (FOCAC) together with 44 African countries, hosting triennial meetings since attended by representatives from 17 other international and regional organizations, including the UN, the EU and the African Union (AU). In 2002, Beijing committed to the Monterrey Conference goals of cancelling developing world debts, writing off USD 1.2 billion owed to China by the 31 least-developed African nations. This was followed in January 2006 by the publication of China's 'Africa Policy' paper, with several substantive aid measures proposed by President Hu Jintao at FOCAC that November: USD 500 million in development grants; a doubling of Chinese ODA to Africa to USD 1 billion by 2009; USD 5 billion in preferential loans and credits for development investors; and numerous tariff reductions for African imports (Harsch 2007; MFA 2006; Xinhua 2006a).

The Export-Import Bank of China (Exim) has been a crucial driver of Chinese ODA, organizing more than 250 government-subsidized loans to African countries at below-market rate since its establishment in 1994. In so doing, Exim has secured resource access for Beijing (as high as 45 per cent of national stocks in some cases) and procurement guarantees for Chinese enterprises (often in the form of machinery contracts; Mohan and Power 2008; Ortiz 2007: 2). Angola, Mozambique, Nigeria, Sudan and Zimbabwe have been the major Exim recipients, with most financing devoted to national-level resource extraction and transportation projects: copper mines in the Congo; oil facilities in Angola and Nigeria; modernization of Port Sudan; restoration of the Central African railway; as well as telecommunications, power and water management programmes (Alden 2007: 4). To complement its financial and technical assistance, however, Beijing has also adopted a relatively new 'soft power' tack. Exim recipients are today given additional incentives, such as medicines (USD 49.3 million in anti-malarial drugs were donated in 2008) and offers to build schools and hospitals (Xinhua 2009a). DAFC has also coordinated several other outreach programmes: Confucius Institutes, for example, providing Chinese language and cultural exchanges; volunteer youth exchange programmes (*Zhongguo qingnian zhiyuan zhe xiehui*); skills training in information technology and Chinese medicine; as well as construction of the new AU Conference Centre in Addis Ababa, Ethiopia (*People's Daily* 2006; MOFCOM 2008b; Xinhua 2009a).

A major reason why developing nations find Chinese aid attractive is that there are rarely other conditions besides resource and procurement guarantees (Lönnqvist 2007: 7–8). Terms such as 'good governance' or eliminating poverty – evident throughout Western aid discourses – are rarely employed by Beijing. Rather, developmental aid explicitly links with national strategic and commercial interests, in addition to propagating anti-colonial or anti-imperial solidarity with recipients (Mohan and Power 2008: 24). Yet Beijing does appear more willing now to occasionally yield on issues in a manner impossible previously for the possibility of abrogating sovereignty in principle and in fact. For instance, though preventing UN action for years on the humanitarian situation in Sudan (allegedly due to its co-ownership of the Greater Nile Petroleum Operating Company with Sudan), in 2008 China allowed several Security Council Resolutions to pass condemning Khartoum on Darfur (UNSC Resolutions 1812, 1828 and 1841). This is, however, far from a sea change. Responding to repeated US calls since 2006 for greater Sino-American energy cooperation in Africa, China has often reverted to an enigmatic stance: '[We] stand ready to cooperate with the US and other countries ... on the basis of equality and mutual benefit' (MFA 2006).

In being selective about and successful in gaining cooperation, despite the emphasis on essentially bilateral aid, China's strategic and commercial focus legitimizes Beijing's autonomy and that of aid recipients through reciprocation. Together with its 'soft power' approach, this may yet give reason for developing countries to provide Beijing with political support as well as resource access: fifty-three African votes at the UN is nothing to sniff at, certainly not for a rising great power (Holslag 2008: 348). Although weak multilateralism is evinced in such measures as FOCAC and regularization of China-AU dialogue, these are simply adaptations of Beijing's logic of complementarity and reflexivity, reinforcing the principle of sovereign inviolability in practice. Accordingly, lower transaction costs for Chinese aid cultivate something of a counter-multilateralism that under-cuts – if not entirely excludes – other, namely Western-led developmental efforts, ultimately serving Beijing's agenda of strategic rebalancing.

Protection: contingent regionalism

Closer to home, Beijing similarly limits its engagement within multilateral frameworks, using ASEAN and the SCO in particular to promote its worldview and reinforce Chinese autonomy. In the context of ASEAN, despite a strong dichotomy between national and regional self-identification being common to Southeast Asian countries, increased politico-economic ties and confidence and security-building measures (CSBMs) have sown the seeds for an 'ASEAN Security Community' (Boisseau and Fort 2005). Beijing's activism in regional discourses, however, ensures that China has a voice in shaping any developments. Conversely, the underlying aim of the SCO, while ostensibly a counter-terrorism and mutual-development pact, is also to preserve a regional order, albeit in Central Asia. Though differing from ASEAN in its conceptions of threat and response, the SCO also pertains less to substantive cooperation than to institutionalizing mutual respect for national sovereignties (Chung 2006: 13). Though there is insufficient room to detail the Six Party Talks concerning North Korea and (de)nuclearization, it is also worth mentioning here briefly. While Beijing seeks stable growth, entailing the resolution of Cold War enmities, maintaining North Korea as a buffer state is another key interest (Wu 2005: 36). Thus, China has shifted from express support for the Democratic People's Republic over the years to conditional assistance, and thence to a push for normalizing East Asian relations; this is highlighted by the convergence of interests with the wider international community (BBC 2009a). While each of the above settings differs somewhat, engagement in weak multilateralism in all these guises ultimately reflects Beijing's inherently conservative worldview and strategic preferences (see Table 10.4).

Table 10.4 Chinese engagement in the ASEAN Regional Forum, the Shanghai Cooperation Organisation and Six Party Talks

	ASEAN	*SCO*	*Six Party Talks*
Relevant mechanisms	ARF and Bali Concord II	Regional anti-terrorism structure	
Security governance system	'Security community'	'Collective defence'/ 'Collective security'	N/A: security dilemma
Security referent(s)	ASEAN member states	SCO member states	Regional states
	'Plus Three' states	State integrity	
	Sovereign inviolability	Political development	Depending on state
	Peaceful coexistence	Economic development	De-nuclearization of DPRK
	Political/economic/ social stability	Social/cultural security	Conflict avoidance/ peaceful unification (?)
	Mutual prosperity	Energy security	Food and energy security (DPRK?)
Function of norms	Sovereign inviolability	Sovereign inviolability	Normalization of peaceful relations
	Peaceful coexistence	Reinforce status quo	
	Mutual non-intervention		
Interaction context(s)	Amity, generally; albeit with latent enmities concerning territorial and resource dispute(s)	Sino-Russian balancing?	Unresolved armistice (1953)
		US/NATO entry into Central Asia	Cold War enmity
		Mutual socio-economic development	

China and ASEAN

Through ASEAN, China has insulated itself from unwanted attention on issues such as Taiwan, Tibet and human rights that are typically raised in its dealings with the West; interactive conditionalities undesirable for many ASEAN members too (Kuik 2005). China's successful relations with ASEAN, shown by its becoming a partner state in 2003 (and thus the first non-ASEAN country to sign the Association's constitutive Treaty of Amity and Cooperation or TAC), have built upon three important and ongoing processes. First, Beijing has long cultivated a normative affinity with its Southeast Asian neighbours based on mutual respect for national sovereignty, non-intervention and peaceful co-existence – principles advanced by China itself since the 1950s as 'good neighbour policy' (*shan jiefang zhence*) and formally enshrined in the TAC. Second, China set itself the goal of becoming ASEAN's largest trade partner, building on the 'Plus Three' framework created in 1997 linking ASEAN, China, Japan and South Korea. Beijing's undoubted success in this has meant that its neighbours are extremely wary of undermining mutual prosperity: ASEAN-China trade, for example, hit the USD 100 billion mark in 2005 and passed USD 202 billion only three years on, exceeding ASEAN-US trade by almost 20 per cent (Xinhua 2008a). Third, China has been one of the most pro-active Asian states pushing for security regionalization. Beijing was a major proponent of the ASEAN Regional Forum (ARF), for instance, created in 1994 as a 'consultative mechanism ... to bring about a more predictable and constructive pattern of relations' (ARF 2005). As an active participant in the ARF and various CSBMs ever since (see Table 10.5), China has thus become a key player in the establishment of the East Asia Summit (EAS)

Table 10.5 Examples of ARF 'Track One' inter-sessionals hosted by China since 1997

Inter-sessional Seminar on Narcotics Controls	Xi'an City	19–21 September 2007
6th ARF Inter-sessional Meeting on Disaster Relief	Qingdao	18–20 September 2006
4th ARF Inter-sessional Meeting on Counter-Terrorism and Transnational Crime	Beijing	26–28April 2006
ARF Seminar on Enhancing Cooperation in the Field of Non-Traditional Security Issues	Hainan	7–8 March 2005
ARF Security Policy Conference	China	4–6 November 2004
Inter-sessional Seminar on Alternative Development	Kunming	7–8 September 2004
Inter-sessional Support Group Meeting on Confidence Building Measures	Beijing	20–22 November 2003
Inter-sessional Seminar on Defence Conversion Cooperation	Beijing	20–22 September 2000
4th Meeting of Heads of Defence Colleges and Institutions	Beijing	6–8 September 2000
ARF Professional Training Programme on China's Security Policy	Beijing	10–19 October 1999
Symposium on Prevention and Treatment of Tropical Infectious Diseases	Beijing	25–27 November 1998
Inter-sessional Seminar on Confidence and Security Building Measures	Beijing	6–8 March 1997

arrangement formalizing security cooperation and 'community-building' between ASEAN Plus Three, India, Australia and New Zealand in 2005. China has also supported various non-governmental initiatives in the region, such as hosting the Boao Forum for Asia from 1999 onwards and assisting several Chinese universities to co-found the Network of East Asian Think-tanks (NEAT) in 2003 with their regional counterparts.

Enmities in Southeast Asia do still exist, however, as highlighted by ongoing spats between Cambodia, Malaysia and Thailand (BBC 2009b). Regionalization is inhibited also by resource and territorial disputes. For example, the Taiwan issue aside, China lays claim over vast swathes of the South China Seas, with the Spratly/Paracel Islands having provided the focus of much bitter diplomacy throughout the 1990s with other littoral states. As with its change in UN approach, however, China has toned down its traditional concerns to become an indispensable component within the regional dynamic. Consequently, Beijing's activism has helped propagate multiple layers of discourse rather than substantial common defence or security commitments; this is not solely due to Chinese activity, but relies also on inputs by regional neighbours as well. Thus cooperation has rarely gone beyond occasional information-sharing and joint counter-terrorism training; and even humanitarian disaster relief, as highlighted by efforts following Cyclone Nargis and the Sichuan earthquakes in 2008, has been patchwork (Simon 2008: 272–82). Though China and its Southeast Asian neighbours have focused upon economic institutionalization rather than security, this has worked for Beijing in reinforcing its worldview and the logic of complementarity. Indeed, ever since China became more 'pro-active' and engaged regionally, ASEAN members have become wary of subscribing to US-led regional security efforts: the US Container and Port Security Initiatives (CSI/PSI) are yet to be adopted throughout Asia; counter-terrorism measures passed by the Washington-dominated Asia Pacific Economic Consortium (APEC) in 2002 have stagnated; while US proposals in 2004 for a Regional Maritime Security Initiative were rejected outright by most ASEAN countries (Christoffersen 2008: 127).

China and the SCO

Beijing has also used the SCO as a counter-balance to US expansion into Central Asia, linking China's regional security concerns in recent years with those of Kazakhstan, Kyrgyzstan, Russia, Tajikistan and Uzbekistan. In contrast to its ASEAN approach, however, not only has China been a driving force of institutionalization, rather than acting on the periphery, it had also determined the SCO to be a security arrangement well before its inception in June 2001. Indeed, the SCO is the culmination of 'Shanghai Five' arrangements established in 1996 (minus Uzbekistan). Based on the Treaty on Deepening Military Trust in the Border Regions signed that year, China pressed for commitments from Kazakhstan, Kyrgyzstan, Russia and Tajikistan to attend annual summits on trust-building and border security. With Uzbekistan later attending the 2001 summit in Shanghai, the SCO was thus formed; the six countries agreeing upon an institutional framework

Table 10.6 Institutionalization of the Shanghai Cooperation Organization

Summit	Location and date	Main purpose of meeting/significant outcomes
Heads of State	Shanghai, 14–15 June 2001	Shanghai Convention Against Terrorism, Separatism and Extremism
	St. Petersburg, 7 June 2002	SCO Charter agreed, RCTS formally established
	Moscow, 28–29 May 2003	Permanent secretariat established, designation of budget and executive
	Tashkent, 17 June 2004	Agreement on combating trafficking of illegal narcotics; observer status for Mongolia
	Astana, 5 July 2005	Declaration on US eviction from C. Asia; observer status for India, Iran, Pakistan
	Shanghai, 15–16 June 2006	2007–9 Action Plan on combating terrorism, separatism, and extremism
	Bishkek, 16 August 2007	Treaty on Long-Term Good-Neighbourliness, Friendship and Cooperation
	Dushanbe, 28 August 2008	Expansion of partnership mechanisms/ discussion of new memberships
	Yekaterinburg, 2009	Regional economic cooperation; Afghanistan; trans-border crime (tbc)
Heads of government/ Prime Ministers	Almaty, 13–14 September 2001	Memorandum of Understanding on SCO goals and cooperation
	Beijing, 23 September 2003	SCO administrative and budgetary mechanisms agreed
	Bishkek, 23 September 2004	Draft SCO concept for multilateral trade and economic cooperation
	Moscow, 26 October 2005	Programme for multilateral trade and economic cooperation agreed
	Dushanbe, 15 September 2006	'Asian Energy Club' mooted; transport infrastructure agreements
	Tashkent, 2 November 2007	Regulations on interactions amongst SCO interbank consortium
	Astana, 30 October 2008	Draft SCO concept of cooperation in environmental protection

for combating the 'three evils' of terrorism, religious extremism and secession-ism (SCO 2001). The formalization of an SCO secretariat with the signing of the organization's Charter in 2002 cleared the way for Chinese and Kazakh joint hostage-rescue and 'anti-terrorism' exercises in 2003, involving 1,300 troops from the two countries. This was followed by the establishment of the permanent

Regional Anti/Counter-Terrorism Structure (RATS/RCTS) in June 2004, after which China and Russia conducted their first-ever joint military exercises (ostensibly for anti-terrorism) in August 2005, dubbed 'Peace Mission 2005'. Observed by the other SCO members, its successful completion led to calls for expanding the military exercises to also include non-SCO countries, such as India (not yet ratified). 'Peace Mission 2007' two years on was a far more substantial anti-terrorism exercise involving all six SCO members and observers from India, Iran, Mongolia and Pakistan: China contributed roughly 1,600 of the 4,000 or so troops deployed to the southern Urals, while Russian fighter aircraft and precision guided weapons were alleged to be used also (Xinhua 2006b). Crucially, the SCO as a regional security mechanism has become increasingly institutionalized, with annual joint exercises matched by more permanent institutional structures and regular meetings at various levels, from head of states and government, to ministerial and departmental (see Table 10.6).

Despite numerous reassurances that the SCO is not directed towards any other state or group of states, its multinational exercises, often involving mechanized infantry and air assault brigades, among other units, have led to comparisons with NATO; not to mention questions about the utility of standard military formations for 'anti-terrorism' (Fels 2009: 26–7). Nevertheless, China's interests in institutionalizing security cooperation in Central Asia are not all that different from its ASEAN approach. Though a primary aim for Beijing is to reduce or counter separatist tendencies in China's Western provinces, the SCO reflects a broader ambition of shaping the regional dynamic, stabilizing regional relations and reinforcing the sovereignty principle through the promotion of interdependence rather than in spite of it. The SCO thus allows Beijing to boost its profile with its Central Asian neighbours, assuaging their concerns about China's economic and military rise by increasing familiarity. That the Organization's objectives have expanded in recent years to include 'advanced cooperation' in politics, economics, energy and the environment, as well as 'the establishment of a new, democratic, just and rational political and economic international order', shows that China and its partners clearly see some other mutual benefits to institutionalization besides military cooperation (Chung 2006: 3). This does not, however, entail reflexive multilateralism and the SCO clearly encapsulates a Westphalian conception of security. Additionally, though the SCO shows a far greater degree of institutionalization than ASEAN in terms of security cooperation, its format is unlikely to change from intergovernmental to supranational. Regular engagement and deepening institutionalization will see to this, barring the exit of either China or Russia from the SCO which would collapse the arrangement altogether.

Compellence: ensuring national sovereignty

That China engages in military exercises with its SCO neighbours is disquieting for some, despite the fact that it has not engaged in any form of militarized conflict in the past 20 years. Nevertheless, according to official figures, Chinese defence expenditure has grown in that time by 16 per cent annually on average;

Table 10.7 Chinese defence spending 1978–2009

Year	Defence expenditure (USD billions)	% of GDP
1979–83	2.74	3.89
1984–8	2.93	1.95
1989–93	4.90	1.43
1994–8	10.71	1.07
1999	15.74	1.20
2000	17.66	1.22
2001	21.09	1.32
2002	24.98	1.42
2003	27.9	1.40
2004	32.17	1.38
2005	36.2	1.35
2006	43.57	1.41
2007	51.99	1.38
2008	61.1	1.40
2009	70.30	–

Sources: Adapted from National Statistics Bureau 2008 and IOSC 2009

Note: Five-year figures for 1979–83 to 1994–8 are period averaged. Conversion from RMB to USD uses Interbank rates by year

and while the veracity of these figures is not the issue for debate here, it suffices to note that even these numbers pose the world's most rapid, sustained rate of increase in military spending (see Table 10.7). Despite Beijing's attempts at greater transparency, such as the biennial publication of Defence White Papers since 1998, anxieties abroad continue to focus on China's historical enmity with Taiwan as a potential flashpoint. Regular PLA/N/AF and Taiwanese 'live-fire' exercises have indeed made brinkmanship a permanent feature on both sides and a substantial proportion of China's order of battle is in fact situated within striking distance of the island (see Table 10.8; Yang 2008: 197; DOD 2009). Moreover, China's most recent military acquisitions have included significant numbers of new short- and intermediate-range ballistic missiles, advanced surface warships, submarines and long-range fighter aircraft – all conventional capabilities of use in a cross-Straits conflict (see Table 10.9). Although Beijing-Taipei relations have seemingly improved more recently (highlighted in late 2008 by the rhetorical switch from 'armed liberation' to 'peaceful liberation' in a speech by President Hu Jintao and the reinstitution of the Association for Relations Across the Taiwan Strait (ARATS)), China's military presence and dispositions have not diminished

Table 10.8 People's Republic of China, force levels (estimated)

Active personnel	Total	Professional	Conscript
People's Liberation Army Forces	2,105,000	1,265,000	840,000
PLA	1,600,000	800,000	800,000
PLAN	255,000	215,000	40,000
PLAAF	250,000	250,000	0
Paramilitary Forces			
People's Armed Police (PAPF)	1,500,000		
Border defence	100,000		
Internal security forces	800,000		
PLAN marines	10,000		
Strategic Rocket Forces			
Intercontinental Ballistic Missiles (ICBM)		46	
Intermediate Range Ballistic Missiles (IRBM)		35	
Short-Range Ballistic Missiles (SRBM)		725	
PLA vehicles and equipment			
Main battle tanks		7,660	
Armoured personnel carriers		3,500	
Armoured infantry fighting vehicles		2,000	
Artillery		17,700	
Multiple-launch rocket systems		2,400	
Surface-to-air missile defence systems		284	
Attack and assault helicopters		475	
Other supporting fires		7,700	
PLAN vessels			
Ballistic Missile Submarines (SSBN)		2 (1 under construction)	
Nuclear Attack Submarines (SSN)		6	
Diesel Attack Submarines (SSK)		51	
Destroyers/Guided Missile Destroyers (DD/DDG)		29	

(continued)

Active personnel	Total	Professional	Conscript
Frigates/Guided Missile Frigates (FF/FFG)	46		
Corvettes/fast attack craft (Coastal Defence)	233		
Amphibious ships (LSD/LST/LPD/RoRo)	74		
Logistics and fleet replenishment ships (AOR/AOE)	204		
PLAAF aircraft and weapons			
Bombers	82		
Fighters	1,179		
Attack	551		
Airborne Early Warning (AEW)	4		
Aerial tanker supports	18		
Transport	296		
Surface-to-air defence systems	1,578		
Tactical air-to-surface missiles	>4,500		
PLAN aviation			
Bombers	130		
Fighters	346		
Attack	296		
Anti-Submarine Warfare (ASW)	4		
Aerial tanker supports	3		
Transports	66		
Helicopters	78		

Sources: IISS 2009, 2008

significantly.

In China's view, military modernization is an inviolable right of sovereign states. Additionally, it redresses the imbalance of American military power in the region and what Beijing sees as an attempt by Washington at encirclement; and US assistance to Taipei is just one irritation among many for Beijing. Chinese anxieties are reinforced also by American sales of advanced arms to others of its neighbours, such as Japan and South Korea, and compounded by substantial force deployments throughout the wider region, as in Korea, Okinawa and Guam. This has often led to tensions and provocative behaviour. For example, US aircraft carrier groups are often interposed between Taiwan and the mainland in times of cross-Straits dispute: in 2001, a PLANAF[1] air defence fighter and US Navy reconnaissance

Table 10.9 Significant PRC military acquisitions since 2005

Ballistic missiles and cruise missiles	Designation	Launcher	Range (est.)
Land-Attack Cruise Missiles (LACM)	DH-10	Land, mobile	4,000 km +
Anti-Ship Cruise Missiles (ASCM)	YJ-62	Land, DDG	300 km +
	YJ-62C	DDG/FFG	150 km +
	SS-N-22	DDG	220 km +
	SS-N-27	SSK	40–300 km
Short-Range Ballistic Missiles (SRBM)	DF-15/CSS-6	Land, mobile	600 km
	DF-11/CSS-7	Land, mobile	300 km
Anti-Ship Ballistic Missiles (ASBM)	DF-21A/CSS-5	Land, mobile	2,500 km
Inter-Continental Ballistic Missiles (ICBM)	DF-31	Land, sited/ mobile	7,200 km +
	DF-31A	Land, sited	11,000 km +
	DF-41	Land, sited	14,000 km +
Submarine-Launched Ballistic Missile (SLBM)	JL-2/ CSS-NX-5	SSBN	8,000 km

PLAN naval vessels	Type	Notes
Shi-Lang	Aircraft carrier	Formerly Varyag
Type 093, Shang-Class submarines	Attack submarine	2 in fleet, 8 planned (total)
Type 094, Jin-Class submarines	Missile Submarine	1 in fleet, 1 testing, 5 planned (total)
Type 052C, Luyang II-Class destroyers	Destroyer	2 in fleet as of 2008, plans for D variant
Type 051C, Luzhou-Class destroyers	Destroyer	2 in fleet as of 2006, plans for D variant
Type 054A, Jiangkai-Class frigate	Frigate	5 in fleet, 1 under construction
Type 022, Houbei-Class fast attack craft	Guided miss. boat	40 in fleet, unknown numbers planned

PLAAF/PLANAF modernization and upgrades

50 Su-33MK2 Flanker: carrier-capable fighter aircraft (transaction stalled as of March 2009)

B-6 (Tu-16) bombers: life extension, range increased and modified for ASCM/LACM launch capability

(*continued*)

PLAAF/PLANAF modernization and upgrades
KJ-200 Airborne Early Warning and Control Aircraft (in development, based on Chinese Y-8 design)
KJ-2000 Airborne Early Warning and Control Aircraft (in development, based on Russian A-50 transport)
34 IL-76 Transports and 4 IL-78 Aerial Refueling Tankers (deal with Russia stalled as of March 2009)

Sources: IISS 2009, 2008; DOD 2009, 2008

aircraft collided in mid-air 70 miles from Hainan Island, leading to heated diplomatic exchanges; in November 2007, a PLAN diesel submarine breached within several hundred yards of the USS *Kitty Hawk* aircraft carrier group in the Western Pacific; and, in early 2009, Chinese ships and US naval survey vessels came to dangerously close proximity in waters claimed by China to be within its exclusive economic zone (Donnelly 2004: 25–27; BBC 2001, 2009c).

Yet Chinese military modernization does not necessarily entail an arms race with the US. Rather, the current focus is on negating Western technological advantages in warfighting through 'unrestricted warfare' (*chao xian zhan*), an asymmetrical counter to America's conventional military power (Qiao and Wang 1999). While considerable investments have indeed been made in modernizing conventional weapons, China has also poured funding into several other key areas: secure command and control technologies; defensive and offensive cyber-warfare and informational systems; anti-satellite weapons; and personnel training to enable their use (IOSC 2009; DOD 2009). While details are lacking, there is nevertheless obvious attention to overall technological advance (see Table 10.10). It is from this that militarized benefits are likely to accrue, culminating in China's own 'revolution in military affairs' or RMA. China's capacity for asymmetrical warfare does appear to be on the rise, highlighted by increases in computer hacking and malware sourcing via Chinese internet nodes, attempts at industrial espionage, the confirmed 'blinding' of a US spy satellite by ground-based laser in 2006, and anti-satellite missile testing in 2007 (DOD 2009; BBC 2007). Augmenting this modernization strategy is an estimated USD 1 billion spent annually on foreign advanced technology imports (often circumventing international dual-use restrictions), which are then integrated into or reverse-engineered for indigenous manufacturing. This has seen, for instance, digitization of Chinese combat vessels using ruggedized French computer components, reverse-engineering of Russian jet engines, purchases of Israeli reconnaissance drones and air-to-air missiles, as well as German drive machinery for civilian vessels copied for use in PLAN warships and submarines (IISS 2008; Medeiros *et al.* 2005). As President Hu elicited in his March 2008 speech to the 11th National People's Congress, this pattern of defence expansion and modernization will continue as a strategic priority, intrinsic as it is to the notion of comprehensive national growth:

'We must improve our capabilities to win high-tech regional wars and keep enhancing the ability of the military to respond to security threats and accomplish a diverse array of military tasks ... based on the achievements of China's economic and social development.'

(Xinhua 2008b)

Another key goal of Chinese defence modernization, much talked about by both academia and the media, has been a 'blue water' capability, with noise-making by senior PLA staff and Chinese think-tanks portraying this as both a strategic and symbolic necessity (AFP 2009). The 60th PLAN anniversary celebrations in April 2009, for example, saw the announcement of a coherent, long-term policy and procurement agenda with a focus on large combat vessels, stealthier submarines, supersonic-cruise aircraft, more accurate guided weapons, and 'informationized' enhancements (Xinhua 2009b). A key feature of this 'blue water' strategy is alleged to be a functional Chinese aircraft carrier. Certainly, there has been substantial Chinese interest in such an asset over the years. In 1983, the former HMAS *Melbourne* was purchased as scrap and disassembled for insight into basic carrier systems such as deck configurations and arrestor gear. Similarly, the *Varyag* – an unfinished, formerly Soviet carrier – was bought from the Ukraine in 1998 for USD 20 million. Refurbishment work appeared underway in 2005, with the ship painted in PLAN colours in June 2007 (*Jane's Navy International* 2009). Furthermore, China has also tried to purchase 50 or so Su-30MK2s navalized fighter aircraft from Russia since 2006; though the deal has apparently fallen through (leading to rumours of a navalized version of indigenously manufactured J-10 and J-7 fighters), it matches reports of PLANAF pilot training at Chinese airbases involving take-off ramps and simulated deck markings painted on the ground (DOD 2009).

Indications are, however, that the refurbished *Varyag* will be a proving vessel. In addition, with huge strides needed in both manufacturing and training, an operational carrier-based force is unlikely within the next several years at least (*Jane's Navy International* 2009). China's shipbuilding infrastructure at least has

Table 10.10 Official scientific and technological activities and spending, 2001–7 (USD billions)

Research	2001–2	2002–3	2003–4	2004–5	2005–6	2006–7
Basic	0.65	0.91	1.09	1.46	1.63	1.68
Applied	2.18	3.06	3.86	4.96	5.37	6.70
Development	10.90	11.99	14.14	17.96	23.37	31.12
Total	13.73	15.96	19.09	24.38	30.37	39.90
% of GDP	0.95	1.07	1.13	1.23	1.34	1.42
Annual change (%)		+16.24	+19.61	+27.71	+24.57	+31.38

Source: National Bureau of Statistics 2008

Note: Conversion from RMB to USD uses Interbank rates by year

the basic capacity: eight Chinese shipyards can build very large or ultra large crude (oil) carriers (VLCC/ULCC), comparable to the dimensions of US super-carriers (Lloyds 2008). Indeed, new military docks at Jiangnan shipyards in Shanghai were opened in early 2009 and visited by experts from Nikolayev South/Mykolaiv in Ukraine (builders of the *Varyag*); dock workers there have allegedly been given contracts for two 60,000-tonne vessels (Chang 2009). Yet, even though a Chinese carrier capability appears imminent, several deficiencies in the wider defence force and industry must also be addressed: surface-to-air defences for fleet protection; secure communications and navigational equipment; propulsive machinery for very large combat vessels; and underway replenishment techniques, among many other things. Relevant doctrine and training would need to be implemented also, since China has no history of joint fleet warfare and captains still operate separately within assigned coastal areas (DOD 2009; Wu and Wang 2004). Without addressing the above, a Chinese-built carrier force would probably be obsolete before commissioning; and even if addressed, it will take more than ten years at least for the PLAN to evolve beyond a littoral force.

Even so, many of the capabilities necessary for carrier support, particularly in logistics and power projection, will also be crucial to securing Beijing's broader developmental strategy, especially as China's economic and resource interests swell beyond the Asian periphery. Indeed, demand for Chinese participation in UNPKO, as discussed above, will require greater Chinese military capacity too. Much was made, for example, of the first-ever 'out-of-area' PLAN deployment to the Gulf of Aden for counter-piracy in late 2008/early 2009; not only by Beijing, but Washington, other world powers, and NATO as well (Xinhua 2009c). If China is to be an 'involved' power taking on global responsibilities, then an increase in its means as well as its political will needs to be accepted abroad. Of course, this depends on other, perhaps unanticipated externalities too, which is a major issue for Beijing since predictability is desirable and the vagaries of American power will continue to affect considerations. China thus perceives US hegemony as an inordinate, unnatural *badao* order: global military reach; entrenched military ties with many of China's neighbours; substantial forward deployments in Japan and South Korea; advanced arms sales to Taiwan; and a litany of military interventions that most recently includes Kosovo, Afghanistan and Iraq (twice). Positive, *wangdao* engagement via diplomacy and trade therefore requires a *Realpolitik* which protects against and undercuts US hegemony. As is clear from the above, this logic is reflected in China's high politics, its approach to cooperation, and military strategy in equal measure.

Conclusions: power, complementarity and reflexivity

China's recent shift to multilateralism is conditional and its strategic concerns still come full circle to Taiwan and the issue of sovereignty. Despite significant changes in recent years, there would appear to be no substantial shift in China's normative motivations, since national integrity and autonomy continue to drive its strategic behaviour (see Table 10.11). Yet, despite defence and security often

Table 10.11 The duality of China's national security culture

Worldview	State sovereignty 'inviolable' and Complementarity, Wangdao reflexivity	• Priority to autonomy, sovereignty, and national defence • Broad securitization entailing cooperation often appropriate
National identity	China as 'Middle Kingdom' and China as 'responsible world power'	• Strategic rebalancing of international order re. civilizational legacy/destiny • Respect for international law, interest in peaceful coexistence and development
Instrumental preferences	Coercive force by necessity and reflexive engagement	• Military force intrinsic to statecraft (*Wu*) • 'Soft power', harmonious conduct (*Wen*), and mutual, virtuous self-governance
Interaction preferences	Unilateralism, 'security' as defence and limited multilateralism, 'security' as contextual, collective responsibility	• 'Unrestricted warfare' doctrine • Still based on status quo interest in national sovereignty and non-intervention

being synonymous in China's worldview, it is also important to understand that this thinking differs somewhat from the rationality implied by Westphalianism. Predating the latter by some margin, Confucian-Taoist implications of proper conduct emphasize complementarity and reflexivity, informing the somewhat romantic, contemporary self-perception of 'China' as a pacific, benevolent and prosperity-seeking *civilization*: The rational conception of 'state' simply has insufficient gravitas. Unpacking this view helps one understand why and how China appears to revert so easily to 'self-interest'. Effective and lasting security must have at its foundation robust national defence, which has purpose discernable only through the lenses of Machiavellian *virtu* (to use the closest Occidental equivalent of *jen-li* morality). Gains from cooperation against unconventional, non-state threats are thus calculated against the need to ensure China's political, social and cultural coherence as well as development and prosperity.

Chinese security culture is heavily influenced by the nation's historical legacy and the meddling of colonial powers in the nineteenth and early twentieth centuries. In addition to a strong, civilizational conception of nationhood, this legacy underpins China's geopolitical stance and its claims concerning such issues as Tibetan 'separatism', Taiwan's 'reintegration' and exclusive resource access in the South China Seas. While this adherence to sovereignty often comes under outside criticism, China's retort is that its detractors, particularly Western nations, are being hypocritical given their own roles in past injustices. This is reflected in Beijing's overriding concern of maintaining autonomy, which heavily influences its instrumental and interactive preferences. What it does not entail, however, is an exclusive aspiration to regional or international domination: China's rise is not a purely rational accumulation of material power, which only partly (and inadequately) resolves the issue of national development. Just as important is the presentation of an alternative moral and normative model to the global discourse – *wangdao* – distinctive from the long-dominant, Western-centric cast of American hegemony. Beijing has thus given greater attention to very particular forms of multilateralism to cultivate acceptance of interactive conditionalities on Chinese terms. For instance, while ASEAN-China trade is substantial, regional dialogues have also helped legitimate China's status and worldview through reciprocation; hence the growing discomfort of neighbouring states concerning US-led regional security initiatives. This preference for contingent multilateralism can be better understood through the logic of complementarity and reflexivity. Beijing understands that its approach might appear selective; but this is – in the Chinese view – only because the contemporary global system is imbalanced, reflecting the *badao* unipolarity of American dominance.

China's message to others is that coexistence can be peaceful and mutually beneficial, without need for threat of coercion or Western (i.e. US) leadership. Its self-perceptions concerning the expression of sovereign rights and strategic modernization are that these are justifiable and rightful actions that cannot be denied to any state. Hence Chinese multilateralism rarely yields common defence or collective security mechanisms – the SCO being a possible exception. Furthermore, even with a seemingly embryonic Asian regional security community emerging via ASEAN, for instance, principles cultivated and reciprocated by China and its neighbours make an analogue of Europeanization in that case unlikely. Ultimately, Chinese multilateralism serves to directly or indirectly reinforce Beijing's competences for maintaining domestic order, stability and growth. Despite interactive preferences being driven by such an inward focus, however, the notions of 'harmonious order' (*hiexie xitong*) and peaceful coexistence do pertain. Chinese goals are not incompatible with those of other countries and there is a duty to respect others' pursuits, just as there is such a duty to safeguard one's own. To use Confucian teachings from *The Analects*, 'Consensus is not harmony. [Only] Gentlemen can disagree in harmony; but petty minds can agree without any at all' (*jun zi er bu tong, xiao ren tong er bu he*; 13.23).

In part, Beijing's strategy is the restoration of a somewhat romanticized self-image of China as the 'Middle Kingdom'. Just as Russia stakes its claim to a regional sphere of influence, so too does Beijing seek to re-establish what it perceives to be a 'natural' regional order with China as the hub and benevolent patron. A legacy stretching back millennia, not just decades, and as rich as that of ancient China serves as an additional legitimizing claim to great power status; more so than does material power alone. As noted above concerning China's conception of 'moral' statecraft, its comprehensive national rise is again not strictly a rational exercise, but reclaims a civilizational destiny. This combination of *jen-li* morality in statecraft, complementarity and strong conception of nationhood sees Beijing sometimes appear flippant and enigmatic; but this oversimplifies what is in fact a nuanced and layered worldview and flexible strategic behaviour. That China is perceived as antagonistic is thus often only realized when fundamental values of sovereignty and non-interference have been undermined, which is only 'fair' or just. Military exercises in the Taiwan Straits, for instance, concern the 'internal' security matter of a rebel province. Similarly, interdiction of US air and naval assets in the Western Pacific physically reinforces Chinese territorial integrity according to what Beijing perceives as a defensible and justifiable interpretation of international law.

Yet even designating this as Westphalianism does not suggest that Beijing limit itself to coercive instrumentality. For all its civilizational aspirations and references, China is also pragmatic. Initiative-taking for certain forms of cooperative security, such as UNPKO and regional CSBMs, highlights Beijing's interest in making peace stable and mutually profitable not only for China, but the international community at large. As reflected in its increasing aid and peacekeeping contributions, for example, extending reach beyond China's periphery has seen substantial diplomatic and 'soft power' efforts by Beijing. While some sceptics see this as a placatory approach to mollify China's critics, it nevertheless successfully promotes China as a political and ideological alternative to the status quo. Drawing such conclusions, however, still leaves substantial grey areas: Chinese defence modernization over the past decade, for example, still gives cause for consternation. The PLA/N/AF is steadily transforming from a conscript-based defensive force into a professionalized one with wide-spectrum capabilities, backed by advanced technologies and nuclear weapons. China's strategic discourse also clearly poses the threat of military confrontation with the US not only as possible, but also likely within 30 years. Since parity with America is impossible in that time, the 'next best' solution for China is to nullify Western technological advantages through asymmetric means, such as area denial and informational attack. Yet anxieties similarly arise in considering how America looks at China. Furthermore, many of China's newer force capabilities, particularly in logistics and power projection, will be crucial not just for China, but for the international community at large, as highlighted by China's participation in UNPKO and regional CSBMs.

More than anything else, it is Beijing's distinct lack of transparency that causes the greatest anxiety for outside observers. Indeed, the emergence of internal, popular pressures for more nationalistic approaches to Taiwan, Japanese reparations and American hegemony – combined with ambitious, potentially destabilizing rhetoric from China's military leadership – muddies the waters further; all while Beijing attempts a moderating effort abroad of peaceful self-promotion. Paradoxically, Beijing's inherent secretiveness has meant that China simultaneously appears pacific and aggressive, yielding equally compelling arguments for containment and engagement. Yet, again, this returns to the issue of Beijing's strategic preferences being founded on a deeply entrenched conception of nationhood. Manifested as a flexible, state-centric approach that maximizes both material and normative gains, Beijing's security referents of political order, social cohesion and economic growth drive the strengthening of national defence so as to establish and protect an autonomous, prospering China. Thus, while China continues to avoid the abrogation of sovereign power whenever possible, it is more accepting of contingent multilateralism and limited cooperation so long as benefits for long-term welfare and status are clear. In addition, despite Chinese security culture remaining inherently conservative, Beijing has more often adapted to cooperation in order to propagate the dual logic of complementarity and reflexivity, and not just to achieve material gain. This may well pose China as a rational, Westphalian state; but its strategic behaviour is more properly understood as a reconstruction of the international system, which seeks to legitimize China's rise by promoting an alternative 'democratic' world order to the imbalanced, Western-dominated status quo.

Note

1   The armed forces of the People's Republic of China comprises the People's Liberation Army (PLA), the People's Liberation Army Navy (PLAN), the People's Liberation Army Air Force (PLAAF), and the People's Liberation Army Navy Air Force (PLANAF). Despite 'PLA' appearing in the title of each, these four branches operate separately. For expedience and to reflect usage in the wider strategic/military studies literature, this chapter uses 'PLA/N/AF' in reference to China's armed forces as a whole, referring specifically to the PLA, PLAN, PLAAF and/or PLANAF where appropriate.

References

AFP (Agence France Presse) (2009) 'China tells Japan it wants Aircraft Carrier', *Wires*, 22 March. Available online at: http://www.google.com/hostednews/afp/article/ALeqM5iLX9Q4jSaza-kDFWyJmogPBGX4dg (accessed 5 June 2009).

Alden, C. (2007) 'Emerging countries as new ODA players in LDCs: The case of China and Africa', *Idées pour le débat* 1, Paris: Institut du développement durable et des relations internationales (IDDRI).

ARF (2005) 'The ASEAN Regional Forum – Establishment, Objectives, Achievements'. Available online at: http://www.aseanregionalforum.org (accessed 28 April 2009).

BBC (2001) 'Who caused the crash?', 5 April. Available online at: http://news.bbc.co.uk/2/hi/asia-pacific/1260290.stm (accessed 5 June 2009).

—— (2007) 'China test sparks space arms fears', 19 January. Available online at: http://news.bbc.co.uk/2/hi/asia-pacific/6278867.stm (accessed 12 June 2009).

—— (2009a) 'Robust message for North Korea', 12 June. Available online at: http://news.bbc.co.uk/2/low/asia-pacific/8098166.stm (accessed 12 June 2009).

—— (2009b) 'Thai troops "cross into Cambodia"', 25 March. Available online at: http://news.bbc.co.uk/2/hi/asia-pacific/7963014.stm (accessed 5 June 2009).

—— (2009c) 'Chinese ships "harass" US vessel', 9 March. Available online at: http://news.bbc.co.uk/2/hi/asia-pacific/7933171.stm (accessed 12 June 2009).

Boisseau du Rocher, S. and Fort, B. (eds) (2005) *Paths to Regionalization – Comparing Experiences in East Asia and Europe*, Singapore: Marshall Cavendish International.

Callahan, W.A. (2004) 'National Insecurities: Humiliation, Salvation, and Chinese Nationalism', *Alternatives*, 29: 199–218.

Chang, A. (2009) 'China ready to build aircraft carrier', *United Press International*, 2 June. Available online at: http://www.upiasia.com/Security/2009/06/02 (accessed 12 June 2009).

Chin, G.T. and Frolic, B.M. (2007) *Emerging Donors in International Development Assistance: The China Case*, Partnership & Business Development Division: Canada International Development Research Centre.

Choedon, Y. (2005) 'China's Stand on UN Peacekeeping Operations', *China Report*, 41(1): 39–57.

Christoffersen, G. (2008) 'Chinese and ASEAN Responses to the US Regional Maritime Security Initiative', in Wu, G.G. and Lansdowne, H. (eds) *China Turns to Multilateralism – Foreign Policy and Regional Security*, London: Routledge.

Chung, C.P. (2006) 'China and the Institutionalization of the Shanghai Cooperation Organization', *Problems of Post-Communism*, 53(5): 3–14.

Dellios, R. (1997) 'How May the World Be at Peace? Idealism as Realism in Chinese Strategic Culture', Humanities & Social Sciences Papers, Bond University, Australia.

DOD (Department of Defense, United States of America) (2008) *Annual Report to Congress – Military Power of the People's Republic of China 2008*, Washington, DC: Office of the Secretary of Defense.

—— (2009) *Annual Report to Congress – Military Power of the People's Republic of China 2009*, Washington, DC: Office of the Secretary of Defense.

Donnelly, E. (2004) 'The United States–China EP-3 incident: legality and *realpolitik*', *Journal of Conflict and Security Law*, 9(1): 25–42.

Fels, E. (2009) *Assessing Eurasia's Powerhouse – An Inquiry into the Nature of the Shanghai Cooperation Organization*, Munich: Taschenbuch.

Gill, B. and Huang, C.H. (2009) 'China's Expanding Peacekeeping Role: Its Significance and The Policy Implications', SIPRI Policy Brief, February, Stockholm International Peace Research Institute.

Harsch, E. (2007) 'Big Leap in China-Africa Ties', *Africa Renewal*, 20(4): 3.

He, Y. (2007) 'China's Changing Policy on UN Peacekeeping Operations', *Asia Papers* (Institute for Security and Development Policy, Sweden): 43–44.

Holslag, J. (2008) 'Commerce and Prudence: Revising China's Evolving Africa Policy', *International Relations of the Asia-Pacific*, 8(3): 325–52.

Huang P.M. (1997) 'Rujia junshi sixiang yu Zhongguo gudai junshi wenhua chuantong' [Confucian military thinking and the military-cultural tradition of ancient China], *China Military Science*, 4: 73–74.

IISS (International Institute of Strategic Studies) (2007) *The Military Balance 2007*, Abingdon, UK: Routledge.

—— (2008) *The Military Balance 2008*, Abingdon, UK: Routledge.

—— (2009) *The Military Balance 2009*, Abingdon, UK: Routledge.

IOSC (Information Office of the State Council, People's Republic of China) (2009) 'China's National Defense 2008', Defence White Paper. Available online at: http://www.gov.cn/english/official/2009-01/20/content_1210227.htm (accessed 25 April 2009).

Jane's Navy International (2009) 'Chinese Aircraft Carrier Capability Unlikely before 2015', 10 April. Available online at: http://www.janes.com/media/releases/pc090401_1.shtml (accessed 5 June 2009).

Kuik, C.C. (2005) 'Multilateralism in China's ASEAN Policy: Its Evolution, Characteristics, and Aspiration', *Contemporary Southeast Asia*, 27(1): 102–22.

Lloyd's Register (2008) *World Shipbuilding Statistics 2008 – Quarterly Reports Compilation*, London: Fairplay.

Lönnqvist, L. (2007) 'China's Aid to Africa: Implications for Civil Society', *INTRAC Policy Briefing Paper 17*, Oxford: International NGO Training and Research Centre.

Medeiros, E.S., Cliff, R., Crane, K. and Mulvenon, J.C. (2005) *A New Direction for China's Defense Industry*, Santa Monica, CA: RAND Corporation.

MFA (Ministry of Foreign Affairs of the People's Republic of China) (2006) 'China's Africa

Policy', 12 January. Available online at: http://www.fmprc.gov.cn/eng/zxxx/t230615. htm (accessed 5 June 2009).

MOFCOM (Ministry of Commerce, People's Republic of China) (2008a) *'Guanxi/fangshi'* [Relations and patterns], 9 January. Available online at: http://yws.mofcom.gov.cn/aarticle/gywm/200606/20060602408464.html (accessed 25 April 2009).

—— (2008b) 'Zhongguo jiben qingkuang de waijuanzhu' [Fundamental situation of China's foreign aid], 30 January. Available online at: http://yws.mofcom.gov.cn (accessed 25 April 2009).

Mohan, G. and Power, M. (2008) 'New African Choices? The Politics of Chinese Engagement', *Review of African Political Economy*, 115: 23–42.

National Bureau of Statistics (2008) *China Statistical Yearbook 2007*, Beijing: China Statistics Press.

OECD Development Assistance Committee (2009), 'Notes on Other Providers of Development Assistance', *Development Co-operation Report 2009*. Available online at: http://puck.sourceoecd.org/vl = 21784158/cl = 12/nw = 1/rpsv/dac09/06/04/index. htm (accessed 20 May 2009).

Ortiz, I. (2007) 'New Developments in South-South Cooperation: China ODA, Alternative Regionalisms, Banco Del Sur', *International Development Economics Associates (IDEA)*. Available online at: http://ssrn.com (accessed 5 June 2009).

Pang, Z.Y. (2005) 'China's Changing Attitude to UN Peacekeeping', *International Peacekeeping*, 12(1): 87–104.

People's Daily (2006) 'Confucius Institute: Promoting language, culture and friendliness', 2 October. Available online at: http://english.peopledaily.com.cn/200610/02/print20061002_308230.html (accessed 28 April 2009).

Qiao, L. and Wang, X.S. (1999) *Unrestricted Warfare*, Beijing: PLA Literature and Arts Publishing House.

SCO (2001) 'Shanghai Convention on Terrorism, Separatism and Extremism', 15 June. Available online at: http://www.sectsco.org/EN/show.asp?id = 68 (accessed 12 June 2009).

Scobell, A. (2002) *China and Strategic Culture*, Washington, DC: Strategic Studies Institute.

Simon, S. (2008) 'ASEAN and Multilateralism: The Long, Bumpy Road to Community', *Contemporary Southeast Asia: A Journal of International and Strategic Affairs*, 30(2): 264–92.

UNDPKO (United Nations Department of Peace-Keeping Operations) (2008) *Ranking of Police and Military Contributions to UN Operations as of July 2008*. Available online at: http://www.un.org/Depts/dpko/dpko/contributors/ (accessed 25 April 2009).

Wu, A. (2005) 'What China Whispers to North Korea', *The Washington Quarterly*, 28(2): 35–48.

Wu, J.N and Wang, G.X. (2004) 'Introduction to Deploying Civilian Vessels in Landing Operations', *Guofang* [Defence], October: 28.

Xinhua (Chinese News Agency) (2006a) 'Full text of President Hu Jintao's speech at the 2006 Beijing Forum on China-Africa Cooperation', 4 November. Available online at: http://news.xinhuanet.com/english/2006-11/04/content_5289052.htm (accessed 12 June 2009).

—— (2006b) 'SCO to stage joint anti-terror military exercise in 2007', 26 April. Available online at: http://news.xinhuanet.com/english/2006-04/26/content_4476403.htm (accessed 1 June 2009).

—— (2008a) 'Trade between China, ASEAN hits $202.6 billion, three years ahead of schedule', 4 November. Available online at: http://news.xinhuanet.com/english/2008-01/16/content_7433400.htm (accessed 12 June 2009).

—— (2008b) 'President Hu: enhancing national defense for world peace', 10 March. Available online at: http://news.xinhuanet.com/english/2008-03/10/content_7760593.htm (accessed 12 June 2009).

—— (2009a) 'President Hu visits five Asian, African nations', Special Report, 2 February. Available online at: http://news.xinhuanet.com/english/2009-02/16/content_10827077.htm (accessed 5 June 2009).

—— (2009b) '60th Chinese Navy Anniversary Special Coverage'. Available online at: http://english.sina.com/z/090416navyfounding/index.shtml (accessed 5 June 2009).

—— (2009c) 'NATO chief praises China's participation in anti-piracy campaign', 20 March. Available online at: http://english.people.com.cn/90001/90776/90883/6577119.html (accessed 12 June 2009).

Yang, A.N.D. (2008) 'The Military of the People's Republic of China: Strategy and Implementation', *UNISCI Discussion Papers*, No. 17: 187–201.

Zheng, B.J. (2005) *Peaceful Rise: China's New Road to Development*, Beijing: Central Party School Publishing House.

11 Japan

From deterrence to prevention

Haruhiro Fukui

Culture, conventionally defined as 'the values, attitudes, beliefs, orientations, and underlying assumptions prevalent among people in society' (Huntington 2000: xv), is widely accepted as a key independent variable in the determination and explanation of human behaviour, whether individual or collective. A particular type of culture, such as a national elite security culture, commonly termed subculture, is likewise a critical independent variable in the determination of the behaviour of the particular group in the particular area of individual or collective human activity. It is thus sensible to assume that the Japanese elite's security culture importantly influences and therefore helps to explain Japanese security policies and practices. In fact, the most interesting and persuasive studies published so far on the subject employ culture, broadly defined, as the key to understanding and explaining Japanese security policy and practice (Katzenstein 1996; Berger 1998; Oros 2008).

A few caveats are in order here, however. First, culture is by no means the only important independent variable in the determination or explanation of human behaviour. Other factors, such as the physical and social environments and, above all, social institutions may affect human behaviour more powerfully, and explain it more effectively, than culture (North 1990). It is therefore not possible to explain what an individual or a group of individuals does (and how in a particular circumstance) exclusively in terms of culture. Second, a subculture is by definition part of a larger culture: a nation's elite subculture is part of that nation's total culture, often juxtaposed and contrasted with its mass culture. In many cases, an elite's actual behaviour may be constrained more by mass culture than by elite subculture, especially in a contemporary democratic society. Third, a subculture may not be homogeneous, not to mention monolithic, but heterogeneous. It may comprise individuals or groups with very different, often even mutually antagonistic, sets of values, attitudes and beliefs. Fourth and finally, culture, like everything else in nature and society, changes over time, though usually slowly and incrementally. It is necessary to keep these caveats in mind in an exercise to explain Japan's security governance policies, or any other nation's for that matter, mainly by its elite security culture.

Moreover, it is not easy to identify and characterize a particular nation's culture or subculture. It could be inferred from careful and systematic observation of its members' actual behaviour or its results. In light of these caveats, however, an explanation of their behaviour based on such inferences can be very misleading and, in any event, would be tautological. We must therefore first identify and characterize the nation's culture or subculture independently of our observations of its members' actual behaviour or its results, which we hope to explain by that culture.

In the following discussion, I will first try to identify and characterize the Japanese elite security culture on each of the four core dimensions – external environment, national identity, instrumental preferences and interaction preferences – and the five dimensions specific to security governance systems – system type, security referent, regulator, function of norms and context of interaction, as defined in the Introduction to this volume, in terms of the two polar ideal types, Westphalian versus post-Westphalian. For this purpose, I will use information culled from recent statements made by members of the Japanese security policy elite and elite institutions. Unfortunately, the limited data available have made it difficult to precisely place the Japanese elite's security culture along the continuum demarcated by the two ideal types. This chapter will therefore be limited to determining whether it may plausibly be identified and characterized as either Westphalian or post-Westphalian, or as a mixture of the two types, i.e. a hybrid. Recent Japanese security policy behaviour will then be reviewed in the four areas of assurance, prevention, protection and compellence, and an estimation will be made as to how consistent the observed pattern of behaviour is with the elite security culture and, therefore, how plausibly it may be explained by the latter.

Japanese security culture

In its official manifesto issued during the 2005 House of Representatives (lower house of the Diet or parliament) general election, the ruling Liberal Democratic Party (LDP) highlighted the serious and growing threats posed to Japanese security by foreign entities, including terrorist and subversive groups potentially armed with nuclear, biological and chemical (NBC) weapons and cyber-warfare capabilities, and promised to strengthen Japan's own defence capability and the military alliance with the US (Jiyuminshuto 2005). Ministry of Defence (MoD, formerly Defence Agency) policy-makers, in particular, perceive, in the classic Westphalian fashion, the security conditions surrounding Japan as characterized by:

- diversity of nationalities, religions, and political systems;
- multiplicity of major powers and a complex structure of conflicting interests;
- persistence of unresolved issues of national unification and conflicting territorial claims and maritime interests; and
- expansion and modernization of military forces by many nations in the region.

(Boeicho 2005: 87)

Recent developments in North Korea and China are particularly alarming in the view of the Japanese foreign policy elite. With regard to North Korea, they have been alarmed specifically by the 1998 ballistic missile tests; the 1999 detection of a suspicious (North Korean) ship off Japan's Noto Peninsula, leading to the first Japanese maritime military action since the end of World War II; the 2001 detection of another suspicious (North Korean) ship off the southwestern coast of Kyushu; and the 2006 ballistic missile and nuclear bomb tests (Boeicho 2005: 168–9; Boeisho 2007b: 64). Furthermore, North Korea is believed to have been actively engaged in espionage and subversive activities against Japan and boasts a 100,000-strong guerrilla/special operations force (Boeisho 2007b: 20). It is also believed to possess NBC weapons and to be working on the development of long-range ballistic and short-range solid-fuel missiles.

With regard to China, MoD policy-makers highlight the 2004 detection of a submerged Chinese nuclear submarine in Japanese territorial waters, which led to the second Japanese maritime military action since 1945; the 2005 enactment of the Anti-Secession Law, which threatened use of military force against Taiwan in the event the latter declared independence; and the 2007 anti-satellite weapons test, potentially aimed at the acquisition of a capability to attack other nations' military or civilian satellites (Boeicho 2005: 165–6; Boeisho 2007b: 64). They also note that China's defence budget is doubling every five years and financing the modernization of a variety of weapons and weapons systems, including new models of ICBMs, cruise missiles, submarines, landing vessels, fourth-generation fighter planes, mid-air refuelling capability, and airborne warning and control systems (Boeisho 2007b: 24–5). China's steady growth as a regional great power is perceived to have profound and disturbing implications for Japanese security (Boeisho 2007b: 26–7).

The 2005 LDP campaign manifesto, however, also pledged that Japan would act responsibly as a member of the international community and that Japan's Self-Defence Force troops would be deployed abroad with a view to defending Japan's national interest within the limits of international cooperation. In a similar vein, Prime Minister Fukuda Yasuo and Foreign Minister Komura Masahiko both pledged their government's commitment to build a Japan dedicated to international peace and cooperation in their January 2008 New Year policy speeches in the Diet (Gaimusho, annual).[1] The Japanese elite's view of the external environment thus appears unmistakably Westphalian but also partially post-Westphalian.

There is no direct evidence of either the LDP or the LDP government's unequivocal commitment to either the Westphalian or the post-Westphalian version of national identity in their recent statements. However, their statements on related issues suggest that they do not subscribe to the classic Westphalian view. For example, the LDP committed itself in its 2005 campaign manifesto to participation in international efforts to solve wide-ranging problems of global interest and concern, such as global warming, poverty and epidemics, etc., mainly through Japan's official development assistance (ODA) programmes abroad, but also through a domestic campaign to change the Japanese people's own lifestyle (Jiyuminshuto 2005). The LDP's coalition partner, the Clean Government Party (CGP), echoed the same commitment in its own campaign manifesto (Komeito 2005).

The CGP's statement also emphasized the importance of economic and cultural exchanges with other nations, especially those in the Asia-Pacific region, for regional and global economic and political stability and peace. The 2008 Ministry of Foreign Affairs (MOFA) 'bluebook' refers to climate change as a problem that the entire international community faces and that 'urgently requires its united action' (Gaimusho, annual).[2] It would be far-fetched to characterize the Japanese elite's security culture on the interaction preferences dimension as 'institutionalized and reflexive multilateralism', but it is evidently not 'unilateralism and contingent cooperation' either. It contains some elements of both and must therefore be said to fall between the two polar types.

The Japanese elite's conception of the security governance system leans more clearly toward the Westphalian model. Ever since the post-World War II Allied occupation ended in 1952, the Japanese elite has unwaveringly stuck to the view that the military alliance with the US, anchored in the 1951 US-Japan Mutual Security Treaty as revised in 1960, is the most important insurance policy against external threats to the nation's security and therefore the central pillar of Japan's security policy (Gaimusho, annual; Boeisho 2007a: 226–7; Jiyuminshuto 2005; Komeito 2005). There has been some movement among the Japanese elite to enlarge and multilateralize the collective defence system, as suggested by Foreign Minister Aso Taro's November 2006 call for creation of an 'arch of freedom and prosperity' among nations in the region that are committed to democracy and the free market economy (Gaimusho, annual). The bilateral alliance with the US nonetheless remains the core element of Japanese security policy.

The most significant security referent for Japan in recent years has been North Korea, which has been treated essentially as an 'adversarial other'. Even the CGP, which tends to be more moderate and internationalist in foreign and security policies than its senior coalition partner, the LDP, declared in its 2005 election campaign manifesto that the development of nuclear weapons by North Korea posed a grave threat to Japan's security and could not be tolerated (Komeito 2005). It went on to declare that, if necessary, Japan should not hesitate to invoke economic and other sanctions against Pyongyang.

With regard to the three other elements of security governance systems, the Japanese elite's security culture incorporates some elements of post-Westphalian type. The formal pacifism embodied in Article 9 of the post-World War II Japanese constitution, known as the 'peace clause' (Fukui 2007: 219), has evidently been internalized by a large segment of the Japanese public. In a May 2007 *Asahi Shimbun* poll, for example, 78 per cent of respondents believed that Article 9 had contributed to peace and, in the same newspaper's poll taken one year later, 23 per cent favoured and 66 per cent opposed amending Article 9 (*Asahi Shimbun* 2007a: 1; 2008a: 14). The Japanese elite security culture may diverge from its mass-level counterpart on this issue. Available circumstantial evidence suggests, however, that conventional war is not considered an acceptable regulator by any significant member of the Japanese elite. The 2005 LDP campaign manifesto espoused 'United Nations-centred peace diplomacy' (Jiyuminshuto 2005). The CGP manifesto issued at that time called for 'diplomacy of peace and humanitarianism' with a view to earning the neighbouring nations' trust and contributing to peace-building in the region (Komeito 2005). In sharp contrast to the perceived identity of its security referent, the appropriate regulator in the security governance system in the

Japanese elite's mind is thus more post-Westphalian than Westphalian, although it falls far short of the ideal that 'states acknowledge the existence and legitimacy of extra-national adjudication of disputes and voluntarily comply with decisions of international or supranational courts and other institutionalized dispute resolution mechanisms' (Sperling 2010: 3).

With regard to the function of norms, the 2005 LDP campaign manifesto called for an active use of the nation's ODA programmes to help promote 'human security', that is, as a means to help solve global problems such as poverty, climate change and epidemics (Jiyuminshuto 2005). The CGP's manifesto said much the same thing, but in substantially greater detail and in a language more clearly post-Westphalian than the LDP's. It stated that Japan, as a member of the international community, has a moral obligation to render assistance to those suffering from poverty, human trafficking, drug abuse, discrimination against women, etc., including accepting more asylum seekers from abroad (Komeito 2005).

As the above discussion suggests, the Japanese elite holds an extremely negative view, verging on outright hostility, of North Korea. At the same time, however, it pledges to strive to improve relationships with all neighbouring nations, solve all outstanding disputes and disagreements in a 'forward-looking' spirit, and build an 'Asian Community' (Jiyuminshuto 2005). In recent years, Japan's top leaders, including Prime Ministers Abe Shinzo and Fukuda Yasuo, have spoken hopefully of building a 'strategic relationship of mutual benefits' with China, a 'partnership based on common strategic interests' with Russia, and a 'comprehensive strategic relationship' with Australia (Gaimusho, annual). Their successor, Aso, pledged, at the end of a December 2008 summit meeting with Prime Minister Wen Jiabao of China and President Lee Myung-bak of South Korea, to strengthen and expand cooperation among the three neighbouring nations not only on economic and financial issues but on a wide range of other issues, including disarmament, non-proliferation, and climate change (*Asahi Shimbun* 2008b: 1). The Japanese elite's conception of the desirable and emergent, if non-existent, security governance system is thus an intermediate type.

The evidence presented above, sketchy as it is, leads this author to conclude that the Japanese elite's security culture cannot be identified categorically with either polar type but only as an intermediate type. The discussion that follows describes Japan's actual behaviour in each of the four categories of security governance and seeks to assess the extent to which the nation's security culture sketched above helps explain salient aspects of Japanese behaviour in each.

Policies of assurance

Post-World War II Japanese security policy has been framed in and constrained by the so-called Yoshida Doctrine, initiated by Yoshida Shigeru, the leader of an early post-war conservative party, the Liberal Party. His view of the prudent foreign and security policies appropriate for the defeated and devastated post-war Japan subsequently evolved into something of a creed governing many of the decisions and actions of a succession of cabinets formed by Yoshida's followers, until it was dubbed a 'doctrine' by a Japanese academic in the 1980s (Nakajima 2006: 5–7, 208–10). It prescribed three interrelated tenets to guide post-war Japanese foreign and defence policies that would give top priority to economic recovery and development, restrain and limit defence spending, and rely primarily on US military power for protection from external threats.

The Yoshida Doctrine, however, has met vocal and sustained criticism and opposition from the beginning, both within and outside the Diet, especially among leaders of a rival conservative and more nationalistic party, known initially as the Progressive Party and later as the Democratic Party. These critics have been calling for a more activist defence policy posture, larger-scale and faster-paced rearmament, and a revision of the post-war constitution, especially its war-renouncing Article 9 (Nakajima 2006: 47–56, 98–115). Under their pressure, abetted by the US government and military, Japan began to undertake re-armament following the outbreak of war on the Korean Peninsula in 1950 and has slowly but steadily expanded its military capability, while consistently defining its mission and limiting its scale as strictly defensive and accordingly calling its military the Self-Defence Forces (SDF).

Throughout the Cold War period, a succession of Japanese governments maintained the view that, while its constitution allowed it to arm itself for strictly self-defence purposes, the SDF could not engage or participate in military operations abroad, even for peacekeeping or humanitarian purposes under the auspices of the UN. Instead, Japan could and did contribute financial support for such operations. In the first major international war of the post-Cold War era, the 1991 Persian Gulf War, however, Japan's generous financial contribution, amounting to about USD 13 billion, earned it no publicly expressed appreciation, not to mention gratitude, from any nation involved in the US-led military intervention (Green 2003: 202; Samuels 2007: 66).

Embarrassed and humiliated by this reaction, or lack of reaction, to its 'cheque book diplomacy', the Japanese government went through painful soul-searching and a serious reappraisal of its introverted and reclusive, if not isolationist, security policy. This led in mid-1992 to the passage through the Diet of the highly controversial International Peace Cooperation Law, or the PKO Law (Gaimusho, annual). This legislation paved the way for the participation of a limited number of Japanese personnel, including SDF troops, in peacekeeping, humanitarian, election-monitoring, and other similarly non-military missions abroad under the auspices of the UN or one or other regional group (Gaimusho, 2009a).

The 1992 law, however, required the existence of an effective ceasefire agreement among parties to a conflict and approval by local authorities of the UN mission and its activities as conditions for the participation of Japanese personnel. It also required prior approval of Japanese participation by the Diet. As a result of these legal restrictions and the persistently cautious parliamentary and public opinion reflected in those restrictions, the actual involvement of Japanese personnel, especially SDF troops, in UN-sponsored and other peacekeeping operations has been highly selective, almost to the point of being grudging. As Table 11.1 shows, a very small number of SDF troops participated in the UN-sponsored peacekeeping

Table 11.1 Japanese troop contributions to UN assurance missions (percentage of total troops)

UN Missions to:	2000	2001	2002	2003	2004	2005	2006	2007
UNDOF (Syria)	2.9	2.9	2.9	2.9	2.9	2.9	3.0	2.9
UNTAET (Timor-Leste)	0	0	10.7	0	0	0	0	0
UNMISET (Timor-Leste)	0	0	17.4	22.4	0	0	0	0

Source: SIPRI 2009

Table 11.2 Japanese contributions to UN peacekeeping operations budget, 2000–6

Year	Japan's share of UN peacekeeping budget (USD millions)
2000	20.6% (437.4)
2001	19.6% (592.9)
2002	19.7 % (443.0)
2003	19.5% (432.4)
2004	19.5% (995.4)
2005	19.5% (916.1)
2006	19.5% (667.0)

Sources: Gaimusho (ed.) (annual); Gaimusho 2009a

operations in Syria in the period 2000–7, and a somewhat more substantial number in Timor-Leste, but only in the 2002–3 period. No SDF troops have participated in any OSCE assurance missions so far. Japanese contributions to international peacekeeping operations have thus continued to be mainly financial and material. This kind of contribution has been very substantial, amounting to about 20 per cent of the total UN peacekeeping operations budget in recent years (see Table 11.2).

Until recently, Japan concentrated virtually all its financial contributions to international projects in its Official Development Assistance (ODA) programmes, implicitly and ambiguously regarding some of them as post-conflict assurance projects. These included grants given since the late 1990s to Bosnia and Herzegovina and Kosovo in the Balkans, the Philippines and Sri Lanka in Asia, Iraq and Palestine in the Middle East, and Sierra Leone in Africa (Gaimusho 2006a). These grants, like most other Japanese ODA grants and loans, were given bilaterally and, in principle, in Japanese Yen rather than US dollars. Most recently, however, Japan has begun to treat some of these programmes explicitly as post-conflict peace-building projects and to fund them in US dollars. In 2006, for example, Japan funded a variety of community-level infrastructure-building and post-conflict rehabilitation and reconstruction projects in several African nations (Sierra Leone, Sudan, Liberia, Congo and Burundi) and the Great Lakes region in East Africa that ranged from about USD 2 million to USD 50 million

(Gaimusho 2006b, 2009a). While very modest both in the amount of aid and the number of recipients involved, these initiatives nonetheless indicate the Japanese elite's growing awareness of and interest in the distinctive category of post-conflict assurance policies.

The Japanese assurance policies thus increasingly focus on international cooperation rather than competition, accept a common definition rather than strictly egoist definition of national interest, and rely on non-military and non-coercive means, even though sovereignty and autonomy remain their salient features. They must thus be characterized as a hybrid and transitional form between the Westphalian and the post-Westphalian types, a form that is consistent with and may be explained, to an important extent, by the Japanese elite's security culture.

Policies of prevention

Japan has so far not been involved in any preventive actions related to civil-military relations or democratization in a foreign country, or conflict prevention by negotiation between foreign countries. Its preventive actions, broadly defined, have been limited to economic assistance to either poor or strategically important developing countries. Japan was the largest ODA donor for a decade up to 2000, but it had fallen to 3rd place behind the US and Britain by 2006, and was projected to fall to 6th place by 2010 (*Asahi Shimbun* 2007c: 1). As Figure 11.1 shows, the ODA share of the Japanese government's annual budget has hovered between about a fifth and a little over a quarter of 1 per cent of the nation's GNP during the last decade.

Japan's share of the total ODA disbursement by the 22 state members of the Organization for Economic Cooperation and Development's Development Assistance Committee (DAC) in 2006 was about 14 per cent, down from over 32 per cent in the 1995–9 period. The bulk of Japanese ODA has gone to the infrastructure and production sectors of recipients' economies, while less than 2 per cent has been channelled to humanitarian projects (OECD 2008). In 2005, Japan

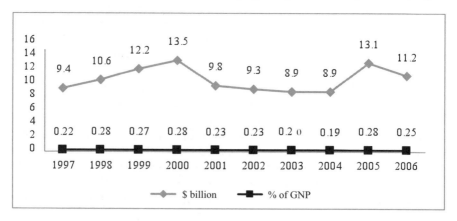

Figure 11.1 Japanese ODA disbursements 1997–2006

Source: Gaimusho (ed.) 2007: 71

Table 11.3 Inflow of asylum seekers into Japan

	1996	1997	1998	1999	2000	2001	2002	2003	2004	2005
Asylum sought	147	242	133	260	216	353	250	336	426	384
Asylum granted (%)	1 (0.6)	1 (0.4)	16 (1.2)	16 (0.6)	22 (1.0)	26 (0.7)	14 (0.6)	10 (0.3)	15 (0.4)	46 (1.2)

Source: Homusho 2007

ranked 15th among DAC's 22 state members in per capita ODA, 16th in the ODA share of GNP, and last place (22nd) in grants as a share of total ODA (Gaimusho 2007: 290–1). Moreover, the lion's share of Japan's ODA has consistently been given to East Asian and Middle Eastern nations, apparently more for geopolitical than charitable considerations. African states' shares have been rising in recent years but, as Foreign Minister Komura frankly explained at a December 2007 cabinet meeting, mainly for 'economic-strategic' reasons rather than humanitarian considerations (*Asahi Shimbun* 2007b: 10). Japanese ODA policy thus must be said to be more Westphalian than post-Westphalian.

Japanese immigration policy in general has been highly restrictive and, as a result, the number of resident foreigners in Japan has been small. Notwithstanding the pledge given in the 2005 lower house election campaign manifesto of the LDP's partner in the ruling coalition, the CGP, to increase the number of asylum seekers granted residence in Japan (Komeito 2005), the number of those seeking asylum in Japan has been very small and the number granted asylum in the nation minuscule, indicating the persisting force of an entrenched culture of insularity and parochialism, which underlies and sustains the Westphalian elements in the Japanese elite's security culture (see Table 11.3).

Policies of protection

Japan has no national institution dedicated to disease control and prevention comparable to the United States Centers for Disease Control (CDC). Nevertheless, health has been progressively securitized in the last few years, with the term and concept of 'medical security' becoming increasingly commonplace in both government documents and the print and electronic media. The growing official recognition of health-related problems as security issues has led, among other things, to the announcement by the Ministry of Health, Labour and Welfare (MHLW) of a Comprehensive Policy for Promotion of Medical Security in 2002, an Emergency Appeal for Measures to Deal with Medical Accidents in 2003, and a report on future medical security (Koseirodosho 2007: 187).

Policing power and responsibility in Japan's central government is shared primarily by three agencies: the National Police Agency (NPA), the Immigration Bureau of Japan (IBJ), and the Japan Coast Guard (JCG). As the modest size of its staff suggests, the NPA is an administrative agency that oversees a nationwide network

Table 11.4 Japanese policing agencies

		NPA	PPH	IBJ	JCG	Total
2000	Personnel	7,640	259,959	2,541		270,140
	Budget[a]	2,702	32,614	309		35,625
	Arrests[b]		309,649	51,459		361,108
	Arrests-narc[c]					
2001	Personnel	7,589	269,910	2,565		280,064
	Budget	2,305	28,961	277		31,543
	Arrests		325,292	40,764		366,056
	Arrests-narc					
2002	Personnel	7,545	274,317	2,663		284,525
	Budget	2,029	26,382	264		28,675
	Arrests		347,558	41,935	4,831	394,324
	Arrests-narc		18,823			18,823
2003	Personnel	7,498	270,809	2,693		281,000
	Budget	2,176	28,438	296		30,910
	Arrests		379,602	45,910	5,154	430,666
	Arrests-narc		17,171			17,171
2004	Personnel	7,481	274,107	2,833		284,421
	Budget	2,379	31,205	315	1,566	35,465
	Arrests		389,027	55,351	4,861	449,239
	Arrests-narc		15,048			15,048
2005	Personnel	7,501	277,611	2,972		288,084
	Budget	2,452	31,869	327	1,563	36,211
	Arrests		386,955	57,172	6,256	450,383
	Arrests-narc		15,803			15,803
2006	Personnel	7,524	280,927	3,120		291,571
	Budget	2,217	28,940	322	1,530	33,009
	Arrests		384,250	56,410	6,691	447,351
	Arrests-narc		14,440			14,440

Sources: Homusho nyukoku kanrikyoku, *Tokei*; Homusho nyukoku kanrikyoku (annual), 2004: 151; 2005: 170; 2007: 107, 110; Kaijohoancho (2007); Keisatsucho, *Tokei*; Keisatsucho soshikihanzai 2007

of prefecture-level police agencies, called the Prefectural Police Headquarters (PPH), which in turn oversee and coordinate police work by their municipal and submunicipal units (see Table 11.4). They handle violations of the narcotics control law as well as criminal law. PPHs' drug law enforcement work is reinforced by parallel work by a few dozen narcotics agents affiliated with MHLW's local branches (Koseirodosho 2008). The IBJ is, like the NPA, a small administrative agency in the central government which oversees policing activities by a network of eight regional bureaus with several local branches each. Japanese practice in this protection policy area is almost totally national in scope, despite the CGP pledge in its 2005 election campaign manifesto to promote cooperation in the international efforts coordinated by the United Nations Office on Drugs and Crime (UNODC) (Komeito 2005).

In domestic counter-terrorism operations, the NPA plays the lead role and has set up several specialized units in recent years (Keisatsucho 2007: 186–9). These include: Special Assault Teams (SAT) housed in eight PPHs; anti-weapons teams at all PPHs to assist SATs in guarding important facilities, such as nuclear power plants; special anti-terrorism teams at nine PPHs; and a Terrorism Response Team (TRT) with a tactical wing for limited overseas operations. The primary responsibility for international anti-terrorism operations belongs to the MoD, but these are focused on assistance to victims of terrorism and refugees, rather than preventing or combating terrorism (Boeisho 2007a: 289–92).

The Japanese government's posture on organized crime reflects and is largely driven by strong public interest in, and concern about, the issue. To highlight the importance of the issue, NPA's 2007 White Paper devoted a lengthy special section to the topic entitled 'Confronting organized gang fund-raising activities'. As Figures 11.2 and 11.3 show, the number of members and affiliates of gang organizations has been relatively small and constant over the last decade, but the number of gang-related criminals arrested for serious crimes has been large relative to the total number of criminals arrested, especially for blackmail, homicide and robbery cases. Yet, the total number of gang-related crimes has declined in the last several years, presumably in response to increasingly aggressive police interventions (see Figure 11.4).

In a nation constantly threatened and frequently devastated by natural disasters, Japanese public and media interest in environmental issues has always been strong and has become even stronger in recent years. SDF personnel and equipment are now routinely used in rescue work in the wake of major earthquakes, volcanic eruptions and heavy rainfalls (Boeisho 2007b: 64–5). These types of natural disasters may thus be said to have been securitized, both in official policy and public and media opinion. However, despite the 2005 LDP election campaign pledge that the Japanese government would deal aggressively with global environmental

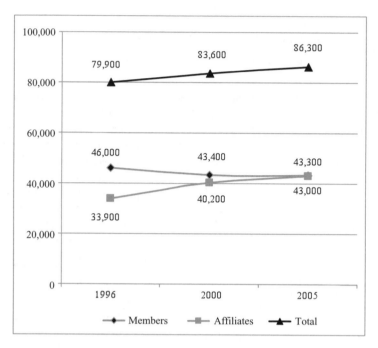

Figure 11.2 Membership of crime organizations

Source: Homusho homu sogo kenkyujo 2006: 103

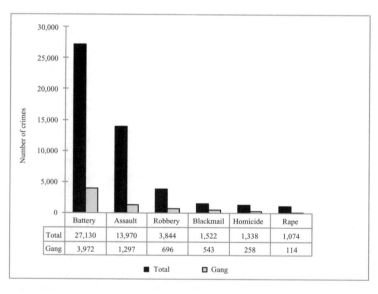

Figure 11.3 Number of criminals arrested for serious crimes 2005

Source: Homusho homu sogo kenkyujo 2006: 105

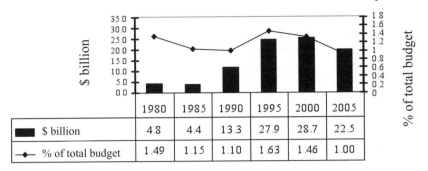

Figure 11.4 MOE budget 1980–2005

Sources: Kankyosho 2007: 284; Somusho tokei kenshujo 2007: 209

problems and exercise leadership in the international effort to reduce greenhouse gas emissions in particular, environmental protection has not enjoyed the level of either staffing or budget allocation that the ruling party's promise suggested (Jiyuminshuto 2005). In 2007, for example, the Ministry of the Environment (MOE) staff numbered only 1,134 personnel. Its share of the central government budget has been as miniscule and has substantially declined in recent years, hitting the 1 per cent level in 2007 (Kankyosho 2007: 284, 306).

In protection policies as a whole, the behaviour of the Japanese elite has thus been pro-active, if not aggressive, within Japan itself, but has remained largely unilateralist rather than multilateral and thus closer to the Westphalian than the post-Westphalian pole of the continuum.

Policies of compellence

Japan deployed its naval ships for an overseas mission for the first time since World War II in the spring of 1992, when several Maritime Self-Defence Force (MSDF) minesweepers were dispatched to the Persian Gulf after the first Gulf War had ended (Boeisho 2007b: 65). The second time that Japan was involved in a post-war overseas military operation was when the MSDF dispatched two destroyers and one fast combat support ship to the Indian Ocean in November 2001 to assist the US and its allies in the multilateral naval operations in and around Afghanistan (the Operation Enduring Freedom Maritime Interdiction Operation). They were subsequently joined or replaced by other MSDF ships in the continuing operations in support of the US war on terrorism, until the last of them was recalled in November 2007 amid rising criticism in Japan of their allegedly unconstitutional involvement in military actions abroad. The only case of troop deployment by Japan for purposes other than peacekeeping operations undertaken under the auspices of either the UN or other multinational regional organizations has been the 4,670 or so SDF troops' participation in the US-led multinational force deployed in Iraq in the 2003–7 period. Japan has not deployed its troops on a permanent or semi-permanent basis abroad since World War II, nor is likely to do so in the foreseeable future, as long as its present constitution remains intact.

Japan nonetheless possesses a substantial military force, albeit euphemistically called the Self-Defence Forces. A succession of LDP and LDP-led governments has taken the position that the SDF and its activities are constitutional. They have, however, not gone so far as to call for acquisition of obviously offensive weapons. The Basic Policy of National Defence adopted by the government in 1957 committed Japan to acquire an exclusively defensive capability, to forswear seeking the status of a military great power, to adhere to the Three Non-Nuclear Principles (not to possess, not to make, and to forbid the presence of nuclear weapons on its territory), and to enforce strictly civilian control of the SDF (Boeisho 2007b: 40–1). In recent years, Japanese defence policy-makers have been shifting their emphasis from the development of deterrence power to the development of ability to respond to diverse domestic and international situations and building a 'multi-functional, dynamic, and efficacious defence capability' (Boeicho 2005: 92–3; 2007b: 45). In order to cope with the apparently hostile and potentially dangerous environment in which Japan finds itself in its elite's perception, the SDF today has as large an arsenal of as advanced weapons and weapons systems as is believed to be compatible with the pacifist constitution. It nonetheless remains an arsenal of defensive weapons and weapons systems. For example, its naval component, the MSDF, does not possess a single aircraft carrier, battleship or cruiser, nor does its air component, the ASDF, possess a single bomber or ballistic missile.

Japan has been bound also by self-imposed restrictions on its export of weapons under the terms of the so-called Three Principles of Arms Export adopted in 1967 and expanded in 1976. Under the original set of principles, arms could not be exported to communist states, to states to which arms exports were prohibited by a UN Resolution, or to states involved or likely to be involved in an international dispute. The 1976 revision added provisions that Japanese firms should refrain from exporting arms even to states that did not fall in any of the three categories listed in the original principles and that the same principles should be applied to export of equipment used in the production of arms (Boeisho 2007a: 429).

As noted, Article 9 of the country's post-war constitution has been the key institutional barrier and the pacifist public opinion the main cultural barrier to a more significant expansion of Japan's compellence power, and these obstacles are not likely to be removed any time soon. The latest developments in the perennial debate among the nation's politicians and in the mass media on the pros and cons of constitutional revision and, more specifically, deletion or drastic revision of Article 9, actually suggest that revisionists are losing and anti-revisionists gaining ground, if only temporarily. The former appeared ascendant during the greater part of the first decade of the twenty-first century under Koizumi Junichiro's (2001–6) and, especially, Abe Shinzo's (2006–7) leadership of the LDP and government. The DPJ's victory and the LDP's defeat in the 2007 upper house election and unambiguous rejection in the 2009 Diet elections, however, have effectively reversed the trend and given the upper hand to anti-revisionists (*Asahi Shimbun* 2008a: 14; *Economist* 2009) Prime Minister Abe appointed an advisory group to push the revisionist campaign but it has become defunct and his plan to create a Japanese

Table 11.5 Japanese defence expenditure

	1990–4	1995–9	2000–4	2005	2006	2007
Share of GDP (%)	0.96	0.97	0.98	0.94	0.93	0.92
Annual rate of change in defence spending		+0.01	+0.01	–0.04	–0.01	–0.01
Distribution of defence expenditures:						
Personnel	41.2	43.6	44.9	44.6	44.5	44.0
Equipment	25.0	19.0	18.4	18.6	17.9	18.1
Infrastructure	3.7	4.2	3.2	2.9	2.4	2.3
Other	27.7	30.3	30.6	31.1	31.5	32.7
R&D	1.7	2.9	2.8	2.7	3.6	3.0
Defence spending per capita in Yen (USD)	36,011 (281.34)	38,609 (341.67)	38,618 (332.91)	37,794 (359.94)	37,427 (314.51)	37,358 (308.74)

Sources: Asagumo Shimbunsha 1992: 233; 2000: 292; 2008: 340–41, 344; Somusho tokei kenshujo (annual), 2002: 192; 2004: 8; 2007: 8, 209; Somusho tokeikyoku tokei kenkyujo (annual), 2008; Ace Consulting Group (2008)

equivalent of the American National Security Council was officially scrapped by his successor, Fukuda (*Asahi Shimbun* 2007d: 2).

As Table 11.5 shows, Japan's annual defence budget has been a modest, and virtually constant, fraction of the central government budget over the last two decades, especially if measured as a share of GNP. The conspicuously low R&D share of the budget reflects the low priority of domestic supply in the acquisition of weapons by the SDF. Given the restrictions on arms export under the 1967 and 1976 Principles of Weapons Export, domestic production suffers from the diseconomies of scale attending short production runs and makes it cheaper for the SDF to buy weapons from foreign makers. Japan thus either imports, mainly from the US, or produces under licences acquired from US firms, the majority of weapons for the SDF. The value of arms production in 2005 accounted for 0.66 per cent of Japan's total industrial production and did not exceed 1 per cent in any industrial sector, except munitions (87.7 per cent), aircraft (53.5 per cent), and shipbuilding (6.9 per cent) (Asagumo Shimbunsha 2008: 360).

Conclusion

The foregoing discussion helps us to evaluate very tentatively the validity of each of the three broad hypotheses addressed in this volume, bearing in mind the several caveats noted in the introduction. The Japanese elite's partially Westphalian and partially post-Westphalian, or hybrid, security culture does match its evident preference for primarily financial contributions to international peacekeeping and humanitarian programmes and actions under the auspices of the UN and other multinational groups, and its conspicuously cautious, or even grudging, attitude towards any action that involves or threatens to involve the use of military force. The SDF's rigidly defensive posture, exemplified both in its extremely limited participation in any type of overseas operations and in the inventory of its arsenal, also fits the characterization of the nation's elite security culture. These observations may be taken to broadly support the hypothesis that national security cultures account for the ways in which threats are securitized and the preferred instruments for meeting those threats.

The data reviewed above, however, also contain a warning against viewing the Japanese elite security culture as a transitional type that is moving progressively away from the Westphalian toward the post-Westphalian type. For one thing, Japanese ODA has not only been a constantly and, by DAC standards, disproportionately small share of Japan's GNP but, according to the nation's top leaders, increasingly and deliberately employed for 'economic-strategic' purposes. Moreover, the focus of Japanese defence policy has been shifting, again according to the nation's leaders, away from simple deterrence to development of a more dynamic and versatile, i.e. potentially offensive, capability. These developments may be attributed, at least partially, to a shift in the nation's elite security culture away from the post-Westphalian and toward the Westphalian type, rather than the other way round.

The highly unilateralist, if not outright egoistic, policies the Japanese elite has pursued in its prevention and, especially, protection policies, such as the treatment of asylum seekers, crime control, and environmental protection, may be attributed, again at least partially, to the Westphalian strain in its security culture. The increasingly multilateralist posture in its assurance policies, on the other hand, may be interpreted as a reflection of the post-Westphalian strain in the same culture. The former has arguably aggravated the collective action problem in Japanese security governance policies, while the latter has mitigated the problem, leading to the Japanese elite's increasing receptivity to international cooperation in some, if not all, types of joint assurance activities. In combination, these actions seem to broadly support the hypothesis that post-Westphalian and Westphalian security cultures mitigate and intensify, respectively, the problem of collective action.

The apparently unflagging determination with which the Japanese elite upholds and strives to strengthen the bilateral military alliance with the US may be considered a corollary of the Westphalian elements in its security culture. On the other hand, that same elite's acceptance of the nation's pacifist constitution, albeit apparently reluctant and possibly only temporary, and its more genuine rejection of military force as the regulator in the security governance system it envisions, as manifested in its assurance and, especially, compellence policies, may be viewed as a product of the post-Westphalian strain in its security culture. These contradictory aspects of their security governance policies thus support the hypothesis that security cultures produce pronounced preferences for specific forms of governance, if only in a general and broad sense of the term. Overall, the Japanese case thus tends to bear out the general sense of each of the three hypotheses linking national security cultures to national security policies across the four domains of assurance, prevention, protection and compellence.

Notes

1 Throughout this chapter, all Japanese names are given in their native order: family name first, given name second.
2 All translations of Japanese texts in this chapter are the author's own and he is solely responsible for any error found in them.

References

Ace Consulting Group (2008) *Gaikoku kawase reto, kinri, kabuka getsumatsu suiihyou* [Table of end of month foreign exchange rates, interest rates, and stock prices]. Available online at: http://www.aceconsulting.co.jp/kawasekinri.html (accessed 1 September 2008).

Asagumo Shimbunsha (ed.) (1992) *Boei handobukku heisei 4-nenban* [Defence handbook, 1992 edn], Tokyo: Asagumo Shimbunsha.

——(2000) *Boei handobukku heisei 12-nenban* [Defence handbook, 2000 edn], Tokyo: Asagumo Shimbunsha.

——(2008) *Boei handobukku heisei 20-nenban* [Defence handbook, 2008 edn], Tokyo: Asagumo Shimbunsha.

Asahi Shimbun (2007a) 'Kempo dai-9-jo wa heiwa ni kouken 78%' [Article 9 of the constitution contributes to peace, 78%], 2 May.

——(2007b) ''07-nenban ODA hakusho: senryakuteki katsuyo wo zenmen ni' [2007 edn ODA white paper: strategic use advocated upfront], 22 December.

——(2007c) 'Nihon no ODA 2010-nen ni 6-i' [Japan's ODA will be 6th in the world in 2010], 19 December, evening edn.

——(2007d) 'Nihonban NSC-koso dannen' [Japanese version NSC plan scrapped], 25 December.

——(2008a) '9-jo kaenai yoron modoru' [Public opinion returns to support of Article 9], 3 May.

——(2008b) 'Nichukan shuno kaigi kisha kaiken Aso hatsugen' [Aso's remarks at the Japanese, Chinese and South Korean leaders' joint press conference], 13 December.

Berger, T.U. (1998) *Cultures of Antimilitarism: National Security in Germany and Japan*, Baltimore, MD: Johns Hopkins University Press.

Boeicho (Defence Agency) (ed.) (2005) *Heisei 17-nen-ban nihon no boei: boei hakusho* [Japanese Defence: Defence White Paper, 2005 edn], Tokyo: Gyosei.

Boeisho (Ministry of Defence) (2007a) *Heisei 19-nenban nihon no boei: boei hakusho* [Japan's Defence 2007: Defence White Paper, 2007 edn], Tokyo: Gyosei.

——(2007b) *Heisei 19-nenban korede wakaru nihon no boei: konpakutoban boei hakusho* [Japan's defence explained: Defence White Paper, 2007 compact edn], Tokyo: Gyosei.

Economist (2009) 'The Vote that Changed Japan', 3 September. Available online at: http://the-economist.com/opinion/displayStory.cfm?story_id = 14363159&source = hptext feature (accessed 30 September 2009).

Fukui, H. (2007) 'Japan: Recasting the Post-war Security Consensus', in Kirchner, E.J. and Sperling, J. (eds) *Global Security Governance*, London and New York: Routledge.

Gaimusho (Ministry of Foreign Affairs) (ed.) (annual) *Gaiko Seisho* [Diplomatic bluebook]. Available online at: http://www.mofa.go.jp/Mofaj/gaiko/bluebook/index.html (accessed various dates).

—— (ed.) (2006a) *Heiwa no kochiku ni muketa wagakuni no torikumi no hyoka: Afghanistan wo jirei to shite* (An assessment of Japanese efforts to contribute to peace-building: Afghanistan as a case study). Available online at: http://www.mofa.go.jp/mofaj/gaiko/oda/shiryo/hyouka/kunibetu/gai/afghanistan/jk05_01_index.html (accessed 13 June 2008).

—— (ed.) (2006b) *Wagakuni no tai-afurika heiwa no teichaku shien: aratana inishatibu no moto de no tomen no shien* (Our nation's assistance for consolidation of peace in Africa: immediate assistance under the new initiative). Available online at: http://www.mofa.go.jp/mofaj/gaiko/oda/bunya/conflict/pdf/statistic02.pdf (accessed 12 June 2008).

—— (ed.) (2007) *Seifu kaihatsu enjo (ODA) hakusho 2007-nenban* [ODA White Paper, 2007 edn], Tokyo: Saeki Insatsu Kabushiki Kaisha.

—— (ed.) (2008a) *ODA: UNDP wo tsujite Kosovo to higashi Timor de jisshi sareta nihon seifu no funsogo enjo* [ODA: Japanese government's post-conflict assistance in Kosovo and Timor-Leste]. Available online at: http://www.mofa.go.jp/mofaj/gaiko/oda/shiryo/hyouka/kunibetu/gai/undp/index.html (accessed 15 June 2008).

—— (ed.) (2008b) *Heiwa no kochiku ni muketa wagakuni no torikumi no hyoka: Afghanistan wo jirei to shite* [An assessment of Japanese efforts to contribute to peace-building: Afghanistan as a case study]. Available online at: http://www.mofa.go.jp/mofaj/gaiko/oda/shiryo/hyouka/kunibetu/gai/afghanistan/jk05_01_index.html (accessed 13 June 2008).

—— (ed.) (2008c) *Wagakuni no tai-afurika heiwa no teichaku shien: aratana inishatibu no moto de no tomen no shien* [Our nation's assistance for consolidation of peace in Africa: immediate assistance under the new initiative]. Available online at: http://www.mofa.go.jp/mofaj/gaiko/oda/bunya/conflict/pdf/statistic02.pdf (accessed 12 June 2008).

—— (ed.) (2008d) *Kokusai Rengo heiwa iji katsudo to ni taisuru kyoryoku ni kansuru horitsu* [Law for cooperation in United Nations peacekeeping and related operations]. Available online at: http://www.mofa.go.jp/mofaj/gaiko/pko/horitu.html (accessed 25 July 2008).

——(ed.)(2009a) *Kokuren PKO no genjo* [Current state of UN peacekeeping operations]. Available online at: http://www.mofa.go.jp/Mofaj/gaiko/pko/katudo.html (accessed 26 June 2008).

—— (ed.) (2009b) *ODA: UNDP wo tsujite Kosovo to higashi Timor de jisshi sareta nihon seifu no funsogo enjo* (ODA: Japanese government's post-conflict assistance in Kosovo and Timor-Leste). Available online at: http://www.mofa.go.jp/mofaj/gaiko/oda/shiryo/hyouka/kunibetu/gai/undp/index.html (accessed 15 June 2008).

Green, M.J. (2003) *Japan's Reluctant Realism*, New York: Palgrave.

Homusho (Ministry of Justice) (2007) *Heisei 19-nen ni okeru nanmin ninteishasu to ni tsuite* [Numbers of refugees recognized in 2007 and related matters]. Available online at: http://www.moj.go.jp/PRESS/080215-2/080215-2-2.pdf (accessed 2 March 2008).

Homusho homu sogo kenkyujo (Ministry of Justice, Research and Training Institute) (ed.) (2006) *Hanzai hakusho (Heisei 18-nenban)* [Crimes White Paper, 2006 edn], National Printing Bureau of Japan.

Homusho nyukoku kanrikyoku (Ministry of Justice, Bureau of Immigration Management) (annual) *Shutsunyukoku kanri* [Immigration control]. Available online at: http://www.moj.go.jp/NYUKAN/nyukan37.pdf (accessed 10 July 2008).

——(2008). *Tokei: Nyukanho ihanshasu* [Statistics: numbers charged with immigration law violations]. Available online at: http://www.immi-moj.go.jp/toukei/index.html (accessed 15 July 2008).

Huntington, S.P. (2000) 'Foreword', in Harrison, L.E. and Huntington, S.P. (eds) *Culture Matters*, New York: Basic Books.

Jiyuminshuto (Liberal Democratic Party) (2005) *Jiminto seiken koyaku 2005* [LDP's promises, 2005]. Available online at: http://www.jimin.jp/jimin/jimin/2005_seisaku/120yakusoku/pdf/yakusokuText.pdf (accessed 20 August 2005).

Kaijohoancho (Japan Coast Guard) (2008) *Kohoshiryo* [Public information]. Available online at: http://www.kaiho.mlit.go.jp/info/kouhou/h15/index.html (accessed 24 July 2008).

Kankyosho sogo kankyo seisakukyoku (Ministry of the Environment, Environmental Policy Bureau) (ed.) (2007) *Kankyo tokeishu (Heisei 19-nenbann)* [Collected statistical data on the environment, 2007 edn], Tokyo: Japan Statistical Association.

Katzenstein, P.J. (1996) *Cultural Norms and National Security: Police and Military in Post-war Japan*, Ithaca, NY: Cornell University Press.

Keisatsucho (Police Agency) (2008) *Tokei* [Statistics]. Available online at: http://www.npa.go.jp/toukei/index.htm#sousa (accessed 12 July 2008).

Keisatsucho (ed.) (2007) *Heisei 19-nenban keisatsu hakusho* [Police White Paper, 2007 edn], Tokyo: Gyosei.

Keisatsucho soshikihanzai taisakubu yakubutsu juki taisakuka (Police Agency, Organized Crimes Policy Department, Drugs and Weapons Division) (2007) *Heisei 18-nenchu no yakubutsu juki josei* [Conditions relating to drugs and weapons in 2006]. Available online at: http://www.npa.go.jp/sosikihanzai/yakubutujyuki/yakubutu/yakutai15/20070427.pdf (accessed 18 July 2008).

——(2008) *Heisei 19-nenchu no yakubutsu juki josei* [Conditions related to drugs and weapons in 2007]. Available online at: http://www.npa.go.jp/sosikihanzai/yakubutujyuki/yakujyuu/yakujyuu1/h19_jyousei_yakujyuu.pdf (accessed 18 July 2008).

Komeito (Clean Government Party) (2005) *Komeito no manifesto 2005* [CGP manifesto 2005]. Available online at: http://www.komei.or.jp/policy/policy/pdf/manifest2005.pdf (accessed 20 August 2005).

Koseirodosho (Ministry of Health, Labour and Welfare) (2008) *Mayaku torishimari-kan* [Narcotics agents]. Available online at: http://www.nco.go.jp (accessed 10 July 2008).

Koseirodosho (ed.) (2007) *Kosei rodo hakusho: heisei 19nenban* [Health, labour and welfare White Paper, 2007 edn], Tokyo: Gyosei.

Nakajima, S. (2006) *Sengo nihon no boeiseisaku: 'Yoshida-rosen' wo meguru seiji gaiko gunji* [Post-war Japanese defence policy: politics, diplomacy, and military affairs revolving around the 'Yoshida Line'], Tokyo: Keio Gijuku Daigaku Shuppankai.

North, D.C. (1990) *Institutions, Institutional Change and Economic Performance*, Cambridge: Cambridge University Press.

OECD (2008). *Aid Statistics* (Paris: OECD). Available online at: http://www.oecd.org/department/0,3355,en_2649_34447_1_1_1_1_1,00.html (accessed 30 June 2008).

Oros, A.L. (2008) *Normalizing Japan: Politics, Identity and the Evolution of Security Practice*, Stanford, CA: Stanford University Press.

Samuels, R.J. (2007) *Securing Japan: Tokyo's Grand Strategy and the Future of East Asia*, Ithaca, NY: Cornell University Press.

SIPRI (2009) *Multilateral Peace Missions Overview*. Available online at: http://conflict.sipri.org/SIPRI_Internet/index.php4 (accessed 6 January 2009).

Somusho tokei kenshujo (Ministry of Internal Affairs and Communications, Statistical

Research and Training Institute) (ed.) (annual) *Nihon no tokei 2007* [Statistical data on Japan]. Tokyo: Nihon tokei kyokai.

Somusho tokeikyoku tokei kenkyujo (Ministry of Internal Affairs and Communications, Bureau of Statistics, Statistical Research and Training Institute) (ed.) (2008) *Zenkoku jinko suii* [Nationwide demographic trends]. Available online at: http://www.e-stat.go.jp/SG1/estat/List.do?lid = 000001035735 (accessed 12 August 2008).

Sperling, J. (2010) 'National security cultures, technologies of public goods supply and security governance', in Kirchner. E.J. and Sperling, J. (eds) *National Security Cultures: Patterns of Global Governance* (London: Routledge).

12 Russia

A global power?

Derek Averre

Few countries have faced such an array of challenges in the area of security governance as post-Soviet Russia. Over the last two decades, Russia has encountered a series of events and trends that – while ultimately re-establishing it as a key player in global and regional affairs – have in many respects shaped quite different perceptions of the global security environment and international politics among its governing elite and society. These include the disintegration of the Soviet Union and subsequent fragmentation of the post-Soviet space, the enlargements of NATO and the European Union into Central, Eastern and Southeastern Europe, NATO's intervention in the FYR over Kosovo, the Chechen wars, and radical changes to the internal political, economic and social foundations of Russia itself. The result is that – while Russia has played a substantive and, in many respects, responsible role in many international issues – and indeed seeks a greater voice in decision-making – it has also challenged important aspects of Western policies over European security governance, creating tension between a 'sovereign' Russia pursuing its national interests and a modernizing Russia seeking to play a constructive part in an interdependent international order. As Mark Webber argued at the end of the first post-Cold War decade, this situation has produced 'an enduring, albeit increasingly problematic accommodation between Russia and the West' (Webber 2000: 33).

This chapter will examine Russia's approaches to security governance within the conceptual framework underpinning this volume. It investigates Russia's performance in the four issue-areas of assurance (peacekeeping, peace-building, stabilization and development aid); prevention (pre/non-conflict economic reconstruction, financial and technical assistance, arms control); protection (internal security tasks, transnational linkages between police/intelligence agencies, federal expenditure on internal security); and compellence (deployment for specific military missions and permanent overseas deployments, armaments programmes, federal budget outlays for defence purposes). It goes on to analyse the hierarchy of threats as reflected in Russian security debates, how these threats are conceptualized and the preferred instruments employed to deal with them; the extent to which Russia has a 'Westphalian' security culture, which inhibits collective action to provide security and, on the other hand, the extent to which it subscribes to 'post-Westphalian' security governance; and preferred modes of international cooperation. Finally, it considers the extent and nature of Russia's involvement in and commitment to shared security governance.

Russian security debates

Russian security thinking is primarily reflected in a series of official foreign and security policy documents (*National Security Concept* 2000; *Foreign Policy Concept* 2008; *Review of the Russian Federation's Foreign Policy* 2007; *Strategy for National Security* 2009) as well as keynote speeches and articles by leading government figures. The *Foreign Policy Concept* is infused with the idea of re-establishing Russia's role as a central player in international affairs and its greater responsibility for global governance in the face of new common security threats and challenges such as international terrorism, drugs trafficking, organized crime, WMD proliferation, regional conflicts, demographic problems, global poverty, energy security, illegal migration and climate change. Its response to these challenges is unequivocal, with the emphasis on strengthening the 'principles of multilateralism in international affairs' and implementing 'network diplomacy based on flexible forms of participation in international structures for the search of joint solutions to common tasks'. However, it also registers Moscow's concerns over heightened 'global competition', stemming from the West's attempts to undermine traditional principles of international law and continue a neo-Cold War 'containment' of Russia, which exacerbates conflicts in Russia's immediate neighbourhood as well as further afield. These concerns are more manifest in the *National Security Concept* (drawn up in the immediate aftermath of NATO intervention in the FYR) and *Strategy for National Security to 2020*. While these documents emphasize the common nature of many security challenges – and in fact deal at length with Russia's internal socio-economic and governance problems – they also point to the weakness of the Euroatlantic security architecture, the growing tendency towards unilateral use of force in the contemporary international environment, and the dangers posed by a new arms race. While Moscow's response focuses very much on non-military instruments, it also highlights the need to rebuild Russia's military capabilities to ensure its defence based on the principles of 'rational sufficiency'.

This uneasy ambivalence between a declared commitment to common approaches to security governance and a deep mistrust over the intentions of the major Western powers lies at the heart of Russian security debates. The breakdown of international institutions, shifts in structural power, and erosion of traditional principles of international politics threaten to produce a situation described by authoritative Russian sources as follows: 'International governance will continue to decline ... [we face] growing chaos and a vacuum of governance and security ... virtually all international security mechanisms that were instituted after World War II or during the Cold War do not measure up to the challenges and threats of the new century' (*The World Around Russia* 2007: 6, 24). These are, of course, not purely Russian concerns; Adam Roberts, among other Western scholars, has eloquently outlined the American shortcomings in terms of upholding 'democratic governance' and the norms and principles on which global politics are based, and the weaknesses of a 'plural order' in dealing with common challenges (Roberts 2008: 347–50). But Russia perceives a substantive threat to its national interests arising from a new division of Europe as result of the dual EU-NATO enlargement (not to mention the EU's neighbourhood policy and its recent more active promotion of the Eastern Partnership); splits within the OSCE as the only universal Euroatlantic institution; and Russia's continuing exclusion from key Western-led institutions. This prompts Moscow to emphasize Russia's role as an independent, sovereign, international player. It has increasingly questioned dominant US and European approaches to security governance and – as a 'normal' great power – sought a greater role in decision-making on important security issues and a system more attuned to collective leadership, with a central role for the UN, regional organizations and informal groupings such as the G8 and the BRIC countries.

Russia's current policies are widely interpreted as a revisionist challenge to the post-Cold War security order (Trenin 2007). Moscow's view, however, is that there is a need not to revise but to revisit security arrangements and base them firmly on principles of international law which were disregarded by the Western powers in the post-Cold War period; its aim is not confrontation but cooperation within a rules-based community – a community of practice rather than of values – in order to secure equal and indivisible security (see Lavrov 2009). President Dmitrii Medvedev's ambitious proposals for a new Euroatlantic security pact are based on these principles: respect for state sovereignty, territorial integrity and independence, inadmissibility of the use or threat of force, equal security, and no exclusive rights for any state or organization for peace and stability (Medvedev 2008; see also Emerson 2008). This is not to underplay the fact that Moscow's vision of Europe differs from that of the Western liberal democracies. But this chapter argues that its challenge is selective; it cooperates over numerous matters of common concern but disputes the position of the leading Western powers on such issues as arms control, US missile defences in Europe, and Kosovan independence. The conflict with Georgia over South Ossetia – the first time that post-Soviet Russia has used military force against another state and questioned its territorial integrity, to which international security organizations were virtually powerless to respond – reflects Moscow's determination both to mount a robust defence of its national interests and to secure a voice in future security arrangements in the wider Euroatlantic area.

Russia's approaches also have a clear normative dimension linked to the key issue of domestic security governance. While subscribing to 'traditional' formal principles of international cooperation between sovereign states – as enshrined in the UN Charter and the Helsinki Final Act – it is highly suspicious of the normative framework that informs Western approaches to foreign policy-making, particularly the 'democratization' and human rights agenda, which are perceived as posing a direct threat to state sovereignty and provoking confrontation along the lines of Cold War 'bloc politics' (Kosachev 2007; see also Averre 2008). As a result, dialogue on democracy and human rights has faced increasing difficulties in the recent period. Moscow accepts certain constraints on its behaviour – for example, those imposed by membership of the Council of Europe – but resists challenges to its domestic legitimacy posed by the Western liberal democracies. Put simply, Russia sees itself as a 'normal' country, accepting many aspects of contemporary security governance while pursuing its own foreign policy interests and defending its own interpretation of the 'rules of the game' within international organizations and regimes. This extends to its sponsorship of regional organizations in the post-Soviet space such as the Collective Security Treaty Organization (CSTO) and the Shanghai Cooperation Organization (SCO) in which the emphasis is primarily on enhancing rather than pooling sovereignty and on regime stability as a means of minimizing potential insecurity.

Policies of assurance

Analysis of military expenditure (see Table 12.1) reflects the extent to which Russia's defence policy remains based on traditional notions of national defence, with minimal commitment to international peace-support operations. President Medvedev has called for a greater international profile in this sphere; the defence budget spending for peacekeeping was increased in 2008 and is projected to rise further in 2009–11, although the allocations are still very small and it is uncertain where they will be spent. Thus, while there are a few exceptions – notably the recent deployments of troops in support of the EUFOR mission in the Central African Republic/Chad (which may prove an interesting development in EU-Russia security relations) and to UNMIS, Russia's participation in assurance missions which might be considered as supporting 'collective milieu goals' has been limited to small-scale contributions – primarily of military observers and civilian police and staff – to UN and OSCE arrangements. This is despite the fact that between 1996 and 2003 Russia was the largest non-NATO contributor of forces to the SFOR and KFOR NATO-led peacekeeping operation, before Moscow's growing disillusionment with what was seen as a flawed operation led to the withdrawal of the Russian contingent.

The vast majority of Russian deployments have been in the Commonwealth of Independent States (CIS), which remains Moscow's priority in terms both of immediate political-military and strategic importance and as a source of transnational security threats (see Table 12.2). Moscow aims to sustain its role as the region's main security guarantor via the presence of 'peacekeeping' troops and provision of military-technical support, and attempts to exclude direct external participation in conflict settlement. Deployments have been made formally as part of CIS arrangements as well as under bilateral agreements. The deployments in Abkhazia and South Ossetia (the latter never sanctioned by the UN) were nominally under a CIS mandate; while portrayed by Moscow as preventing conflict, they were widely seen as biased and coercive in the sense that they guaranteed the autonomy of these separatist territories. In the aftermath of the conflict with Georgia and Moscow's recognition of the independence of Abkhazia and South Ossetia, Georgia withdrew its support for the peacekeeping forces in the two territories, thereby terminating them. As a result, Moscow's deployment has effectively been transformed into an allied contingent, bolstering their defence in the face of Georgia's territorial

Table 12.1 Draft Russian defence expenditure 2009–11 (billion roubles)

National defence	2009	2010	2011
Armed forces of the Russian Federation	913.3	1,045.5	1,107.3
Mobilization of external forces	6.6	6.1	6.1
Mobilization of the economy	4.7	4.9	6.3
Collective peacekeeping	0.12	0.12	0.13
Military nuclear programmes	22.5	27.5	29.1
International treaty obligations	2.8	2.9	3.0
Applied R&D	164.8	157.8	153.7
Other	163.6	146.7	174.8
Total national defence	1,278.5	1,391.8	1,480.5
Additional defence-related security expenditure			
Internal troops	66.3	76.2	82.8
Security organs	185.4	201.2	219.5
Border troops	84.4	93.3	83.5
Other	289.9	331.0	327.8
Total defence-related expenditure	1,904.5	2,093.5	2,194.1
As % of total federal expenditure	21.1	20.2	19.4

Source: IISS 2009: 215

claims. Moscow has also blocked the roll-over of the UN observer mission to Georgia (UNOMIG). Russia's role in the trilateral Joint Control Commission peacekeeping force in Transnistria has also been seen as prejudiced in favour of the latter territory, with Moscow again insisting on a decisive role in resolving the conflict. The CSTO has also initiated multilateral peace operations in the Central Asian region with Russia's participation, as well as counter-narcotics and counter-terrorist operations, via the Collective Rapid Deployment Force, and plans to step up collective efforts to deal with illegal migration and emergency situations in the near future.

The EU's Eastern enlargement and the European Neighbourhood Policy (ENP) have been described as 'two major policies of assurance – represent[ing] cases of the EU as a successful and relatively autonomous foreign policy actor' (Kirchner and Sperling 2007: 218). While EU political-military involvement in the Eastern neighbourhood has been negligible, conflict prevention is becoming an increasingly important part of its external security policy. It is seen as a potential security provider by some ENP countries; the EUJUST-Themis rule of law mission in Georgia and EUBAM assistance mission on the Moldova-Ukraine border have been followed by the EU monitoring mission in Georgia, established after the

Table 12.2 Russian contributions to multilateral assurance missions 2008

		Police	Military observers	Troops	Civilian staff
UN peacekeeping	UNTSO		4		
	MINURSO		15		
	UNOMIG	x	5		
	UNMIK	x	1		
	MONUC	x	27		
	UNMEE (terminated 2008)		x		
	UNMIL	x	6		
	UNOCI		11		
	MINUSTAH	x			
	UNMIS	x	13	123	
	UNMIT	x			
UN political	UNAMA				x
	UNAMI				x
	UNIOSIL (terminated 2008)		1		
	UNMIN (observers withdrawn 2008)		x		x
CIS	Moldova/Transnistria			*1,278	
	(South Ossetia			3,800)	
	(Abkhazia			3,800)	
OSCE missions	FYR Macedonia				x
	Georgia				1
	Dushanbe				x
	Bosnia-Herzegovina				4
	Kosovo				2
EU	EUFOR CAR/Chad			100–120	
CSTO	Collective Rapid Deployment Force			1,200	

Sources: SIPRI 2009: 130–58; IISS 2009: 226–7

Notes:
x   Number not known
*   Total including Moldovan

South Ossetia conflict, and the EU has also considered a peacekeeping operation in Moldova to address the Transnistria issue. These 'policies of assurance' do not, however, assure Moscow; while there may be shared concerns between the EU and Russia and engagement over issues of 'low' politics, including post-conflict reconstruction in the region, Moscow is wary of any external political-military involvement in regional security governance in the CIS. Indeed, the EU-Russia common external security space – one of four 'common spaces' agreed in 2007 as the vehicle for bilateral negotiations – has been limited largely to political dialogue on issues of international concern and has conspicuously failed to generate shared decision-making or even far-reaching cooperation, apart from the EUFOR CAR/ Chad mission and Russian cooperation with the EU Atalanta naval operation to fight piracy off the Somalian coast (see *EU-Russia Common Spaces* 2009). Indeed, the EU's Eastern Partnership initiative, the establishment of which was brought forward in response to the South Ossetia conflict, has excited suspicions in Moscow that some new EU member states view it as a partnership against Russia.

Ongoing problems over the CFE Treaty and Russia's resentment of NATO's Eastern enlargements – not least in view of its recognition of Ukraine and Georgia as future Alliance members – have, of course, also caused confrontation with NATO. Again, however, Moscow has proved cooperative on a range of issues, resulting in incremental progress on assurance-related matters through the consultative NATO-Russia Council. Regular consultation and joint threat assessments on terrorism, as well as civil emergency planning for terrorist attacks, have expanded to related areas such as border control (including counter-narcotics activities), non-proliferation, airspace management and nuclear safety. In December 2004 NRC foreign ministers approved a comprehensive Action Plan on Terrorism. Russian vessels were deployed in 2006 and 2007 to support Operation Active Endeavour, NATO's counter-terrorist operation in the Mediterranean. Russia has facilitated land transit across its territory of non-military equipment in support of the NATO-led International Security Assistance Force (ISAF) in Afghanistan. Practical cooperation in the protection against nuclear, biological and chemical weapons is ongoing. Dialogue in the area of theatre missile defence has included a study to assess the possible levels of interoperability among the theatre missile defence systems of NATO Allies and Russia and the holding of command post exercises. Progress has also been made on a Cooperative Airspace Initiative. In the area of military-to-military cooperation, a programme has been set up to develop interoperability, including training and exercises, furthered by the 'Political-Military Guidance Towards Enhanced Interoperability Between Forces of Russia and NATO Nations', approved by NRC defence ministers in June 2005. The Partnership for Peace Status of Forces Agreement has facilitated further military-to-military cooperation, including the deployment of forces participating in joint operations and exercises, as well as Russian logistical support to ISAF. The NRC has taken steps to prepare for possible future cooperation in crisis management, notably through the approval in September 2002 of 'Political Aspects for a Generic Concept for Joint NATO-Russia Peacekeeping Operations'. Other areas of cooperation include search and rescue at sea, defence industrial and research cooperation, and joint action in response to civil emergencies and developing capabilities to manage the consequences of terrorist attacks ('NATO's relations with Russia' undated).

Policies of prevention

In the first post-Soviet decade Russia was more a receiver than a donor of financial and technical aid. However, recent official communiqués suggest an increasing commitment to policies of prevention in the area of humanitarian and post-conflict assistance. The emphasis appears mainly to be on debt-burden relief and assistance in development, education and public health in Africa; USD 12 billion has reportedly been written off in debt and USD 33 million is to be made available to the International Development Agency for 2007–14, though other allocations are small in scale ('Russian Relations with Sub-Saharan African Countries' 2007). Russian legal and normative documents do not yet include the concept of official development assistance, but Russia is planning to increase funding in this area further to USD 400–500 million per year (*Russia's Participation in International Development Assistance* 2007). It is also reportedly developing an interagency programme to create a pool of professionals to support peace-building activities.

As a global power aiming to balance its national interests and international obligations, Russia plays a prominent role in many international organizations and regimes, including those linked with arms control and disarmament agreements (see SIPRI 2009: 493–541). In the nuclear sphere, as well as engaging in strategic arms control talks with the US to establish an agreement to replace the START-I Treaty, which expires in December 2009, and affirming the principle of cooperative monitoring which underlies the verification regime, Moscow has ratified the CTBT – unlike the US – as well as undertaking initiatives such as trying to multilateralize the INF Treaty and joining the Russian-American Global Initiative to combat acts of nuclear terrorism. It is also party to IAEA safeguards agreements under the NPT and has signed an additional safeguards protocol.

As suggested earlier in this chapter, however, Moscow has in the recent period sought to revisit certain security arrangements in an attempt to regain what it perceives as losses it suffered in the immediate post-Cold War period. As a result, talks on the Adapted CFE Treaty have stalled, with NATO member states refusing to ratify it and Moscow placing a moratorium on its CFE commitments, threatening to create a substantial gap in security governance arrangements in Europe and reflecting the deeper divisions outlined earlier in this chapter. Moscow's concern – that the US and NATO are not observing the regulatory aspects of CFE, with NATO moving treaty-limited equipment to new bases in Romania and Bulgaria and the US planning to deploy missile defences in Europe – is reciprocated with NATO member states' concerns over Russia's non-observance of flank limitations and Moscow's continuing refusal to honour political commitments made at the 1999 OSCE Istanbul Summit to withdraw its troops stationed on Moldovan and Georgian territory. This impasse – and the danger of re-creating two opposing groups of states if the Adapted CFE Treaty does not come into force – has only been exacerbated by the conflict over South Ossetia and Russia's deployment of forces in the separatist regions (Oznobishchev 2008: 53–60). The crisis may, however, present an opportunity to rethink conventional arms control and associated codes of conduct on political-military aspects of security in Europe.

One area where it is possible to talk of preventive security governance is Russia's contribution to the Global Partnership, conceived in 2002 to boost the Cooperative Threat Reduction programme and deal with the Soviet legacy of weapons of mass destruction (WMD). Moscow pledged USD 2 billion over ten years, primarily for chemical disarmament (Russia's 40,000 tonnes of chemical weapons stockpiles are to be destroyed by April 2012, as stipulated by the Chemical Weapons Convention) and nuclear submarine dismantlement, with some funds envisaged for fissile material security. As the Russian economy began to recover, federal budget allocations increased, and by 2006 Russia had spent around USD 1.27 billion on these projects. Further allocations have since been made; however, in view of the global financial crisis there is some doubt on whether the CWC deadline will be met and whether Russia can continue to sustain its Global Partnership pledges.

A similar situation obtains in the sphere of non-proliferation export controls, where Moscow has generally been cooperative in the fight against terrorist use of WMD. The adoption of normative legal documents has been accompanied by a White Paper detailing Russia's international commitments (*The Russian Federation and Nonproliferation of WMD* 2006). Russia's export control system now conforms closely to international practice and its lists of controlled goods and technologies have been brought into line with those of international control regimes, most of which – with the exception of the Australia Group, which deals with chemical and biological items – now include Russia as a member. A three-year project established direct contacts between Russian and EU export control officials in 2006 and work is ongoing on harmonizing Russian legislation with the EU export control system. In the last few years alone over 60 criminal cases involving charges relating to unauthorized exports of controlled items have been brought and more than 30 attempts by foreign entities to smuggle sensitive items have been forestalled. The problems facing Russia in this sphere – political disputes between states (the case of nuclear cooperation with Iran being a prominent case in point), striking an appropriate balance between trade and security, a poorly equipped and corrupt customs service, lax enforcement and a lack of understanding of export controls among exporters – are common to many countries and there have been substantive improvements in Russia's performance in recent years (Averre 2009b).

Policies of protection

Despite a greater degree of secrecy surrounding budget funding of the 'power agencies' – a generic term covering ministries, agencies, services and forces concerned with national security, public order and the defence of the realm – it is possible to establish trends over the recent period from the above data and to assess the Russian government's priorities. In absolute terms funding allocations for protection have increased markedly (see Table 12.3). This reflects a key policy concern under

Table 12.3 Power agencies (PA) in the federal budget (millions roubles)

	1999	2000	2001	2002	2003	2004	2005	2006	2007	2008	2009*	2010*
FSB, SVR, FSO	8,555	13,668	24,593	34,477	47,510	51,862	66,000	91,539	116,836	147,709	178,328	205,632
Border service	5,562	10,501	13,912	19,280	25,066	30,711	35,908	48,798	53,786	64,921	79,936	77,607
FSTEK							19	22	188	22	23	27
Total security	**14,117**	**24,168**	**38,506**	**53,756**	**72,576**	**82,572**	**101,927**	**140,359**	**170,811**	**212,652**	**258,287**	**283,266**
MVD	18,444	31,517	39,242	50,916	70,794	115,510	147,805	166,029	189,781	243,089	268,763	265,849
VV MVD	5,050	12,974	15,923	15,446	19,382	23,580	26,987	38,383	46,791	54,740	59,341	65,449
Penal system	10,961	17,856	26,440	33,822	46,644	14,538	61,494	78,369	93,505	119,633	140,160	145,087
Procuracy	2,436	4,269	6,835	9,397	11,797	48,201	20,734	27,332	34,475	39,996	50,394	49,493
Justice	891	1,938	2,945	3,968	7,288	8,254	19,600	28,016	39,527	50,445	39,682	37,646
FSKON/tax police	1,346	1,911	3,766	5,406	3,381	7,585	9,064	11,250	13,041	16,513	19,130	18,828
Courier service	130	209	282	375	647	1,063	1,347	1,582	1,787	2,000	2,476	2,510
Total public order	**39,256**	**70,674**	**95,433**	**119,330**	**159,932**	**218,730**	**287,029**	**350,959**	**418,905**	**526,416**	**579,946**	**587,862**
MChS	1,289	2,175	3,053	4,062	5,791	6,537	9,527	n/d	20,920	no data	no data	30,942
GUSP	2,522	2,653	3,859	4,727	7,158	9,334	12,543	n/d	21,459	no data	no data	29,283
Total emergencies	**3,811**	**4,828**	**6,912**	**8,790**	**12,949**	**15,871**	**23,070**	**29,722**	**42,379**	**49,923**	**57,236**	**60,225**
'National defence'	**115,594**	**191,728**	**247,703**	**295,393**	**355,692**	**429,999**	**581,144**	**681,803**	**831,875**	**1,040,840**	**1,216,083**	**1,253,154**
All power agencies	**172,779**	**291,397**	**388,554**	**477,269**	**601,149**	**747,172**	**993,171**	**1,202,843**	**1,463,970**	**1,829,831**	**2,111,552**	**2,184,507**
Total budget	**666,931**	**1,029184**	**1,321,903**	**2,054,194**	**2,358,546**	**2,698,867**	**3,514,348**	**4,281,329**	**5,986,562**	**7,566,639**	**10,051,377**	**9,886,921**

(continued)

	1999	2000	2001	2002	2003	2004	2005	2006	2007	2008	2009*	2010*
PA as share of total	**25.91**	**28.31**	**29.39**	**23.23**	**25.49**	**27.68**	**28.26**	**28.10**	**24.45**	**24.18**	**21.01**	**22.09**
security	2.12	2.35	2.91	2.62	3.08	3.06	2.90	3.28	2.85	2.81	2.57	2.87
public order	5.89	6.86	7.22	5.81	6.78	8.10	8.17	8.20	7.00	6.96	5.77	5.94
emergencies	0.57	0.47	0.52	0.43	0.55	0.59	0.66	0.69	0.71	0.66	0.57	0.61
national defence	17.33	18.63	18.74	14.38	15.08	15.93	16.54	15.93	13.90	13.75	12.10	12.67
PA as share of GDP	**3.58**	**3.99**	**4.35**	**4.41**	**4.54**	**4.40**	**4.59**	**4.49**	**4.42**	**4.39**	**5.22**	**5.06**
security	0.29	0.33	0.43	0.50	0.55	0.49	0.47	0.52	0.52	0.51	0.64	0.66
public order	0.81	0.97	1.07	1.10	1.21	1.29	1.33	1.31	1.26	1.26	1.43	1.36
emergencies	0.08	0.07	0.08	0.08	0.10	0.09	0.11	0.11	0.13	0.12	0.14	0.14
national defence	2.40	2.62	2.77	2.73	2.68	2.54	2.69	2.55	2.51	2.50	3.01	2.90

Source: Cooper 2009

Notes:
* 2009 = budget; 2010 = draft budget.

FSB – Federal Security Service; SVR – Foreign Intelligence Service; FSO – Federal Protection Service; FSTEK – Federal Service for Technical and Export Control; MVD – Ministry of Internal Affairs; VV MVD – Internal troops of the MVD; FSKON – Federal Service for the Control over the Circulation of Drugs; MChS – Ministry of civil defence, emergencies and liquidation of natural disasters; GUSP – Main Directorate for Special Programmes (mobilization preparedness).

Vladimir Putin, namely the re-establishment of internal order in Russia following the 'systemic crisis' in the 1990s and a renewed emphasis on the state as a provider of public goods (see Putin 2008), as well as Russia's much improved economic performance over the period under review. However, apart from a slight rise in 2000–1 and 2004–6 – possibly caused by the second Chechen campaign, which ended in 2007 – they have remained fairly constant as a percentage of total budget expenditure. There was a notable, though hardly excessive, overall increase in spending on security as a percentage of GDP over the last decade, though it appears to have stabilized in the recent period. Analysis of the share of allocations for the power agencies shows that spending on internal security and public order has increased, partly at the expense of the Armed Forces, while again having remained more or less constant in the second half of the current decade (see Table 12.4).

Russian spending on 'traditional' security and defence substantially exceeds that on health, education and social policy, in contrast to the correlation in developed countries (Table 12.5). The shares of budget allocations are projected to remain more or less constant in all these categories, suggesting no great change in the priorities of the Medvedev administration. Nevertheless, as is evident from the *Strategy for National Security to 2020*, the Russian leadership is well aware of the internal challenges the country faces; modernization and development demand more investment in social programmes. A slight increase in spending on health care, which has translated into only partial improvements in the main indicators of public health, and in fact to a decline in some areas, reflects a major public policy concern in Russia over the poor health and high mortality rates of sections of the population, which contribute to what is widely seen as a demographic crisis (see Table 12.6). With structural deficiencies in the economy having been only partially remedied over the last two decades – reflected in the impact of the global financial crisis, which is currently hitting Russia harder than many other developed states

Table 12.4 Share of total funding by security category 1999–2010 (%)

	Security Services	Public Order	Emergency Provision	National Defence
2010*	13.0	26.9	2.7	57.4
2009*	12.2	27.5	2.7	57.6
2008	11.6	28.8	2.7	56.9
2007	11.7	28.6	2.9	56.8
2006	11.7	29.2	2.4	56.7
2005	10.3	28.9	2.3	58.5
2004	11.1	29.3	2.1	57.5
2003	12.1	26.6	2.1	59.2
2002	11.3	25.0	1.8	61.9
2001	9.2	22.8	1.7	66.3
2000	8.3	24.2	1.7	65.8
1999	8.2	22.7	2.2	66.9

Source: Cooper 2009

Note:
* budget figures

Table 12.5 Structure of federal budget expenditure 2005–10 (% of GDP)

	2005	*2006*	*2007*	*2008*	*2009*	*2010*
General state matters	1.4	1.3	2.1	2.1	1.9	1.8
Expenditure on interest	1.0	0.6	0.5	0.5	0.5	0.6
National defence	2.7	2.5	2.7	2.7	2.7	2.7
National security/law enforcement	2.1	2.0	2.2	2.2	2.3	2.2
National economy	1.2	1.3	1.6	2.1	2.0	1.2
Education	0.7	0.8	0.9	0.9	0.8	0.8
Culture, cinema, media	0.2	0.2	0.2	0.2	0.2	0.2
Health care and sport	0.4	0.5	0.7	0.6	0.6	0.6
Social policy	0.8	0.7	0.7	0.8	0.9	1.0
Total expenditure	**16.3**	**15.9**	**17.8**	**18.8**	**18.8**	**18.1**

Source: Cooper 2007

Table 12.6 Russian budget expenditure on health care and sport

	1995	*2000*	*2005*	*2006*
Expenditure billion (1995: trillion) roubles	41.0	153.4	797.1	962.2
Percentage of total expenditure	8.4	7.8	11.7	11.5
Percentage of GDP	2.9	2.1	3.7	3.6

Source: Federal State Statistics Service 2009: http://www.gks.ru/bgd/regl/b07_34/IssWWW.exe/Stg/
d02/07–04.htm (accessed 15 October 2009)

– and with traditional security concerns still high on the agenda, the Medvedev government faces difficult choices in the coming period.

Analysis of the crime data in Table 12.7 suggests that, with some exceptions, the increased spending on internal security and on the judiciary has produced a reduction in serious crimes in Russia and more effective policies of protection over the present decade; increases in other crimes such as robbery and drugs offences may be a result of higher levels of detection and greater intervention by the courts. Additional data on crime provided by the Russian Ministry of Internal Affairs (MVD) for 2008 in Table 12.8 suggest that criminal activity, which might be considered transnational or closely related to key domestic security concerns – terrorist crimes and serious economic criminal activity – is falling, though there was a sharp increase in extremist activity registered and investigated by the MVD.

The establishment of transnational cooperation between police enforcement and intelligence agencies suggests a more comprehensive approach, linking external and internal security. A joint cooperation plan for 2007–10 was established between the EU's FRONTEX and the Russian Border Service, covering risk analysis and

Table 12.7 Recorded crimes (in thousands)

	1992	1995	2000	2002	2003	2004	2005	2006	2007
Homicide and attempted homicide	23.0	31.7	31.8	32.3	31.6	31.6	30.8	27.5	22.2
Intentional serious injury/rape	67.6	74.2	57.7	66.6	65.2	66.2	67.1	60.3	54.3
Robbery/burglary/theft	1,846.0	1,547.0	1,481.0	1,141.0	1,398.0	1,583.0	1,981.0	2,094.0	1,907.0
Terrorist attacks		1.0	135.0	360.0	561.0	265.0	203.0	112.0	48.0
Drug abuse	29.8	79.9	244.0	190.0	182.0	150.0	175.0	212.0	231.0
Total recorded crimes	**2,761.0**	**2,756.0**	**2,952.0**	**2,526.0**	**2,756.0**	**2,894.0**	**3,555.0**	**3,855.0**	**3,583.0**

Source: Federal State Statistics Service 2009: http://www.gks.ru/bgd/regl/B08_12/IssWWW.exe/Stg/d01/11–01.htm (accessed 15 October 2009)

Table 12.8 Criminality in 2008

	Registered		Investigated	
	total	*% change*	*total*	*% change*
Terrorist	642	−15.4	550	−16.8
Extremist	46	+29.2	430	+98.2
Appropriation/embezzlement	72,142	−1.8	66,299	−2.5
Extortion	9,953	−13.8	8,105	−10.6

Source: Ministry of Internal Affairs 2009

information exchange, approaches to illegal immigration, and joint border management activities. There has also been cooperation between EUROPOL and Russian law enforcement authorities on illegal immigration, human and narcotics trafficking, and currency crimes (with ongoing dialogue on data protection); discussion between EUROJUST and the Russian Procurator's Office and judicial cooperation in civil and commercial matters; a Memorandum of Understanding between the Russian FSKON and European bodies on control over the circulation of drugs; developing contacts between the European Police College (CEPOL) and Russian agencies; and expert level meetings on counter-terrorism (*EU-Russia Common Spaces* 2009; *Review of EU-Russia Relations* 2008). Owing partly to Russian sensitivities over sovereignty, these activities to date have been largely confined to information-sharing and limited joint activities rather than to the establishment of common regulatory mechanisms and far-reaching institutional changes in Russia.

Multilateral governance arrangements in the post-Soviet space – though their effectiveness in some areas is limited, again owing to national sovereignty concerns – form an important part of Russia's protection policies. While Russia places greater emphasis on bilateral relations, it has been keen to develop regional frameworks such as the CIS – threatened by fragmentation but still strongly supported by Moscow – the CSTO, whose remit covers multilateral security relations across most of the states in the region, and the SCO. President Medvedev has called for an increase in the military capability of the CSTO. In September 2008, its Secretary-General, Nikolai Bordyuzha, announced the intention to create a new military formation in addition to the CSTO Collective Rapid Deployment Force, which currently numbers around 4,000 troops from Russia, Kazakhstan, Kyrgyzstan and Tajikistan. Within the framework of the SCO, which operates on an interstate rather than supra-state basis and is not concerned with military or peace operations, Russia participates in the Regional Anti-Terrorist Structure, a permanent organ established as a coordinating and information-sharing structure to deal with terrorism, extremism and separatism in the SCO member states, and has conducted large-scale anti-terrorist manoeuvres, officially designated as 'peace missions' (Aris 2009). The SCO Charter reflects its member states' normative preoccupation with regime security and mutual non-interference in matters of domestic governance as a means of ensuring stability and dealing with non-traditional transnational security issues; although the SCO deals with economic and other issues, for Moscow its utility is to a large extent as an instrument to manage instability in the wider Central Asian region (Bailes *et al.* 2007). Neither the CSTO nor the SCO is concerned with the promotion of security sector reform or good governance.

Policies of compellence

In some cases Russia's military presence in the CIS may be considered to fall into the category of compellence. Though there was, until August 2008, no direct military action against states and deployments were insufficient for large-scale military action, the presence of Russian troops demonstrated political commitment and guaranteed Moscow a prominent part in conflict resolution. There are still substantial deployments in Armenia, Kyrgyzstan, Tajikistan and Ukraine, with infrastructure in Belarus and Kazakhstan (IISS 2009: 226–7).

The conflict with Georgia appears to have signalled a radical change in Russia's approach, however. Moscow's legal and normative argument for its invasion of Georgia – self-defence against the illegal use of force against Russian peacekeepers, Georgia's violation of the peace process, and the protection of Russia citizens abroad – has been challenged: 'The strong impression remains that Russia is picking and mixing its legal argument … if it is accepted that interests can be advanced through compliance with international norms, then Moscow appears to be indicating an increasingly revisionist stance and a declining regard for the social benefits to be derived from complying with broadly held norms in the international community' (Allison 2008: 1155). Moscow has adduced the case of Kosovo and re-emphasized its argument that the whole edifice of post-Cold War security governance has been undermined; it is prepared to isolate itself over the issue of independence for the separatist territories, even though this has not been sanctioned by the UN – formerly a sine qua non of Russian views of the international order – to assert its claim to shape its security environment.

There have been substantive problems with defence reform in post-Soviet Russia. These have stemmed partly from the inevitable difficulty of downsizing huge standing forces but have been exacerbated by divergent views between the civilian government and conservative figures among the senior military, who – despite changes in Russia's security priorities – have been reluctant to move away from traditional Cold War defence postures. They have consistently criticized reform plans as leaving Russia vulnerable to the strategic challenge posed by NATO enlargement to Russia's borders and US plans to station missile defences in Europe, as well as to instability caused by unpredictable neighbours and the continuing threat of Islamic radicalism (Solov'ev and Ivanov 2009). Priorities have thus not always been clear and progress towards establishing 'networked' asymmetric warfare capability has been retarded, as was evident in the conflict with Georgia. Nevertheless, a reduction is planned in conscript liability to 12 months in 2008–9 and the Armed Forces are to be reduced from 1.1 million to 1 million by 2013. The professionalization of the Armed Forces has continued, with more than 30 additional formations to be established by 2010, though there will continue to

Table 12.9 Russian nuclear forces in January 2009

Designation	Number deployed	No. of warheads
Strategic offensive	620	2,787
Bombers	77	856
ICBMs	383	1,355
SLBMs	160	576
Strategic defensive (anti-ballistic)	1,968	701
Non-strategic		1,346
Land-based bombers	524	648
Naval attack aircraft	179	237
Sea-launched cruise missiles		276
Anti-sub warfare and SAMs		185
Total strategic defensive/non-strategic		2,047
Total		**4,834**

Source: SIPRI 2009: 354–5

be a mixed contract/conscript army for the foreseeable future.

Far-reaching defence modernization plans also extend to Russia's strategic nuclear forces, regarded as the ultimate deterrent against both nuclear and large-scale conventional attack. Russia currently has around 4,800 warheads (see Table 12.9) with over 8,000 in reserve. In 2007 it began flight tests of new road-mobile MIRVed missile and missile defence penetration aids, and the MIRVed Topol is expected to be deployed in 2009. Six new Borey-class submarines are to be deployed starting in 2008 as part of plans to continue upgrading sea-based strategic forces. Another priority is the resumption of long-range patrols of strategic aviation; one additional long-range Tu-160 bomber was introduced in 2008 and the aim is to have a total of 30 by 2025–30. In 2007 Russia continued to reduce its strategic nuclear forces in line with Strategic Offensive Reduction Treaty (SORT) commitments and as part of a doctrinal shift away from a 'substantially redundant' towards a 'minimally sufficient' deterrence posture, which can be maintained until 2015–20 within force ceilings imposed by SORT, even if the US develops a BMD system, though strategic forces will need qualitative improvements to enhance survivability and ability to penetrate missile defences in the future.

Projection of Russian power abroad is mainly realized through the Navy. In this respect, it is significant that Moscow hailed the completion of a two-month deployment of a battlegroup from the Northern Fleet – including in the Mediterranean – in February 2008 as the restoration of Russia's naval presence abroad. In October 2008 there was also deployment in the Mediterranean and Caribbean of a nuclear-powered missile cruiser, with joint training with the Venezuelan Navy, and

Moscow announced the construction of a Russian naval facility at Tartus on the Syrian coast (IISS 2009: 207). Controversially, Moscow is also bidding to retain its Black Sea Fleet base in Ukraine beyond the expiry of the leasing agreement in 2017 in the face of Ukraine's refusal due to concerns over sovereignty and the ability of the BSF to destabilize relations between the two countries, even though Russia is expanding its base at Novorossiisk.

As for conventional air power, two regiments of Su-27 fighters were due to be operational by the end of 2008; a fifth-generation fighter is also being developed for 2013–15 and the Su-35 multi-role fighter is to enter service by 2010. There are also plans for major conventional arms for the ground forces, with a new main battle tank to be introduced after 2010, although the T-90 main battle tank is likely to remain the main component until 2025. Between 2010 and 2015 the Armed Forces will purchase 116 combat aircraft and a large number of helicopters, 700 tanks and 1,000 APCs; the Navy will receive 12 new surface ships, with the aspiration to rival the US and deploy six carrier groups within the next 20 years.

In line with global trends, Russian expenditure on the military has risen sharply over the last decade, though it should be noted that it has hardly increased at all as a share of GDP (see Table 12.10). It may be that the global financial crisis will scale down Russia's arms procurement ambitions. Nevertheless, the planned substantial re-armament programme – aiming at 'a qualitatively new look for the Russian Federation armed forces' (*Strategy for National Security* 2009) and to make amends for under funding the Russian defence industry in the immediate post-Soviet period – is likely to be maintained. The armaments programme announced by Putin in 2002 focused initially on R&D, expenditure on which increased in subsequent years. But now funding is starting to shift from R&D into procurement; 70 per cent of the defence budget will be spent on weapons procurement, repairs, R&D and testing by 2015, up from 30 per cent in 2006. The latest programme to 2015 is classified but reportedly covers a USD 150 billion procurement, upgrades and maintenance effort, with the aim of replacing 45 per cent of existing equipment. While Russian security conceptions discount the likelihood of major warfare, Moscow's views on the current international environment, as well as the future need to project its influence abroad, mean that Russia has to build up its defensive capabilities with the aim of maintaining strategic stability and being able to respond with operational and battle preparedness to the array of potential challenges to its sovereignty and territorial integrity.

Table 12.10 Estimated Russian military expenditure 1999–2008 (in constant 2005 USD)

	1999	2000	2001	2002	2003	2004	2005	2006	2007	2008
% GDP	3.4	3.7	4.1	4.3	4.3	3.8	3.7	3.6	3.5	n/a
USD billions	14.0	19.1	21.2	23.6	25.1	26.1	28.5	31.2	34.8	*38.2

Source: SIPRI 2009: 235, 242

Note:
* USD 58.6 billion in current prices (2008)

Conclusion

In their previous work on EU security governance, Emil J. Kirchner and James Sperling (2007: 238) concluded 'Yet any assessment of the EU's success or failure as a security actor in these four security policy arenas [assurance, prevention, protection and compellence] remains heavily dependent upon the yardstick employed to do so'. When analysing the case of Russia, the problem is compounded; not only is it difficult to establish comparable metrics to assess its performance in terms of security governance, but there is also a tendency in much writing on Russian security policy to use EU – or European or Western liberal-democratic – conceptions of security governance as the 'yardstick' against which to measure Russia, whereas the complex and dynamic nature of the international and regional security environment makes these conceptions highly conditional or restrictive. Put simply, where Moscow's attempts to assert its influence clash with Euro-centric or Western-centric norms (even though these are often the subject of contestation among the Western states themselves) it is automatically seen as 'defecting' and, as often as not, mischief-making.

A second issue is that of legitimacy. As suggested earlier in this chapter, a non-democratic domestic constitutional order is often seen as a barrier to effective pursuit of collective security governance (see Averre 2009a); certainly, the controversial nature of the 'Putin regime' has become central to any discussion of Russia's foreign policy. A state's security policies are undoubtedly determined not only by its security environment but also by the domestic balance of forces arising from its historical experience and, in Russia's case, its peculiar path of reform or 'modernization' in the post-Soviet period. Russia does face substantive challenges to effective internal security governance – indeed, as mentioned earlier, official pronouncements place far greater emphasis on internal than on external security issues; these challenges, and the corporate interests of the Russian 'state capitalist' bureaucracy, often combine to frustrate adherence to commonly accepted rules and constrain moves towards greater political pluralism (Arbatov 2007). Equally, as outlined earlier, there is a strong emphasis in Russian foreign policy rhetoric on 'sovereign' norms and competing values systems. Moscow's vision of the international order contrasts sharply with the 'post-Westphalian' European security system promoted by the Western liberal democracies.

Important differences over security governance arrangements have thus arisen. A genuine collective perception and definition of threat, underpinning common purpose in state policy and a common understanding of 'solidarist' norms and rules, has foundered on a lack of trust and mutual respect about the legitimacy of the policies pursued by the other. Thus the West's questioning of Russia's commitment to democracy and human rights, notably over Chechnya, has led Moscow to accuse it of 'double standards' in the fight against terrorism and to criticize the preoccupation of the OSCE with the 'humanitarian basket' and bias over election monitoring in the East (Entin and Zagorsky 2008). While the West has challenged Russia's support for undemocratic regimes in the countries of the shared neighbourhood, Moscow has countered by supporting norms of stability and in turn challenging the West's support for the Saakashvili regime. Moscow (hardly alone among the non-Western powers) has contested the West's interpretation of the core principles of international law over NATO's intervention in the FYR and Kosovo's declaration of independence, while the West has condemned Russia's invasion of Georgia and recognition of the independence of South Ossetia and Abkhazia. Finally, regulatory and normative failures in arms control treaties – which, given the actions of the US over the ABM Treaty and missile defences in Europe, are hardly all on Russia's side, despite its own shortcomings over CFE Treaty commitments – have created a climate of mistrust which technical negotiations, even if successful, will only partly dispel.

However, Russia has not always hampered the pursuit of collective 'milieu goals' but has respected many of the criteria for shared governance that mitigate the 'security dilemma'. It accepts normative constraints on the use of force and the primacy of political and diplomatic instruments in statecraft, and – despite the contentious claims of some commentators – does not seek to recreate 'empire'; it sustains a military capacity largely oriented towards defensive sufficiency; and it supports international law as the basis of conflict resolution and formal institutional mechanisms to adjudicate within-group conflict. Most (apart from a few conservative ideologues) would now accept that Russia no longer pursues an unalloyed, ideological anti-Western security policy. While substantive problems have arisen in the recent period, it is facile to say that Russia's leadership (though its decision-making is sometimes erratic) is wholly cynical and follows a purely interest-driven external policy. As cooperative efforts across a range of issues indicate, Moscow's rhetoric about sovereign autonomy (which is often for internal consumption) masks a higher degree of commitment to shared security governance, as distinct from purely instrumental, 'primitive' forms of multilateralism, than is generally supposed in terms of all three – the normative, intentionality and regulatory – dimensions identified by Mark Webber (Webber 2000).

Exceptionalism is not imprinted on the DNA of Russia's security culture: its current international behaviour is a response to specific circumstances and a particular reading of the international environment. There are deep-rooted domestic problems and 'gradual ideational assimilation' appears to be a long-term prospect. Nevertheless, the evolution of a common security culture between Russia and its Western partners across the issue areas dealt with in this book might be further explored both empirically and conceptually.

References

Allison, R. (2008) 'Russia Resurgent? Moscow's Campaign to "Coerce Georgia to Peace"', *International Affairs*, 84(6): 1145–71.

Arbatov, A. (2007) 'Bureaucracy on the Rise', *Russia in Global Affairs*, 2 (April–June).

Aris, S. (2009) 'The Shanghai Cooperation Organisation: "Tackling the Three Evils". A Regional Response to Non-traditional Security Challenges or an Anti-Western Bloc?', *Europe-Asia Studies*, 61(3): 457–82.

Averre, D. (2008) 'Russian Foreign Policy and the Global Political Environment', *Problems of Post-Communism*, 55(5): 28–39.

——(2009a) 'Competing Rationalities: Russia, the EU and the "Shared Neighbourhood"', *Europe-Asia Studies*, 61(10) (December 2009): 1689–1713.

——(2009b) 'Written Evidence for House of Commons Foreign Affairs Committee Report', *Global Security: Non Proliferation*, 3 June, ev. 219–22. Available online at: http://www. publications.parliament.uk/pa/cm200809/cmselect/cmfaff/222/222.pdf (accessed 20 July 2009).

Bailes, A.J.K., Dunay, P., Guang, P. and Troitskiy, M. (2007) *The Shanghai Cooperation Organization*, SIPRI Policy Paper No. 17, Stockholm International Peace Research Institute, May.

Cooper, J. (2009) 'The Funding of the Power Agencies of the Russian State', Centre for Russian and East European Studies, University of Birmingham.

Emerson, M. (2008), *The Struggle for a Civilised Wider European Order, Elements for a European Security Strategy*, Centre for European Policy Studies Working Document No. 307, October.

Entin, M. and Zagorsky, A. (2008), 'Should Russia leave the OSCE?', *Russia in Global Affairs*, 3 (July–September).

EU-Russia Common Spaces Progress Report 2008 (2009). March. Available online at: http://ec.europa.eu/external_relations/russia/docs/commonspaces_prog_report_2008_ en.pdf (accessed 17 September 2009).

Federal State Statistics Service (2009). Available online at: http://www.gks.ru/ (accessed 2 July 2009).

Foreign Policy Concept of the Russian Federation (2008). 12 July, unofficial translation. Available online at: http://www.mid.ru/ns-osndoc.nsf/0e9272befa34209743256c63004 2d1aa/cef95560654d4ca5c32574960036cddb?OpenDocument (accessed 11 May 2009).

IISS (2009) *The Military Balance 2009*, Abingdon, UK: Routledge.

Kirchner, E.J. and Sperling, J. (2007) *EU Security Governance*, Manchester and New York: Manchester University Press.

Kosachev, K. (2007) 'Russia and the West: Where the Differences Lie', *Russia in Global Affairs*, 4 (October–December).

Lavrov, S. (2009) 'Speech at Brussels Forum 2009', Brussels, 21 March. Available online at: http://www.mid.ru/brp_4.nsf/0/EE1043EE8ED70F8CC325758A002571B7 (accessed 9 June 2009).

Medvedev, D. (2008) 'Speech at Conference on World Politics', Evian, 8 October. Available online at: http://www.kremlin.ru/text/appears/2008/10/207422.shtml (accessed 12 January 2009).

Ministry of Internal Affairs (2009). Available online at: http://www.mvd.ru/files/ PUeh34ZSL9gjacp.pdf (accessed 2 July 2009).

National Security Concept of the Russian Federation (2000). Approved by Presidential Decree No. 24, 10 January, English translation. Available online at: http://www.mid.ru/ ns-osndoc.nsf/0e9272befa34209743256c630042d1aa/b8d88f7503bc644fc325752e0047 174b?OpenDocument (accessed 11 May 2009).

NATO, 'NATO's relations with Russia' (undated). Available online at: http://www.nato. int/cps/en/natolive/topics_50090.htm (accessed 15 May 2009).

Oznobishchev, S. (2008) 'Arms Control in Europe', *Russia: Arms Control, Disarmament and International Security, IMEMO Supplement to the Russian Edition of the SIPRI Yearbook 2007*, IMEMO RAN, Moscow.

Putin, V. (2008) 'Speech at Session of the State Council on Russia's Development Strategy to 2020', 8 February. Available online at: http://www.mid.ru/brp_4.nsf/0/531C812CE37 C337AC32573EA00271F54 (accessed 6 May 2008).

Review of EU-Russia Relations, Communication from the Commission to the Council (2008). COM(2008) 740 final, Brussels, 5 November.

Review of the Russian Federation's Foreign Policy (2007). 27 March. Available online at: http://www.mid.ru/brp_4.nsf/sps/3647DA97748A106BC32572AB002AC4DD (accessed 4 May 2007).

Roberts, A. (2008) 'International Relations after the Cold War', *International Affairs*, 84(2): 335–50.

The Russian Federation and Nonproliferation of Weapons of Mass Destruction and Delivery Systems: Threats, Assessments, Problems and Solutions (2006). Center for Nonproliferation Studies, 20 July. Available online at: http://cns.miis.edu/pubs/other/rusfed.htm (accessed 10 November 2008).

Russian Embassy in China, 'Russian Relations with Sub-Saharan African Countries' (2007). 4 June. Available online at: http://www.russia.org.cn/eng/?ID=117 (accessed 20 July 2009).

Ministry of Finance (of the Russian Federation), *Russia's Participation in International Development Assistance* (2007). 14 June. Available online at: http://www.minfin.ru/common/img/uploaded/library/2007/06/concept_eng.pdf (accessed 20 July 2009).

SIPRI (2009) *SIPRI Yearbook 2009: Armaments, Disarmament and International Security*, Oxford and New York: SIPRI/Oxford University Press.

Solov'ev, V. and Ivanov, V. (2009), 'Reform sets off on an unpredictable path', *Nezavisimoe voennoe obozrenie*, 29 May.

Ministry of Foreign Affairs (of the Russian Federation), *Strategy for National Security of the Russian Federation to 2020* (2009). 12 May. Available online at: http://www.mid.ru/ns-osndoc.nsf/0e9272befa34209743256c630042d1aa/8abb3c17eb3d2626c32575b50 0320ae4?OpenDocument (accessed 18 May 2009).

Trenin, D. (2007) *Russia's Strategic Choices*, Carnegie Endowment for International Peace Policy Brief, May.

Webber, M. (2000) 'A Tale of a Decade: European Security Governance and Russia', *European Security*, 9(2): 31–60.

The World Around Russia 2017; An Outlook for the Midterm Future (2007). Report by the Council on Foreign and Defence Policy, State University Higher School of Economics and RIO-Center, November.

13 Conclusion

Structure, agency and the barriers to global security governance

Han Dorussen, Emil J. Kirchner and James Sperling

The post-Westphalian hypothesis provides a structural explanation for the deviation of states from the Westphalian norm with respect to the content and form of security policy. Just as important, it explains the structural dimension of the willing abnegation of sovereignty by some states, particularly those in Europe, and the jealous protection of state sovereignty in others, particularly those in Eurasia. Moreover, the structural characteristics of the post-Westphalian state explain the process of (de)securitization, the material dissolution or (un)intentional legal blurring of national and system boundaries, and the intensification and broadening of collective action problems across the security spectrum. The national security culture hypothesis captures the role of agency in security governance policies. It captures the purposes and means of national security policies, particularly the preference for relying upon the 'soft' or 'hard' elements of power. It also captures the reflexive interaction preference that shapes the national affinity for (non-)institutionalized security cooperation and governance, or for bilateral or unilateral action.

The technologies of public goods supply hypothesis focuses on the intrinsic nature of the public good as either a barrier or facilitator of security governance cooperation. This hypothesis permits meaningful measurement and statistical testing, unlike those pertaining to the post-Westphalian state and national security culture. We test the technology of public goods supply hypotheses relying upon data measuring participation in and contributions to UN missions and programmes. Such an empirical test may:

- generate indirect evidence supporting the proposition that national security cultures and the emergence of the post-Westphalian states shape national responses to security governance challenges;
- explain variations in behaviour between states with similar structural characteristics or identify a complementary explanation for the patterns of global and regional security governance;
- provide a basis for rejecting the structural characteristics of the post-Westphalian state or agency, embedded in a national security culture, as a significant explanatory variable.

Systems of security governance

The forms of security governance range from a primitive balance of power to highly institutionalized security communities.[1] The structural characteristics of the post-Westphalian state impels states to seek highly institutionalized forms of security governance, while a national security culture demarcates the range of security governance systems compatible with national preferences and purpose. The preference for one form of governance over another reflects not only systemic imperatives but also the (in)compatibility of national security cultures with the intrinsic nature of a specific system of security governance. Any governance system has four distinct components – the referent, the regulator, the normative framework, and the interaction context – that fall along a broad spectrum of values (see Table 13.1). The precise content and combination of these components will generate a system of security governance falling along a continuum bounded by a balance of power and a fused security community.

The *security referent* identifies the target of the security arrangement. The security referent may be directed inwardly towards the contracting states (as in a collective security system) or outwardly towards an 'other' (as in an alliance) or the regional milieu (as in a security community). Where the role of power dominates interstate relations, even among states sharing a common identity, security arrangements will be outwardly directed towards an 'other' or the regional milieu. The *system regulator*, in turn, identifies the types of conflict-resolution mechanisms that range from the rule of war to the rule of law. As the utility or legitimacy of war declines, so too does the willingness of states to rely on it to regulate conflict; likewise, as national identities coalesce with a broader collective identity, sovereign recognition will become less important, providing the space for constructing effective institutional mechanisms for conflict resolution. The *normative framework* of a governance system captures the function norms play in the calculation of states' interests and behaviour. The mere existence of international norms does not reveal whether those norms are intrinsic or extrinsic to

Table 13.1 Constituent elements of security governance system

	Captures	*Range of values*
Security referent	Target of security concern	'within-group', an 'other', or both
Regulator	Mechanism for conflict resolution	Warfare to binding arbitration within well-defined institutional framework
Normative framework	Role of norms in defining national or group interests	Instrumental and disconnected from interest definition to substantive and intrinsic to the definition of interest
Interaction context	Security dilemma and relational orientations	Enmity and intense security dilemma to amity and the absence of a security dilemma

Source: Sperling 2008: 109

state calculations or how binding those norms are likely to be. Where system-level norms govern within-group interactions, the sovereignty principle is necessarily discounted and a reliance on force delegitimized. When those conditions are met, system-level norms become intrinsic to the calculation of interest, and produce outcomes seriously at a variance with material interests or the structure of power. When those conditions are not met, narrow national interests will trump system norms when they collide. The *interaction context* refers to the level of amity and enmity in the system and the intensity of the security dilemma. Where states have lost or ceded sovereign control and discounted sovereign prerogatives to international or regional institutions, the security dilemma is likely to dissipate, and amity will characterize interstate relations. Similarly, where states retain sovereign prerogatives and treat sovereignty as inviolable, then the security dilemma will remain acute, war remains a viable option, normatively and instrumentally, and states retain a narrowly defined national interest. The range of values assigned to these four constitutive elements for any system of security governance provides a mechanism for testing the proposition that there is an elective affinity between categories of security governance and national security cultures (see Table 13.2).

Table 13.2 A typology of security governance systems

	Security referent	Regulator	Normative framework	Context of interaction
Impermanent alliances	Great powers	War and balancing of power	Limited to rules of war	Neither a permanent state of amity nor enmity towards any state; classic security dilemma
Concert	Great powers	Multilateral consultation, managed balance of power	Limited to supporting existing regimes, qualified renunciation of war within group	Conditional amity; mitigated security dilemma
Collective defence	Identifiable enemy outside the group	Balancing, deterrence, force or war	Qualified or contingent commitment to aid ally	Amity within group; enmity without; security dilemma intact
Fused security community	Within group	International law, institutional conflict resolution mechanisms	Deep, broad, and binding; voluntary compliance; eroded juridical sovereignty	Deep amity derived from a positive or collective identity; a common set of norms have been internalized; security dilemma atrophied

Source: Sperling 2008: 111

National security cultures and security governance

The states surveyed in this collection do not neatly conform to the two ideal-type national security cultures outlined in the Introduction. Instead, the national security cultures of these states must be placed along the continuum demarcated by these two ideal types *and* there is empirical evidence that national security cultures are not homogenous or internally consistent: some national security cultures share the characteristics we have ascribed to a post-Westphalian state while others are more closely aligned with a Westphalian security culture. Despite such incongruities within national security cultures, however, there is an elective affinity between the structural characteristics of these states and the content of the national security culture. The precise admixture of values or properties defining a national security culture is at least partially, if not totally, independent of where a state falls along the Westphalian continuum: a Westphalian state is unlikely to participate in a governance system requiring the sensibilities and affinities of a security culture that embody a cosmopolitan identity or other-regarding definition of self-interest, whereas a post-Westphalian state is likely to do so.

Three of the powers investigated in this collection – China, Mexico and Russia – provide relatively unambiguous examples of states with Westphalian security cultures and the structural characteristics of a Westphalian state. Similarly, Italy and Germany present equally clear cases of post-Westphalian structures and security cultures consistent with the ideal-type. France, Japan and the UK present mixed cases, although in the cases of France and the UK the persistence of the Westphalian character of their national security cultures reflects the rhetorical miasma of past glories, and the possession of significant power-projection capabilities conjoined to the political will to use them. But at the same time, the policy choices and actions of these states outside compellence missions locates them towards the post-Westphalian end of the spectrum; i.e. much closer to Germany and Italy (and the European Union) than to the US.

Japan presents an even more complex case than Britain or France. Arguably, Japan possesses a schizophrenic security culture: Japan has renounced war as an instrument of statecraft and suffers from the structural vulnerabilities of a post-Westphalian state, yet prefers bilateral to multilateral action and has a largely egoist definition of interest. The US is the most difficult case in many respects. It is clear that the perception of threat has often been militarized in the national political discourse despite the American dedication of resources and reliance upon the 'soft' elements of power to meet a broad array of security challenges. Unlike the other major powers examined in this collection, the US is a core participant in a number of regional governance systems that range from a balance of power (Northeast Asia) to collective defence (the transatlantic region) to a bilateral security community (with Canada). Finally, despite the American proclivity to act unilaterally, American resources and diplomacy have supported regional and global multilateralism since 1945.

The origins of these nations' security cultures have deep roots in their national historical experiences and memories, particularly the lessons learned from national traumas. While German and Italian elites emerged from World War II with different historical memories than their counterparts in France and the UK, elites in all four countries have since developed a remarkable level of trust in each other; they believe that a recurrence of intramural war is highly unlikely or simply beyond the pale, and have internalized the principle of collective security cooperation. This element of post-war cooperation, such as through NATO, has also resulted in the development of a transatlantic security community between Europe and the US and Canada; it is of course also a long-standing feature of Canadian-US relations. Carrying a historical legacy comparable to that of Germany and Italy, post-war Japan developed a culture of restraint, if not pacifism, in matters of security. But Japan differs from Germany and Italy insofar that its bilateral security treaty with the US not only affects its view with the outside world, but has also removed any incentive to explore institutionalized forms of regional security multilateralism.

The historical experiences of these seven countries differ from those of China, Russia and Mexico. Chinese security culture is heavily influenced by the nation's historical legacy, particularly the 'century of shame' brought about by European, American and Japanese colonialism in the nineteenth and into the twentieth centuries, and a persistent fear of US geopolitical encirclement since the founding of the People's Republic of China. This legacy underpins China's uncompromised attachment to Westphalian sovereignty stance and contingent security multilateralism. The dissolution of the Soviet Union and the West's empty promise of equal partnership in the 1990s have forced the Russian Federation to adopt a similarly assertive position with respect to autonomy and sovereignty. History is also an important factor in Mexico, where nineteenth-century experiences with the US have scarred the Mexican foreign policy elite's collective memory: they continue to reassert and uphold the Westphalian principle of non-interference in the domestic affairs of other countries.

Keeping these caveats in mind, we can now ask the question: Do empirical narratives support the national security culture hypotheses developed in the Introduction to this volume?

- H_1: *National security cultures account for the securitization of threats and the preferred instruments relied upon to meet them.*

Historical events, geographic location and political traditions in turn affect the securitization of threats and the mode of response across the four security dimensions: assurance, prevention, protection and compellence. Securitization occurs when an issue is framed as one of a security, i.e. it is defined as a threat in a national security statement as found in defence or security White Papers, when there is a marked increase in the allocation of resources (budgetary and personnel), when the legitimizing rhetoric of budgetary expenditures is securitized, or when there is a transfer of prerogatives from a civilian to a security agency or ministry, either permanently or temporarily in times of crisis.

Data from the ten countries reveals differences in the degree of securitization of threats and the means adopted to cope with the perceived threats. With regard to policies of assurance, all ten states (except Mexico) frame the reconstruction and rebuilding of conflict-torn countries as a security issue, but do not use the same means to deal with these situations. Civilian means (e.g. aid and technical assistance, and democratization programmes) are much preferred by Canada, Germany, Japan and Italy, with France, the UK and the US being more willing to mix these with military efforts (peacekeeping) than Germany and Japan. China and Russia have no reticence over the use of military personnel in peacekeeping operations and, in many ways, choose this as their main form of engagement in post-conflict environments.

Policies of prevention have been gradually securitized, from the definition of a 'priority zone' for aid and for action against failed states to the gradual involvement of police and even the military in the struggle against illegal immigration, such as in France. Conflict prevention has taken the form of milieu goals for the four European countries, Canada, Japan and the US, in which the emphasis is on persuasive rather than coercive methods of statecraft. In contrast, China, Mexico and Russia, with significantly smaller aid programmes, place greater stress on the commercial or raw materials objectives rather than the stability and democratic measures advanced by the other seven countries.

There has been an accelerated securitization of threats in all the countries reviewed since 2001. A number of heretofore domestic challenges have been transformed into security threats: terrorism, cyber-security, natural disasters and public health. In several countries a link has been forged between organized crime, border control and immigration policies. In response to these securitized threats, the four European countries, Canada and Japan have introduced structural mechanisms equivalent to the US Department of Homeland Security; they have also substantially increased the budgets and number of personnel dedicated to those tasks. In addition, both the British and the French have introduced a doctrine of 'resilience' to enable public authorities and society to respond to a major crisis and rapidly restore normal functioning.

Unlike policies of assurance, where either peacekeepers or civilian personnel are involved, and unlike policies of prevention, where the emphasis is mostly on technical assistance, policies of compellence and protection became increasingly blurred as the severity of the perceived threats to national security, identity or integrity was deemed to require a military response in the form of external peace-making or peace-enforcement missions. Issues of international terrorism, regional conflicts and the proliferation of weapons of mass destruction feature prominently in national defence and security White Papers. However, there are differences in how the ten countries have securitized these threats and, more so, the instruments deemed necessary to meet them. Germany and Japan, which, after World War II, committed themselves exclusively to a defensive capability and renounced the status of being a military great power, have a long-standing culture of 'reticence' to engage in external peace-making or peace-enforcement operations. This reticence is subsiding as elites in both nations recognize the necessity of developing a multifunctional, dynamic and efficacious defence and security capability. Similarly, the Canadian and Italian national security cultures view the use of force as a last resort, an orientation espoused in the EU's European Security Strategy. Mexico adheres strictly to the non-interference principle. By contrast, the use of force is deemed a core state prerogative for China, Russia, France, the UK and the US. France and the UK, however, are less likely to act outside a multilateral context or without a legitimizing UN mandate.

Thus, the data on the four security dimensions confirms the hypothesis that national security cultures do account for the securitization of threats, the preferred instruments relied upon to meet them, and the variations between states with similar power resources and interests in international order.

- H_2: 'Post-Westphalian' security cultures mitigate the problem of collective action, while 'Westphalian' security cultures intensify the problem of collective action in the provision of security.

The degree to which states embrace or reject a strong national identity influences national attitudes towards the importance of autonomy as a national goal, the preference for multilateralism, bilateralism or unilateralism, or the willingness to pool sovereignty. It indicates whether states retain Westphalian characteristics or exhibit post-Westphalian ones. The Chinese security culture, for example, exhibits a strong civilizational conception of nationhood, which translates into a jealous regard for unfettered sovereignty, territorial integrity and national defence. Russia, under the leadership of Vladimir Putin, emphasized similar national attributes, but Russia lacks the long-standing historical grievances found in China. The Mexican identity is expressed not so much in the positive sense of 'self' but rather in the negative sense of how the Mexican and American identities differ. The openness of transactions within the EU and the existence of a number of common policies have affected both the identity and sovereignty of EU states; it requires collective action to safeguard the fruits of the European project and to meet common external threats defined collectively. High levels of openness and a concern with milieu goals, rather than particularistic national security goals, conventionally conceived, also characterize Canada, Japan and the US. This preoccupation with milieu goals is reflected in the way these seven countries conduct policies of assurance and largely applies to policies of prevention. Less progress, in terms of collective action, has been achieved in policies of protection, where national identity persists more stubbornly. Vestiges of undiluted national sovereignty still constrain common action, even where the threat is collectively acknowledged as common, and even within the EU. This constraint binds more tightly in Canada, Japan and the US and dominates policies in China, Russia and Mexico. A more varied picture emerges from the ten countries with regard to policies of compellence, where a mixture of institutionalized collective action (ESDP and NATO missions) and 'coalitions of the willing' (Operation Iraqi Freedom and Operation Enduring Freedom) hold sway, but where also a majority of countries, including France and the UK, refuse to abnegate the right to unilateral action – possibly reflecting the material capability to project force autonomously and the possession of a nuclear deterrent.

According to the evidence gathered from the ten countries, only Germany and

Italy would appear to possess post-Westphalian cultures, with the other eight states manifesting Westphalian traits. However, on the policy dimensions of assurance and prevention, the behaviour of five of the eight states classified as Westphalian conform to the expectations of a post-Westphalian state. Both France and the UK, together with Germany and Italy, have internalized EU norms and standards, which has created an 'other-regarding' identity eroding the national identity. In other words, the EU has helped these four countries to forge, at least to some extent, a common identity. Similarly, these four countries think about their interests in terms of what is good for the EU as a whole. They portray the EU as a big family and do not countenance intramural war. While not of the same intensity, the practice of international codes has also affected the identity and the sense of 'other-regarding' in Canada, Japan and the US.

Thus a differentiated picture emerges with regard to the second hypothesis. Post-Westphalian security cultures, as existing in Germany and Italy, mitigate the problem of collective action. However, Canada, France, Japan, the UK and the US have in practice adopted security culture traits similar to those of Germany and Italy. There is evidence, therefore, that these nations' national security cultures have mitigated the problem of collective action. In contrast, the Chinese and Russian emphasis on the national identity and autonomy, which reflects the behaviour of a classical Westphalian state, has intensified rather than mitigated the problem of collective action in Eurasia, the Pacific and North America. The same characteristic holds for Mexico in the North American context.

- *H₃: National security cultures produce preferences for specific systems of security governance that, in turn, facilitate or inhibit international cooperation.*

In the post-war period, particularly within the institutional evolution of the EU, France, Germany, Italy and the UK have relied increasingly on collective security measures, persuasive rather than coercive foreign policy instruments, and multilateral rather than unilateral modes of interaction. These states seek to promote regional and global stability based on democratic principles consistent with those introduced and promoted by the US in Europe (e.g. the role of NATO) and in Asia (bilateral mutual defence treaties with Japan and South Korea). Similar sentiments also prevail in Canada. Hence, the four European countries, Canada, Japan and the US are signatories to collective defence or bilateral security arrangements and increasingly substitute collective milieu goals for particularistic national security goals, conventionally conceived.

While the US participates in a large number of collective defence and security arrangements, it has not always made a substantial effort to subordinate unilateral prerogatives with multilateral obligations. In this respect, US foreign policy behaviour sets itself apart from that of the four European countries, Canada and Japan. Moreover, its superior military strength, geopolitical presence, and global interests have put it at loggerheads with China and Russia, which, after periods of stagnation and retrenchment, are trying to reconnect with past glories. Both countries are determined to establish themselves as central players in international affairs and to reshape the content and form of global security governance. Both pursue revisionist agenda: rebalancing the international power structure through a system of collective leadership; rejecting the obligation to intervene; eschewing human rights doctrines; advocating a policy of non-interference in the sovereignty of other states; promoting multilateralism; and insisting upon a central role for the UN. However, both countries seek to pursue particular forms of multilateralism to cultivate acceptance of interactive conditionalities on Chinese or Russian terms.

These countries collectively fall along the entire spectrum of interaction preferences. The security cultures of France, Germany, Italy and the UK are consistent with the requirements of a fused security community, while the security cultures of Canada, Japan and the US are compatible with collective defence. Russian and Mexican security cultures appear to restrict participation in highly institutionalized systems of security governance and are most compatible with a concert, while China emerges as a country with a nineteenth-century security culture best suited to the compulsions of the balance of power.

Technologies of public goods supply: burden-sharing in UN operations and programmes

Westphalian and post-Westphalian national security cultures coexist in the international system and, given the dynamics of rising globalization, states with different security cultures find themselves more often in need of collaboration. The UN is perhaps the most prominent arena for interstate cooperation, providing examples of collective action across the security governance spectrum: protection, assurance, prevention and compellence. The production technologies of these public goods may either provide barriers or facilitate cooperation on security governance. The technology of public goods supply hypothesis suggests accordingly that burden-sharing in security governance varies across security policies.[2] Burdens will be shared less evenly if, in a particular category of security governance, on balance, the goods are less 'public' and asymmetries more relevant. Consequently, equal burden-sharing is expected for protection and assurance because of their respective weakest-link and summation aggregation technologies conjoined to symmetric costs. In contrast, large countries are expected to shoulder the costs of prevention and compellence. The technology of summation also describes prevention, but asymmetry of costs is expected to lead to uneven burden-sharing. Uneven burden-sharing is predicted for compellence because of its best-shot aggregation technology, where a committed effort of the major players is often decisive. Moreover, issues lending themselves to coercion often involve asymmetric threats and the marginal costs of a military operation are spread unevenly as well.[3] The well-known exploitation hypothesis should thus only apply to compellence policies. Olson and Zeckhauser (1966) have indeed found evidence that alliances, such as NATO, are likely to provide a suboptimal level of defence with burdens mainly imposed on large allies with disproportionate benefits and relatively low marginal costs. In the context of EU security governance, Dorussen *et al.* (2009) find that the smaller EU members disproportionately shoulder the costs of assurance and protection, while wealthier EU members carry a somewhat disproportionate burden in the provision of prevention, and larger EU members do so in the provision of compellence. Since asymmetric marginal costs largely explain any uneven burden-sharing, their main conclusion is that the aggregated burden of collective security governance in the EU is shared quite evenly.

A comparison of participation in and contributions to UN missions and programmes not only provides a further test of the technology of public goods supply hypothesis, but it also allows us to assess the relative importance of the proposition that national security cultures and the emergence of the post-Westphalian states shape national response to security governance challenges. The test requires us to make three preliminary determinations: those activities included in the calculation of burden-sharing; the allocation of those activities to the various dimension of security governance; and the appropriate benchmarks for defining equitable burden-sharing. Regarding the first point, we exclude the assessed and mandatory contributions which primarily apply to the regular UN budget and the financing of UN peacekeeping operations. Instead we focus on the voluntary contributions to the different UN funds and programmes and deployments to UN peacekeeping missions.

The UN Development Programme (UNDP) covers a wide range of humanitarian and development assistance programmes falling under prevention policies. Voluntary contributions to the UNDP budget were USD 1.1 billion in 2008. We use bilateral contributions to the regular budget as well as co-financing arrangements. Protection concerns policies of internal security such as policing and crime. The remit of the UN Office on Drugs and Crime (UNODC) is to enhance regional and international cooperation to stem the flow of illicit drugs, to strengthen the rule of law, and to fight human trafficking, corruption and money-laundering. We test for burden-sharing in the voluntary contributions to the UNODC budgets which in 2007 amounted to approximately USD 64 million. The defining aspect of assurance policies is the emphasis on persuasion to sustain order in post-conflict environments, particularly efforts to improve domestic governance. The UN Peacebuilding Fund (UNPBF) as well as the civilian contributions to UN peacekeeping operations (UNPKO) correspond most closely to the assurance policies at the global level. We test for the deposits made to the UN Peacebuilding Fund up to 2009. The UN distinguishes between deployments of police, military observers and troops to peacekeeping operations. We recognize that deployment only partly reflects the actual burdens involved. Some missions are clearly more risky or logistically demanding than others. The UN provides reimbursements for the deployment of peacekeepers as a flat payment per soldier. For some poorer countries, the reimbursements actually present a net gain. The primary tool to cover UN peacekeeping expenses is assessed on the basis of member state GDP and UN status. However, member states regularly fall short in their contributions, occasionally resulting in delays in reimbursements to troop-contributing member states. In addition to deployment to peacekeeping missions, we also use data compiled by Shimizu and Sandler (2002) on the actual cost of peacekeeping burdens. Unfortunately, these data only exist for OECD countries up to 2000. Compellence focuses on coercive measures to resolve conflict. For the period covered by our study, the commitment of troops to Afghanistan under a UN mandate represents a global policy of compellence.

It is obviously important to reflect on the baseline to assess the 'fairness' of contributions. Equitable burden-sharing is defined relative to capacity (total gross domestic product, GDP) as well as to wealth (GDP per capita). The Kendall tau test is an appropriate non-parametric statistical test to evaluate burden-sharing relative to the ability to contribute. Kendall tau tests rely on a comparison of rankings and assume ordinal-level data. Since it does not require any assumption about normality of the error terms, it is less affected by the small number of observations. The null hypothesis is that there is no correlation between the ranking on resources available and the ranking of share of resources committed to collective security policies. The Kendall tau statistic ranges from -1 to $+1$. If tau < 0, states with more resources contribute a smaller share of their resources, and if tau > 0, they contribute a larger share. A rejection of the null hypothesis therefore suggests a positive (negative) relation indicating exploitation of the strong (weak) by the weak (strong). Contributions to protection and prevention policies as well as some of the indices for assurance policies are in monetary terms, making it appropriate to measure share of resources relative to GDP. The Kendall tau test compares the ranking of member contributions relative to their economic size (Contribution$_i$/ GDP$_i$) with their GDP ranking. Instead of capacity, it is also appropriate to use wealth (measured as GDP per capita) as a baseline. Contributions to assurance and compellence mission are generally in person-years and measured as share of population.

We have compiled information on contributions to UN missions for the 21 UN member states mentioned by UN Secretary General in his yearly reports since 2000 as the main contributors to the UN peacekeeping budget. The list of countries includes all the countries examined in detail in the case studies: Canada (p), China (w), France (w/p), Germany (p), Italy (p), Japan (w), Mexico (w), Russia (w), UK (w/p) and the US (w). It further includes: Australia (w), Austria (p), Belgium (p), Denmark (p), Finland (p), Republic of Korea (w), Netherlands (p), Norway (p), Spain (p), Sweden (p) and Switzerland (w). Following the criteria outlined previously, countries that are followed by 'w' are classified as Westphalian, while those with 'p' are classified as post-Westphalian. France and the UK are recognized as mixed cases and initially classified as Westphalian. Next, they were reclassified as post-Westphalian and the tests were repeated. In a few instances, which will be discussed below, this affected the results, but the findings were generally robust with regard to the reclassification of individual countries.

Table 13.3 gives the value of the Kendall tau statistics as well as their statistical significance for each of the ten indices. It allows for a comparison across security policy dimensions as well as between Westphalian and post-Westphalian countries. Finally, it provides Kendall tau statistics assessing proportionality of burden-sharing relative to capacity (GDP) as well as wealth (GDP per capita). Considering the full set of 21 countries and comparing burden-sharing relative to capacity across the four security dimensions (column 1), the Kendall tau statistics clearly indicate

Table 13.3 Burden-sharing of deployment and contributions to UN initiatives relative to population, wealth and size of the economy (Kendall rank-order tests)

		Time period	Capacity (GDP)			Wealth (GDP pc)		
			(1) All	(2) Westphalian	(3) Post-Westphalian	(4) All	(5) Westphalian	(6) Post-Westphalian
Protection								
UNODC UN Office on Drugs and Crime[1]	Contributions/ GDP	2006–7	−0.486 (0.002)	−0.244 (0.371)	−0.455 (0.062)	0.410 (0.010)	0.511 (0.049)§	0.236 (0.350)
Assurance								
UNPBF UN Peacebuilding Fund[3]	Contributions/ GDP	2006–9	−0.376 (0.019)	−0.045 (0.928)	−0.418 (0.087)	0.310 (0.053)	0.090 (0.788)	0.418 (0.087)†
UNPKO Peacekeepers (all)[4]	Deployment/ Population	2000–7	−0.486 (0.002)	−0.289 (0.283)	−0.600 (0.013)	0.295 (0.066)	0.333 (0.211)	0.127 (0.640)
UNPKO Peacekeepers (police)[4]	Deployment/ Population	2000–7	−0.333 (0.037)	−0.067 (0.858)	−0.346 (0.161)	0.410 (0.010)	0.378 (0.152)	0.382 (0.120)
UNPKO Contributions[5]	Contributions/ GDP	2000	−0.333 (0.058)a	−0.429 (0.230)	−0.309 (0.213)b	0.085 (0.649)a	−0.048 (1.00)b	−0.018 (1.00)
Prevention								
UNDP UN Development Programme (total)[2]	Contributions/ GDP	2000–7	−0.448 (0.005)	−0.156 (0.592)	−0.527 (0.029)	0.410 (0.010)	0.556 (0.032)	0.200 (0.436)

(continued)

	Time period	Capacity (GDP)			Wealth (GDP pc)		
		(1) All	(2) Westphalian	(3) Post-Westphalian	(4) All	(5) Westphalian	(6) Post-Westphalian
UNDP UN Development Programme (regular)[2]	Contributions/ GDP	2000–7	−0.486 (0.002)	−0.156 (0.592)	−0.636 (0.008)	0.486 (0.002)	0.644 (0.012)	0.382 (0.120)[†]
UNDP UN Development Programme (co-finance)[2]	Contributions/ GDP	2000–7	−0.448 (0.005)	−0.111 (0.721)	−0.455 (0.062)	0.448 (0.005)	0.600 (0.020)	0.273 (0.276)
Compellence								
ISAF/OEF Afghanistan[6]	Deployment/ Population	2003–7	0.014 (0.952)	0.598 (0.023)	0.236 (0.350)	0.462 (0.004)	0.092 (0.786)	0.273 (0.276)
			N = 21	N = 11	N = 10	N = 21	N = 11	N = 10

Sources:

1 UNODC Annual Report 2007, 2008;
2 UNDP Annual Report 2001–8;
3 http://www.unpbf.org;
4 http://www.un.org/Depts/dpko/dpko/contributors/index.shtml;
5 Shimizu and Sandler 2002;
6 The Military Balance 2003–7
GDP is in current dollars from the Penn World Tables, version 6.3

Notes:

a   17 observations
b   8 observations
§   Non-significant if France and UK are coded as post-Westphalian
†   Significant at 0.05 if France and UK are coded as post-Westphalian

that the smaller countries generally contribute disproportionally to protection, assurance and prevention policies, while the contributions to compellence appear to be even. At first sight, these findings may appear surprising given our theoretical expectations that burden-sharing in protection and assurance would be even, while for protection and compellence larger countries would contribute disproportionally. In Dorussen *et al.* (2009), we found similarly that smaller countries tend to contribute disproportionally as long as the absolute contributions are relatively small. Comparing burden-sharing relative to wealth for all 21 countries (column 4), the Kendall tau statistics show that for all four dimensions of security policies, richer countries contribute disproportionally. Interestingly, with the exception of contribution to peacekeeping missions, these findings remain robust if we exclude China and Mexico, the poorest countries in our sample. The most striking finding is, however, that there are only minor differences in burden-sharing across the four security policy dimensions. This suggests that technology of public goods provision only has a minor impact. Interestingly, compellence is the exception to this general finding.

Distinguishing further between countries with Westphalian and post-Westphalian security cultures, some interesting differences in burden-sharing emerge. The theoretical expectations for the impact of technology of public goods provision on burden-sharing are derived from rational choice models assuming self-regarding utility functions and these predictions should thus apply in particular to countries with a Westphalian security culture. The Kendall tau statistics in columns 2 (for capacity) and 5 (for wealth) indeed confirm these expectations. Larger countries disproportionally contribute to compellence security policies, while large and small Westphalian countries share the burdens evenly with respect to protection and assurance policies. Contrary to our theoretical expectation, they also share the burden of prevention policies evenly, but here we find that richer Westphalian countries contribute disproportionally. On the other dimensions, rich and poor Westphalian countries share the burden evenly, which is only somewhat surprising for compellence. However, it seems eminently reasonable to argue that capacity is a more relevant criterion for compellence while wealth is more relevant for prevention.

Countries with a post-Westphalian security culture appear to differ systematically in willingness to contribute to collectively provided security. Evaluating burden-sharing proportional to capacity for the post-Westphalian countries (column 3), the Kendall tau statistics indicate that smaller countries tend to contribute disproportionally to protection, assurance and prevention, while they carry a 'fair' burden of compellence policies. Relative to their wealth (column 6), post-Westphalian countries contribute proportionally on all four security dimensions. It is only in comparing relative to wealth that the classification of France and the UK as Westphalian or post-Westphalian has some impact, making the pattern somewhat more consistent if they are coded post-Westphalian. The national security cultures of these states may lead politicians in these countries to be more aware of the value of the collective provision of security, more willing to contribute proportionately, and to do so according to a calculus dominated by a logic of appropriateness. It is even possible that they are more other-regarding ('altruistic') in their calculation of costs and benefits. Various competing explanations suggest themselves for the behaviour of these post-Westphalian countries. Politicians may have realized that their – in absolute terms – small contributions provide dispro-portional influence on the direction and content of collective security policies. At this stage, these explanations are clearly tentative and even somewhat *ad hoc*. They suggest, however, interesting areas for further research.

Conclusion

The empirical evidence presented in *National Security Cultures* supports two of the three theoretical claims made in the introduction: the distinction between the Westphalian and post-Westphalian state provides a structural explanation for vari-ations in state behaviour with respect to global (and regional) security governance; and variations in security cultures explain the patterns of behaviour of national elites in the formulation and execution of security policies across the governance spectrum. The third claim, that the technology of public goods supply would have a differentiated impact on the level of each category of governance policy supplied, was only sustained in one (compellence) of the four domains of security govern-ance. Interestingly, the technology of public goods supply appears to explain better the behaviour of Westphalian states.

The data used for the statistical analysis undertaken in this chapter provided a 'difficult' case for all three hypotheses: the UN is a collective security organiza-tion that has generated an (admittedly imperfect) pattern of security cooperation across the four elements of security governance over a 60-year period, the major (post)-Westphalian states are either permanent members of the Security Council or seeking such status, and a mutually agreed upon scale of contributions has defined member state obligations that is likely to shape national contributions to UN programmes even where the contributions are voluntary. The results of the statistical analysis, in conjunction with the case-study national narratives, provide strong evidence that national security cultures and the evolution of the Westphalian state explain variations in contributions to global and regional security governance.

Post-Westphalian states make disproportionately large contributions to global protection, prevention and assurance policies; this behaviour provides, at a mini-mum, indirect evidence that national security cultures account for that divergence. The precise elements of the national security cultures accounting for those dif-ferences are difficult to determine from the statistical analysis, but the narratives in the country chapters provide ample evidence that those states tending towards the post-Westphalian end of the spectrum are more rather than less likely to view security threats as collective rather than national, to operate in a highly institution-alized context to address those security governance challenges, and to place greater reliance upon policies of assurance, prevention and protection as compared to compellence. Similarly, the disproportionately large contributions of Westphalian states to UN compellence policies support the hypothesis that these states' security cultures make national elites more prone to rely upon the military instrument and that their policy is animated by differentials in power capabilities.

National Security Cultures provides a conceptual and empirical foundation for exploring the barriers and opportunities for regional security governance. While we do not claim to have unequivocally established or proven that the national security culture or the evolutionary trajectory towards the post-Westphalian ideal-type determines the precise content of any state's approach to security governance, we have provided a set of interrelated and testable hypotheses that provide the foundation for future, comparable studies that, in the end, could make a contribution to our collective empirical and conceptual understanding of security governance in an increasingly turbulent and dangerous world.

Notes

1 This section draws on Sperling (2008).
2 Buchanan (1965), Hirshleifer (1983) and Sandler (1977, 1992) have developed the joint-product analyses.
3 Dorussen *et al.* (2009) elaborate these arguments in the context of EU security governance.

References

Buchanan, J. (1965) 'An Economic Theory of Clubs', *Economica*, 32 (125): 1–14.
Dorussen, H., Kirchner. E. and Sperling, J. (2009) 'Sharing the Burden of Collective Security in the European Union', *International Organization*, 63(4): 789–810.
Hirshleifer, J. (1983) 'From Weakest-Link to Best Shot: The Voluntary Provision of Public Goods', *Public Choice*, 41(3): 371–86.
Olson, M. and Zeckhauser, R. (1966) 'An Economic Theory of Alliances', *Review of Economic Statistics*, 48(3): 266–79.
Sandler, T. (1977) 'Impurity of Defense: An Application to the Economics of Alliances', *Kyklos*, 30: 443–60.
——(1992) *Collective Action: Theory and Applications*, Ann Arbor, MI: University of Michigan Press.
Shizumu, H. and Sandler, T. (2002) 'Peacekeeping and Burden-Sharing, 1994–2000', *Journal of Peace Research*, 39(6): 651–68.
Sperling, J. (2008) 'State Attributes and System Properties: Security Multilateralism in Central Asia, Southeast Asia, the Atlantic and Europe', in Bourantonis, D., Ifantis, K. and Tsakonas, P. (eds) *Multilateralism and Security Institutions in an Era of Globalization*, Abingdon, UK: Routledge.

Index

Abkhazia 268, 270, 284
Aceh 50, 71, 88, 107, 134
ACP (Lomé Convention) 110–11, 122
Afghanistan 21, 26, 34–7, 43, 50–1, 57–8,
  64, 67, 69–72, 76, 79–81, 89, 91–2; 98,
  106–8, 118, 122, 133, 135, 138–9, 143,
  150–1, 167, 172–3, 175–8, 180–4, 200,
  208, 220, 222, 229, 237, 257, 271, 297,
  299
Africa 26–7, 29, 35–6, 39, 49, 71–2, 84,
  106, 131, 133, 137–8, 223–5, 251, 253,
  272 ; African Union 107–8, 135, 224;
Al-Qaeda 76, 172–3, 176–7, 186, 191,
  200
Albania 50, 64, 72–3, 75, 88, 185
Algeria 29, 71, 75
anthrax 56, 76
Armenia 254, 259, 274, 281
ASEAN 110, 213, 225, 226–8, 230, 239;
  Regional Forum 226; ASEAN Plus
  Three 228
Australia 136, 228, 249, 297; Australia
  Group 273
Austria 136, 297
axis of evil 176, 199

Balkans (Western Balkans) 26, 36, 72,
  80–1, 87, 106, 108, 117, 178, 200, 251
Ballistic Missile Defence 43; programme
  140
bilateralism 12, 178, 224, 293
bioterrorism 33–4, 166
Bolivia 133, 155
Bosnia and Herzegovina 36, 50, 57, 64,
  70–2, 81, 88–9, 98, 107–8, 116, 118,
  150, 178–9, 22, 251, 270
Brown, G. 85, 86, 90, 93–4, 99
Bush, George W. 59, 93, 165, 167, 172–3,
  175–7, 180, 183–4, 186, 191–2, 194–5,

197, 199, 208; security doctrine 105,
199

Calderón, F. 154, 160, 164–5, 197
Canada 127–51, 159, 165–6, 171, 182,
  207–8, 241, 290–5, 297; ATA 141,
  148; Canada Corps 134; CEFCOM 142,
  147–8, 151; Canadian International
  Development Agency 132–4, 143,
  146–7, 149–50; Defence White Paper
  129; Security Intelligence Service 129,
  141; CANSOFCOM 141, 147, 151;
  Department of National Defence 137,
  143, 150–1; Department of Public
  Safety and Emergency Preparedness
  142; DFAIT 132, 143; Free and Secure
  Trade (FAST) 140; International
  Development Research Centre (IDRC)
  132
Caucasus 51, 108, 117
CBRN 116, 176, 19
Chad 25, 35–6, 48, 57, 70, 81, 116, 268,
  270–1
Chechnya 178, 283
China 39, 65, 90, 92, 174–5, 177, 198–9,
  213–44, 246–7, 249, 290–5, 297,
  300; ARATS 231; Court and Judicial
  Agency 218; CPCTC; National People's
  Congress 235; Defence White Paper
  23; Export-Import Bank 224; Ministry
  of Commerce's Department of Aid
  to Foreign Countries (DAFC) 223;
  Ministry of National Defence 219;
  People's Armed Police Force 215, 218,
  232; People's Liberation Army 218,
  232, 244
Commonwealth of Independent States
  (CIS) 268, 270–1, 279–80, *see also*
  Russia and Soviet Union

civil liberties 3, 127
civilian power 43, 47, 57, 62–3, 67, 72, 82, 121, 156
climate change 100, 248–9, 266
Clinton, W. 176–7, 183, 186, 188, 192, 199
Cold War 21–4, 35, 37–9, 44, 54, 66–8, 77, 87, 96–8, 106, 109, 127, 129, 131, 135–8, 142, 145, 153, 156, 167, 173, 175–7, 183, 186, 197–8, 200–1, 213, 218, 222–3, 225–6, 250, 265–7, 272, 280
collective memory 152, 291
Collective Rapid Deployment Force 269–70, 279
Commonwealth 89, 91, 93, 98, 135
conditionality 226, 239, 295
conflict prevention 27, 49, 51, 79, 90, 103, 110, 116, 119, 157, 184, 252, 269, 292
conflict resolution 8–10, 43, 47, 131, 280, 284, 288–9
Congo 49, 50, 224, 251; DR 48, 50, 57, 71, 81, 9, 106–7, 116–18, 134, 207, 220
Cooperative Threat Reduction 186, 188–9, 208, 273
corruption 35, 75, 106, 157, 162, 196, 217, 296
counterfeiting 35, 217
crisis management 26, 68, 110, 118, 271
Croatia 45, 71, 88, 178–9
CSTO 268–70, 279–80
CTBT 24, 272
CTF 138–9, 150–1
Cuba 156, 171
cyberspace 191–2, 195, 208
cybervandalism 176, 188
cyberwarfare 194, 235, 246
Cyprus 70, 80, 87, 98, 220

Darfur 48, 50, 91, 107, 207, 225
debt relief 29, 132–3, 186–7
democracy promotion 106, 133, 156, 168
democratisation 18, 29, 79, 106, 110, 112, 131, 133, 156, 252, 267, 292
Denmark 118, 144, 297
development assistance 112, 132, 182

Egypt 71, 80, 88, 107, 184
El Salvador 154–5, 157
energy security 226, 266
environmental degradation 6, 10, 129, 154, 159, 167, 176
epidemics 56, 176, 247, 249
epidemiological surveillance 14, 33, 113–14
espionage 130, 192, 235, 247

Ethiopia 48, 133, 221, 224
EU 3, 5, 23, 36, 45, 71, 74, 85, 103–23, 134, 156, 176, 265, 290; action plans 114; *aquis* 104, 112, 119; Amsterdam Treaty 112–13; association agreement 110, 112; battle groups 80, 103, 117, 119; Border Missions 106; CEPOL 279; CFSP 25, 46, 108; Civilian Crisis Management 108; Commission 109–10, 112, 120, 182; Cooperation Agreements 110; Council 76, 105, 111; Eastern Partnership 267, 271; ECHO 108–11; Economic Partnership Agreements 110; EIDHR 108–11; enlargement 91–2, 110–12, 267, 269; ENP 105, 110–12, 267, 269; ESDP 29, 36, 43, 47, 49, 57, 69, 71, 79–81, 87, 103, 106–8, 116, 118–19, 293; ESS 49, 103–6, 109–10, 112, 117–20, 293; EU3+3 51; EUBAM 50, 88, 269; European Arrest Warrant 114; European Defence Agency 103, 117–19; European Defence Community 117; ESS 49, 103–6, 109–10, 112, 117–20, 293; EUFOR 35, 51, 57, 70, 81, 88, 116, 118, 268, 270–1; EUJUST 26, 50, 71, 107, 269; EUROFOR 80; EUROGENDFOR 48, 108; EUROJUST 114–15, 279; EUROMARFOR 80; EUROPOL 55, 114–15, 279; FRONTEX 49, 114, 227; IFS 108–11

failed states 4, 8, 98, 108, 110, 120, 130–1, 292
food security 181, 226
Forum on China-Africa Cooperation 224–5
France 21–42, 49, 51, 58, 66, 73, 77, 110, 114, 119, 172198, 207–8, 290–5, 297, 299–300; Aid and Cooperation Department 27; COFOG 31–2; French Development Agency (AFD) 27, 33; Ministry of Defence 23, 27, 33–4, 37–8; Ministry of Foreign Affairs (MAE) 27–9, 32–4; Ministry of Health 33; Ministry of Identity, Immigration and Development Solidarity 28, 30
Fukuda, Y. 247, 249, 259

G8 54, 66, 76, 133, 267
Gaza 88, 107, 134
Georgia 39, 48, 50, 64, 71, 88, 107, 168, 188, 220, 267–72, 280, 284
Germany 25, 32, 43–66, 73, 78, 98, 106, 110, 114, 172, 175, 188, 207–8, 219, 235, 290–5, 297; Bundesrat 53;

Bundestag 56–7, 59; Bundeswehr
57–8; Center for International Peace
Operations 49; unification 43–6, 49, 52,
56
Global Partnership Against the Spread
of Weapons and Materials of Mass
Destruction 188, 273
global warming 144, 166, 247
greenhouse emissions 54, 151, 257
Gulf War 138, 143, 250, 257

Haiti 133, 136, 138, 166, 220, 222
HIV/AIDS 33, 133, 184–5
Hobbes, T. 173, 175, 202
Hu-Jintao 224, 231
human rights 3, 21–2, 39, 49, 73, 93, 108,
127, 130, 133–4, 154, 164, 167, 181,
226, 267, 283, 295
Hussein, Saddam 176, 186

India 65, 80, 90, 92, 136, 198, 218, 228–30
Indonesia 65, 71, 88, 107, 133–4, 199
information sharing 14, 34, 114, 116,
159–60, 167, 228, 279
information technology 3, 192, 224
information warfare 176, 188
Intercontinental Ballistic Missile (ICBM)
208, 232
Intermediate-range Nuclear Forces (INF)
Treaty 272
International Bank for Reconstruction and
Development 223
International Criminal Court 49, 150
International Development Agency 132,
143, 272
International Security Assistance Force
(ISAF) 59, 64, 67, 80–1, 118, 135,
138–9, 177, 180–1, 200, 208, 271, 299
Iran 25, 51, 72, 92, 110, 172, 176–7, 186,
188, 197, 199, 229–30, 273
Iraq 21, 24, 26, 43, 45–6, 50–1, 56–7, 59,
69–70, 72, 77, 79, 81, 89–90, 92, 98,
105–7, 117, 122, 133–4, 154–5, 167,
172, 176–8, 180–4, 186, 197, 199–200,
207, 221–2, 237, 251, 257, 293
Iraq Relief and Reconstruction Fund
(IRRF) 181, 183
Iraqi National Development Strategy 181
Islamic extremism 34, 76, 95, 30, 175–6,
280
Israel 48, 80, 11, 155, 174, 184, 208, 235;
Israeli–Palestinian conflict 43
Italy 32, 66–84, 114, 198, 207–8, 290–2,
294–5, 297; CIMIC 79; Counter

Terrorism Committee 76; Ministry of
Defence 80–1, 84; Ministry of Foreign
Affairs 76, 84; Ministry of Health 77

Japan 49, 174, 199, 207–8, 213, 219,
227, 233, 237, 240, 245–64, 290–5,
297; Basic Policy of National Defence
258; CGP 247–9, 253, 255, 263;
Comprehensive Policy for Promotion
of Medical Security 253; Emergency
Appeal for Measures to Deal with
Medical Accidents 253; Immigration
Bureau of Japan (IBJ) 253; Japan Coast
Guard (JCG) 253; Ministry of Defence
246; Ministry of the Environment 257;
Ministry of Health 253; National Police
Agency (NPA) 253; National Security
Council 259
jihad 76, 176
just war 67, 218

Kant, I. 1, 202; optimism 173, 175
Kazakhstan 176, 188, 228, 279–80
Kosovo 45–6, 48–51, 57, 59, 64, 70–1, 73,
77, 87–9, 98, 103, 107–8, 118, 122, 138,
143, 178–9, 220, 222, 237, 251, 265,
270, 280, 284
Kosovo Force (KFOR) 26, 35, 64, 70, 81,
118, 200, 268
Kyoto Protocol 32, 54, 77, 145
Kyrgyzstan 188, 228, 279–80

Lebanon 35–6, 48, 70–2, 79–80, 134, 207,
220, 222
Liberia 48, 220–1, 251
Lisbon Treaty 120

Macedonia 50, 57, 64, 71–2, 81, 88,
107–8, 111, 116–18, 185, 270
Mediterranean 8, 29–30, 35, 71–2, 110,
117, 271, 281
Medvedev, D. 39, 267–8, 276–7, 279
Mérida Initiative 165, 197
Merkel, A. 54, 56
Mexico 110, 130, 152–71, 290–4, 297,
300; Beta Groups 159; Biological
Laboratories Program 166; FAI 162,
164; Federal Attorney General 162;
Federal Organized Crime Act 160;
Federal Preventive Police 162, 164;
Health Act 160; HLSC 160; Interior
Secretariat 162; National Security
Council 159; Secretariat of National
Defense 156

Middle East 71, 84, 108, 11, 131, 138, 220, 251, 253

migration 27–30, 35, 46, 52–3, 70, 73–4, 84, 91–3, 95, 110, 119, 140, 154–5, 157–60, 164–5, 178–9, 183, 188, 191, 253, 266, 269, 279, 291

military capacity 49, 117–18, 129, 145, 237, 284

Moldova 50, 64, 71, 88, 107–8, 188, 269–72

Morocco 29, 71, 75, 80

Mozambique 51, 133, 221, 224

multilateralism 12–13, 24–6, 39, 68, 105, 119, 128, 174, 177–8, 200–1, 207, 215, 223–5, 230, 237–40, 248, 266, 284, 290–1, 293, 295

Mutual Security Treaty US-Japan 248

NAFTA 153

NATO 21–2, 24–6, 36–8, 45–6, 49, 58–9, 64, 67–9, 76–82, 84–6, 89, 91, 96–9, 104, 111, 117–19, 122, 128–9, 131, 135–9, 143–5, 151, 172, 174–5, 180, 181–83, 197–8, 200–1, 222, 226, 230, 237, 265–8, 271–1, 280, 284, 291, 293–5; enlargement 265, 267, 271, 280

non intervention 154, 156, 167, 219, 226–7, 238

non-interference 168, 213, 239, 279, 291, 293, 295

NORAD 129, 131, 140, 145

norms 3, 7–9, 23, 47, 57, 100, 103, 119, 194, 201, 226, 246, 259, 267, 280, 283, 288–9, 294

North American Plan for Avian and Pandemic Influenza 165

North Korea 176–7, 186, 188, 199, 213, 225, 246–9

nuclear deterrence 21–2, 24, 36, 198

Obama, B. 172–3, 176–7, 180–1, 184, 186, 188, 191, 194, 207–8

ODA 49, 51–2, 64–5, 73, 90–1, 99–100, 111–12, 122, 131–3, 145, 150, 181–2, 186–7, 218, 223–4, 247, 249, 251–3, 260, 272

OECD 28, 52, 72–3, 90–3, 111, 113, 157, 182, 186–8, 223, 252, 296; DAC 111, 223, 252

Operation Enduring Freedom 36, 59, 138–9, 150, 172, 183, 200, 257, 293, 299

Operation Iraqi Freedom 172, 180, 183, 200, 293

Organization of American States 160

organized crime 6, 10, 14, 23, 34–5, 54–5, 75–7, 93, 96–6, 105–6, 112–14, 130, 139, 152–4, 157, 159, 160, 162, 168, 176, 183, 191–2, 195, 255, 266, 292

OSCE 14, 26, 64, 68–9, 71, 79, 87–9, 99, 108, 111, 134–5, 150, 174, 178, 207, 251, 267–8, 270, 283, ; Istanbul Summit 272

Pakistan 80, 92, 150, 173, 177, 181, 184, 229, 230

Palestine 50, 71–2, 107, 111, 251

peacekeeping 9, 26–7, 36–7, 69, 77, 79, 84, 87–8, 106, 116–18, 122, 128–9, 131, 135–6, 138, 154, 166, 168, 178–80, 213, 218–19, 223, 240, 250–1, 257, 260, 265, 268–71, 280, 292, 296–7, 300

Persian Gulf 172, 197–8, 201, 250, 257

Petersberg Tasks 117–18

pollution 31–2, 144

poverty 55, 70, 72, 89, 105, 133, 167, 171, 224, 247, 249, 266

pre-emptive attack 199; war 218

preventive engagement 103, 110, 117, 120

proliferation (non-proliferation) 5, 27, 51, 105, 109–10, 112, 129–31, 176–7, 186, 188–9, 266, 273, 292

Proliferation Security Initiative 191

Putin, V. 276, 282–3, 293

refugees 46, 48, 52–3, 57, 73, 93, 106, 130, 140, 155, 178–9, 183, 255

Regional Anti-Terrorism Structure (RATS/RCTS) 226, 230, 279

Romania 75, 185, 272

rule of law 29, 67, 69, 106–8, 127, 130, 134, 154, 156, 162, 165, 168, 181, 183, 269, 288, 296

Russia 13, 39, 57, 75, 151, 175–7, 183, 186, 188, 190, 198–9, 201, 207–8, 226, 228, 230, 235–6, 239, 249, 265–86, 290–5, 297; Action Plan on Terrorism 271; Black Sea Fleet 282; Chechen war 265, 276; Ministry of Internal Affairs (MVD) 275–5, 277

Russian Border Service 277

Russian-American Global Initiative 272

Sarkozy, N. 21, 39

Schengen Convention 110, 112

securitization 1, 4–5, 13, 21, 25, 30–1, 33, 44, 54, 59, 66, 74, 82, 99–100, 105, 119,

133, 153, 157–9, 175, 186, 188, 191, 194, 200, 238, 287, 291–3
security; cyber- 177, 193–5, 292; dilemma 7, 226, 284, 288, 289; harmonization 140; holistic approach to 188; knowledge based 37
Serbia 51, 64, 71–2, 88, 134, 178–9
Serious Organised Crime Agency (SOCA) 95–6
Shanghai Cooperation Organization (SCO) 213, 226, 229, 268
Sierra Leone 51, 89, 98, 135, 207, 221, 251
Six Party process 188; talks 225–6
Slovenia 45, 80
Smart Border Initiative 139–40
soft power 66–7, 122, 128, 174, 218, 224–5, 238, 240
Solana, J. 105, 110, 112, 120
Somalia 81, 92, 116, 138, 271
South Korea 199, 227, 233, 237, 249, 294
South Ossetia 267–8, 270–1, 273, 284
Soviet Union 45, 58, 112, 129, 134, 175–7, 183, 186, 188, 198, 222, 265, 291
Stability and Association Policy (SAP) 106
Stability Pact for Southeastern Europe 51, 106, 108
Stabilization Force in Bosnia and Herzegovina (SFOR) 81, 268
START-I Treaty 272
Strategic Arms Reduction Treaty 188
Strategic Offensive Reduction Treaty (SORT) 281
Sub-Saharan Africa 29, 84, 223, 272
Sudan 48, 80–1, 90–2, 107–8, 138, 207, 220, 224, 251
Support for East European Democracy (SEED) 178–9, 185
Syria 72, 251, 282

Taiwan 213, 222–3, 226, 228, 231, 233, 237–40, 247
Tajikistan 64, 88, 188, 228, 279–80
Taliban 172–3, 176, 200
terrorism 6, 10, 14, 23, 34–5, 43, 54–6, 75–6, 93–5, 99, 105, 111–14, 129–31, 139, 141–2, 151, 154, 159–60, 165, 168, 172, 174, 176–7, 183–4, 186, 191–6, 199, 208, 213–14, 225–30, 255, 257, 266, 271–2, 279, 283, 292; messianic 130; religious 130, 229; war on 176, 184, 257
terrorist attacks 23, 34, 56, 76–7 109–10, 130, 140, 191–3, 271–2, 278; 11 September 21, 43, 55–6, 76, 94, 154,

158, 198, 213; London 55, 94–5, 117; Madrid 55
Timor Leste 48, 166, 220–1, 251
trafficking, drugs 35, 95–6, 112, 114, 153–4, 159, 162–5, 167–9, 176, 195, 229, 266, 279; humans 95, 216–17, 249, 296
Treaty on Conventional Armed Forces in Europe (CFE) 134, 271–2, 284
Trident 97, 99
Turkey 55, 92

Ukraine 50, 87–8, 107, 11, 150, 176, 188, 236–7, 269, 271, 280, 282
UN 24, 32; -centred peace diplomacy, 248; Charter 123; Department of Peacekeeping Operations 79; International Bill of Human Rights 134; MINURSO 48, 79–80, 220, 270; MINUSTAH 79, 136, 220, 270; UN Verification Mission in Guatemala 166; UNAMID 76, 107–8; UNDGITF 181, 209–10; UNDP 182, 296 298–9; UNFICYP 70, 79–80, 220; UNHCR 84, 93, 155; UNIFIL 36, 48, 79, 220, 222, 223; UNIKOM 221–2; UNMIH 222; UNMIK 26, 48, 70, 79, 220, 270; UNMIS 220–1, 268, 270; UNMOGIP 79–80; UNODC 255, 296, 298–9; UNODC 255, 296, 298–9; UNOMIG 48, 220, 269–70; UNOMIL 221–22; UNPBF 296, 298–9; UNPROFOR 36; UNSAS 219, 222; UNTAG 222; UNTSO 79–80, 220, 222, 270
UN Security Council 24–5, 45, 85, 87, 99, 136, 154, 159–60, 167, 181, 188, 194219, 222–3, 225, 301
unilateralism 12, 45, 175, 219, 248, 293
United Kingdom 36, 25, 31–2, 49, 51, 66, 73, 77–8, 85–102, 110, 114, 135, 175, 198, 207–8, 290–5, 297, 299–300; CONTEST 93; DfID 86, 89, 91; FCO 86, 89; Home Office 86, 93–5; Ministry of Defence 86, 89, 96, 102;
United States 18, 34, 36, 118, 150, 165, 172–209; CDC 193, 202, 253; CNTF 181; coalition of the willing 89, 180; Container Security Initiative 191; as conventional power 197; CPR 194; Department of Defense 188, 190–2, 197–9, 208–9; Department of Energy 188, 190–1; Department of Health and Human Services 166, 191, 193–4;

United States (*continued*)
Department of Homeland Security
158, 191, 292; Department of Justice
191, 193, 195, 208–9; Department of
Treasury 195; Development Assistance
and ESF 184–5; FBI 192, 195–6, 208;
FinCEN 195; Immigration and Customs
Enforcement 165; Law and Order Trust
Fund (LOTF) 181; National Intelligence
Strategy (NIS) 177; National Security
Council 194; Patriot Act 192; TFI 195;
State Department 178; US-Mexican War
1846–48 155; US-Mexico Voluntary
Repatriation Program 159

weapons of mass destruction 27, 78, 97,
105, 109–10, 112, 130–1, 186, 189, 199,
266, 273, 292
World Bank Iraq Trust Fund (WBITF) 181
World War II 22, 45–46, 66, 96, 128,
142–3, 153, 174, 247–9, 257, 266,
291–2